▶ Editing as
Cultural Practice
in Canada

## TRANSCANADA SERIES

The study of Canadian literature can no longer take place in isolation from larger external forces. Pressures of multiculturalism put emphasis upon discourses of citizenship and security, while market-driven factors increasingly shape the publication, dissemination, and reception of Canadian writing. The persistent questioning of the Humanities has invited a rethinking of the disciplinary and curricular structures within which the literature is taught, while the development of area and diaspora studies has raised important questions about the tradition. The goal of the TransCanada series is to publish forward-thinking critical interventions that investigate these paradigm shifts in interdisciplinary ways.

Series editor:
Smaro Kamboureli, Avie Bennett Chair in Canadian Literature, Department of English, University of Toronto

*For more information, please contact:*

Smaro Kamboureli
Avie Bennett Chair in Canadian Literature
Department of English
University of Toronto
170 St. George Street
Toronto, ON  M5R 2M8
Canada
Phone: 416-978-0156
Email: smaro.kamboureli@utoronto.ca

Siobhan McMenemy
Senior Editor
Wilfrid Laurier University Press
75 University Avenue West
Waterloo, ON  N2L 3C5
Canada
Phone: 519-884-0710 ext. 3782
Fax: 519-725-1399
Email: smcmenemy@wlu.ca

# ► Editing as Cultural Practice in Canada

Dean Irvine | Smaro Kamboureli
editors

WILFRID LAURIER
UNIVERSITY PRESS

Wilfrid Laurier University Press acknowledges the support of the Canada Council for the Arts for our publishing program. We acknowledge the financial support of the Government of Canada through the Canada Book Fund for our publishing activities. This work was supported by the Research Support Fund and by Smaro Kamboureli's Canada Research Chair in Critical Studies in Canadian Literature Program.

Library and Archives Canada Cataloguing in Publication

Editing as cultural practice in Canada / Dean Irvine and Smaro Kamboureli, editors.

(TransCanada series)
Includes bibliographical references and index.
Issued in print and electronic formats.
ISBN 978-1-77112-111-8 (paperback).—ISBN 978-1-77112-093-7 (pdf).— ISBN 978-1-77112-094-4 (epub)

1. Editing—Social aspects—Canada. 2. Editing—Political aspects—Canada. 3. Editors—Canada. I. Kamboureli, Smaro, editor II. Irvine, Dean, 1971–, editor III. Series: TransCanada series

PN162.E35 2016             808.02'70971             C2015-908618-3
                                                     C2015-908619-1

Cover image by P.K. Irwin, untitled 1958 oil pastel (Trent University Art Gallery). Cover design by Scott Barrie. Text design by Angela Booth Malleau.

This book is printed on FSC® certified paper and is certified Ecologo. It contains post-consumer fibre, is processed chlorine free, and is manufactured using biogas energy.

Printed in Canada

Every reasonable effort has been made to acquire permission for copyright material used in this text, and to acknowledge all such indebtedness accurately. Any errors and omissions called to the publisher's attention will be corrected in future printings.

*In Memoriam*

*Ellen Seligman*

# Contents

# Acknowledgements

The preparation of this volume has taken longer than expected, so, first and foremost, we would like to thank all the contributors for their patience. We are also grateful to Lisa Quinn, our editor at Wilfrid Laurier University Press, for her own patience, as well as for her support and exceptional professionalism throughout the process of producing this book.

Dean Irvine would like to express his profound gratitude to the TransCanada Institute and the University of Guelph for hosting the Editing as Cultural Practice workshop in October 2011. Special thanks are owed to two project administrators at Dalhousie University, Vanessa Lent and Emily Ballantyne, who coordinated Editing Modernism in Canada's financial and logistical contributions to the workshop and this edited collection. Matt Huculak, who worked with EMiC as a Postdoctoral Fellow from 2010 to 2012, delivered expert Web support for the circulation of workshop versions of papers and bibliographies and for facilitating internal communication among participants via blog posts. Yale University's Macmillan Center and Department of English provided institutional support through their sponsorship of the Bicentennial Canadian Studies Visiting Professor program. EMiC's research initiatives have been made possible through a Strategic Knowledge Cluster grant from the Social Sciences and Humanities Research Council of Canada. Additional support for EMiC and its cluster director has been provided by the Faculty of Arts and Social Sciences and the Provost and Vice-President Academic at Dalhousie.

Smaro Kamboureli would like to express her indebtedness to Karen Bygden, the Administrative Assistant at the TransCanada Institute (2004–2013), who oversaw the logistical details of hosting the Editing as Cultural Practice workshop, and did so with great aplomb. She is indebted as well to Hannah McGregor, who, as a TransCanada Doctoral Fellow and Research Assistant at the time, was the mainstay of the project at different levels, from helping with the compilation of material for the grant application to the collation and preparation of the manuscript, and also to Mishi Prokop, the undergraduate Research Assistant, for the various kinds of help she provided. She would also like to express her deep appreciation to all those who attended the workshop and made valuable contributions to the discussions: University of Guelph colleague Jade Ferguson, Simon Fraser Professor Emeritus and editor Roy Miki, Sheena Wilson from the University of Alberta, and Linda Warley from the University of Waterloo; TransCanada Institute Postdoctoral Fellow Katherine McLeod and former Canada Doctoral Fellow and University of Toronto Postdoctoral Fellow at the time Robert Zacharias; and the University of Guelph School of English and Theatre Studies graduate students, Leslie Allin, Alexandra Guselle, Robert Ian Jones, Marcelle Kosman, Jessica Riley, Jodie Salter, and Paul Watkins. These students deserve special thanks for sharing their workshop experience in the post-workshop seminar she held at the TransCanada Institute. Hosting this event and publishing this volume would not have been possible without the support provided by her Canada Research Chair, Tier 1, in Critical Studies in Canadian Literature and a Social Sciences and Humanities Research Council of Canada Aid to Research Workshops and Conferences grant.

Both editors of this volume would like to extend their deep thanks to Robert Bringhurst, George Elliott Clarke, Kateri Akiwenzie-Damm, Frank Davey, Roy Miki, and Daniel David Moses for agreeing to read from their work and join the roundtable discussion about the practice and poetics of editing in Canada on opening night, an evening open to the public and made possible through a Canada Council grant, as well as financial support from the Office of the Dean of the College of Arts, University of Guelph.

For assistance with securing permission to reproduce on the cover P.K. Irwin's untitled 1958 oil pastel (photograph by Eric Onasick), we would like to acknowledge Neal Irwin, Trustee of the Estate of P.K. Page, Zailig Pollock, Literary Executor of the Estate of P.K. Page, and the Trent University Art Gallery. Excerpts from the introduction and Chapter 6 of Robert Lecker's *Keepers of the Code: English-Canadian Literary Anthologies and the Representation of Nation* (University of Toronto Press, 2013) have been reprinted with permission of the publisher.

# Introduction

## Dean Irvine and Smaro Kamboureli

### EDITING AS CULTURAL PRACTICE

*E**diting as Cultural Practice in Canada* addresses editorial work as a manifold activity that has shaped the production of Canadian literature and its formation as a scholarly discipline. Originating in a workshop organized by two partner projects, the TransCanada Institute and Editing Modernism in Canada, this edited collection brings together a diverse group of scholars and writers, all of whom have served as editors of different kinds of Canadian literature, from the nineteenth century to the contemporary avant-garde, from canonized texts in critical editions to anthologies of minoritized authors and the oral and print literatures of the First Nations. Their contributions demonstrate that editing has been consistently integral to the creation, organization, and dissemination of knowledge in the arts and humanities, even though its indispensable function has not always been readily acknowledged or appreciated. It is precisely the fundamental operations of editing across the domains of scholarship and cultural creation that this collection examines. More specifically, it deals with the multilayered character and politics of cultural transmission and editorial practices that are particular to the editing of Canadian literatures in English, and in doing so sets out to theorize various aspects of the editorial process by interrogating inherited paradigms of literary and scholarly values. It engages as much with specific cases of Canadian editorial production as with the existing conceptual frameworks that have influenced the direction of editorial practices. Principles of authorial intentionality and textual authority, models for genetic and socialized editions, contingencies of textual production and reception, construction and pedagogical use of anthologies, formations of canonical and minoritized literatures, prototypes of digital tools and computational methods—these are the subjects around which this collection revolves. Essential to the handling of these subjects is the recurrent consideration of what constitutes the responsibilities of the editor as interpreter, mentor, facilitator, and co-creator. Collaboration, as a crucial aspect of the editorial process and a proliferating research model for scholarship in the arts and humanities, is one of the signal contexts within which this collection situates editing.

Indeed, our shared interest in collaboration as an integral element of editing, and vice versa, prompted us to organize the October 2011 workshop Editing as Cultural Practice. Our different but overlapping engagements with literary and scholarly work initiated a series of theoretical and practical questions that have emerged as much from our experiences in editing as from our direction of collaborative research projects. Our respective projects, Editing Modernism in Canada and TransCanada Institute, were designed specifically to foster collaborative research, whose outcomes relied as much on the enactment of editorial practices as on the theorization of different modalities of editorial labour. That a significant part of our careers includes editing diverse genres—magazines, journals, literary texts, scholarly editions, essay collections, anthologies, publication series, and digital repositories—has made us acutely aware of the vicissitudes of this mode of literary and scholarly production. By staging a workshop, we placed ourselves in an apt state and station to reflect on the ways in which our own editorial labours and those of our assembled collaborators manifest themselves as cultural practice.

As an ethnographic term, cultural practice denotes the collective traditions and customs of a given people. Operating as a mode of communal labour and agency, cultural practice brings forth collective products of lived experiences. In presenting editing as cultural practice, this book does not attempt to construct an ethnography of editorial practices. Instead, we seek to stress the role editors play in activating the sociality of literary and scholarly work, a role manifested across different registers. Insofar as editing is a working concept—one whose process-oriented definition is iterative, and so inscribed incrementally in practice—so, too, is culture. In other words, editing is a mode of cultural practice in which its customs and traditions—say, for instance, the compilation of literary or scholarly material, the arcana of proofreading marks, the arbitration of anonymous peer review, or the design of house styles—are working concepts constituted by the social relations among authorial and editorial agents and by the transactions of their literary and scholarly labour. Editing puts working concepts of culture into practice and thus inserts cultural production into collective spaces of employment—co-op, workshop, publishing house—but it can also identify a void, and rectify it by making visible what dominant forms of cultural production render invisible or inconsequential. By generating the conditions necessary to create new spaces for cultural work and, in the process, creating alternative perspectives that expand established cultural idioms, editing as cultural practice reflects both the custodial role that editors play and their ability to see beyond the cultural imaginaries that have shaped existing literary traditions or genres.

Editors as cultural practitioners do not merely ensure that a book goes through a carefully monitored and executed editorial and production process. Aware of how cultural, market, and institutional ideologies and practices shape what is deemed to be publishable, they can play a role in destabilizing or expanding these practices. For example, the wave of anthologies about diasporic authors in Canada published in the early 1990s exemplify editing as cultural practice in that they were responsive to Canadian literature's systemic obliviousness to voices other than those of mainstream white Canadian authors. Anthologies such as *Voices: Canadian Writers of African Descent* (1991), edited by Ayanna Black, and *Many-Mouthed Birds: Contemporary Writing by Chinese Canadians* (1991), edited by Bennett Lee and Jim Wong-Chu, constitute significant instances of editing as cultural practice. Edited by writers who were embedded in the communities their anthologies represented and who were active in anti-racist and cultural work intended to produce, in Larissa Lai's words, a "radical relationality that recognizes the necessity of coalition across racialized categories" (90), these publications played an instrumental role—especially when considered from our present vantage point—in recalibrating the Canadian literary terrain. As Lai demonstrates in *Slanting I, Imagining We: Asian Canadian Literary Production in the 1980s and 1990s*, the editing of special issues of journals and magazines, as well as that of anthologies, can result in "groundbreaking ... anti-racist cultural production" (65). The capacity of editing as cultural practice to transform cultural discourses by providing the stimulus to think differently is similarly evident in various realms and constituencies. Whether the process involves founding journals like *Tessera* and *West Coast Line*, or gathering essay collections like *Gynocritics/Gynocritiques*, edited by Barbara Godard, and *Looking at the Words of Our People*, edited by Jeannette Armstrong, or the establishment of small presses like Mawenzi House (previously known as TSAR Publications) and Theytus Books, editing as cultural practice can spawn new avenues and venues for the production and dissemination of literary and intellectual work, at once critiquing the limits of existing discourses and conferring legitimacy to previously marginalized voices. Editing as cultural practice, then, entails an interactive and collaborative process, a materialist approach whereby editors, aware of how literary production can metabolize in different ways, simultaneously occupy different sites, be they cultural, activist, or pedagogical.

While not all editors operate as cultural practitioners, most kinds of editorial labour share many of the qualities of editing as cultural practice. Whether employed by presses or periodicals to make decisions about the acquisition of texts, engaged in the collaborative process of revising manuscripts, setting criteria for anthology selections, marking up electronic documents, organizing multimedia repositories online, or establishing principles for the presentation of texts in print or digital media, Canadian literary and scholarly editors occupy a multiplicity of distinct, yet frequently overlapping, positions. Despite this extensive range of editorial activity, and even though the development of Canadian literature as a disciplinary formation has been shaped to a large extent by editorial work, there is a dearth of critical material on the theory and practice of editing in Canada. What little exists—*Editing Canadian Texts* (1975), edited by Francess G. Halpenny, and *Challenges, Projects, Texts: Canadian Editing / Défis, projets et textes dans l'édition critique au Canada* (1993), edited by John Lennox and Janet Patterson—revolves exclusively around case studies of editing scholarly editions of individual authors. *Editing as Cultural Practice in Canada* likewise engages with case studies, a strategy necessary to tease out the implications of various editorial methods, but it also moves beyond particular instances to examine the irreducibly varied and complex roles that editors play, as well as the canonical, pedagogical, materialist, and theoretical significance of editing as both a scholarly and creative activity. This collection examines some of the gaps in the field of editing Canadian literatures in English and contributes more generally to contemporary theoretical discussions about editing in both print and digital media. Coming from different yet intersecting fields, nearly half of our contributors—Robert Bringhurst, George Elliott Clarke, Frank Davey, Kate Eichhorn, and Darren Wershler—are both literary authors and scholars; one, Kateri Akiwenzie-Damm, is a poet and publisher; and the rest—Irene Gammel, Carole Gerson, Paul Hjartarson, Robert Lecker, Benjamin Lefebvre, Hannah McGregor, Heather Milne, Laura Moss, Zailig Pollock, Harvey Quamen, Cynthia Sugars, Bart Vautour, and Christl Verduyn—are literary scholars. Like the editors of this volume, there are two things that they have in common: they have edited and been edited by others. Having occupied both sides of the publishing process, we all have a profound appreciation for and intimate understanding of the exigencies of editing—experiences that we have collectively recalled and relived in the process of writing and editing this collection.

## WHAT IS AN EDITOR?

"What did the most famous, sought-after woman of her time do in order to escape the limelight forever and basically cease to exist in the public eye? Simple: She became a book editor" (Barber). If Jackie Kennedy Onassis, the woman in question, sought refuge from the limelight by becoming an editor, it is because traditionally many editors remain invisible. House editors especially work in the shadow of the authors whose writing they restructure, rewrite, and polish. No serious book, be it literary or scholarly, ever reaches the reader before undergoing an editorial process. In fact, it is not uncommon for the finished book to be drastically different—in length, structure, setting, style, or point of view—from an author's original submission. Yet most readers remain oblivious to what this long-standing and essential practice entails. They have to go to the acknowledgements section, if there is one, to discover who the editor was; such editors may be thanked profusely, but rarely, if at all, are any details forthcoming about the nature of their work. House editors are the invisible hand that turns a manuscript, no matter how finished its author considers it to be, into the final product that reaches the reader. Even "when the author with whom the editor is associated is … highly visible," as Lorraine York writes, and "some of that visibility inevitably rubs off," the "measure" of that visibility is usually "produced by and dependent on the celebrity with whom he or she is associated" (69).

This process can also be reversed. House editors may be so well known—indeed, celebrities in their own right—that appearing under their imprint or being edited and published by them bears its own stamp of recognition. Malcolm Ross, for instance, is synonymous with McClelland and Stewart's New Canadian Library, the influential series of paperbacks for which he served as general editor from 1958 to 1978. Of more recent vintage, Louise Dennys, Executive Publisher of Knopf Random Canada, Ellen Seligman, McClelland and Stewart's Publisher (Fiction) and Vice-President, and Douglas Gibson, formerly McClelland and Stewart's President and Publisher, may be renowned editors who have been instrumental in shaping the canon of Canadian fiction but, as their job titles indicate, they are principally recognized by the institutions that employ them as publishers. In such cases, too, little is divulged about the actual editorial processes in which they are involved. Partly the result of the conventions that regulate the cultural industries—Scribner's legendary editor Maxwell Perkins famously said that "an editor serves as a handmaiden to an author … he creates nothing" (qtd in Berg, *Max* 6) and "should strive for anonymity" (qtd in Bower)—this secrecy safeguards the writer's authorial signature and thus maintains the mystique of writerly authority. We may recognize that the texts we read are the result of an elaborate and intensely collaborative process that involves such players as literary agents, anonymous readers of manuscripts, book designers, and copy editors, but our reading act tends to bypass what transpires during the editorial and production stages.

What Darcy Cullen calls "the 'middle' part of the publishing process," editing remains "sandwiched between acquisitions and sales, … often closed from view, or viewed as closed off, even though it is here that the manuscript's metamorphosis into book occurs" (3). Metamorphosis is the operative word in this account, for it encapsulates one of the fundamental roles of editors. Their historical invisibility has long been viewed in conventional feminized terms: they are indispensible yet cast in the role of a "midwife" (Tartar xiii). Nevertheless, the work of house editors does not necessarily fade into total obscurity; even if their names may not always be familiar, literary archives are replete with evidence of the ways in which their editorial hands have shaped the texts we read. While Lorne Pierce of the Ryerson Press, for instance, is by no means forgotten, he is likely remembered as an early- to mid-twentieth-century publisher rather than as an editor. Other house editors at mid-century, however, such as Ellen Elliott at Macmillan and Claire Pratt at McClelland and Stewart, are less likely to be remembered for their editorial work, even if the former can be credited with discovering and mentoring the young P.K. Page in the mid-1940s and the latter is recognized for helping put the final touches on Sheila Watson's historic 1959 novel, *The Double Hook*.

This inconspicuousness, however, does not apply to all editing. Scholarly editors not only have been producing landmark editions of Shakespeare and Joyce and anthologies that have wielded power to shape and reshape literary traditions but also have been instrumental in advancing methods and theories about editing. Minor cultural industries have developed around the publication of competing editions of canonical authors and anthologies of national literatures. As Irene Gammel and Benjamin Lefebvre document in their chapter, Lucy Maud Montgomery, one of Canada's iconic literary figures, has stimulated the growth of a globalized tourism, popular culture, publishing, and scholarly industry, one that has sustained the production of myriad editions ranging from mass market paperbacks to critically annotated multi-volume series and that has given rise to the institutionalization of Montgomery studies. Editing has increasingly gained similar clout by modelling new modes of scholarly practice, as evidenced by the momentum in humanities research toward collaboration, a scholarly activity that more often than not results in edited volumes such as this one or Cullen's *Editors, Scholars, and the Social Text*. Moreover, as social media have transformed the ways in which scholars relate to the world and to one another, so has the role of editors come to be understood as that of "an active participant in the making and dissemination of texts" (Cullen 4). Even so, the profession of scholarly editing, as Cullen admits, has not always been "benign to editors"; reduced to "the status of containment," they are often seen as caretakers of an author's oeuvre, their agency confined at times to the detective work necessary to establish the authenticity and chronology of print and archival materials or to map the networks among various agents involved in the composition, revision, and dissemination of texts. Editors may play a major role in institutionalizing an author's work and upholding or expanding a given tradition, but their visibility is frequently attached to the discovery of error in an edited text. "It's a common trope," Cullen notes, "that editors are only noticed when they make a mistake" (10). Editors, so it seems, should expect to remain behind the scenes to serve as instrumental agents of institutions that typically conceal their functional necessity and reserve the currency of publicity for authors.

Even less noticeable to consumers of mass market and trade publishing, the editors of small literary presses are characteristically known only to other similarly situated authors, publishers, and editors as well as to those scholars who undertake research on emergent, alternative, or avant-garde literatures. Small press editors are most often authors who have taken on the complementary role of curating and disseminating the work of the literary communities in which they circulate. Curating in this instance refers to an editor's readiness to scout for new talent and take on authors whose work does not meet the profit expectations of mainstream publishers, but it can also refer to an editor's ability to imagine a manuscript when none yet exists or to acts of mentoring that foster the creation of a work. Such editors typically make this effort without expecting remuneration beyond what is necessary to continue publishing the output from a given literary collectivity, however loosely or narrowly defined. In Canada, these presses (both not-for-profit and for-profit) have included Hilda and Laura Ridley's Crucible Press (1938–58), John Sutherland's First Statement Press (1945–56), Raymond Souster's Contact Press (1952–67), Dennis Lee, Dave Godfrey, and Margaret Atwood's House of Anansi Press (1967–74), bill bissett's Blewointment Press (1967–83), and NeWest Press (1977–), founded by, among others, literary authors Rudy Wiebe, Henry Kreisel, and Douglas Barbour. As Frank Davey points out in this collection, bpNichol's small press work included editing books, chapbooks, and pamphlets with his own Ganglia Press (1965–88), with the Underwhich Editions collective (1978–90), and with Coach House Press (1966–96). Darren Wershler, who has worked as an editor for the renamed Coach House Books (1997–), takes a candid look in his chapter at the present-day dysfunctionality of cultural policy, the publishing industry, and the state's governance of scholar-editors in Canada. He attributes that dysfunctionality to "ethical incompleteness" (Miller, *Well-Tempered* ix), namely, to structural conditions of lack, precarity, and dependency that arise out of contradictions at the conjuncture of democracy and neoliberalism, contradictions that produce divided civic-minded citizens and consumer-minded subjects. With a similar economic bent, but with a focus on feminist editors and editing, Kate Eichhorn and Heather Milne in their chapter take account of "affective economies" (Ahmed, "Affective" 119) of editorial labour and their collaboration on a 2009 anthology of women's avant-garde poetry and poetics for Coach House Books.

While most of the contributors to this volume have earned recognition at one time or another for their literary scholarship, and while several of the chapters in this collection carry the insights of literary authors, publishers, and translators, their collective work as editors has not commanded comparable attention. This is not to suggest that their editorial labour is somehow less distinguished than their other literary activities, but that the other modes of scholarship in which they are most accustomed to writing—theory, criticism, history, biography—have become partitioned from the field of editorial scholarship. Crossing over this partition, Christl Verduyn's opening chapter on the intersections of literary and editorial theory draws attention to the ways in which her scholarly editions of Marian Engel's notebooks and novel *Elizabeth and the Golden City* were informed by the author's reading of Maurice Blanchot in the process of writing her 1973 novel *Monodromos*. By calling attention to the ways in which French structuralist and poststructuralist theory in the later twentieth century emerged out of an intellectual tradition that did not divert its editorial and textual scholarship into a separate stream, Verdyun performs a crucial task in identifying and traversing the disciplinary and institutional gaps that developed when scholarly editing was severed from literary theory in North America. Her instructive overview of the principal traditions in international scholarly editorial theory and practice—intentionalist, social-text, and genetic—provides a primer on those editor-theorists who resurface in subsequent chapters. At least by rate of recurrence, Jerome McGann's championing of social-text criticism and editorial practice, initiated by his *A Critique of Modern Textual Criticism* in 1983, and D.F. McKenzie's *Bibliography and the Sociology of Texts* in 1986, establish a common point of theoretical reference for the majority of this collection's chapters on scholarly editing (see Verduyn, Gammel and Lefebvre, Pollock, McGregor, Hjartarson and Quamen, Vautour, and Moss and Sugars). Not least of McGann's relevance to the scholars gathered here is his emphasis on the historicity and sociality of texts and their collaborative production. McGann's prolific career over the past three decades as a textual scholar, editor, and theorist simultaneously reconnects the conduits between critical and editorial theory and documents the transition in recent practice from print to digital media.

## EDITING CANADA

Although Canadian literatures have not often been part of international debates in editorial and textual scholarship, Canada has played host to a long-running conference series on scholarly editing at the University of Toronto. Since its inception in 1965, the Conference on Editorial Problems has on three occasions hosted events and published proceedings dedicated to editing Canadian literary texts. The 1972 conference staked out the territory for editors and editions of Canadian literary texts. Its published proceedings, *Editing Canadian Texts*, called attention to the absence of any semblance of editorial principles articulated in modern paperback editions of early literary Canadiana—the majority of which were non-critical editions, some abridged, others facsimile, and still others based on untrustworthy copy texts and riddled with errors. Edited and introduced by Francess G. Halpenny, the proceedings offered no decisive statements from its editor, though this was unlikely foremost in her mind: her commentaries on editing Canadian literary texts indicate a preoccupation with the absence of scholarly editions rather than a call for definitive standards and guidelines of the sort that characterized the contemporaneous work of the Modern Language Association's Center for Editions of American Authors (1963–75) and its Committee on Scholarly Editions (1976–).

Indeed, if there was one thing that characterized this slim yet historically important volume, it was the collective emphasis on the editor's responsibility to contribute to the making of the Canadian literary tradition "as a worthy field of study" (3). Hence the recurring emphasis on a strategically selective past that reflects a linear, foundationalist approach. In that scheme of things, "minor works and minor authors" (Halpenny 8) were strategically ignored—considered not marketable enough—and the emphasis was placed on developing a publishing and institutional climate conducive to "the elucidation and confirmation of eighteenth and nineteenth century poetic, dramatic, fictional, and non-fictional prose texts" (New 15–16). What was deemed to be editorially important at that time was establishing a "record of our culture given form and ... of literary progress" (31). This, in effect, was a call for the kind of editorial activity that would rectify the dire absence of bibliographies and biographies and of "a fully indexed union list of Canadian manuscript holdings" (Nesbitt 45). As preserver and facilitator of the Canadian literary tradition, the Canadian editor in the 1970s was assigned the task of "authenticating and clarifying the texts themselves" (New 25), a process involving the collation of variant texts and the compilation of interpretative annotations.

Among the more notable absences in *Editing Canadian Texts* is the apparent disconnection between scholarly editors in Canada and the international field. None of the major theorists at the time enter into the conversation; either none of the presenters had ever heard of the likes of W.W. Greg or Fredson Bowers, or perhaps they felt—in keeping with the cultural nationalism of the early 1970s—that these debates in Anglo-American textual scholarship were divorced from the conditions of editing Canadian literatures. Given that the period's stock lexicon of variants, authorial intention, and copy texts enters into just one of the papers—Bruce Nesbitt's "Lampmania," which suggests at least some peripheral awareness of the Greg–Bowers textual scholarship circulating elsewhere—the 1972 conference demonstrates only a premonition of theoretical engagement with the discourse and practice of scholarly editing.

After nearly two decades, when the Conference on Editorial Problems series returned to the topic of Canadian literatures, the francophone and anglophone editors who travelled to Toronto for the 1989 conference brought with them a broadened range of theoretical approaches to scholarly editing. As evidenced by John Lennox and Janet M. Paterson's bilingual edited collection *Challenges, Projects, Texts: Canadian Editing / Défis, projets et textes dans l'édition critique au Canada,* the level of theoretical sophistication and diversity of methodologies is indicative of the turn to theory that transformed Canadian literary and editorial scholarship beginning in the 1970s and 1980s. Here the international debates over competing traditions of scholarly editing at last found their proxies in Canadian literatures. Representatives from projects to produce scholarly editions of French and English literary texts that emerged in the 1970s and 1980s came together to report on their progress. Editors from the major multi-edition series active at the time—Jacques Allard from l'Édition critique de l'oeuvre d'Hubert Aquin, Gwendolyn Davies from the Centre for Editing Early Canadian Texts, Jean-Louis Major from le Corpus d'éditions critique, Zailig Pollock from the Collected Works of A.M. Klein, Paul Wyczynski from Les Oeuvres complètes de François-Xavier Garneau—were joined by Malcolm Lowry scholar and editor of his two-volume collected letters, Sherrill Grace.

Most of the editorial projects discussed in Lennox and Patterson's collection recall its predecessor from the 1970s in their continued alignment of the task of editorial work with the recovery and preservation of literary traditions in Canada and Quebec. In Major's words, the editor's task is delimited by the double imperative to rescue and safeguard—"une opération de sauvegarde et … de sauvetage" (75). At the same time, however, there is a concerted effort not simply to describe editorial work or to address its challenges but also to conceptualize how this particular kind of scholarly endeavour relates to that of literary criticism and theory. As Grace asked poignantly, "What, finally, is an editor, where does he or she differ from a literary critic?" (27). Though she did not provide a cogent answer—perhaps wisely so—her essay exemplifies that an editor is not merely a discerning reader who authenticates and preserves literary manuscripts by comparing variants or working with copy texts; she or he *is* a literary critic, and a theorist to boot. What is more, as Pollock's account of editing Klein demonstrates, the editor is also a "storyteller" (54). If the storyteller, as Walter Benjamin writes, relies on experience, and if "half the art of storytelling [is] to keep a story free from explanation as one reproduces it" (84, 89), then the editor as storyteller is certainly not a handmaiden. Editing as storytelling speaks not only to the diverse paths—literal and intellectual—that an editor is compelled to pursue but also to how these trajectories are inscribed in the work edited, and beyond it. Some of these routes may be rendered invisible in the process, but their inconspicuousness does not mean they are insignificant; it attests to the editor's art.

While the 1972 and 1989 conferences on editing Canadian literatures manifested similar concerns regarding the institutional structures and material conditions that can hamper or foster editorial work, there was a decisive shift at the latter event away from editing as a blunt instrument of disciplinary and pedagogical formations of the nation and national literatures and toward the adoption of critical editing strategies that foreground their own complicities in and disruptions of the nation's ideological-cultural apparatuses. This change signals a significant departure in the history of editing Canadian literatures insofar as the editor's task is no longer seen in national or nationalist terms but rather in ways that engage the larger cultural and institutional systems within which literary texts are produced and circulated. Among the contributions to *Editing as Cultural Practice in Canada*, Robert Lecker's study of a series of Canadian literature anthologies since the early 1980s and Laura Moss and Cynthia Sugars's reflections on assembling their 2009 anthology track this period of transition from the articulation of residually imperialist, Eurocentric narratives of nation to the disarticulation of nation under a "postcolonial ethos" that coordinates "multicultural, multiethnic, multiracial, and multilinguistic" identities (181, 174). Similarly, Gerson's account of editing the three-volume *History of the Book in Canada / Histoire du livre et de l'imprimé au Canada* negotiates its alignment with other contemporaneous national histories of scribal and print culture and, at the same time, speaks to its adaptation to the conditions of a settler colony that developed into a nation-state that officially recognizes bilingual and bicultural origins and accommodates cultural, ethnic, racial, and linguistic multiplicities. Calling attention to the ways in which the history of the Canadian nation-state is largely synonymous with the subjugation of Indigenous peoples in Canada, the present collection stages a dialogue between Indigenous and non-Indigenous editors through Kateri Akiwenzie-Damm's reflections on First Nations editing and publishing as part of a contemporary movement toward Indigenous literary sovereignty, as well as through Robert Bringhurst's meditation on his own transnational migrations, First Nations art and literature as cultural heritage of the commons, and intercultural exchanges transacted in the histories of collecting, editing, and translating traditional Haida narratives over the course of the twentieth century. Such disarticulations of the nation are equally evident in George Elliott Clarke's prolegomenon for a new anthology of African-Canadian literature, which seeks to dismantle canonical narratives and national literatures of the Black Atlantic in the establishment of a diasporic "archive" of Black Canadian authors.

If the 1989 Toronto conference and its published proceedings pointed to the reorientation of editing Canadian literatures toward modes of critique and self-critique, it did so at a time when the gravitation to critical theory was prompting literary scholars to undertake self-reflexive interrogations of disciplinary and institutional formations, thereby calling into question not just normative, dominant, and exclusionary narratives of nation but also those of class, gender, race, and ethnicity. At a moment when literary scholars were summoning theoretical frameworks from an expansive corpus of international and transnational intellectual traditions to facilitate socio-political modes of critique, it seems logical that their editorial counterparts working on Canadian literatures should have equally committed themselves to crossing linguistic and geopolitical borders in their intricate navigation of social, legal, and institutional systems. Such systems, as we have already suggested, mediate the making and dissemination of literary texts and their implementation of scholarly apparatuses to render visible those processes of textual production that remain hidden behind the publicity screens of publishers and their authors.

For the 2010 Conference on Editorial Problems, which was hosted by Editing Modernism in Canada, co-organizers Colin Hill and Dean Irvine invited presentations by researchers working in the fields of anglophone and francophone literatures as well as theatres in Canada, transnational modernist studies, and the digital humanities. Featuring  scholars who locate their research at the intersection of digital technologies and the editing of modernist literary texts from Canada and beyond, the 2010 conference situated the editing of Canadian literatures in relation to the practices of digital modernist studies. Although the conference series brought together editors using computers as early as 1984 (see Butler and Stoneman), it would take nearly two more decades before computational and digital approaches to editing Canadian literary texts were showcased. While the 1984 conference demonstrated the growth of humanities computing in Canada through the 1970s and early 1980s and exhibited Canadian-based projects alongside international ones, none of the invited speakers addressed the nascent field of computer-assisted editing of Canadian literary texts. Even among Canadianists, there has been scarce recognition of literary critics and scholarly editors in the 1960s, 1970s, and 1980s who worked on humanities-computing projects that involved Canadian literatures. Since the 1984 conference, theories and practices of editing Canadian literary texts have been increasingly aligned with the uptake of digital technologies and computational methods among researchers working in the transdisciplinary field of humanities computing—or, as its practitioners came to rebrand it at the turn of the century, the digital humanities.

Exemplary of this technological transition, Zailig Pollock—the only presenter at both the 1989 and 2010 Toronto conferences, and a participant at the Editing as Cultural Practice workshop—has not only worked through changes to method and theoretical alignments in print editions through the 1980s and 1990s but also adapted his practice to prototype collaborative, Web-based critical editions of E.J. Pratt and P.K. Page over the past decade. In doing so, he testifies to the importance of intergenerational mentorship and training for scholars just entering the disciplinary nexus of scholarly editing and the digital humanities. One of the emerging scholars at the workshop whose research extends to the digital humanities was Bart Vautour, who delineates theoretical approaches to the conjuncture of politics and editing that serve as a preamble to his ambitious collaborative work with Emily Robins Sharpe on their blended print and digital research project, Canada and the Spanish Civil War. As a member of the Editing Modernism in Canada Collaboratory at the University of Alberta (EMiC UA), Hannah McGregor provides a description of her experience as part of this team of researchers and digital-tool developers that takes up the question of collaborative authorship in the context of her study of short fiction published in mid-century periodicals under the name "Martha Ostenso." As the respective leaders of EMiC UA's editorial and digital initiatives, Paul Hjartarson and Harvey Quamen come together in their chapter to represent the collective effort of literary scholars, programmers, librarians, and archivists who have combined forces to undertake the digitization, transcription, dating, and annotation of the correspondence of mid-century modernist authors and domestic partners, Sheila Watson and Wilfred Watson. This intergenerational cross-section of digital scholarship and scholarly editing opens up to public view the formal and informal networks of pedagogy and intellectual exchange necessary for collaborative editorial initiatives.

## FROM WORKSHOPPING CANLIT TO WORKSHOPPING CANADIAN LITERATURES

While conferences have been the most common venues for scholars to meet and share ideas about editing, one of the precedents for the Editing as Cultural Practice workshop took place several decades earlier. Among her accomplishments as the director of the Centre for Editing Early Canadian Texts (CECCT), Mary Jane Edwards hosted a public workshop on scholarly editing at Carleton University in May 1983 (Edwards, *Public Workshop*). Modelled on the Modern Language Association's push in the 1970s and 1980s to standardize scholarly editions and consolidate the institutional presence of an Anglo-American tradition in textual scholarship, the goals of the CECCT workshop to establish guidelines for the editors of individual volumes produced by the centre might seem remote to the social, political, economic, and technological concerns of editors at the Editing as Cultural Practice workshop. Perhaps the two workshops diverge at the idea that standardization of method and centralization of authority to regulate observance of standards should serve as horizons for scholarly editorial practice. At the same time, the two workshops occupy—despite the three decades that separate them—astonishingly similar circumstances with respect to the integration of digital technologies and computational methods into editing and publishing workflows. Designed in part to facilitate the creation of computer programs and text-encoding protocols to perform editorial and publishing procedures, the CEECT workshop anticipated many of the concerns voiced by digital-media editors at the Editing as Cultural Practice workshop regarding the need to adopt best practices for the exchange and interchange of interoperable data, metadata, and tools. Rather than legislate mandatory standards for the production of uniform editions, which is effectively what the CEECT workshop accomplished, the call to adopt best practices is predicated on an openness to alternatives and adaptation.

CEECT's public workshop may have assembled an international group of editorial and computer experts, but the project's ultimate resolution to develop a centralized, project-specific, in-house model for computing and programming proved too localized; it led to the design and implementation of more than seventy computer programs for mainframe-based word processing, collation, typesetting, and publishing—none of which ever left the Carleton campus (Edwards, "Centre" 158–59). CEECT's once innovative experimentation with "mainframe linguistic-oriented computing" (Laird 65) has been superseded by a generation of scholarly editors for whom computing takes place on desktop, laptop, and mobile devices—not on local terminals linked by telecommunications and time-sharing programs to a mainframe that performs computations—and more often than not for whom open-source programs, encoding protocols, and best practices are shared and maintained by an extensive international community. That this ambitious editorial initiative started at a time of extraordinary change with the introduction of mainframe computing to the humanities and the publishing industry should serve as a cautionary tale to editors working at the present moment, in which the same institutions are under pressure to adapt to rapid transformations in information technologies.

In retrospect, CEECT's model may best illustrate the consequences of leveraging too much of the workshop's operative functions and too little of its cultural dynamics. This signals yet another way in which the CECCT workshop and Editing as Cultural Practice diverge. Designed with the express purpose of systematizing editing, the former did not engage directly with the cultural-materialist and socio-political conditions that affect the production and dissemination of literature. Intent on developing project-specific pragmatic and technological solutions, it did not have the mandate to address precisely what framed the dialogue at Editing as Cultural Practice between the cultural and material particularities outside a text that shape its production, publication, and circulation with those inscribed in it, a dialogue primed as much by recent developments in editorial methodology as by the important changeover from a presumably homogeneous CanLit tradition to Canadian literatures. If there was a single driving force that led to Editing as Cultural Practice, it was the desire to examine editing as a "discipline" that is inextricably related not only to the various mediating processes that produce, or reproduce, a published text but also to the discursive and material manifestations of the making of Canadian literature as a diverse corpus. The participants—including Daniel David Moses and Terry Goldie, who could not contribute to this volume—moved fluidly from their role as critics and/or literary authors to that of editors, and vice versa. As the chapters gathered in this volume demonstrate, they practise a kind of nomadism that allows them to roam across adjacent terrains. The workshop proved to be an ideal setting to examine how editors who are also literary authors and/or critics migrate from one kind of praxis to another, an instance of an assembly that animates cultural practice.

The history of the workshop as an economic and social institution for individual and community labour and as a mode of cultural practice for groups of artists and intellectuals is a far more complex and nuanced one than its present-day and everyday occurrence in the arts and academia might indicate. Despite its utilitarian versions in technology and commercial sectors that place emphasis on the workshop's materialist functions—which typically provide vocational and research training, focused on specialized skill and knowledge acquisition—its cultural variants in the arts and humanities coordinate the socio-economic concerns of artistic and scholarly production with the imaginative and creative dimensions of aesthetic and research practices. "What is needed," as art historians Till Förster and Sidney Littlefield Kasfir write, "is an informed understanding of the interrelationship between the workshop as an economic and social institution and the workshop as a space where individual and collective agency meets" (19). As a heterotopic space for cultural practice, the workshop lends itself most readily to critical exchanges among its participants, who negotiate the relationships among the customs and traditions of the multiplicity of communities from which they originate. Attended as it was by graduate students and scholars other than those included in the program, as well as by Lisa Quinn, our house editor at Wilfrid Laurier University Press, and including public readings by the participating literary authors and follow-up sessions with students, the Editing as Cultural Practice workshop materialized how editing brings together what Jim McGuigan calls "critical intellectuality and practical intellectuality" (39), two different yet complementary kinds of labour that operate as relations of exchange. *Editing as Cultural Practice in Canada* is not designed to offer a consensus about editorial policies regarding the editing of Canadian literatures and scholarship. But it does convey—at least this is our joint editorial view—a sense of the dynamic dialogue that took place at the workshop, which, we hope, will spur readers and editors to explore further the issues raised here.

# Literary and Editorial Theory and Editing Marian Engel

Christl Verduyn

> "L'expérience qu'est la littérature est une expérience totale."
> Maurice Blanchot, *Le Livre à venir*, 1959

> "The experiment which is literature is a total one."
> Marian Engel, *Cahier XXVI*, 1972–73

When Marian Engel jotted down into her 1972–73 writing notebook a translation of French theorist Maurice Blanchot's statement that "the experience that is literature is a total experience" (Blanchot 2003, 209), she would not have been thinking, as we have been invited to do, about the "cultural, social, economic, canonical, pedagogical, materialist, and theoretical significance of editing as a creative and scholarly practice in the field of Canadian literary studies" (Editing Modernism in Canada). She was wrestling with the form for what would become her third and most structurally demanding novel, *Monodromos* (1973). Engel read French fluently and was deeply interested in the new, modernist thinking about literature and critical theory. She was dissatisfied with the traditional form of the novel; she wanted to "cut the novel up in ... a Godard-ish way ... cut loose from the conventional plot" (Verduyn, *Lifelines* 96). These aims and ambitions, together with Engel's lifelong interest in philosophy, made Blanchot, the "novelist-philosopher" (Hart and Hartman 10), an ideal choice for her literary-critical explorations. Blanchot is perhaps less familiar in English-speaking academia than thinkers and theorists such as Emmanuel Lévinas, Roland Barthes, Michel Foucault, and Jacques Derrida,[1] whose work he influenced (Hart and Hartman 14) and with whom he was among the vanguard of those asking, in the modernist period:

> What is the nature of the literary work (text, object)? What is an author, and what authority does the author have over the work? What are the work's

relationships to its social contexts? to its modes of composition, production, and distribution? to its reader? How do these relationships affect a reader's or critic's views of the work?

Some readers may recognize these as the opening questions of Michael Groden's essay, "Contemporary Textual and Literary Theory." They are questions that literary critics and theorists have been asking for years. As Groden notes, though, textual theorists have asked these questions as well, yet there has been relatively little contact between the two groups, and "not much recognition of common interests" (259). I agree with Groden that this has been regrettable, because there is much to be gained from a greater exchange between literary critics and textual critics and a cross-fertilization of their work. "Textual and literary theorists and critics would be much better off," Groden states, "with more interest in and understanding of each other's theories and activities" (281).

It is in this spirit, and with this strategic objective, that I consider two of my scholarly editing[2] projects on the work of Marian Engel (1933–1985) in light of contemporary discussions and theories of editorial practice. This chapter traces the hybrid editorial practice that I employed in the projects: an approach that combined literary and editorial theory, integrating aspects of the latter drawn from both Anglo-American and continental European traditions.[3] I begin with a brief account of key features of these editorial traditions, and then turn to the two editing projects in question. The first project involved Engel's writing notebooks, or *cahiers* as she called them. It resulted in the publication of the volume *Marian Engel's Notebooks: "Ah, mon cahier, écoute ..."* (1999). The focus of the second project was a novel that Engel was working on at the time of her death. My edition of it appeared 2010 as *Marian and the Major: Engel's Elizabeth and the Golden City* (2010). These projects presented at once similar and different opportunities and challenges for editorial work. Both emerged out of archival holdings and were animated in the first instance by feminist and life writing theories, complemented by the argument for the cultural, social, and historic significance of the materials. The archival component of the projects was integral to the editing practices they involved. Peter Shillingsburg identifies as scholarly editions those "which preserve or rescue a work of artistic, social, intellectual or historical importance" (4).[4] This describes both *Marian Engel's Notebooks* and *Marian and the Major*. The volumes recover from archival fonds materials of literary, social, and historical value and make them available in published form for the first time. In so doing, they fulfill an initial editing goal identified by George C. Rogers Jr.: making a new corpus of material available. They also illustrate a second editing goal that Rogers describes: "readability and usability" (4). Finally, they exemplify Shillingsburg's statement that "the purpose of any edition determines what editorial principles will be followed" (3).

The Editing as Cultural Practice workshop has provided a welcome opportunity not only to return to these projects but also to explore its objective of bringing editorial theory and practice to the fore. In the process, I hope to illustrate how an integrated approach combining literary and editorial theories best suited not only my editing projects on Engel's work but also the literary and critical theory contexts and interests of the writer herself.

▼

The postwar period saw the emergence of new ideas about literature and about literary and critical theory, as well as about editorial theory and methodology. Anglo-American 1950s New Criticism eliminated the author as a source of interpretation (Groden 265),[5] while on the European continent, French *modernité* and structuralism—and critics like Roland Barthes—announced the death of the author. Those involved in the "total experience that is literature" (Blanchot, *Book* 284)—from writers and readers to critics and editors—witnessed the atomic schism of literature into "work" and "text." Intense discussions and debates followed, in English and French academic circles alike, about these and related terms and concepts, from the author, authority, and agency, to language and discourse. Blanchot's 1959 *Le Livre à venir* (*The Book to Come*) was part and parcel of the discussions and reimaginings of literature, especially in terms of key "framing" or explanatory concepts such as process, open-endedness, fragmentation, and plurality. These notions were inspiring to Engel and helped shape her novel *Monodromos*. They were also influential in the development of editorial theory in continental Europe, in particular French *critique génétique*—genetic criticism—as represented by Louis Hay and Almuth Gresillon.

New developments in editorial theory emerged on both sides of the Atlantic at the same time, but they evolved in different directions, with different emphases, tenets, and principles. Following from W.W. Greg, the Anglo-American tradition privileged authorial intention, identifying copy text as that which is determined to be closest to the author's intentions based on an examination of all versions of the authoritative text. Such an approach, it was viewed, minimized the risk of personal and interpretive editorial practice. This might see an editor "corrupt" a text by emending or intervening in its composition or stylistics in order to express the meaning she or he considered most appropriate. Authorial intention remained a dominant characteristic of Anglo-American editing theory and practices even as these evolved and developed through the work of such scholars as Fredson Bowers, G. Thomas Tanselle, David Cheetham, Peter Shillingsburg, George Bornstein, Michael Groden, and Jerome McGann. For example, McGann's concept of social/sociological editing expanded editing theory beyond the author's intention to include influences exerted by other players in the production of a text, such as editors, publishers, institutions, and technology. For McGann, "literary works are social rather than personal or psychological products" (*Critique* 43–44, qtd in Irvine, "Editing" 75–76). Moreover, an author's identity is not singular: "Authors do not have, *as authors*, singular identities," McGann declared; "an author is a plural identity" (*Textual* 75, qtd in Irvine, "Editing" 74).

Whether singular or plural, authorial intention was not a dominant concern in developing continental European editorial theory. Rather, interest lay with the "genesis" of a text, from its draft to its print version, through various stages and processes of its production. These included a wide array of materials—the writer's notes, drafts, manuscripts; the author's correspondence at the time and on the subject; and the typescripts, proofs, and various published versions of the text. The focus was on the extended and varied process of writing itself rather than on the identification of a "final," authoritative text. By focusing on the concept of "text as process," these theorists privileged "production over product, writing over what is written, textualization over the text, multiplicity over uniqueness, possibility over the finite" (Bushell 103). Genetic criticism resonated with new ideas and theories about literature proposed by theorists such as Barthes and Blanchot. The latter's "book to come," for example, envisioned the literary text as an ongoing process in which texts are contingent, open-ended, and potentially subject to rewriting (Bushell 101).

Genetic criticism's interest in "text in process" and "avant-texte" is also conceptually, and crucially, compatible with the vast field of archival and life writing materials, out of which the Engel editing projects emerged. Indeed, genetic criticism is greatly facilitated by the availability of and access to archival materials, especially when these include notes about and early drafts and versions of texts. Archival materials can facilitate the work of genetic critics, but they can be equally helpful to editors who seek to establish authorial intention and authoritative versions of a text.[6] Archival documents and manuscripts may record an author's intentions about a text. The divergent roles that archival resources can play in the editing process model the possibility for divergent editorial practices within a given editorial project. This is the case for the projects on Marian Engel's notebooks and manuscript novel.

*Marian Engel's Notebooks: "Ah, mon cahier, écoute ..."* is a 575-page volume presenting the novelist's writing *cahiers*. There are over forty notebooks preserved in the Marian Engel Archive at McMaster University—unpretentious, inexpensive school-exercise booklets that Engel kept from her teenage years until her death in 1985. Filled with a lifetime of notes, thoughts, and reflections on writing and life, the notebooks became part of my research for a critical study of Engel's fiction, *Lifelines: Marian Engel's Writings* (1995). They were extremely useful for the insights they provided into the author's published work. But they were compelling in their own right as well, and eventually led me to pursue their publication, a project that required both literary and editing rationales. The former were solidly provided by feminist theory and by the new ideas about life writing that emerged during the 1980s. The latter proceeded from the particular combination of Anglo-American and European editorial theory that this chapter is exploring.

Beyond the valuable information that Engel's notebooks presented about her published novels and short stories, I perceived that they represented a powerful and consequential example of life writing. In my introduction to the notebooks, I reported that the volume was "inspired by a sense of excitement about life writing's capacity for an evolving notion of the literary text" (Verduyn, *Notebooks* 4). Life writing was theorized anew in the 1980s as a genre and critical practice with the potential to expand and change the understanding of what constitutes literature and the literary text. Marlene Kadar defined life writing as a "genre of documents or fragments of documents written out of a life, or unabashedly out of a personal experience of the writer" (5), while Helen Buss described it as a process "that borrows from every other mode of writing to make new vehicles for self-expression" (11). Life writing was seen to have the capacity to encompass and blend a wide range of writing forms: from the traditional and familiar to the marginal and experimental; from (auto)biography, memoirs, diaries, and letters to fragments and occasional writing, however fleeting, incomplete, or inconsistent. This description aptly applied to the contents of Engel's writing notebooks.

In addition to outlines and drafts, character sketches and concerns about structures for her novels and short stories, and the insights these offered for their published versions, Marian Engel's *cahiers* include a wealth of life writing materials: philosophical reflections on life, research notes on reading and writing, investigations into cultural theory, personal introspection, descriptions of people and places, recipes, back-of-the-envelope budgets, and lists of everything from groceries, to colours, flowers, birds, and words. For the most part, this material is neither dated nor presented chronologically. Indeed, the *cahiers* might best be described by Engel's own word for them: "scrambled" (Cahier IX, 23). This trait is intensified by her frequent return to, and use of, blank pages in earlier notebooks.

The theory and practice of life writing—and the notebooks' compelling illustration of these—thus formed a second powerful rationale for their publication. Life writing extended the work and challenge that feminist theory had posed to literary conventions and canons. "The analysis of the relation between genre and gender," I wrote of the *cahiers*, "has resulted in an expansion of the literary canon to include forms that frequently, though not exclusively, have been practised by women" (*Lifelines* 22). Life writing accommodated and valorized the "feminine forms" of diaries, letters, memoirs, autobiographies, and less familiar or formal forms, such as Engel's *cahiers*. The "scrambled" nature of the notebooks did not disqualify them as worthy of publication nor diminish their literary value in and of themselves. Indeed, they qualified as a unique accomplishment of literary modernism, in the same way that Elizabeth Podnieks had conceptualized the diaries of novelists Virginia Woolf, Antonia White, Elizabeth Smart, and Anaïs Nin.

A third rationale for the project to publish an edition of Engel's notebooks was their socio-historic value as "one woman's record of an important era in Canadian literature history ... the post-war period ... a time of significant cultural and social change as experienced by a woman determined to live as an artist in Canada" (Verduyn, *Notebooks* 5). Engel was part of a generation of women—women writers in particular—who sought viable alternatives to the more traditional social roles and professions as wives and mothers, nurses and teachers. For a woman of Engel's generation, life as a writer could present precarious personal and practical challenges. Engel's *cahiers* offer an "insider's" account of these challenges—from concerns about lack of income as a writer to the absence of career or professional role models and a supportive community of other writers. As such, the notebooks illuminated a broad social spectrum and historical era.

In sum, a combination of social, historic, cultural, canonical, and literary considerations and frameworks valorized my intention to publish an edition of Engel's notebooks. This array of rationales, in turn, shaped my strategic approach to editorial decisions. As I summarized in my introduction to the notebooks, "material was retained which best illustrated the *cahiers* as life writing, social and historical document, philosophical and personal reflection, and template of the creative process" (*Notebooks* 16). The concept of the notebooks as a blueprint for the creative process brings the edition into the realm of genetic criticism.

Genetic criticism distinguishes between the production of a text and text as product, valuing the former over the latter. This perspective is very much in alignment with my own conception of the notebooks as maps of the development of Engel's novels and short stories. As mentioned, the *cahiers* contain many drafts and versions of texts that eventually appeared in published form. The project undertook to present the notebooks *tel quel*, in their full, fragmented, multifaceted form, as a rich source for investigating the production of Engel's publications. As it turned out, this proved not to be fully possible due to practical editorial factors beyond an author's intention. It is worth pausing here to consider what Jerome McGann has usefully identified as "external" influences in his theory of the social constraints on the production of text.

Publishers—and the very real economic pressures that they work under—are obvious and substantial influences on the production of texts. For example, a prime consideration is "how big a book" a publisher might reasonably be expected to take on, given the costs of paper, printing, shipping, and editorial production. In today's publishing world, a 250- to 300-page volume is the standard or norm. This presents a considerable constraint for pursuing a major project on an author's extensive life writings. There are also questions of "canon," which can constrain market considerations. A publisher might be ready to publish as "big a book" as necessary, depending on how "big a name" or reputation an author may enjoy, or the level of his or her status in the cultural or literary canon. As Neil Fraistat and Elizabeth Bergmann Loizeaux, together with Rachel DuPlessis, ask, "Which works get reproduced and edited in the first place?" and "Whose work gets reproduced in expensive multi-version editions?" (Fraistat and Loizeaux 10). In addition to gender, there are issues of race and class, which today are no longer in the "margins of the text" (Greetham). Who is "in" and who is "out"—or more generally, canonical issues—are important "external" influences on editorial projects.

I was extremely fortunate to find a publisher willing to take on the sprawling, open-ended, fragmented notebooks belonging to Marian Engel, a novelist admittedly without the canonical clout of a Virginia Woolf or a Margaret Atwood. Engel had published seven novels, two collections of short stories, children's books, essays, and newspaper columns; she had been the first chair of the Writers' Union of Canada and had played a lead role in the creation of public lending rights for writers; she had enjoyed close friendships with such well-known Canadian writers as Margaret Laurence, Margaret Atwood, and Timothy Findley. Notwithstanding all this, her work is not among the first to come to mind when discussing Canadian literature. I remain grateful to Sandra Woolfrey, then director of Wilfrid Laurier University Press, for her commitment to publish Engel's *cahiers*. At nearly six hundred pages, *Marian Engel's Notebooks* is a "big book." Even so, it is not a complete edition of the *cahiers*. There were further external factors influencing the ultimate character and content of the project. In particular was the concern of living individuals—family or friends—about material they might regard as "sensitive." This concern was a determining influence with regard to material in the notebooks to be left "out" or "in" the final version.

On this question, I was influenced by—among other theorists, arguments, positions, and perspectives—Diane Wood Middlebrook's view that "what is ethical is not the same as what is legal" (128). As Middlebrook explains, "once a person's lifework is terminated by death, the circumstances surrounding the life and the work can be asked every kind of question" (128). For the living, though, such questions may raise issues other than legal ones. Engel's *cahiers* contain entries about individuals in her life—in particular her children—that I decided to leave out of the published edition. This does not mean that these entries are hidden or inaccessible. As I point out in my introduction to the volume, the notebooks in their entirety are available and open to the public at McMaster University's archives (*Notebooks* 8). In total, I set aside approximately 9 percent of the material as "sensitive" and personal to members of the Engel family. Dream recordings that were especially fragmented and difficult to follow accounted for another 10 percent, as did repetitive passages.[7] One concern at this workshop is whether and how decisions to keep material "in" or "out" stand up to the light of textual theory. I am proposing an answer that draws on elements from both major textual editing traditions.

On the one hand, following genetic editorial precepts, the *Notebooks* project was an open-ended one, a "text-in-process." This offered the conceptual, theoretical, and practical basis for publishing an edition of Engel's notebooks that did not claim to be the full and final authoritative copy text. That said, it would have been impossible to make editing decisions about Engel's notebooks that did not constitute a judgment or interpretation of the material. Literary, cultural, social, and historical theoretical justification notwithstanding, editing decisions about Engel's notebooks constitute a judgment or interpretation of the material. As such, the project also aligned with Anglo-American editorial theories of editing as interpretation.

The project raised other questions about editorial interpretation and intervention besides whether and how to excise material. In preparing the edition, I relied on—and in some instances departed from[8]—the archival organization of the notebooks. Archivists count among McGann's "collaborators" in the social production of texts. As an editorial "collaborator," the archivist injects expertise—and interpretation—into the organization of archival materials. For Engel's notebooks as well as for her novel-in-progress, *Elizabeth and the Golden City*, McMaster University archivist Kathleen Garay was the first to examine and apply archival expertise to the largely undated and unchronological material. Citing McGann, Dean Irvine writes of the "editor-archivist" ("*Marchbanks*" 950). While he is referring to the archival aspects of online hypertext, the notion of the editor-archivist applies readily to traditional archival print projects, in which an editor working with unpublished archival material stands to gain considerably from archival theory and from the expert practice of the archivist.

As an open-ended, fragmented, some may say flawed edition, *Marian Engel's Notebooks* is subject to criticism from future editors, who might argue against all and any excisions that were made. Indeed, their critique could well extend to decisions taken about the typeface used in the publication. The edition I prepared presents material from the notebooks in typeface that reproduces as much as possible the written layout on the notebook page. This accounts for the unusual breaks and blanks in the text, the extensive use of short forms (e.g., "&" for "and"), and odd spellings, which are marked [*sic*] except when they are obvious typos (e.g., "shcool" instead of "school"), in which case they are "silently corrected" (*Notebooks* 17–18). Another editor might object to these practices. I would not be offended by this. The edition I produced is one of any number of possible editions that might have been or might still be produced (assuming willing publishers, co-operative family members, and other influential factors in the editing experience). My view is that many of the editorial challenges presented by the project on Engel's notebooks could be—and were—addressed through the use of a combination of literary and textual theories and practices. From the perspective of a hybrid editorial theory and practice, excisions from the Engel *cahiers* are not a matter of material being held back, especially given that the notebooks are open to access at McMaster University's archives. Rather, these decisions reflect an understanding that any edition is ultimately one version among others that may be produced as a text. In sum, in editing Engel's notebooks, decisions based on cultural, social, and canonical reasons, supported by feminist and life writing theories, are further strengthened by and in their combination with textual theory. The same holds for the editing of Engel's last, unpublished novel: *Elizabeth and the Golden City*.

Beyond admiration for Engel's writing, what would motivate or embolden an editing project that tackled not just an unfinished and unpublished novel but one that its author described at one point as "4,000 pages [of] MESS" (Verduyn, *Marian and the Major* 63). The pleasure of reading Engel's writing was decidedly a factor in taking on an edition of her final novel-in-progress. Engel's late-life prose is crafted and clever, and so is the tale it tells. *Elizabeth and the Golden City* brings together the fascinating real-life story of a nineteenth-century Welsh immigrant to Canada, Major William Kingdom Rains, and Engel's engaging fictionalized version of it. Neither story is complete: many details of Rains's life have been lost to history, and Engel died before she finished the novel. But the stories complement one another in compelling ways, and one of my aims in producing *Marian and the Major* was to cement and present that complementarity in print.

Major William Kingdom Rains (1789–1874) was born in Wales on the eve of historic times. He fought in the Napoleanic Wars, during which he met the poet Byron. He was married to Ann Williams (1790–1883), with whom he had six children before leaving for Canada without her, to settle on St. Joseph Island in northern Ontario with two sisters left under his guardianship: Frances and Elizabeth Doubleday. Each sister had a family with him. This domestic arrangement caught the attention and imagination of, among others, the nineteenth-century British travel writer Anna Jameson (1794–1860), the Swiss-born naturalist and explorer Louis Agassiz (1807–1873), the American poet William Cullen Bryant (1794–1878), and the novelist Marian Engel when she and her family camped in the area in 1969.

Rains's unusual story inspired Engel in a number of writing projects. These included an early radio play, her Governor General's Award–winning novel, *Bear* (1976), in which Rains is the model for Colonel Cary, and her last novel project—*Elizabeth and the Golden City*. Rains's story gave Engel the opportunity to act on her long-standing interest in the creative and literary possibilities offered by family life and social history. In a beguiling blend of fact and fiction, history and literature, she transposed the story of the major and the sisters from mid-nineteenth-century pioneer Ontario to mid-twentieth-century Montreal, where she had been a student at McGill, and then to 1960s and 1970s Toronto, where she was part of the Canadian literary scene.

As this brief summary suggests, *Elizabeth and the Golden City* is an example of how literature can be formed from life and how real-life events, times, places, and people can be transformed into stories and fictional figures. The parallels between the real-life William Kingdom Rains and Engel's major, and between the sisters Frances and Elizabeth on pioneer St. Joseph Island and Engel and her years in Montreal and Toronto, add in interesting new ways to our knowledge of Canadian social history. The multiple drafts and versions of *Elizabeth and the Golden City* in the Marian Engel Archive presented two further reasons for the project of editing the unpublished and unfinished novel. First, they demonstrated substantial aesthetic-literary and historical-cultural merit. Second, the project offered another powerful example of literary genesis and production.

As in the notebook project, the project to edit Engel's unpublished novel emerged from the archives, where archivist Kathleen Garay had organized into archival files and boxes the author's "4,000 page [of] MESS." My task was to turn this into a manageable, "readable" text. I "edited down" the material to a 308-page book, which I titled *Marian and the Major: Engel's Elizabeth and the Golden City*. Clearly, significant editorial intervention—and interpretation—was involved in this editing project. But on what theoretical and practical bases did I proceed?

In my introduction to *Marian and the Major*, I outline the approach I adopted:

> There is no attempt in the current undertaking to finish Engel's work-in-progress for her.... What follows is not a novel in the traditional sense, nor is the scholarship concerned with detailing its many versions. By this I mean that it is not the purpose of this book to present a detailed comparison of the various drafts, noting each change in wording or style. Rather, guided by the initial ordering of the papers by archivist Kathleen Garay, and by my earlier studies of Engel's fiction and writing (Verduyn 1995, 1999, and 2004), I have retained what appear to have been the closest to complete of the chapters-to-be. This means that earlier versions of the chapters preserved in the archives have not been included here, accounting for the numerical difference between the "4,000 page [of] MESS" that Engel joked about in

her letter to [her agent Virginia] Barber and the 250 pages of "Elizabeth and the Golden City" presented in this volume. I have focused on the chapters or parts of the novel that are nearest to the structure Engel sketched for the work and that read today as the most complete, which is not the same as "completed." As Engel's quip about "4,000 pages [of] MESS" suggests, and as the multiple drafts in the archives clearly demonstrate, the process of finishing a novel is far from neat and tidy. (63–64)

The novel did not always unfold according to the outlines Engel envisioned for it and, as the *cahiers* reveal, she struggled with its structure until the end. "Discontinuity," she recorded six months before she died, "is best for me with this kind of material. So I may break through. Different form could get rid of set-piece 'characters' […] A joy to invent [but] Trollope did them better. Perhaps he has finally shown me the end of realism." (64)

As described, the project to bring the unpublished and incomplete novel into publication was sustained by a combination of theoretical perspectives and editorial approaches that I am characterizing as a pragmatic and hybrid practice. The production of *Marian and the Major* involved both authorial intention and editorial interpretation. I accepted the theoretically informed reality that this was very much a "text-in-progress," and I combined this perspective with the use of two sets of literary theoretical principles and practices—both Engel's ("Discontinuity is best for me") and my own (drawn from feminist and life writing theory). The result, I believe, is a particular and defensible kind of overall unity of fragments.

The literary and editorial theoretical foundations of *Marian and the Major*, I am arguing, are solid and legitimate. This does not mean that the volume is the only possible "completed" version of the novel-in-progress. Nor does it rule out the possibility of different (or even better) versions that might be produced in the future. As in the case of the notebooks, another editor might very well produce a different edition (provided, of course, a willing publisher, cooperative family members, and so on). From the editorial perspective of "text-in-process," the possibility of another, different edition is not at issue. As with the notebooks, my edition of *Elizabeth and the Golden City* is one version—and, I believe, a compelling, effective, and useful one—but it is not necessarily a final, authoritative exemplar.

▼

This workshop has provided a useful opportunity for me to revisit two editorial projects that I completed and published, to reflect on the theoretical and practical strategies of how I pursued them, and to take stock of editorial theory and practice, including my own. At the time, the projects to edit novelist Marian

Engel's writing notebooks and her final novel-in-progress were informed and supported first and foremost by feminist theory and by theories of life writing. In the "literary/textual theory" divide that Groden identifies, the "literary theory side" was decidedly the more prominent approach in my work. Returning to the projects in the context of this workshop has brought editorial theory to bear, and to balance the weight of literary theory. In hindsight, a combination of literary theory and editorial theory usefully and effectively addresses the practical and ethical challenges that arose during the completion of these two projects, such as decisions about the inclusion or exclusion of "sensitive" material. An integrated approach to literary theory and textual criticism lies at the heart of answering editorial questions considered initially and primarily from the perspectives of feminist and life writing theories.

In much the same way that the ideas of French literary theorists like Blanchot helped Engel think through and achieve the innovation she aimed for in her writing practice, combining literary theory with editorial theory deepens and enriches the understanding and practice of textual editing. Certainly, it has heightened my self-consciousness about my contribution to that practice—the editing of Marian Engel's *cahiers* and her manuscript novel *Elizabeth and the Golden City*.

# "We think differently. We have a different understanding": Editing Indigenous Texts as an Indigenous Editor

Kateri Akiwenzie-Damm

## INTRODUCTION

> "The consciousness of ourselves as Indigenous cultural beings is very important to our Existence as speaking-writing Indigenous peoples. In fact, cultural consciousness is the bottom line."
>
> Simon Ortiz, "Speaking-Writing Indigenous Literary Sovereignty" (xi)

For the past two decades an increasing amount of attention has been given by Indigenous and non-Indigenous writers, scholars, academics, and theorists to questions around the analysis and criticism of Indigenous literatures. Currently, Indigenous literary nationalism is one of the most hotly debated areas of scholarship in the field of Indigenous literature. Indigenous literary nationalism places nation-specific Indigenous intellectual and cultural values at the centre of literary analysis, not in the margins. It centres the study of tribal literatures in the physical and intellectual contexts from which those literatures emerge, on the understanding that Indigenous nations have powerful, sophisticated intellectual foundations and that place figures predominantly within them. At the forefront of this movement are some of the most intellectually astute and engaged Indigenous scholars in North America. Among them is Daniel Heath Justice, Canada Research Chair in Indigenous Literature and Expressive Culture at the University of British Columbia. According to Justice, Indigenous literary nationalism is one of the most controversial debates that he and other scholars of Indigenous literature are engaged in at this time, especially in terms of "the degree to which Native literary criticism can (and should) be grounded in the social, cultural, historical, and political contexts of Native nations" (Akiwenzie-Damm, "Daniel Heath Justice" n.pag.).

Strangely, as this debate is raging very little attention has been paid to the editorial processes that occur before Indigenous literary works make it to print. I say *strangely* because the editing process plays a role in whether a manuscript is published and, if it is, by which publisher, and more importantly, whether its cultural integrity and authenticity are retained, presented in an appropriate way, and expressed to the extent of that writer's abilities and understanding. If the editing process is not undertaken with sensitivity and some knowledge and understanding of Indigenous cultures (and in particular that of the writer)— including, for example, Indigenous protocols, concepts of intellectual property, traditional or Old Time Stories, our literary traditions and canons, Indigenized forms and genres, and Indigenized forms of English—there is always the possibility that the editing process will risk intentionally or unintentionally excising or misrepresenting cultural aspects of the writer's work. There is also the risk that the editing process itself will break down irreparably over issues of cultural difference and/or power dynamics between the author and editor and not because of the quality of the writing or because of clashes strictly to do with the manuscript itself (if such a distinction can be made).

When Indigenous authors in Canada submit their work to a publisher it is always in the context of a colonial history built on exclusion, segregation, abuses of authority, domination, and official policies of assimilation meant to destroy Aboriginal languages and cultures, remove Aboriginal peoples from their lands, disrupt familial relationships, and eliminate the special legal status of any remaining "Indian" peoples. Education policies of the federal government, which has jurisdiction over "Indians and lands reserved for Indians" (Canada, Constitution Act), have been disastrous. For more than a century the federal government-funded, church-run Residential School system forced First Nations children to attend Christian boarding schools purposely located far from their homes and parental and cultural influences. These schools, which were grossly underfunded and poorly monitored, failed to provide students with the skills, including the English-language skills, for which they were ostensibly intended. Punished for speaking their own language, many students left the schools having suffered neglect and physical, emotional, and sexual abuse, and unable to express themselves effectively either in their own language or in English. Of those few who were able to retain knowledge of traditional storytelling or who had the abilities and skills to tell their own stories,[1] few found opportunities for getting published. Indeed, until the 1980s very few Aboriginal writers were published in Canada. Those who were include George Copway, E. Pauline Johnson, Duke Redbird, Howard Adams, Maria Campbell, Sarain Stump, Basil Johnston, and Harold Cardinal.[2]

In a still-colonial, post–Residential School era, when an Indigenous person submits a manuscript to a publisher, it is an act of defiance and faith, one that potentially carries with it the opportunity to both heal some aspects of historic trauma (not only for the individuals involved but also for the communities involved) and to provide advocacy and agency for Indigenous creative and cultural expression that has not been widely available or accessible in the past. Or it can continue to extend or re-create historic harms. Warren Cariou, an accomplished writer of Métis ancestry and Canada Research Chair and Director of the Centre for Creative Writing and Oral Culture at the University of Manitoba, notes that

> there is such a long and unfortunate history of Aboriginal stories being appropriated, expurgated, and distorted in colonial culture, and these abuses have often occurred under the guise of "editing." It is very important for editors to be aware of that history and to work very hard to ensure that their editing practises do not (consciously or unconsciously) continue to create such distortions. (Cariou n.pag.)

The Indigenous publishing industry in Canada is still in its early stages. In 1980, Theytus Books (a First Nations publishing house located on the Penticton Indian Band in British Columbia), now the oldest Aboriginal-owned and -controlled publisher in Canada, began publishing Aboriginal literature. There are only three other established Aboriginal publishing houses in Canada: Pemmican and the Gabriel Dumont Institute (both of which focus exclusively on Métis writing) and Kegedonce Press.[3] To the best of my knowledge, Theytus Books is still the only Aboriginal publisher to receive block-grant funding through the Book Publishing Industry Development Program[4] of the Department of Heritage.[5] This is despite the sometimes intense lobbying by the Circle of Aboriginal Publishers / Aboriginal Book Publishers of Canada[6] for assistance in establishing and maintaining an Aboriginal publishing industry in Canada. Among other activities,[7] such an industry would require require developing and training Indigenous editors, not only to work with these publishers but also to work with non-Indigenous publishers in the Canadian publishing industry, specifically with those who publish books by Indigenous authors and/or about Indigenous peoples, cultures, history, or knowledge. Despite these efforts, little has changed in the fifteen or so years since Indigenous publishers in Canada joined forces to lobby for understanding, support, and assistance. For all intents and purposes, Indigenous publishing in Canada remains isolated, underfunded, in many ways, excluded from the Canadian mainstream cultural marketplace, and under sometimes intense pressure to conform to imposed mainstream publishing values, aesthetics, and goals. That our own might be equally valid and valuable is continually challenged and denied.

Without support, and despite being penalized in some ways for taking on the work to develop our own publishing industry,[8] Indigenous publishers in Canada, like Kegedonce Press, must try to find and develop their own Indigenous editors who will support their goals and those of their authors, and who can balance cultural awareness and sensitivities with the ability to provide required technical and editorial advice. Furthermore, these editors must understand when editorial interventions are necessary in the larger socio-political context. In other words, they must be able to simultaneously ensure that "the fundamental mechanics of writing and presentation" (Justice n.pag.) are considered and that the cultural integrity of the manuscript is respected and protected. As Cree writer, painter, and academic Neal McLeod says, "I think that there are two key elements to editing: i. the mechanics of the writing, and ii. cultural imagery and nuances of writing" (n.pag.). Balancing those two elements in a culturally attuned way is essential.

## CHALLENGES

There are many challenges facing Indigenous writers and, to a lesser extent, non-Indigenous editors of Indigenous literature. While none are insurmountable, the challenges for non-Indigenous editors are more profound.

### Positioning

In all cases, editors of Indigenous Literature must be awareof their position in relation to both the writer and the writing. They must also be aware of the context in which this cultural practice is occurring. By this I mean that they must be aware of the colonial history that may come to bear upon the process and upon their relationships with Indigenous writers. They must know and acknowledge that Indigeneity is varied and diverse. There are many different Indigenous identities not only in terms of general groupings (e.g., First Nations, Métis, Inuit) but also tribally, culturally, linguistically, and legally.[9] They must have knowledge of Indigenous history, and traditional and contemporary Indigenous cultures, and literatures, especially those specific to the authors with whom they are working.

For Indigenous editors, awareness of their position in relation to the writer and writing generally would be less of an issue than it might be for non-Indigenous editors. Cherokee writer and academic Daniel Heath Justice explains that

> there's a real benefit to the relationship between Indigenous writers and Indigenous editors, in that there's (ideally) a common ground of understanding that can be a very fertile ground for ongoing development and growth—you don't have to educate one another about the "why" of things that are cultural. (letter, n.pag.)

Similarly, Warren Cariou has found that working with Indigenous editors

> has been very productive and effective.... There is, in a way, a feeling of relief that I have known from early on they are going to "get it," that they will understand what I'm trying to do. There is less of a sense of hierarchy and power dynamics in the relationship, and that helps me to not only feel comfortable, but I think it also frees me to be more creative and even more experimental in what I write. I have had a sense that these Indigenous editors are more my partners in creation than they are judges. (n.pag.)

Being Indigenous is not a "free pass" for an editor, however. One has to bring those Indigenous perspectives, knowledge, and protocols to bear as an *Indigenous* editor. For this reason, "it's important that they [Indigenous editors] are comfortable with their own Indigeneity within the editorial process—i.e., that they do not simply inhabit a persona of the red-pencil-wielding editor but that they acknowledge to the writer that they also have a particular cultural (tribal, linguistic) position" (Cariou n.pag.).

For non-Indigenous editors, it requires an honest and open assessment of both the privilege and the lack of knowledge they bring to the editing process. Cariou believes that

> it's also important for non-Indigenous editors to understand their own cultural position in the editing process, and to recognize that that position might resonate with some negative experiences for the writer (experiences with non-Native authority figures in various aspects of our still-colonized situation). Being aware of that is important if the editor and writer are to move beyond that colonial deadlock. (n.pag.)

He goes on to say that "the primary responsibility for breaking down that kind of deadlock lies with the editor, who needs to demonstrate a willingness to learn and a humility in relation to the cultural traditions of the writer" (n.pag.).

Also required is a willingness to learn about Indigenous history and culture, not only insofar as it directly relates to the literature but also in terms of developing trust, effective communication, and shared goals with the writer. It is incumbent on non-Indigenous editors working with Indigenous writers "to make efforts to learn as much about the writers' cultures as possible. And this of course means more than simply book-learning; visiting and meeting people are in many ways more important" (Cariou n.pag.).

### Relationship

The relationship between author and editor may also pose challenges. Indigenous authors almost always expect a non-hierarchical relationship in which they retain authority over their manuscript while learning and developing under the guidance of someone who will assist them in making the manuscript ready to be published. In this type of relationship, editors are expected to point out errors, inconsistencies, structural issues, and other problems in a manner that is respectful. The emphasis is not so much on the editor "fixing" problems but on providing thoughtful and thought-provoking insights, and suggesting various ways of addressing any identified issues so that the author can decide what, if anything, to do to resolve each of them

In my work as an editor and publisher, I have tried to ensure that the Indigenous writers (and Indigenous designers and artists) who work with me feel respected, empowered, validated as artists, treated as equals, and heard. As an editor, I see myself as a partner helping to create a book that meets the shared goals of those involved—that is, the writer's, the publisher's, and my own. I view this relationship as one in which each partner brings invaluable expertise and a wealth of knowledge to the process. Unless both the writer and the editor bring the full scope of their abilities and knowing to the editorial table, it will not be a complete success.

McLeod sees the editor's role as that of a "mentor" or part of a mentoring process that can include the oral tradition as well. Cariou sees the editor as "more of a helper" and "guide" who allows and assists the writer "to go where she or he wants to go," while maintaining the writer's "own agency and integrity but also offering help to make the journey as successful as possible (successful in the writer's terms)" (n.pag).

On the other side of the relationship, Indigenous writers working in a culturally engaged editing process must participate fully in that process in an open and reciprocal way. The writer must be willing to consider suggestions and ideas but also is expected to protect the integrity of the work—including its cultural integrity, when necessary—through respectful discussion. When the relationship is one in which the writer has power and authority and is also heard and respected, while the editor demonstrates interest in and knowledge of the writer's culture and is honest and humble, conflicts and deadlocks are far less likely to occur even when sensitive areas are discussed. Furthermore, the writer should understand that the editor is also working on behalf of a publisher. In some instances, for the sake of both writer and publisher, the editor should make the writer aware of decisions that may affect the potential "success" of the book in terms of sales and marketing.[10]

## Defining Success

The ways in which success for an author and a book is defined is another potential area of cultural conflict and challenge. Cariou notes that an editor of Indigenous writing ought to guide the writer in such a way as to make the process as successful as possible in the writer's terms. Obviously, the process must then include some way of coming to an understanding of shared goals and definitions of success. For Indigenous editors this may be an informal and indirect or intuitive process that occurs in the course of sharing ideas, building the relationship, and discussing the project generally, or during the editing itself. For the non-Indigenous editor it may be necessary to discuss the writer's goals and aspirations in a more direct way, keeping in mind that Indigenous communication often differs from non-Indigenous modes of exchange in that it often tends to be indirect, spiralling around issues rather than attacking them head-on. It is also important for non-Indigenous editors to recognize that Indigenous values promote the community and collective good over individual advancement.

From my perspective as an Anishinaabe writer, editor, and publisher, I believe that success cannot be defined except in terms of the collective goals and aspirations of the group or community. At Kegedonce Press, our authors, publishing assistant Renée Abram, and I often refer to those of us involved with the press as "the Kegedonce family."[11] That term reveals just how much each of us cares about our work and one another, and how we measure success in terms of relationship, which can be seen as a form of kinship, a "family" or community operating on shared goals and values for the betterment of the whole. For us, this is a large part of our measure of success. In practical terms, we often see this in action when those involved with the press become mentors, collaborators, advocates, and helpers to others in the group and/or helpers, supporters, and promoters of the press as a whole. Often this help and support continues even if the writer publishes with another press or has not published in some time.

I also recognize that an author may carry the collective goals of his or her community, along with, or even instead of, individual aspirations. So, for example, a writer may be motivated to publish by a desire to pass on or contribute to Indigenous cultural knowledge. Indigenous authors also tend to define success less in terms of book sales and more in terms of giving voice to their people, dispelling stereotypes and misrepresentations through truth telling, increasing awareness of certain issues, reaching specific markets, resisting oppression, and/or, as Jeannette Armstrong has said, "affirm[ing] toward a new vision for all our people in the future" (241).

Given all of this, it is not surprising that recognition and acceptance from within the Indigenous community is often seen as a marker of an author or book's success that, I would argue, is of primary importance to Indigenous authors. Without it, success in the mainstream (awards, bestseller status, "fame" and popularity) lacks meaning, and may be seen as empty or even as a sign of the author "selling out."

## CULTURALLY BASED PRACTICES

In addition to the culturally attuned practices discussed above—recognizing colonial harms and distortions and committing to not making them worse; positioning oneself honestly within the editorial process; learning about the author's Indigenous culture; creating a non-hierarchical relationship based on Indigenous values of cooperation and respect in which the editor acts as a guide, mentor, and partner; and defining success collaboratively with the author in a way that recognizes and supports Indigenous values and goals—there are other practices to consider when editing Indigenous texts. According to Greg Young-Ing, Cree poet, Assistant Director of Research at the Truth and Reconciliation Commission of Canada, and managing editor of Theytus Books,

> some of the culturally-based practices that are being used or adopted in editing Indigenous texts are utilizing principles of the Oral Tradition within the editorial process, respecting[,] establishing, and defining Indigenous colloquial forms of English, incorporating Indigenous traditional protocol in considering the appropriateness of presenting certain aspects of culture, and consulting and soliciting approval of Elders and traditional leaders in the publishing of sacred cultural material. (68)

To this list, I would add respecting and upholding Indigenous intellectual and cultural property rights, which includes appropriately acknowledging all contributors to a manuscript.[12] In terms of editing anthologies, I would add that being conscious of representation and inclusivity within the parameters of the anthology when selecting material is an important aspect of this particular editorial process.

### Culturally-based Principles[13]

Principles to guide (Indigenous) editing of Indigenous writing include the following:

*Acknowledgement of the Editor's Cultural*      *Nbwaakaawin/Wisdom and*
*(Tribal, Linguistic) Position*      *Gwekwadziwin/Honesty[14]*

"I think it's important that they [editors] are comfortable with their own Indigeneity within the editorial process—i.e., that they do not simply inhabit a persona of the red-pencil-wielding editor but that they acknowledge to the writer that they also have a particular cultural (tribal, linguistic) position" (Cariou n.pag.).

*Non-Hierarchical Relationships*      *Dbadendizwin/Humility and*
*with Authors*      *Mnaadendiwin/Respect*

It is essential that editors not replicate power imbalances by situating themselves as the "experts" in the editorial process. Indigenous authors must be seen and see themselves as having power, autonomy, and expertise to contribute. As Cariou notes,

> viewing their role as more like a helper than an authority figure or judge is also a good thing, I think, and one that also fits in well with Indigenous approaches to pedagogy in general. I am not meaning to say that the editor should act like an Elder if he or she is not one, but I think it is important for each Indigenous editor to consider the ways that Elders have taught us important lessons and guided us through difficult challenges. The editor as guide is perhaps a good comparison: allowing and helping the writer to go where she or he wants to go—maintaining the writer's own agency and integrity but also offering help to make the journey as successful as possible (successful in the writer's terms). (n.pag.)

*Empowerment of Those Involved*                           *Zaagidiwin/Love*

This involves engaging with the writer in a dialogue about writing and editing, particularly with regard to the specific manuscript being edited, and providing suggestions that will help the writer improve not only the quality of that manuscript but their work in general. Writers should feel respected and supported by the editorial process, not judged, attacked, or misunderstood. In some cases, especially where there is historically based distrust of authority figures, this may not be possible. Some writers, especially emerging writers, may tend to see any edits or suggestions as negative judgments rather than as attempts to help. Daniel Heath Justice notes that some Indigenous writers could "mistake necessary revisions for attacks on culture." Through the editing process, writers should learn skills and methods that will improve their ability to self-edit their future work.

Editors, too, should be empowered through the process. By engaging in discussions with Indigenous writers who are acknowledged as experts and colleagues, the editor should be able to improve his or her editing and communications skills and learn about other Indigenous peoples, communities, knowledges, and histories.

Both writer and editor should have a sense of belonging to a community or team with shared values, ideals, and goals, and of making positive and important contributions to the process of upholding those values and ideals and attaining those goals.

*Non-interference*                           *and Dbadendiziwin/Humility*

The principle of non-interference is providing guidance or support while respecting another's personal autonomy, decision-making, and free will. Editors of Indigenous writing should ask questions; point out inconsistencies; examine the structure of the work to point out areas that may be problematic; challenge the writer to rethink and, if necessary, rework problem areas; make suggestions or provide options for rewrites or other approaches; and encourage and support the writer's efforts to improve the manuscript. The primary goal should always be to bring out the absolute best of that author's writing through a respectful dialogue and exchange of ideas. This demands an understanding that it is ultimately the author who makes the final decisions about the text and who takes responsibility for those decisions.

One way I put this into practice as an editor is by being careful not to attempt (intentionally or unintentionally) to push writers or their writing to be something they are not simply because convention demands it or, in my opinion, it might be better in some way. This principle is also evident in Cariou's assertion that "as an editor, it is not my place to coax a writer into writing for a 'mass market' or a non-Indigenous audience if they are not interested in doing that" (n.pag.).

## Linguistic Accuracy                                                     Debwewin/Truth

This is necessary whether the language is a colonial language (English or French), an Indigenous language, or Indigenized forms of English or Anglicized forms of Indigenous languages. This is of particular note because working with Indigenous-language material is not only important to the continuation of these languages, but also quite rare. As McLeod says, "our Indigenous languages deserve to be written as accurately as any other language" (n.pag.).

Linguistic accuracy is also essential when working with material in Indigenized forms of English or Anglicized forms of Indigenous languages. In the past, these forms of language have not been accepted, edited to conform to conventional English, altered in ways that did not recognize their cultural and linguistic underpinnings, or caused the manuscript to be rejected altogether. Editing out these forms of language is offensive.

## Protection of the Integrity of Indigenous Knowledge           Aakde'win/Bravery

Writers and editors should work together to ensure that Indigenous knowledge is protected—that is, that it is not misrepresented or misused. At the same time, when necessary, elements that for cultural reasons might need to be excluded from public dissemination should be removed from the manuscript (McLeod n.pag.).

## Commitment to the Collective Well-being                            Zaugigae/Love
## of Indigenous Peoples

This requires an understanding that "Indigenous writing and literature does not just serve individual interests but rather collective sites of memory and knowing" (McLeod n.pag.). The commitment to collective well-being requires that editors "help create a space for Indigenous consciousness and thinking … and take the time to mentor emerging writers (even if this may take a great deal of time)" (McLeod n.pag.). It also requires that editing promote the presence, not absence, of Indigenous peoples, and that it contribute to our "survivance" rather than our domination and erasure. Anishinaabe writer and theorist Gerald Vizenor says that "the commercial stories of Native absence and victimry perpetuate dominance" (Akiwenzie-Damm, "Survivance" 27). Editors of the work of Indigenous writers must acknowledge and be aware of this and instead support and affirm "stories of survivance" by Indigenous authors: "Stories of survivance are stories of resistance and a creative sense of presence" (27).

# Toward Establishing an—or *the*—"Archive" of African Canadian Literature

George Elliott Clarke

No history is straightforward (unless it is over), but some are more disorderly than others.[1] Consider, for instance, the chronicle of a literature that I describe as "African-Canadian" but that some others prefer to label—as is their wont—as "Black Canadian." For contemporary critics reviewing or studying works of Canadian African/"Negro" provenance, the blatant—and salutary—bias is to understand them as a "recent" categorization, as a "now" literature penned by "arrived" writers (like the Canadian-by-choice Dionne Brand [1953–] or the Canadian-by-birth Lawrence Hill [1957–]). For many readers—and even for some scholars—there is no African/Black Canadian literature, especially if we mean "creative writing," before "Bajan" native Austin Chesterfield Clarke's first novel appears in 1964. There's a wanton simplicity in such a chronological and cultural-critical assertion: one is freed from having to spelunk into the darkest, dustiest, dirtiest depths of archives. Furthermore, one may presume—with one's readers—that even if there are earlier novels out there, authored by African-heritage colonial settlers of British North America or by citizens of the Dominion of Canada, they cannot be worth recovering. After all, what could such dead-and-buried works have to say to us today that is of any import, even as sociology, never mind as story? The writer and scholar M. NourbeSe Philip expresses precisely such a *noble* reservation when she feelingly complains of "a great Canadian void" (*Frontiers* 45), that is to say, the absence of significant, Black Canadian literary production before the onset of significant Afro-Caribbean immigration, 1955–present. "Until now"—essentially from the 1970s onwards—she *seems* to say, there is no African-Canadian literary history that is lustrous enough to bear reading, reprinting, and even riffing upon. A peculiar but problematic amnesia underscores such pronouncements. As antidote, one must recall Michel Foucault's assertion that "a revolutionary undertaking is directed against the rule of 'until now'" (*Language* 233), meaning, presumably, that a revolutionary must appreciate that to deem existing circumstances as "new" is propaganda against insurgency.[2] In other words, there are always precedents, antecedents, ancestors. However, it is seldom in the interest of the ruling class or its disciples to *remember*, let alone applaud, the cultural works of disempowered minorities. Thus, again, when Philip argues that early African-Canadian writing—sermons and religious tracts—is "not literature" (*Genealogy* 73n22), one feels her consternation that black settlers and illiterate ex-slaves in early Canada did not—or could not—bother to pen novels, plays, and verse collections. Indeed, there are only a few extant slave narratives that one can list, unblushingly, as "Canadian" (either by authorship or by publication). Formidably, then, Philip calls into question the rationale for exhuming early black writing in Canada and daring to call it "literature," when it is obviously "less than" such. This point is especially so if we set, say, Phillis Wheatley, the first African-American poet to publish a book (1773), against a figure like Susannah (Susana) Smith, once of Virginia, then of Nova Scotia, and finally of Sierra Leone, who wrote—or spoke and saw transcribed—a letter, dated 12 May 1792, asking for "Sope" (Fyfe 24). To compare Wheatley's achievement to Smith's is to compare publishing with handwriting. Nevertheless, one might posit that "literature" is not strictly a synonym for "creative writing," and recognize that religious texts—even sermons—may find themselves anthologized and their (collective) authors taught in university English classes. Canons do, it would appear, interpenetrate, not necessarily "each after its own kind," but rather in flagrant miscegenation, so that the Holy Bible migrates from Departments of Theology to English classes where it appears as "the Bible as Literature," or, say, *The Autobiography of Malcolm X* (1965) violates the boundaries of political science and history and ends up in a graduate English seminar. In the wake of deconstruction, who can be sure about what texts to exclude *qua* literature, anyway? (Any text can be literature, but only the *studied* text constitutes "good" literature?) To sum up my long introduction here, the *project* of properly constituting an African/Black Canadian literature is one that entails mining archives, to extract "legitimate" texts and authors for study, but also to reconstitute history as a base—shifty, yes, but not an abyss.[3] Indeed, I think we need to understand that the project of assembling any anthology is, implicitly (sometimes even explicitly), a challenge to the "canonical" parameters established by previous anthologies, whether they be—to refer to my own project—African-Canadian, Canadian, African-American, West Indian, British, French, French-colonial, and so on. To propose a new, national anthology of "early" African-Canadian literature is to also push against (or even push aside) previous anthologies of *other* literatures or canons.

To oppose any suggestion that, by advocating retrieval of the antique and the forgotten and the lost, I am also fetishizing, ironically, the "new," the "discovery," I will remark that I follow Smaro Kamboureli's sage comment in her introduction to her anthology, *Making a Difference: Canadian Multicultural Literature* (1996), that her attempt to offer "a historical overview" is intended to dispel "the notion that multicultural writing is only a recent phenomenon" (xxii). At the same time, she is conscious that "any anthology that intends to offer a historical overview can only function as an allegory of literary history, can only map out yet another narrative path by which we can enter that history" (xxii). Bearing these *bons mots* in mind, I want to argue that to catalogue black books and black writers, of Canadian location, from before the 1960s, is to also identify "firsts": the first poets, playwrights, and novelists. By doing so, we also note their initial grappling with the pernicious subtlety of Canadian racism, in both its social and state guises, and to ascertain their strategies for presenting themselves and representing their communities despite official narratives that, resenting their presence, strove to erase their existence. Should we examine these pioneering "Black Canuck"[4] scribes, we might also find that their works serve to emphasize certain essential trends, leitmotifs, and themes still *au courant* within *our* literature.

Notwithstanding the preceding paragraphs, one recognizes that the scholar or historian of African-Canadian literature is stuck with the problem of having to declare a genesis wherever he or she feels best able to set this "debut" (while remembering—strictly—that all such origins are never fixed). Our strategy here affirms the Franco-Ontarian critic René Dionne's intuition in *La Littérature régionale aux confins de l'histoire at de la géographie* (1993) that "une littérature régionale possède déja un corpus d'oeuvres au moment où ses promoteurs la proclament comme un domaine littéraire particulier" (38). Just as the critic of Franco-Ontarian—or Acadien or Québécois—literature must prove the existence of such literatures by carving them out of the larger corpus of French, French-Canadian, and world francophone literature, so must the student of Black Canadian writing seize his or her texts from the libraries and canons of Africa, African America, America, the Caribbean, South America, Europe, and European Canada. Ultimately, one declares his or her authority to claim a text or writer as constitutive of a "new" régime of reading, and one must stand prepared to defend this syllabus, just as the founders of a "new" nation must first declare its existence and then present a defence of it. In a crucial article, African-American scholar Nahum Dimitri Chandler assures us that "in order to displace hegemonic institutions"—such as, let us say, totemic canons—"one can only carry out a full displacement by crossing the threshold from open criticism to a declaration of authority" (87). To fuse—but not confuse—the thought of Dionne and Chandler, African/Black Canadian literature truly *arrives* as the consequence of brazen, authoritarian, unilateral, retroactive, self-conscious, and defensive (offensive?) annunciation of a canon and a chronology. In other words, ya gotta come with the truth—or just sit your ass down: "Without assuming power according to some existing institution within the status quo, any project of criticism is always open to a quite worldly and unkind intervention" (87). If you don't search and research, you don't found no "church." Then again, to cite Richard Sher, "each book has its own peculiar way of coming into the world and inhabiting it" (58). It's the same thing for *a* literature.

In *Odysseys Home: Mapping African-Canadian Literature* (2002), I compiled a bibliography of the literature, canvassing anglophone and francophone texts, from 1785 to 2001–2. Introducing the compilation, I recorded a few "firsts," despite the good-intentioned objections of scholar Rinaldo Walcott, who urges that Black Canadian intellectuals "refuse the seductions of 'firstness' and engage in critique, dialogue and debate, which are always much more sustaining than celebrations of originality" (xiv).[5] Yet the novels of Martin Robinson Delany and Amelia Etta Hall Johnson, the poetry of Nathaniel Dett and Anna Minerva Henderson, and the drama of Lennox Brown, to use only a few, English-language examples, serve to introduce—inaugurate—a resonant, Canuck interrogation of "blackness" and "national" identity, and these concerns *still* animate African/ Black Canadian writers and their critics "now." Moreover, these authors step into the "void" (cf. Philip) and assume both authority to speak and, indeed, to disrupt or dispute discourses, usually negative, about Africa and Africans and "Negro" *being*. Decades intervene between these authors, and they experience different socio-economic and political conditions. Somehow, however, they answer consistently questions that bedevil us still. Excepting the dyed-in-the-wool African-American Delany, these writers sure are obscure. Nevertheless, they jet an inkling of Black Canuck literature, even if we are oblivious to this achievement. Undeniably, these "accu(r)sed" progenitors of African-Canadian literature penned a set of esoteric publications, all existing in splendid independence from each other, but all also participating in the conversations of their times, from abolitionism to temperance, from Afrocentrism to integration, and also echoing respective literary movements, from romanticism to modernism. Still, these writers are also projections to black readers of the future, though not necessarily African-Canadians.

Certainly, one *echt* distinction between early African-American and African-Canadian authors is that the former can hope for an Indigenous readership, while the latter, generally, cannot. For this reason, most early African-Canadian authors do not address Canadians of any complexion, except obliquely. (The startling exception is Henderson, though she, pointedly, in speaking to her immediate New Brunswick audience, veils her racial identity and marginalizes "blackness.") Thus, when Franck Fouché publishes his poetry collection,

*Message*, in Port-au-Prince, Haiti, in 1946, he has no reason to expect a bibliog-rapher to come along, three-plus generations later, to claim his work, addressed first to Haitians, then to French readers, and finally to African-Americans, as the first francophone African-Canadian work of verse. Yet to read *Message* from an African-Canadian vantage point lends it more value than to read it simply as a mid-century Haitian—later Haitian-Canadian—poet's debut. Starkly put, in his native Haiti, Fouché may be a middling writer of piddling notice. But in African-Canadian bibliography, he is of signal importance, having been the first—proto-Canadian—francophone to author a book of poems and a play.

Another oddity that marks early African-Canadian texts is that they are sel-dom *real* "books." Instead, one novel is a newspaper serial (Delany's *Blake*), pam-phlet-length chapbooks serve as poetry collections (see Henderson's *Citadel*), and mimeographed typescripts represent drama (see Brown's plays). To turn to Sher again, he proposes that "each [book] is unique, and none can be made to fit a prefabricated mold" (58). Who's to say that we cannot treat "non-books" as if they were—unique—books? Sher points out, helpfully, that "books serve as homes for text, but they are also physical artifacts, commodities, status symbols, and more. They come in a variety of sizes and shapes, are published and mar-keted in different ways, and vary in other respects" (42). It would be repressive to rule out early African/Black texts as "books" just because they lack cloth covers. Too, the physical status—or artifact—of the "book" is an essential aspect of its meaning, purpose, and audience "pivoting." Even so, all African-Canadian liter-ary production desiring public consumption shares in the idea that print creates, says Claire Hoertz Badaracco, "a public culture of aesthetic and political signif-icance" (15). For the foundational literary writers of Black Canuck presence, that "public culture" is debates around slavery, family life, racism, colonialism, temperance, education, religion, and community development, but also aes-thetics and existentialism. In *Trading Words: Poetry, Typography, and Illustrated Books in the Modern Literary Economy* (1995), Badaracco observes that "poets, typographers, book designers, advertising illustrators, printers, publicists, and journalists share a common purpose in the modern literary economy—per-suasion linked with sales" (195). If we extend the notion of African-Canadian modernity back to 1859, when Delany's *Blake* is serialized and forward to 1965 when Brown's first play, "The Captive," is issued by the Ottawa Little Theatre, we affirm that "persuasion"—even propaganda—is the principal interest of the "first" African-Canadian texts. Arguably, then, even Susannah Smith's humble request for "Sope" is not distinct from Amelia Johnson's plea for temperance and obedience to Anglo-Protestant Christian morality or Henderson's implicit integrationism.

To open up the book format of Martin Robinson Delany's *Blake; or, The Huts of America: A Tale of the Mississippi Valley, the Southern United States, and*

*Cuba*, arguably the *first* African-Canadian novel, is to confront an expression of ardent anti-slavery and passionate pan-Africanism. Written in Chatham, Canada West, now Ontario, between 1856 and 1858, the novel began to appear in the New York-based *Anglo-African Magazine* between January and July of 1859. The serialization was interrupted by Delany's expedition to Africa in May 1859, and not resumed, in the now *Weekly Anglo-African*, until December 1861, and concluding in early 1862. Delany (1812–1885) is a central figure in African-American literature, where he is credited as being an "early Afrocentric ideologue" (Austin 205) and as the fount of "an African American literary river" (206). However, despite his three years in Canada West (where he relocated to flummox the evil US Fugitive Slave Act of 1850 and to promote a project of African-American emigration to either South America or Africa), and despite his authorship of *Blake* on Upper Canadian soil, he has been granted no place in English-Canadian literary history. *Blake* is the third African-American novel, so it is read in that culture as a response to American slavery and European imperialism in Africa. Yet it may also be viewed as a radical, African-Canadian response to the same issues, one that could be read profitably in relation to George Brown's anti-slavery agitation in the Toronto *Globe* newspaper or even in Susanna Moodie's settler memoir *Roughing It in the Bush* (1852), which includes an account of the lynching of a black barber and cleaner, Tom Smith, somewhere in Canada West, for marrying an Irish woman (Moodie 211). Thus, *Blake* should be seen as an African-Canadian entry in an international debate over slavery whose North American resolution had national consequences for British North America. (Lest we forget, the military elimination of African servitude in the United States served as a stimulus to Canadian Confederation in 1867, thanks to the threat of American military revenge against British North America for British imperial support for the now-defeated Confederacy during the US Civil War.)

Born in 1812 in Charles Town, (West) Virginia, to a slave father and a free mother, Delany grew up with an intimate knowledge of his African roots, for "his Mandingo grandmother (who died at the age of 107)" used to "chant[] about her homeland," and his father was "the son of a Golah chieftain" (Takaki 83). Given his innate pride in his African ancestry as well as his failed bid for admission to Harvard Medical School, plus his scorn for slavery, Delany soon fixed upon black emigration as the appropriate reply to white oppression. Because blacks were a suppressed minority in the United States, they would have to relocate to exercise self-determination. Although Delany removed to Chatham, Canada West, in 1856, he viewed Canada as only a temporary haven. Even so, he was very aware of the impact of racism upon "coloured Canadians," and he does not hesitate to excoriate white Canadian liberalism for its hypocritical attacks on American slavery, even while it restricted Black Canadian education and economic opportunity. Hence, it is easy to place Delany's black nationalism and pan-Africanism alongside the similar solid position of Philip (1947–) or the less definite, more playfully sinuous, mixed-race postmodernism of the poet Wayde Compton (1972–). Likewise, Delany's Byronic, revolutionary hero may be juxtaposed with Dionne Brand's existentialist rebel heroines in her novel, *In Another Place, Not Here* (1996). As well, Delany's polyphonic prose, one akin to the "unique … argot formed of Latinate polysyllables, puns, translationese, stray associations, archaic English phraseology, and … slang" (characteristics that Alan J. Peacock identifies in US poet Ezra Pound [Peacock 97]), is a style that many African-Canadian authors adopt.[6] So long as there are African-heritage Canadian writers, Delany will never truly die.

Delany differs from other early African/Black Canadian authors on the question of Christianity. Many passages in *Blake* complain about its hypocrisy. Thus, Henry Blake asks, rhetorically, "What's religion to me? My wife is sold away from me by a man who is one of the leading members of the very church to which both she and I belong" (112). With deliberate irony, Henry later asserts, "Well, I'm a *runaway*, and from this time forth, I swear—I do it religiously—that I'll never serve any white man living!" (130). Writing to American abolitionist William Lloyd Garrison on 14 May 1852, Delany says "Heathenism and Liberty, before Christianity and Slavery" (Takaki 94). For Delany, black liberation means building truly free black communities, not slavishly adopting "white" religion. Strains of this thought persist in Brand and Philip.

In contrast to Delany's reservations regarding "religion," Anglo-Christian attitudes determine the fiction of the first African-Canadian novelist native to British North America, Amelia Etta Hall Johnson (1858–1922). Born to African-American parents in Canada West in 1858, and educated in Montreal, Johnson moved to Baltimore, Maryland, where at age sixteen she married the Reverend Harvey Johnson, DD. In 1877, she began writing poems for what her biographer, I. Garland Penn, describes as "race periodicals" (Penn 422). Next, Johnson issued, in 1887, an "eight-page, monthly paper," *The Joy*, "containing original stories and poems" (422–24). Johnson's stories and poems also appeared in *The National Baptist*, "one of the largest circulated white denominational journals in the [United States]" (424). Like Delany, who had written for Frederick Douglass's abolitionist newspaper, *The North Star*, from December 1847 to the summer of 1849, and who edited another newspaper in 1875, Johnson became a "creative writer" after first playing the roles of editor and journalist. Penn delights to note that "in 1889–90 [Johnson] reached the place for which she had been aiming and preparing herself. She wrote for publication a manuscript, which was purchased by the American Baptist Publication Society, one of the largest publishing houses in America," thus making her "the first lady author whose manuscript has been accepted by this society" (424). Her next success was the "first Sunday-school library book written by a colored author" (425).

Johnson's first novel, *Clarence and Corinne; or, God's Way*, published in Philadelphia in 1890 by the American Baptist Society, is an odd work, at least from a postcolonial and postmodern and Afrocentric perspective: all of her characters are white, or so the illustrations attest. Not only that, her novel is a Christian comedy: the saved lead good lives and, when troubles interrupt their not unpleasant progress, they rally, resituate themselves on the narrow path of righteousness, and achieve marriage, family unity, and relative prosperity. Johnson's fiction reads like the Book of Job—if it were authored by Jane Austen. In her introduction to the 1988 reprint edition of *Clarence and Corinne*, African-American scholar Hortense Spillers recognizes its status as "barely disguised tractarian writing. In other words, the narrative presses its polemical point by way of the story, which provides an occasion for the theme of social uplift" (xxvii). Moreover, "nothing ... earmarks this work specifically as one written by a 'black woman writer,' or an 'Afro-American,' and ... there is very little or no evidence in the novel itself to suggest that Amelia E. Johnson wrote according to the putative urgencies of coeval black life in the United States" (xxvii). Correctly, Spillers advises that Johnson's decision to write fiction using only white characters reflects the feeling, as recorded by the African-American newspaper the *Baptist Messenger*, that such writing "is one of the silent, yet powerful agents at work to break down unreasonable prejudice, which is a hindrance to both races" (qtd in Spillers xxviii). By using white characters, Johnson hints that blacks rival whites in terms of writing and religion, psychology and insight. Thus, she calls racial categories into question at the historical moment when they are most rigid. Moreover, it is unlikely that the American Baptist Association could have—would have—published a Christian novel featuring boldly black characters. Accepting this reality, Spillers reclaims and redeems Johnson for African-American literature by stating that "it is unimportant exactly *what* and *how* [Johnson] wrote, but altogether significant *that* she did" (xxviii). Certainly, "her contemporaries saw the testimonial, exemplary force of her work as an instance of sociopolitical weaponry: 'the author of "Clarence and Corinne" feels confident that there are those among the race who need only to know that there is a way where there is a will, to follow her example, and *no doubt far surpass this, her first experience in bookmaking*; and she is happy in knowing that come what may, she has helped her people' (Penn, p. 426; emphasis mine)" (Spillers xxvii–xxix). In the novel, then, "race disappears ... as human community loses specificity, except for its deeply embedded error" (xxx).

Yet it is not an attempt to "smuggle in race"—as Spillers alleges that Johnson's readers do (xxxii)—to assert that a novel about poverty, familial angst, runaway fathers, and foster mothers refers to the legacy of slavery, just as it warns against the sins of city life. Thus, the hovel in which Clarence and Corinne spend their first years resembles any slave shack of yore:

> Dismal as was the outside of this wretched abode, still more so was the inside. The floor, devoid of carpet, and unacquainted with soap and water, creaked underfoot, and in places was badly broken.
>
> The two or three rickety chairs, a rough pine table and crazy bedstead could hardly be dignified with the name of furniture. Some chipped plates and handleless cups were piled in confusion on the table....
>
> A rickety stove, that was propped up on bricks, which did duty for legs, was littered with greasy pots and pans. Ashes strewed the hearth, and the few unbroken lights in the windows were so begrimed with dust as to be of little use, so far as letting in the daylight was concerned. (6)

To complete this slavery-like portrait, Johnson tells us that Clarence and Corinne were hovel "inmates" (Johnson 6). Their mother is "the mistress of all this misery" (6), and upon her "countenance was stamped despair, and judging from her swollen eye, one also was the victim of ill-usage" (7). Now a shiftless husband hits her; formerly, a slavemaster or an overseer might have done so. When Clarence cries out, "Oh, how I wish we could dress decently, and go to school again like other children" (7), his plea for equality is a matter not only of class, but also of race, for segregation is pushing Southern blacks out of classrooms and back onto plantations, a regression enforced by Ku Klux Klan terrorism.

*Clarence and Corinne* is, then, like most Bible-based writing, an allegory—one that connects urban ills to moral lapses, yes, but also one that subtly reminds readers that the struggling, just-freed black men and women require social uplift as well as spiritual liberation. Thus, alcoholism replaces racism as the prime evil: the father of Clarence and Corinne is a mean drunk, and his violence and addiction kill his wife and disperse his children. The bottle stands in for the bullwhip; the inebriated daddy replaces the power-drunk "massa." Other aspects of slavery also appear. When Corinne has to live with the miserly Miss Rachel Penrose, who believes "a bright fire ... [is] a waste, and enough to eat entirely unnecessary" (Johnson 42), Corinne experiences "nothing but hard work from morning until night" (47). One later learns that "the scanty food and poor clothing the child received was but little reward for the quantity of labor required of her" (68). "The poor little thing is overworked and underfed" (74). Moreover, like the archetypal Gothic masters, Miss Rachel, to establish Corinne's obedience to her severe economy and exacting standards, forces her to read only the Bible verses—"such as the twenty-eighth or twenty-ninth of Numbers, all about sacrifices, etc." (58), while ignoring "the beautiful stories of 'Joseph,' 'Daniel,' 'Samuel'" (58). Intriguingly, these latter stories supply the plots and imagery of many anti-slavery spirituals. Again, subtly, Johnson asks us to read the brutal-izing effects of industrialization and urbanization, fuelled by lust, greed, and alcohol, as being akin to the degradations perpetrated by slavery.

The evidence suggests that *Clarence and Corinne* is domestic missionary work. Johnson seeks to truly "civilize" the United States. If the secret subject of the novel is the continuing damage wrought by now-abolished slavery upon American morale and social mores, its secret mission is to repair the Christian abolitionist alliance of blacks and whites, now sundered by post-Reconstruction politics. Moreover, its secret intertext is Harriet Beecher Stowe's Christian abo-litionist novel *Uncle Tom's Cabin, or Life Among the Lowly* (1852), which—radi-cally—presents the slaves as *naturally* more moral than the slaveholding whites. In writing of black suffering via "whiteface," then, Johnson repeats Stowe's argu-ment that redemption is available to all who struggle against evident immorality: slave days then; slum life—with its vices—"now." From this perspective, *Uncle Tom's*—Christian—*Cabin* has been reduced to the alcoholic's hovel in which Clarence and Corinne experience dispossession. Too, though their faces, illus-trated, are white, their speech and subjects could come straight from Negro minstrelsy: "Yes'm," says Clarence (Johnson 11), among other locutions; and the "silk handkerchief" that he gives his sister is, in reality, "an old bandanna ... comically dilapidated" (10).

Though Johnson has been partly claimed by African-American scholar-ship, she belongs *by birth* to the African-Canadian canon. Moreover, her use of white characters foresees Suzette Mayr's fiction more than a century later. In *The Widows* (1998), Mayr narrates the attempts of three elderly German women to baptize themselves into new lives by tumbling over Niagara Falls in a barrel. By succeeding, they also find redemption for the weight of the sufferings that their nation engendered by instigating the Second World War and committing crimes against humanity—including genocide. Championing elder empower-ment, feminism, and lesbianism, the novel is also an oblique commentary on racial exclusion. In André Alexis's short fiction and novels, too, there is a ten-dency to deploy a multicultural and multiracial cast, ignoring *caste*, so that one must question just how much "colour" can be said to truly determine anyone's character.

Although James Madison Bell can be claimed for the African-Canadian canon, he was an African-American poet who worked as a plasterer in Canada West, only from 1860 to 1865. Born in Ohio in 1826 and dying there in 1902, Bell has only a tenuous connection to African-Canadian and Canadian liter-ature. He squeezes in references to Canada in "Modern Moses, or My Policy Man," penned in the Confederation year of 1867, by mentioning "debauchees wherever found / from Baffin's Bay to Puget's Sound" (200). Yet Bell's true subject is American politics.[7]

Thus, let us consider the probable first collection of poems to be published by a black author born in Canada, namely, Robert Nathaniel Dett's *Album of a Heart*, published in 1911 in Jackson, Tennessee. Raised in Drummondville— now Niagara Falls, Ontario—Dett (1882–1943) is significant to African-American musicology, for as a scholar of the Negro spiritual, he also published two essential compilations: *Religious Folk-Songs of the Negro as Sung at Hampton Institute* (1927) and *The Dett Collection of Negro Spirituals* (1936). Importantly, Dett launched (or followed) several African-Canadian tendencies. *Album of a Heart* utilizes both "dialect" and standard English, just as Black Canadian poets, novelists, and playwrights do today. The poem "Conjured" is practically ragtime in rhythm:

> Couldn't sleep last night!
> Just toss and pitch!
> I'm conjured! I'm conjured!
> By that little witch!
>
> … Whenever I try to think;
> Side track and switch
> My thoughts do; and finally
> Dump me in the ditch. (46)

The diction is ragged too, more related to blues and the brothel than to the college where Dett was ensconced when his book was published. Yet in the same volume as "Conjured," there is the stately, Tennysonian "At Niagara," a fairly Victorian piece of *vers libéré*, or loosened blank verse:

> No! No! Not tonight, my Friend,
> I may not, cannot go with you tonight.
> And think not that I love you any less
> Because this now I'd rather be alone. (12)

The poem is rather mysterious; it could be about spiritual disaffection, homoerotic confusion, or suicidal brooding:

> Urge me no further, now that you understand.
> A nobler friend than you none ever knew
> But not this time. Tonight I'll be alone.… (13)

In "Pappy," Dett displays his familiarity with the then-popular Plantation tradition in American poetry: "When I was a pickaninny / many years ago, / I members how my mammy used ter call me …" (19). One can almost imagine

Al Jolson, in blackface, performing this "number." But, being Canadian, Dett produces "Au Matin" (31)—a bit of Hardyesque drivel about ghostly dawns and gone love—and also "Au Soir" (32), which, being a better poem, exudes a rag-time feel about copulation:

> Now does joy
> Its bounds transcend—
> Would the night
> Might never end!
> O soft shine on us
> From above,
> Beauteous Night
> Of perfect love. (33)

So, there you have it: the first published—at book-length—African-Canadian poet in English authors pop-song-styled lyrics and formal verse, alludes to French, and indulges in dialect verse. In addition, Dett was an expatriate intellectual, pursuing a career in the United States, presumably because there was no room in Canada—the Great White North—for a black man of his talents. A composer as well as a scholar, he remains a seminal Harlem Renaissance figure in the United States, but remembered here mainly in the prestigious, Toronto-based, eponymous Nathaniel Dett Chorale.[8]

The first African-Canadian woman to publish a book of poems was Anna Minerva Henderson (1887–1987), who was a retired civil servant, aged eighty, when her chapbook, *Citadel*, appeared in the Canadian Centennial year, in Saint John, New Brunswick. A New Brunswicker by birth, she is notable for having been a stellar pupil—really, an intellectual—in a time when there were few serious educational opportunities for blacks in general and for black women in particular. Indeed, Henderson obtained a teacher's certificate, taught school in Nova Scotia, and then, in 1912, at age twenty-five, was hired into the federal civil service after writing an entrance test and earning *the third-highest grade in the Dominion*. While in Ottawa, she wrote a column for the Ottawa *Citizen* titled "The Colyum" or "Just Among Ourselves" (Shadd 3). By the time she was fifty, Henderson was publishing her verse in little magazines. The biographical note attending the publication of her sonnet, "Parliament Hill, Ottawa," in *Canadian Poetry Magazine* in 1937, allows only that she is unmarried ("Miss") and "a civil servant of Ottawa" ("News" 63). A year later, when this poem is reprinted in *New Harvesting: Contemporary Canadian Poetry, 1918–1938*, edited by Ethel Hume Bennett, the "Biographical Notes" remain laconic: "Anna M. Henderson, of Ottawa, has published verse in periodicals and magazines" (Bennett 194). When Henderson self-publishes *Citadel*, a slim booklet of thirty-one pages, she does not offer us either a "collected" or a "selected" poems. Indeed, one of her best poems, "Parliament Hill, Ottawa," is missing from the collection. The latest dated poem in the book is from the winter of 1965 (Henderson, *Citadel* 30)/ and the earliest (presumably) refers to 18 May 1947 (9). Yet some of the poems appeared before 1947. This fact indicates that *Citadel* is a crafted chapbook focused on Saint John's cityscape and history, the British connection, faith, and the strife between artist and critic: it is neither a hodgepodge of musings nor a select batch of the author's "best." Instead, it must be considered her forceful entry into her city's literary culture, though it is doubtful that most readers would have known the author was black. Henderson's poems are mainly sonnets or quatrains; seldom does she allow *vers libre* to darken her pages. She comments on Loyalist history, the foggy look and soggy feel of Saint John, and, almost inaudibly, on race and racism. She sounds more like John Milton than she does Little Milton, for, likely, she wishes to prove—against racist and/or sexist nay-sayers—her (*race's*) competence in the field of letters. The key to Henderson's low-key style is "Mount Mansfield, Vermont": in this sonnet, the speaker exults in climbing the mountain—in a ski resort—and feels "singing happiness." Her exultation prefaces the claim, "This now we know— / That nevermore can level valley-ways / Shrouded in mist and sheltered far below, / Suffice to hold us captive through our days" (19). Superficially, the speaker is pleased to be at the summit of a redoubtable mountain, and feels that she may repeat the experience. But, in solid metaphysical tradition, Henderson moves the poem toward allegory: "And in the valley, dark in dreams below / Gleam here and there the twinkling lights of Stowe" (19). As it turns out, the Vermont resort is named after Stowe, whose *Uncle Tom's Cabin* (1852) served to ignite the American Civil War. Most subtly, Henderson is likening the mountain climb (prescient of the Reverend Dr. Martin Luther King's imagery in his final sermon of 4 April 1968) to the dream of freedom once held by slaves, who looked to abolitionists like Stowe for inspiration. But the successful "escapee," now at the summit, basks in the moon's "floods of silver light" (19). A generation ago, a few Black Canadian critics chastised writer and playwright Alexis for not being, in essence, "black-identified enough" to merit their approval. Well, what will they do with Henderson, who made her singular poetry quite without any black support, but still found it possible to forward an African-Canadian voice, albeit in neoclassical registers?

The first African/Black Canadian to publish a play achieved that distinction only in 1965, but the circumstances were auspicious: Lennox John Brown (1934–), a native of Trinidad, won a competition, then run annually by the Ottawa Little Theatre, to seek out and publish the best "new" Canadian plays in English. (If one counts Fouché's pre-emigration publications in Haiti, then he was the first Black Canadian to publish a play in French. I refer here to *Un fauteuil dans un crâne* [1957].)[9] Brown was only in Canada a decade or so before moving on to the United States, although his later biography is rather sketchy. What can be said is that *The Captive* (1965) was issued not as a book, but rather as a bound typescript, fifty-seven pages in length. Also notable is that Brown, as an Afro-Caribbean immigrant to—or long-term resident in—Canada, sees as "early" as 1965 that African-Canadians are superbly variegated, so that prospects for unified action are difficult. His *dramatis personae* include Clarence—"a Negro medical student from Jamaica" (Brown, "The Captive" 1), Oseka—"an African student from Kenya" (1), Jimmy—"a Negro from Harlem" (1), and Norm—"a Canadian Negro" (11). These four black men have kidnapped a white man, an anonymous southerner from the United States who has been trying to organize a Canadian chapter of the Ku Klux Klan. Their unity in this effort, though it violates the liberty and life of another human being, suggests possibilities for a concerted, joint political movement throughout the African Diaspora. But Brown's elaboration of the men's backgrounds soon reveals their "unity" to be paper-thin. "JIMMY, the Harlemite, is tense, lithe and athletic ... [He] is essentially a man of action" (4). "OSEKA ... is cool, businesslike and efficient. He is that dangerous combination of thought and action" (4). "CLARENCE ... is a dreamer. He has an indecisive passive quality that suggests weakness" (4). "NORM"—tellingly the born Black Canadian—is not a student, but a "railway porter" (11), who "*appears* to be an outgoing type who laughs easily" (11; my emphasis), and, who, when we first see him, has been "drinking and is a bit tipsy" (11). Like Jimmy, he is "mercurial" and can be "quite violent—even to the people closest to them" (11). Brown's portraiture is both clichéd and complex. The two working-class types are American and Canadian, but the latter is more degraded, presumably because he has no political and economic power (unlike Oseka and Clarence) and no cultural influence (unlike Jimmy). Oseka and Clarence, one African and the other Caribbean, are either middle-class already or middle-class in aspiration. They are not the sons of disempowered minorities, but representatives of new nations, just freed from Caucasian-shaded imperialism. That these four should unite to terrorize a supposed member of a white terrorist organization *could be* read as propagandistic posturing. But Brown complicates—no, negates—this possibility by, first, showing that Oseka and Clarence are rivals for the affections of "JOAN ... an unusually attractive white girl of about 22. Her long blonde hair and fair skin give her a fairy-like impression" (25). Her brother, John, also a character, is a liberal white who befriends the Negroes. Shortly, the kidnapped man dies, and his captors are wracked by guilt and fear—of the noose (capital punishment is still legal in Canada in 1965). Joan and John are torn by what to say to the police, if they dast say anything; and Oseka admits his love for Joan, who—sorrowfully for him—reaffirms her love for Clarence. The play is sharply written, and the lines attain a prose poetry that lifts it high above the Civil Rights Movement events that may have informed its development. Brown's characters are compelling, though the playwright seems dismissive of Norm as the Black Canadian drunkard—a symbol of black failure—whereas Jimmy exemplifies black struggle. This portraiture—caricature—is affirmed by Brown's 1972 statement that "there is no substantial Black culture in Canada" (Brown, "A Crisis" 8).

However, as this short summary of some "early" African/Black Canadian texts demonstrates—indelibly, there always was—just as there is—some form of "substantial Black culture" in Canada, especially if we recognize that Canadian "Black culture" has always been variegated due to different periods of incoming-black arrival in disparate parts of the *evolving* state under very distinct protocols. We also need to suspend the notion that there is a monolithic "Black culture" that is identifiably the *same* as the forms of African Diasporic identity that have arisen elsewhere in the Americas (or even in Britain or in Europe.) It is partly my position here that the special and specific "Black *cultures*"—yes, plural—in Canada can better be accessed, assessed, and appreciated, if we bother to recuperate the commentaries and creative work of the early—or the *first*—African-Canadian writers, even if they had no concept of such an identity. We must construct a *national* anthology of such works, to perceive the ideational imperatives of African-Canadian literature from its inception. Theoretically, the establishment of an—or *the*—"archive" of African-Canadian literature will make discussion of even current texts more coherent, if not "literate."

Twenty years after publishing *Fire on the Water: An Anthology of Black Nova Scotian Writing*, in two volumes; fifteen years after publishing *Eyeing the North Star: Directions in African-Canadian Literature*; and a decade after publishing *Odysseys Home: Mapping African-Canadian Literature*; I remind myself that the purpose of an anthology (or bibliography) is to marshal evidence—proof—of the existence of a canon that *has always been*, but, at the same time, *has always been overlooked*. Yet as soon as the anthologist or bibliographer compiles or selects this *provisional* canon, he or she exposes it to potentially fatal interrogation of its worth. Once such a body of texts has achieved "the light of day," so to speak, why should anyone give it "the time of day"? It is in answering this question that the anthologist or bibliographer proves his or her acumen, mettle, and, to use Chandler's term, "authority." It is his or her editing, his or her selection or compilation of texts, that makes the argument for the worth of the *de facto* canon. His or her editing itself *is* the argument for the texts or authors that *depend* on the introductory matter (a defensive apparatus that may also extend to the provision of explanatory notes, suggested timelines or periodizations, identifications of "schools," biographies or bio sketches, and even references to other critical works). Too, in arguing for the merits of discrete texts and authors, the anthologist (or bibliographer) is also challenging the borders or margins of other canons, reminding us that canonical status, of whatever form, is not fixed, but open-ended. If the anthologist—or bibliographer—puts a set of texts and authors on trial, so to speak, his or her selection or compilation is, itself, proof of the subjects' canonicity.

# Project Editing in Canada: Challenges and Compromises

Carole Gerson

## PREAMBLE: WHAT IS AN EDITOR?

Editors, for all their power in shaping literature and scholarship, have seldom been specifically addressed in general, let alone in Canada.[1] As Susan L. Greenberg notes in the introduction to her recent collection of interviews with editors, "editing, as a subject in its own right, is not talked about very often—not even by the people who do it" (1). This absence may be due to the imprecise nature of the category, which ranges from substantive editors (or copy editors) who polish manuscripts, to literary editors at major magazines and newspapers, to acquisitions editors who work within publishing houses and often establish their direction. While most such people receive little public recognition, some achieve considerable status and influence, such as the legendary nationalist Lorne Pierce, who directed Ryerson Press for forty years (see Campbell, *Both Hands*); the modernist advocates W.A. Deacon—long-time literary editor at *Saturday Night* and *The Globe and Mail*—and William Toye at Oxford University Press; and more recent individuals such as Douglas Gibson at McClelland and Stewart.[2] The category also includes scholarly editors who prepare definitive editions of literary works as with the CEECT series of early Canadian prose works or classroom editions such as the three recent Norton editions of canonical Canadian books;[3] academics like Malcolm Ross[4] who oversee publishers' series; and, finally, the many (like myself) who occasionally practise what I call "collection editing," for want of a better generic term. Likewise wrestling with terminology, Jeffrey R. Di Leo recently responded to William Germano's distinction between an anthology as "a gathering of previously published, or mostly previously published, work" and a collection as "a gathering of new or mostly new writing" by choosing "anthology" as the inclusive term for the various types of edited and collected works whose preparation involves shaping multiple primary or secondary texts into a final volume ("Analyzing" 4). However, as most Canadian scholars probably share Dean Irvine's view that "an anthology is by definition a text by several authors" ("Editing" 69), I think the term "collection" better serves the present purpose because its range extends from the edited works of a single author to large multi-volume projects. Despite the ubiquity of anthologies and collections in academic culture, their editorial production remains curiously invisible, as indicated by their absence from Darcy Cullen's recent collection of articles, *Editors, Scholars, and the Social Text*.

Published discussions of editing in Canada tend to focus on influential career editors like Deacon or on problems of textual editing, as in the two volumes of articles emanating from conferences at the University of Toronto in 1972 and 1989.[5] Less common have been discussions of collection editing and project editing, enterprises that share a somewhat different set of concerns.[6] Embarkation on a venture of collection editing such as an anthology, a writer's collected or selected works, or a project that produces one or more volumes of critical texts by multiple authors, presupposes an outcome that is balanced, or unified, or otherwise coherent in some discernible way; the appearance of "Canadian" in the title usually implies an explicit or implicit national vision.

Anyone who engages in collection editing quickly discovers that the preparation of such books creates a narrative of compromise between the initial vision that inspired the project and the pragmatics of publication in relation to such matters as permissions, copyright, the dimensions of the page, and the size of the volume (as I have learned from gathering overlooked primary texts into tomes that I hope have had some impact on the understanding and canonization of Canadian literature.)[7] Other chapters in this volume, by colleagues who have similarly engaged in recuperative editing, examine theoretical and practical issues common to such projects, touching on some of the editorial issues that I have raised in the past about such matters as national vision, gender balance, and masculine modernism.[8] Conceptual issues of inclusion and exclusion are writ even larger in the big collaborative projects that have shaped Canadian knowledge since the 1960s. These include the *Literary History of Canada*, whose first volume appeared in 1965; the *Dictionary of Canadian Biography*, whose first volume appeared in 1966; and the *Historical Atlas of Canada*, whose first volume appeared in 1987. Accounts by their editors[9] discuss many of the challenges and concerns, from defining the scope of their project to the delights and travails of working with idiosyncratic scholars, that were also encountered by the editors of the most recent such enterprise, the three-volume *History of the Book in Canada* (2004–7). The following analysis of that project's editorial questions and solutions draws on my experience as a member of the overall editorial team and as co-editor of Volume 3, which covered the period from 1918 to 1980.

## WHAT IS BOOK HISTORY?

For more than three centuries, Western cultures have taken for granted the notion that the history of printed materials represents the history of knowledge. While bibliographers, historians, and literary scholars had long paid attention to selected aspects of the many products of the printing press, it was only in the 1980s and 1990s, when it became apparent that the hegemony of print was being seriously challenged by new technologies, that interdisciplinary groups undertook large-scale collaborative efforts to track the significance of print as an "agent of change" (to cite the title of Elizabeth Eisenstein's monumental study) and the role of "the book as a force in history" (Darnton 9). As with so many scholarly movements of the second half of the twentieth century, the examination of book history began in France, with *L'apparation du livre* (1958; translated into English in 1976) by Lucien Febvre and Henri-Jean Martin. This study inspired French scholars to embark on the *Histoire de l'édition française*, whose first four volumes were released in 1982, the same year that Robert Darnton published his foundational essay, "What Is the History of Books?" Basing his analysis on the book trades of eighteenth-century France, Darnton outlined a model of production and reception involving authors, publishers, sellers, distributors, and readers; whether accepted, modified, or contested, during the past thirty years Darnton's diagram has underscored scholarly analysis in the field variously known as book history, print culture, book culture, or book studies. Even though Darnton concludes his article by cautioning that "books themselves do not respect limits, either linguistic or national," that many authors belong to "an international republic of letters," and that "the history of books must be international in scale and interdisciplinary in method" (22), the following two decades saw the rapid development of book history projects that were conceived and organized within specific national frameworks.

This national focus may be attributed in part to the state-based model for book history already established in France as well as to the influence of Benedict Anderson's theorization of the ways that "print-languages laid the bases for national consciousnesses" (44). Also in play were the identity politics and nationalist sensibilities of the late twentieth century that motivated the editors of scholarly projects for Ireland, Scotland, and Wales to dissociate their book cultures from that of England, despite inevitable overlap with the seven-volume *Cambridge History of the Book in Britain* and the three-volume *Cambridge History of Libraries in Britain and Ireland*. For example, to rescue the history of the book in Wales from being merely "an appendix to the history of the book in Britain" (Jones and Rees xiii), Welsh editors and scholars foregrounded the rich history of texts written in the Welsh language. The dictum "to know ourselves," popularized in Canada as the title of the 1975 Symons report on Canadian studies, seems to have implicitly motivated national book history projects in other jurisdictions.

For scholars working on the print history of monolingual major powers such as France, Britain, and the United States, the national and the international often coalesce; however, in a small country like Canada, whose local print cultures interweave with external cultural empires, tensions between the national and the international are constantly in evidence. In general, whatever the geographical range of a book history endeavour, national issues cannot be ignored. While books, readers, and authors have cavalierly disregarded national boundaries, the world of print has been regulated by political jurisdictions through licensing, taxation, censorship, customs offices, public education, and the like, and has also received government support through grants and other benefits to libraries, publishers, authors, translators, and similar players in the book trades. Ideally, then, the narratives of national book histories should be contextualized within the international dimensions of print culture, and international studies need to take full cognizance of the impact of national policies and structures.

## EDITORIAL CHALLENGES OF A MAJOR PROJECT: *HISTORY OF THE BOOK IN CANADA (HBIC)*

The initiation of *History of the Book in Canada* followed the establishment of national book history projects in Britain, Scotland, Wales, Ireland, Australia, and the United States during the 1990s, all of which would produce many weighty volumes of collected essays by multiple expert authors. Inspiration and encouragement originated with the Bibliographical Society of Canada / Société bibliographique du Canada, which sponsored a landmark founding conference in Ottawa in 1997. Patricia Lockhart Fleming at the University of Toronto served as overall director;[10] she and Yvan Lamonde at McGill were the general editors who oversaw all three volumes, with additional volume sites for other members of the editorial team. For Volume 1, Gilles Gallichan maintained a site at the Library of the National Assembly in Quebec City. For Volume 2, Fiona A. Black had an office at the University of Regina, followed by one at Dalhousie University when she took up a position there. Volume 3 was generously supported with facilities and infrastructure at the Université de Sherbrooke, where Jacques Michon held the Canada Research Chair in book and publishing history, and at my home institution of Simon Fraser University. At Dalhousie, Bertrum MacDonald, editor of electronic resources, oversaw the construction of five databases, now housed at Library and Archives Canada, to support the inquiries of authors and editors and to establish infrastructures for ongoing research.[11] At the outset, the general editors established an illustrious Advisory Board that included international scholars from other book history projects and an Editorial Committee of senior scholars and figures from the Canadian book community who provided valuable consultation at various phases of conception and implementation. The whole undertaking was funded by a $2.3 million Major Collaborative Research Initiatives grant from the Social Sciences and Humanities Research Council (SSHRC), supplemented by a translation grant from the Canada Council and additional resources from our universities. Most of the funds went to support more than sixty graduate research assistants and five postdoctoral fellows; other major budget lines covered our regular newsletters, travel to editorial meetings, the mounting of six conferences (two for each volume), and the salary of Judy Donnelly, our project manager extraordinaire.

With the initial grant period of five years extended to seven, the editorial team maintained a rigorous publication schedule. Volume 1 (*Beginnings to 1840*), edited by Patricia Lockhart Fleming, Gilles Gallichan, and Yvan Lamonde, appeared in 2004;[12] Volume 2 (*1840–1918*), edited by Lamonde, Fleming, and Fiona A. Black, was published in 2005;[13] and Volume 3 (*1918–80*) which I co-edited with Jacques Michon, followed in 2007.[14] The books were issued in English by the University of Toronto Press and in French by les Presses de l'Université de Montréal, two publishers with a history of collaboration; their commitment to produce attractive and relatively affordable volumes[15] was secured at the time of the initial grant application. From the outset, it was agreed that the books would be printed in Canada's first roman typeface, Cartier Book, initially developed by Carl Dair in 1967 to commemorate Canada's Centennial and subsequently adapted by designer Rod McDonald for computer typesetting. Named to honour Jacques Cartier's "discovery" of Canada's mainland, the font's title now seems appropriate for reasons different from the celebratory perspective of 1967, given our current recognition of the role of print in suppressing Canada's Indigenous people.

*HBiC*'s editorial team included librarians, bibliographers, literary scholars, and historians, a combination leading to fertile interdisciplinarity. Altogether the project benefited from the collaboration of 172 authors, ranging from graduate students to retired scholars, many of whom wrote more than one text. Most contributors participated in one or more of our six conferences which enabled the editors to test the design of each volume in a first conference, and to workshop authors' drafts in a second. In addition to ensuring that texts were read by many eyes, these conferences created a strong sense of camaraderie, bringing together doctoral students, mid-career scholars, non-university specialists, and seasoned professors.

Book history proved a new approach for many of our authors, as some were more accustomed to literary analysis while the practice of others was to collect information without developing much narrative to connect the details. Even though we worked hard to recruit scholars whose areas of expertise matched the project's needs, as editors working to firm deadlines we found that substantive intervention was often necessary, and we rewrote many texts, regardless of the status of their assigned author. As a result, *HBiC* proved an instructive site for experiencing at ground level the contested nature of authorship. Some authors grumbled at our changes, some graciously requested that editors' names be added as co-authors, and some simply took credit for work that was not fully theirs. Despite having signed contracts, some potential contributors never fulfilled their commitments, leaving us to recruit replacements on short notice. On several occasions, graduate student researchers were asked to write case studies on topics that were entirely new to them and fully rose to the occasion.

As the editorial team designed the volumes, we wrestled with many issues that can be gathered under the general headings of scope, language, and cultural significance. Situating our project within the environment created by the other national histories of the book then under way heightened our awareness that the history of print culture in Canada was inflected by several features unique to this country's history and geography. Most major projects, such as those in Australia, Britain, France and the United States, concentrate on the history of print in just one language. Interestingly, editors in Wales and Ireland took opposite approaches to the handling of dual-language national book cultures in order to foreground their Celtic identities. The one-volume *A Nation and Its Books: A History of the Book in Wales* (1998) includes sections about the history of writing in Welsh and the importance of its maintenance as a spoken language during the twentieth century. On the other hand, the editors of the multi-volume *Oxford History of the Irish Book* separated their volume dedicated to *The Printed Book in Irish, 1567–2000* from the three volumes covering *The Irish Book in English* over the same time period. In Canada, we chose to integrate the cultures of the two major languages, in line with our national policy of bilingualism, and to strive for balanced attention to their respective book histories in relation to their differing identity narratives. Further complicating the dissemination of print in Canada is the population's dispersal across a vast land mass, with most Canadians residing within 200 kilometres of the American border, rendering American economic and cultural domination inescapable. In addition to a prolonged colonial link to Britain that inhibited the development of domestic publishing until the twentieth century, all aspects of English-language book history in Canada have been influenced by the looming presence of the United States, an expansionist foreign power with ten times our population. Canada's French-language book history, by contrast, was shaped by a sense of isolation that often led to protectionist self-sufficiency. To trace the history of the book in Canada, therefore, required continual pursuit of two narrative streams, one English and one French. These stories sometimes run parallel to each other, sometimes follow differing paths, and sometimes merge.

## QUESTIONS OF SCOPE

From the outset, *HBiC*'s editors agreed that Canada's present-day borders would determine our geographical domain—unlike the American project, whose volumes tend to introduce states and territories as they joined the Union.[16] Volumes 1 and 2 of *HBiC* include maps to illustrate the changing boundaries of the British North American colonies and the expanding nation as provincial demarcations evolved. Although Newfoundland did not enter Confederation until 1949, we cover the island's print history from the time of first European contact in the sixteenth century.[17] Challenges of distance, transportation, and communication continuously affected our book history: printing presses were set up in remote areas, and books were carried to readers by every vehicle imaginable. In Canada as in the rest of the world, print culture tends to concentrate in urban centres. However, our project also addressed regional activity—each volume sought to represent the geographical spectrum of production and consumption during its period, a goal that expanded with the spread of newcomers into the West and the North after the middle of the nineteenth century. Outside Quebec, publishing in French occurred in the Acadian communities of Nova Scotia and New Brunswick as well as in Ontario and the West. Although the major centres of English-Canadian production have been the largest cities of Montreal and Toronto, pockets of publishing activity flourished in all provinces and territories, from pioneer times to the surge in the 1960s and 1970s supported by new government funding programs. Authors tend to reside in or near the major publishing centres, but book buyers and readers are everywhere.

Because the territory that became present-day Canada has historically been a crossroads of British, French, and American culture, we situate the Canadian experience within the colonial triangle created by these three powers, and within the global environment resulting from their empires. The focus of *HBiC* is not the history of the *Canadian* book—which would have been relatively limited in scope—but the history of the book *in Canada*, which requires attention to the high proportion of material read by Canadians that was written and/or produced abroad. Within this international framework, the structure of the Canadian project addresses most aspects of Darnton's production circuit, positioned within the contextual approach outlined by Thomas Adams and Nicholas Barker. Interestingly, we discovered that it was Volume 3 that could follow Darnton most faithfully, as his model presupposes an established cycle of production and reception that was not fully in place in Canada until the twentieth century. In her review of this volume, Candida Rifkind found its structure inflected by "Pierre Bourdieu's work on the field of cultural production and the sociology of literature" (170), an influence that was implicit in our overall conceptualization.

In all three volumes, *HBiC* looks at authors, printers and publishers, distributors (involved in importing, exporting, and bookselling), and readers, examining these agents within the larger contexts of government, religion, technology, and international relations. The volumes' draft tables of contents were frequently revised in our efforts to embrace this ambitious range of material within our page limits. To enhance the longer inclusive sections, we used case studies to highlight key figures or events; as well, we chose visual images that would add to the discussion rather than simply illustrate major sections of text (leading Roy MacSkimming to lament the scarcity of portraits of authors and publishers in his review of Volume 3 in *The Globe and Mail*). In Volume 3, for example, Jack McClelland's publicity stunts are encapsulated in the caption to a photo of one such event, and Frank Newlove's innovative cover designs for the first volumes of the New Canadian Library are described in the caption to a display of four images.

Within each volume, content balance was shaped by the volume's editors in accordance with its historical framework. Because book publishing was slow to develop in Canada before the beginning of the twentieth century, the topic receives more attention in Volume 2 than in Volume 1 and constitutes a major portion of Volume 3. On the other hand, newspapers, periodicals, and the many kinds of occasional materials produced by print shops are more visible in the first two volumes. As well, the first two volumes pay more attention than the third to music publishing and to technologies of illustration. Given *HBiC*'s overall focus on print in the life of Canadians, it would have been wonderful to have had the research resources and page space in Volume 3 to examine department store catalogues and telephone books, two print formats that people consulted far more widely than the literary texts that dominate the conventional analysis of Canada's print culture. Unlike most other national book history projects, *HBiC* devotes considerable space to library history: in the first two volumes, personal libraries receive attention, whereas the third focuses on the development of public and institutional library services. Across the project, the editors felt that the history of libraries offered an important window onto the elusive history of reading, a feature of book history that we would have liked to cover in greater detail.

As we made these decisions about scope and contents, we confronted the indeterminacy of the notion of "book history." If "the book" is regarded as a concept rather than a material artifact and is to extend beyond the codex form, how far can it be taken? To include every form of literacy and system for conveying messages, including singly produced "texts" such as tombstones and "livres d'artiste"?[18] To communication practices that are closer to "aides-memoire" than to formalized systems based on language or images? All our volumes include reading materials commonly associated with books, such as newspapers and magazines. Volume 1 also looks at many other printed items, from currency to election materials, business forms, and health notices;[19] Volume 2 includes sheet music, cookbooks, and posters and handbills.[20] While Volume 3 does mention railway timetables,[21] by the twentieth century, print had become so ubiquitous that it was necessary to narrow our focus to books and allied materials, despite the vast range of utilitarian and occasional printed products among the everyday paraphernalia of modern life.

Our periodization reflects developments related to print production: the year 1840 divides the first two volumes because it marks the establishment of the first press west of Ontario and the subsequent expansion of print into the West and the North, as well as the introduction of responsible government into the colonies. The third volume begins with the year 1918, the end of the First World War, a date commonly regarded by Canadian historians as a threshold for various political, economic, social, and cultural developments that accompanied peacetime prosperity, including changes in copyright legislation. To maintain some historical distance, we close this volume in 1980, a year that marked many changes in the book world occasioned by the introduction of new technologies, and in Canada by the shift from a national to a more global perspective represented by NAFTA, the North American Free Trade Agreement of 1985.

The apparent tidiness of this periodization scheme belies the reality that not all our topics share the same chronological benchmarks. Centuries, decades, wars, and other major events (such as Confederation) present markers that appear to offer convenient narrative frameworks, yet use of these dates often threatens to distort the larger picture by severing stories from their origins or later developments. Beginning Volume 3 in 1918 seemed a safe decision as the end of the First World War is a recognized turning point in much of Canada's social and cultural history. But not for anglophone publishing, whose twentieth-century story begins before the war, when changes in copyright regulations encouraged four large British publishers to set up branch plants in Toronto.[22] During the same years, the foundations were laid for the two major Canadian-born publishing houses of the twentieth century, Ryerson Press and McClelland and Stewart. Fortunately, we were able to obviate discontinuity by having the same author deal with English-Canadian publishing in both Volume 2 and Volume 3; George Parker expertly stickhandled the volumes' chronological divisions by shaping the story for Volume 3 in relation to the agency system.

Another editorial concern as the project's conceptual framework evolved was how to recognize the many Aboriginal groups whose sign systems preceded the arrival of European printing. As eloquently pointed out by Germaine Warkentin (a member of our Editorial Committee), in contrast to other settler colonies such as Australia and New Zealand, Canada was colonized by Europeans who arrived without printing presses. Nearly two hundred years of scribal culture in New France preceded the first newspaper produced by Bostonian immigrants to Halifax in 1752. In her essay "In Search of the Other," she argues that Canada's book history should include the many forms of writing—both colonial and Aboriginal—that enabled communication before the arrival of printing and that continued alongside it for many centuries, especially in Native cultures. Such questions forced the editorial team to confront *HBiC*'s disciplinary boundaries, as we felt that to do justice to Canada's many Indigenous sign systems would require a different framework and indeed a different project, one led by Aboriginal scholars along with historical anthropologists and communications specialists. At the same time, we did our best to acknowledge the Indigenous presence; hence pre-contact systems of cultural transmission through petroglyphs, pictographs, wampum belts, bark and hide scrolls, totem poles, and hieroglyphics are briefly surveyed at the beginning of Volume 1.[23] Subsequent texts create a thread that traces Aboriginal interactions with the world of print through all three volumes, from the textualizing of Native languages by missionaries in the seventeenth century to the growth of Aboriginal control over authorship, publishing, and reading in the second half of the twentieth.[24]

If the determination of our beginning point proved controversial, so too did the selection of our date of conclusion. The original plan was to end with 2000, a year that looked tidy but proved difficult. While other book history projects, such as those in Australia and the United States, bring their narratives into the twenty-first century, we decided to change our end date from 2000 to 1980, with a coda to summarize the last two decades of the twentieth century. This adjustment enabled us to manage a number of concerns. First of all, we felt that the effort to follow all our narrative threads up to a present year that would be outdated by the time of publication would have diminished our perspective: not knowing the outcome of current stories in this era of technological transition, such as the effect of the Internet on bookselling or the fate of publishers and authors in the brave new world of e-books, meant that we would have had to devise vague conclusions. Narratives inevitably assume trajectories of success or failure, and it would have been embarrassing to mispredict the future.

## LANGUAGE MATTERS

Despite Canada's official bilingualism, bilingual scholarly projects are surprisingly rare in the humanities. A wave of such ventures occurred in the late 1960s and early 1970s in response to the rise of Quebec nationalism and with the support of translation grants from the Canada Council. This period saw the founding of the Association of Canadian and Quebec Literatures / L'Association des littératures canadiennes et québécoise as well as the appearance of Ronald Sutherland's comparative critical studies of English- and French-Canadian literatures and his establishment of the journal *Ellipse* (Sherbrooke, 1969–), which is dedicated to publishing Canadian poetry in translation (see Fischman). Hence the bicultural nature of *HBiC* is one of its most distinctive features; we worked in both French and English, with each volume's pair of editors comprising an anglophone and a francophone. Like the country itself, the project is asymmetrical, as evidenced in its very title—*History of the Book in Canada / Histoire du livre et de l'imprimé au Canada*—and we were challenged to balance our representation of the two founding language groups. As a cultural entity, Quebec is more self-contained than English Canada; as well, it has more thoroughly researched and documented itself, through such bodies as GRÉLQ (Groupe de recherche sur l'édition littéraire au Québec), founded in 1982 by Jacques Michon at the Université de Sherbrooke. Another significant undertaking unmatched in English-speaking Canada is the cultural history *La vie littéraire au Québec*, housed at Laval University, which has issued six volumes to date. At the government level, the mandate of the Bibliothèque et Archives nationales du Québec (BAnQ) is to collect all Quebec imprints and publications concerning Quebec, maintaining a retrospective and current bibliography. Hence its electronic catalogue offers an inclusive database that makes it possible to quantify genres, languages, authors, publishers, and the like. For the rest of Canada, there is no similar resource.

The editorial team was conscious of the continual need to address multiple narratives and fully aware that the asymmetry of Canadian history would be evident across the entire project. In Volume 1, French Canada receives substantial attention due to the primacy of French settlement. By Volume 3, English Canada dominates by virtue of its larger population and greater geographical spread. Through all three volumes, we sought to acknowledge duality and difference as in the following examples, whose contrasts illuminate the kinds of choices we faced in editorial management and decision-making.

The dominance of the Catholic Church in Quebec, in contrast to the Protestantism of most English-speaking regions, has played out differently with regard to religious publishing, educational publishing, and censorship. Institutionalized religion also affected library history, as Quebec's Catholic hegemony rejected the liberal principles that accompanied the public library program established by the American benefactor, Andrew Carnegie, at the beginning of the twentieth century. Some regions benefited enormously from his bequest: between 1901 and the early 1920s, 125 Carnegie-supported libraries sprang up in Canada: 111 in Ontario and the remainder mostly in the expanding communities of the West. But none were built in Quebec,[25] where francophone readers depended on parish libraries whose small collections were carefully monitored by the Church. These circumstances inspired Quebec's Protestant anglophones to establish separate institutions for their own communities. Some proved very stable, such as the Fraser-Hickson Institute, a Montreal subscription library active from 1885 to 2007, and the still vibrant Westmount Public Library, founded in 1897 in commemoration of Queen Victoria's Diamond Jubilee as a "Free Public Library and Reading Room" that would "be forever free to the use of the inhabitants and ratepayers of the Town" ("History").

While French Canada lagged in the realm of public libraries, its development of a distinct children's literature was more rapid, beginning in 1921 with the establishment of the landmark periodical *L'Oiseau Bleu* (Montreal, 1921–40). English Canada did not reach a comparable threshold until 1967, with the founding of Tundra Books, the country's first dedicated children's book publisher. Located in Montreal, Tundra was interested in bilingual publishing and issued many books with side-by-side texts in French and English. In the field of children's literature, as in most aspects of print culture, English Canada has continually struggled to assert control and foster local authorship and publication in resistance to a constant torrent of imported books and magazines, largely from the United States. French Canada, however, has been sufficiently protected by language and religion to provide moral if not material support for local production in most genres of print; as well, the development of French-language radio, television, and film led to additional opportunities for francophone writers and publishers. Quebec's cultural sovereignty has been cultivated through various provincial policies, such as a massive program of school prize books that flourished from 1856 to 1964 and that guaranteed large markets for selected publishers and canonical authors. In the 1960s, the Quebec government introduced programs to protect French-language, Canadian-owned bookstores and other book-related businesses. In the rest of Canada, the book trades have been less fortunate.

As these examples demonstrate, interweaving the book histories of Canada's "two solitudes" proved to be one of this project's most exciting editorial challenges. In the words of reviewer Fernande Roy, "les deux univers ne se croisent pas: ils s'ignorent plutôt" (277–78). Although Hugh MacLennan originally selected *Two Solitudes* as the title of his 1945 novel in order to describe a balanced relationship between Canada's foundational European cultures, the experience of the *HBiC* editorial team confirms its now common use to represent cultural division: French and English university-based researchers such as historians, bibliographers, and literary scholars tend to function within separate linguistic circles, with surprisingly little crossover. It appears to me that the linguistic bifurcation of our cultural history is in part the creation of those who study it—including those participating in the present project on cultural editing in Canada (in contrast to the 1989 University of Toronto conference on Canadian editorial problems, whose published proceedings carefully balance French and English projects and views; see Lennox and Paterson). With *HBiC*, we found that many scholars met their limits when they obligingly attempted to cover their topic in the other language, only to discover the superficiality of their knowledge; several others preferred not to try. With Volume 1, I was given three weeks to research and write the section on "English Literary Culture in Lower Canada" when the volume's editors learned belatedly that the francophone expert contracted to write about the early literary culture of Quebec would not deal with anything English.

Managing this linguistic chasm posed a consistent editorial conundrum. In Volume 3, while larger topics such as book publishing merited separate sections for each language, we didn't want to fracture the entire volume into separate entries for English and French coverage of every topic. Hence in the editorial offices at the Université de Sherbrooke and Simon Fraser University, we developed our own methodology and terminology to handle this problem. We referred to the longer, parallel separate texts as "twin bed" entries; for other topics, we created a number of "double bed" entries by "marrying" two shorter texts, one originally written in English and one in French. These were linked by opening and closing sections written by editors, thereby creating shotgun co-authorship among scholars who never met in person. In addition to dealing with issues of content and translation, our practice of working in two languages encountered technical questions arising from different editorial conventions. But we also found that the process of translation improved both readability and veracity; in the apt words of Patricia Fleming: "Nothing points up the flaws in a text more effectively than putting it into another language. Imprecisions that we let pass in a first edit would come back from translation either misunderstood or so much improved that we were shamed into revising the original" ("National" 41).

In addition to maintaining balance between Canada's dual lineage of English and French, ongoing reconceptualization of the makeup of the country shaped our attention to the print activities of the many immigrant communities that set up presses in their own languages, as well as our consideration of printing in Native languages. However, before 1980 there had been scant collection of data concerning the country's unofficial languages, beyond census counts of immigrants' mother countries. Moreover, statistical accounts of print activity tended to group all allophone languages as "other." To construct the print history of these "others" entailed a consistent cross-volume effort. Volume 1 looks at printing in German and in Gaelic; Volume 2 adds Icelandic, Yiddish, and Chinese. For Volume 3, it was a challenge even to identify the many languages that new Canadians read, wrote, and printed. Particularly helpful was the monumental

*Encyclopedia of Canada's Peoples*, whose appearance in 1999 documented the recent dramatic shifts in Canada's cultural identity. The editors of this hefty volume identified 119 ethnocultural groups, one of which—Aboriginal Peoples—they subdivided into twelve entries.

Immigrant communities share a common pattern of first producing newspapers and serials for local consumption, with other genres added as numbers and circumstances warrant. So distinctive was this feature of Canadian life that in 1937 Stephen Leacock commented: "The publication of foreign language newspapers in the Prairie Provinces of Canada has, far as I know, no parallel in the world. The only thing one could compare it to would be a cocktail party of the League of Nations at Geneva" (157–58). Some groups became internationally significant, linking Canada's print history with that of global communities. For example, between 1898 and 1920, acclaimed poetry written in Alberta by Stephan Stephansson, an Icelandic immigrant, was sent back to Reykjavik for publication.[26] During the Soviet era, the prairies were an internationally recognized site for publishing in Ukrainian. More recently, after the Soviet invasion of Czechoslovakia in 1968, exiles Josef Škvorecký and Zdena Škvorecká-Salivarová maintained their homeland's literary voice with their Toronto publishing house, 68 Publishers (founded in 1969), which produced books that were smuggled behind the Iron Curtain.

## CULTURAL SIGNIFICANCE

The broad approach taken by the editors of the *History of the Book in Canada / Histoire du livre et de l'imprimé au Canada* has enabled contributors and readers to learn much about themselves. Yvan Lamonde's summary of the project's "percées" includes new information about the print culture of New France before the arrival of the printing press, analysis of relations between print and politics in the nineteenth century, the iconography of the book in Canada over the centuries, the continuity of stories such as the history of religious publishing across all three volumes, and the challenge to scholars to situate their knowledge of regional specifics within the larger frameworks of national and international developments. Most reviewers of the published volumes (who tended to be book historians or literary scholars), both francophone and anglophone, congratulated the editors for the overall integration of the project. Some would have preferred a different organizational structure, such as fewer case studies or more integrated overviews; others found coverage of some areas disappointingly thin, such as the treatment of Gaelic in Volume 1 (Finkelstein, Rev. 67), or the same volume's account of "l'évolution de la presse coloniale" (Harvey 141). Reviewers of Volume 2 called for more attention to the cultural history of reading (Winship 464) and to individual publishers, as well as a more nuanced understanding of gender (Campbell 409). In *The Globe and Mail*, Roy MacSkimming found Volume 3's treatment of newspapers and magazines "especially skimpy" ("Charting" D25). Many reviewers cited case studies they particularly enjoyed, and Margery Fee took impish delight in compiling a list of unexpected "snippets of information" gleaned from Volume 3 ("Canucks" 22).

Less tangible than the published books, the coast-to-coast scholarly network that evolved may ultimately prove to be one of the project's most lasting and significant results. While the substantial format of the six hefty volumes may make them appear definitive, the editorial team was always fully aware that with most topics we were just skimming the surface. One reviewer asked, "cette collection se veut-elle vraiment un point de départ pour la recherche ou constitue-t-elle plutôt un point d'arivée?" (Ducharme 554). The answer is both: our goal was to establish a foundation, not a monument, and to inspire subsequent scholarship to probe deeper and further. Evidence that this is occurring is well demonstrated with the example of Penney Clark's research on English schoolbooks in Canada. Paul Aubin had spent many years documenting the history of French textbooks in Quebec and was the obvious person to deal with this topic in all three volumes of *HBiC*, yet no one had given much thought to the production history of the English-language textbooks used in the rest of Canada, despite their obvious importance in social and cultural formation and their economic value to Canadian publishers. We were fortunate to recruit Clark, an education professor at UBC, who took on the topic of educational publishing for Volumes 2 and 3 of *HBiC* and has since developed the history of English-Canadian school texts as her major research area, for which she has received substantial funding from SSHRC. Others have used *HBiC*'s deficits as starting points from which to launch new lines of inquiry. In *The Surface of Meaning* (2008), Robert Bringhurst laments *HBiC*'s lack of attention to "the visual and sculptural aspects of Canadian books" (12), thereby identifying the knowledge gap to be filled by his own study of book design in Canada.

## GLOBAL DIMENSIONS

The phrase "as Canadian as possible, under the circumstances" (Gerson, "Question") applies as much to *HBiC* as to most aspects of Canada's cultural history. The history of the book in Canada is implicitly also the history of a culture oscillating between colonialism and nationhood in its struggle for identity and autonomy. Standing outside such projects, it is easy to challenge national histories of the book: we all know that authors, books, and readers are notorious disrespecters of national boundaries and that "the spotlight on 'nation' can obscure as much as it reveals" (Gross 118). But we also need to recognize the occasions when nations—including middle powers such as Canada—have touched international communities of print. From Canada the world has received print in many Indigenous languages, largely using the roman alphabet, but also in the hieroglyphic script of the M'ikmaq (dating from 1676) as well as the syllabic script of the Cree (first printed by James Evans in 1840), which was soon adapted to create the Inuktitut syllabary in use today ("Inuktitut"). The many volumes of *Jesuit Relations* sent from New France to Paris (1632–72) were avidly read for information about the New World and also as travel literature. In the twentieth century, Canadians invented the regional library system, pioneered in the 1930s in the Fraser Valley of British Columbia.[27] Before the era of Booker Prizes (won by Michael Ondaatje in 1992, Margaret Atwood in 2000, and Yann Martel in 2002), our international literary contributions ranged from John McCrae's "In Flanders Fields" (1915), seldom identified as Canadian by the millions around the world who recite this poem every 11 November, to major interventions in popular culture likewise not often known to have originated in Canada. Ontario's Leslie MacFarlane was the first real person to write under the "Franklin W. Dixon" pseudonym credited as author of the Hardy Boys and other popular series produced by the American Stratemeyer syndicate.[28] L.M. Montgomery's *Anne of Green Gables* (1908), specifically but not insistently set in Prince Edward Island, continues to attract millions of readers in dozens of languages. The global empire of Harlequin romances began in the middle of the Canadian prairies and now has its headquarters in Toronto.[29]

Several reviewers appreciated the continual efforts of *HBiC*'s editors to contextualize Canada's book history within an international framework. David Finkelstein opined that the entire project presents "a narrative arc charting not so much a national history as a trans-national history" ("Cold" 23), a comment echoed in Roger Osborne's review of Volume 3, which he felt will "make a significant contribution to the emerging interest in transnational histories of the book" (368). Underlying these comments is the shift that has occurred in book history from the national to the post/trans/inter-national. As the various multi-volume national book histories began to release their first publications during the late 1990s and into the twenty-first century, the turn of scholars to international aspects of the field became visible in the growing number of recent volumes whose titles proclaim their scope: *Across Boundaries* (Bell, Bennett, and Bevan), *Worlds of Print* (Hinks and Armstrong), *Books Without Borders* (Fraser and Hammond), *Books between Europe and the Americas* (Howsam and Raven), and the five-volume collection of transnational essays, *History of the Book in the West* (Weedon). All include passionate scholarly arguments about the need to expand or overcome the boundaries of national book histories that serve as "vehicles for nation-state construction" (Wirtén 3), and call for examination of the overarching issues of international book history as well as attention to interstitial concerns and figures that fall between the cracks of national paradigms (Shep). It is difficult not to concur with Eva Wirtén's view that the large-scale national projects are not just important in themselves—they should also be regarded "as repositories of knowledge about *what needs to be done in the future*" (4; emphasis in original).

What is the place of Canada and of Canadian elements in the new enterprise of post/trans/inter-national book history, as it exists to date? The above-named volumes contain a total of some 180 essays, just two of which directly concern Canada, both written by participants in *HBiC*. Otherwise these collections, edited by major international scholars in the field, overlook Canada almost entirely, except for passing mention of several Canadian sites among the places that participated in the US-based North American book trade. The picture isn't entirely bleak; several recent book history projects link Canada to the outside world, such as Alison Rukavina's analysis of Canada's role as a market for colonial editions from British publishers during the last decades of the nineteenth century, and Leslie Howsam's *Cambridge Companion to the History of the Book* (2015), in which two essays make use of *HBiC* to bring Canada into discussions of the international book trade and of bibliographical methodologies for book history.[30] As well, literary scholars sometimes address the international peregrinations of Canadian fictional characters, from Haliburton's Sam Slick (Edwards) to Anne Shirley of Green Gables (Gammel).

Although Rukavina disputes Simon Eliot's view that national book history is necessary to lay the groundwork for international book history (8), the case of Canada supports Eliot: without the volumes of *HBiC* to show that Canada has a book history (however imperfectly it may have been researched and written) and many expert book historians, international scholars and editors would be even more likely to ignore us. Hence in creating a book history for Canada, *HBiC* carved out a faintly visible Canadian space on the international map of print culture, no mean feat at a time when participating in post-national or global intellectual endeavours too often means yielding to foreign cultural hegemonies.

# Editing in Canada: The Case of L.M. Montgomery

Irene Gammel and Benjamin Lefebvre

> "One should not try to write a book impulsively or accidentally, as it were.
> The idea may come by impulse or accident, but it must be worked out
> with care and skill, or its embodiment will never partake of the essence
> of true art."
>
> L.M. Montgomery, "The Way to Make a Book" (138)

"I was born to be an editor. I always edit everything. I edit my room at least once a week," Margaret Anderson proclaimed in her 1930 autobiography, *My Thirty Years' War* (58), drawing a playful yet deliberate link between the editing of an avant-garde periodical, *The Little Review*, and her passion for interior decorating. Refusing to see editing as a "passive facilitation of others' works," as Jayne E. Marek observes in *Women Editing Modernism* (61), Anderson and her co-editor, Jane Heap, championed editing as a way of shaping modernism itself. In taking this view of editing as a bold and dynamic cultivation of ideas and movements, this essay proposes to explore editorial practices in a Canadian context with the creation and consolidation of L.M. Montgomery studies as an academic field.

The case of Montgomery is timely given her impressive upward trajectory over the course of a century. Montgomery's work has been translated into over thirty-five languages; it has figured in international libraries more than that of any other Canadian author, including such luminaries as Margaret Atwood; and it has spawned a multimillion-dollar industry in entertainment, tourism, and spinoff products. This essay proposes that crucial to the development of Montgomery's name as a world-renowned author has been the development of high-quality critical editions, volumes of scholarly essays, and trade editions—a domain that has remained underexplored in both editorial and Montgomery studies.

Thus this essay begins by exploring Montgomery's own editorial practices and the degree of her authorial control in the editing of her most famous novel, *Anne of Green Gables*, and its sequels. It then turns to the posthumous and monumental editing of Montgomery's personal journals and correspondence, the editing of scholarly volumes theorizing about Montgomery's oeuvre over the past two decades, and finally the publication of a trade variant that has supplanted an earlier expurgated published edition. In pursuing these editorial themes and in exploring diverse editorial models and concerns in Montgomery studies, this essay takes as its point of departure Jerome J. McGann's influential book *The Textual Condition*, affirming that editing is always imbricated in social institutions and designed to serve changing social functions. Thus, this essay ultimately argues that the editing of Montgomery's fiction and non-fiction texts reflects the multiple needs of myriad groups and institutions across space and time, illuminating an editing industry that frequently pulls in different directions, revealing tensions and controversies but also fulfilling an array of differing needs. Just as Anderson and Heap edited and shaped *The Little Review* into an international organ, so too has innovative and rigorous editing helped launch L.M. Montgomery studies around the globe.

## L.M. MONTGOMERY'S AUTHORIAL AND EDITORIAL PRACTICES

Like Anderson, L.M. Montgomery (1874–1942) was a born editor. Until the publication of *Anne of Green Gables*, she worked on developing her fiction in the isolation of small-town Cavendish, Prince Edward Island, yet she was connected to a global community through the popular magazines of the era. She edited her prose carefully, using as her model popular genres found in glossy mass-market periodicals such as *Godey's Lady's Book* and *The Delineator* as well as in ephemeral Sunday School newspapers such as *Zion's Herald*, which provided ample instruction for both editing and home decorating (see Gammel, *Looking* 207–19). Anderson's metaphor for the editor as interior decorator is especially apt for Montgomery, who edited her short stories and novels as she edited her rooms, fashions, hairstyles, and social behaviour. She exercised the utmost care in her craft, as reflected in her instruction to her readers in our epigraph, "One should not try to write a book impulsively or accidentally." Following her motto in the same article to "be your own severest critic" (139), she scrupulously studied and applied the formats and prescriptions for success throughout a lengthy apprenticeship culminating, in 1905, in the writing of *Anne of Green Gables*, published to great acclaim three years later.

In this inspired first novel, as in all of her best fiction, Montgomery developed an exquisite balance by spinning a conventional formula with brilliant creativity and emotionality, producing a fiction that uplifts and resonates with readers a century after its initial publication. She enlisted a double discourse within her texts (Rubio, "Subverting"), subverting conventional plots by injecting them with wit and satire along with sharp observations of characters and incidents often drawn from her own journals. Like her Romantic predecessors Byron, Shelley, and Keats, who relied on invisible appropriations of ephemeral erotic literature in their love poetry (McGann, *Textual* 35), so Montgomery relied on popular periodicals and the more ephemeral newspapers to supply the immediate precursors for Anne Shirley. Her handwritten manuscript of *Anne*, now housed in the Confederation Centre Art Gallery and Museum in Charlottetown, documents just how carefully she edited her work, devising her own intricate, alphanumerical notation system to track her editorial changes (see Epperly). When Montgomery died in 1942, she left her readers with what scholars have come to see as a highly controlled output of writings that she meant to survive, systematically destroying notebooks, correspondence, and other papers that might have been of interest to scholars and editors. Montgomery was a painstaking editor who exerted considerable editorial pressure over the Anne books. Her personal journals reveal similar tactics of selection, arrangement, and exposition, but they also display the subversive author's unconventional and progressive personal battles. Though Montgomery revised and rewrote the journals throughout her life, themes of intense female friendships and dissatisfaction with her husband survive in the journals, suggesting traces of expurgated material that would support the conclusion that beyond the romantic ideals of Montgomery, the author and editor as staged on the pages of this record, exists a fractured female psyche that belies the fragmentation of the modern self (see Gammel, "Staging"). These themes offer a barely visible glimpse of complex processes of self-editing that were only exaggerated by the vigorous interventions of subsequent editors on her body of work.

Montgomery's relationship with her Boston editor and publisher L.C. Page, a womanizing, manipulative Svengali (Rubio, *Lucy Maud Montgomery* 225–38), has become legendary. Page was certainly a man of questionable ethics, but he was also a genius in securing posterity for a good book by developing sequels and in cajoling authors to comply with his directives in order to produce bestsellers. Thus, from 1907 to 1915, his remarkably productive editorial collaboration with Montgomery spawned some of her most popular texts, such as *Anne of Avonlea* (1909) and *Anne of the Island* (1915). Though none of the sequels would trump the popularity of *Anne of Green Gables*, the collaboration provided a creative tension that may have fuelled some of Montgomery's best writing and that certainly prompted her to write faster (Gerson, "Seven Milestones" 20). When her third novel, *The Story Girl* (1911), did not progress at a rate that satisfied him, he persuaded her to put the project on hold and expand a five-instalment serial, "Una of the Garden," as her third novel, *Kilmeny of the Orchard* (1910); when her writing of novels was delayed by life events (including her marriage to a minister, a honeymoon abroad, her relocation to rural Ontario, and her first pregnancy), he agreed to her proposal that she rewrite a selection of her best short stories as *Chronicles of Avonlea* (1912) in an attempt to capitalize on the sales success of *Anne*. Although his suggestions ensured that Montgomery had a new book out every year, she opted to slow her pace after she switched to McClelland, Goodchild, and Stewart (Toronto) as her Canadian publisher and Frederick A. Stokes (New York) as her American publisher, and with only a few exceptions she published a new novel every second year until her final novel, *Anne of Ingleside*, in 1939.

In addition to the acrimony over her exceedingly low royalty rate, Montgomery was distressed over Page's unilateral insistence on publishing a collection of leftovers from the *Chronicles* volume as *Further Chronicles of Avonlea* (1920), which included extracts and material that she had reworked into some of her then-published novels as well as changes he had made without her consent. Asserting her authorial control, Montgomery fought his unscrupulous editing, arguing in court that Page threatened to damage her integrity as an author. Adding insult to injury, the eight-year lawsuit occurred after Montgomery had sold all remaining rights to her first seven books to Page in an attempt to sever ties with him completely. Although she continued to draw an income from books published with McClelland and Stokes, she was forever barred from royalties from novels published by Page, including *Anne of Green Gables*—a fact that rankled deeply given that her early Page books continued to outsell her later novels. Their acrimonious separation is aptly mirrored in the divergent fates of typescript and manuscript in Canada and the United States. The typescript, which had been prepared by Montgomery and was the basis for the June 1908 edition of *Anne*, was kept by Page but eventually discarded, either before or after the L.C. Page & Company was sold to Farrar, Straus, & Cudahy, Inc. in 1957, a year after Page's death. Montgomery retained and carefully preserved the manuscript, which would become crucially relevant for recent critical and scholarly editions, an important editorial tool in extending Montgomery's legacy into the twenty-first century.

Although some of Page's editorial practices disregarded the creative integrity of his authors, he must be credited with producing attractive collectors' editions, such as the twenty-fifth (silver) anniversary edition of *Anne of Green Gables* in 1933 adorned with a silver-coloured cloth, as well as popular editions featuring the stars of the 1919 and 1934 film adaptations; Page was always keen to revive the appeal of *Anne* when its readership seemed to wane. Thus Montgomery's story is one of editorial complexities in which the editor is likewise a collaborator, a not uncommon phenomenon of editing, as McGann describes: "As the process of textual transmission expands, whether vertically (i.e., over time), or horizontally (in institutional space), the signifying processes of the work become increasingly collaborative and socialized" (*Textual* 58). Just so, Montgomery was unable to control the proliferation and permutation of her novel throughout her lifetime, given that she had no say or involvement in the marketing or design of her work that drew readers to her text, and this lack of control has only intensified in the seven decades after her death, due to advances in technology and digitization and to the expiration of copyright. This process, whereby the author's control becomes diluted, is perhaps inevitable, as McGann elaborates: "Texts and their editions are produced for particular purposes by particular people and institutions, and they may be used (and reused) in multiple ways, many of which run counter to uses otherwise or elsewhere imagined" (*Textual* 47). Nowhere is that principle more evident than in the myriad editions produced of Montgomery's *Anne of Green Gables*.

## EDITING *ANNE OF GREEN GABLES* ACROSS A CENTURY

Although Montgomery left as her literary legacy twenty-two books of fiction (in addition to 530 short stories, 500 poems, eighty-five essays, and ten 500-page ledgers of journals), all of her novels, beginning with *Anne of Green Gables*, have remained in print since their initial publication between 1908 and 1939; most of them have never been out of print. The ready availability of Montgomery editions obviously solves the problem of access, but it also raises questions of visual editing, since each permutation of the text contends with unique aesthetic goals in accordance with its intended audience. Despite the relative consistency of texts, the success story of *Anne of Green Gables* has been its editorial adaptability and translatability for multiple audiences and institutions, as reflected by the fact that the market now offers editions abbreviated for children, editions to accompany adaptations for television, and collector's editions in which new internal illustrations replace the original illustrations by M.A. and W.A.J. Claus. Notably, the 100th anniversary edition of *Anne of Green Gables* in 2008, authorized by the heirs of Montgomery and published in hardcover by Penguin Canada, did include the original internal images as well as the original cover image by George Gibbs (although it used the 1925 Harrap edition as its copy text). When *Anne of Green Gables* was first published in June 1908, Page presented the novel as a family text, with the famous Gibson girl drawn from a 1905 cover image in *The Delineator*, a New York fashion magazine (Gammel, *Looking* 231–32), and most of its reviews in periodicals in Canada, the United States, and the United Kingdom celebrated the book as one that would appeal primarily to adult readers ("*Anne*"). In the course of the twentieth century the novel evolved into a more one-dimensional children's text within trade publishing, a process reflected in the increasingly neotenous covers, as seen, for example, in the first Canadian edition, published by Ryerson Press in Toronto, which by the 1960s featured an iconic cover image drawn by Toronto illustrator Hilton Hassell (see McKenzie 146–48; Creelman and Gammel). The mass-market Seal paperbacks (which, since the 1980s, comprise the only complete set of Montgomery's books in English) opt for cover images suggestive of a conventional set of sentimental novels in which heterosexual romance figures prominently, attesting to the works' returned status as crossover novels for both children and adults. This shift is likewise reflected in the austere New Canadian Library (NCL) edition of 1992, published by McClelland and Stewart, which was favoured by many scholars during the 1990s but which has since been replaced with a broad choice of more recent critical editions. While the NCL cover illustration depicting a local choir has little to do with the plot of *Anne of Green Gables*, the painting's creator, Robert Harris (1849–1919), is well known for his work *The Fathers of Confederation* (1884), so the cover indeed reinforces the notion of *Anne* as a Canadian icon—just as she was being championed during the 1990s.

For many recent scholarly editions, the June 1908 version is the authoritative text because the novel was published with only minor changes, as Cecily Devereux notes in her 2004 Broadview edition of *Anne of Green Gables*: "the variations between the manuscript and the 1908 text do not indicate highhanded editing on the part of the company; changes tend to be made at the level of the comma … and of national conventions of spelling" ("Note" 46). In fact, it would appear that Page went out of his way to incorporate British spelling, even though Montgomery tended to use a great deal of American spelling during the Cavendish years of her writing, and Devereux conjectures that Page may have wanted to highlight the Canadian content (although this inclination was clearly silenced in the 1919 and 1934 Hollywood movie script versions, which Americanized the story, much to Montgomery's dismay). Still, there are two other early editions that have been used as copy-texts for later editions: the 1925 British edition by Harrap, which regularizes British spelling and seems to have relied on uncorrected proofs of the Page text; and the 1942 Canadian edition by Ryerson Press in Toronto, which also uses Page's text but a post-1925 version, when the 1908 plates had been replaced, so that the Canadian text differs from the original June 1908 *Anne* slightly (Devereux, "Note" 44).

Since the 1990s, the presence of multiple critical editions of *Anne of Green Gables* documents neatly the idea of editing as a social, collaborative, and transformative activity, as McGann asserts: "When we edit we change, and even good editing … necessarily involves fundamental departures from 'authorial intention,' however that term is interpreted" (*Textual* 53). Thus each critical edition subscribes to its own ideology in line with the expected users, depending on whether an edition is trying to reach the "general" reader, the scholarly reader, the student reader, the female reader, the child reader, or a combination of these groups. It is these critical editions and their relationships with their readerships that deserve a closer look given also the ways in which they are imbricated in the expanding scholarly field of Montgomery studies.

In 1997, Oxford University Press in New York published *The Annotated Anne of Green Gables*, edited by a team of scholars, Wendy E. Barry (an American) and Margaret Anne Doody and Mary E. Doody Jones (sisters born in Nova Scotia, though Margaret Anne teaches at the University of Notre Dame). Creating a new text out of the 1908 Page edition, the 1925 Harrap edition, and Montgomery's handwritten manuscript, *The Annotated Anne* uses British spelling and features as a cover image *Caller Herrin'* (1881) by English Pre-Raphaelite painter and book illustrator Sir John Everett Millais, thus dressing the edition in a code of historical fiction and the Victorian cult of childhood. Boasting encyclopaedic annotations and an impressive apparatus of appendices that explore the material culture of the era, the edition pays homage to the local Canadian Maritime tradition with its forceful connections to the New England states, especially Massachusetts. This characteristic is distinctly different from a second critical edition, published by the independent Canadian scholarly publisher Broadview Press, which presents as its cover a sepia-toned rural classroom scene of the Nisbet School in 1908, the photograph drawn from the Provincial Archives of Alberta, ostensibly establishing a cross-Canada connection. The look complements editor Devereux's exploration of the political dimensions lurking underneath a children's text, such as the decidedly conservative and maternal feminism underlying the novel (Devereux, Introduction 30), a critical and theoretical approach aimed for the university textbook market.

A third critical edition comes in the 2007 W.W. Norton *Anne of Green Gables*, edited by Mary Henley Rubio and Elizabeth Waterston, editors of seven volumes of Montgomery's journals. Its cover is adorned with a lovely green-hued painting depicting two girls engaged with each other at the beach, with a rock formation in the background representing the Canadian Maritimes. As with the NCL edition, the cover of this Norton edition was painted by Robert Harris, but the edition also pays tribute to several decades of L.M. Montgomery scholarship in Canada, the United States, Sweden, and Japan by reprinting and excerpting scholarly essays. With its apparatus of notes detailing the various editions and variant spellings, the Norton edition expands and refines earlier critical editions. Of course, there are considerable overlaps too. All of the scholarly editions, for example, note the inconsistent spelling of Lover's Lane, which continues to create confusion in the editing of *Anne*, given the ambiguity of the apostrophe in the original manuscript and first edition (occasionally "Lovers' Lane").

Although not a critical edition, nor an example of Canadian editing, noteworthy too is the 2008 Modern Library paperback edition (published in New York and set from the original June 1908 Page edition with silent corrections and sans interior illustrations), whose stated goal it is to elevate *Anne of Green Gables* into the canon of "the world's best books," as noted on the back cover. Jack Zipes's introduction situates *Anne* beside such classics as Salinger's young adult novel *The Catcher in the Rye* (1951) and even evokes the eminent German philosopher Ernst Bloch's *Das Prinzip Hoffnung* (1954–59) to describe Anne as the embodiment of the principle of hope for the future. As Zipes observes: "Home is not the past; it is our destination that we can only partially reach because the social conditions that we have created do not allow for the easy fulfilment of our hopes and desires" (xviii). The cover of the Modern Library edition provides the perfect crossover image: the back of a girl's head as she gazes at a field of lilacs, her brilliant tussle of crimson-auburn hair brimming with nubility at the same time it is affixed with a prepubescent lilac bow. She is both child and adult, contemporary and timeless, the perfect surface for viewer projection. The reading guide at the book's end appeals to the book club reader, those many educated fans of Anne, often adults who happily return to re-experience the novel anew. It is to them that Zipes appeals when he observes: "Today, scholarly critics who take the works of so-called children's literature seriously generally consider *Anne of Green Gables* a classic crossover novel, that is, one that appeals to and is read by both young and adult readers" (xx).

In the face of this proliferation of editions, then, is there one that should be crowned the definitive edition? Is any one of these texts superior to or more authentic than another? The simple answer is no. Despite qualitative differences, these texts reflect the depth and diversity of Montgomery studies by fulfilling different needs for different functions and readerships. Consequently, they also illustrate what McGann posits as the law of change, whereby editions, as he observes, "will exhibit a ceaseless process of textual development and mutation—a process which can only be arrested if all the textual transformations of a particular work fall into nonexistence" (*Textual* 9). Since this law of change is tightly linked to readership, what ultimately does the barometer of reception indicate about the spatial and temporal conditions of production? Or in other words, why are some editions more successful than others at certain points in time?

## POSTHUMOUS EDITING OF MONTGOMERY'S PERSONAL WRITINGS

Although the first posthumous Montgomery publication, a 1960 volume of letters to Ephraim Weber titled *The Green Gables Letters*, was celebrated as "one of the most important literary contributions of the year" by *The Globe and Mail*

(Dumbrille 21), one that "whets one's appetite for more such collections of letters by Canadian writers," according to the *Dalhousie Review* (Pacey, review 429), it is interesting to note that the efforts to republish primary fiction and non-fiction texts culled from magazines did not meet with the same success. *The Alpine Path: The Story of My Career*, a 1974 republication in book form of a writing memoir that Montgomery had published in seven instalments in *Everywoman's World* in 1917, was pronounced "Scrap from the Barrel" by the *Vancouver Sun*, its sentimental moments "embarrassing and dreary" (Dawe 30A). As for *The Doctor's Sweetheart and Other Stories*, a volume of short stories selected by Catherine McLay and published in 1979, *Books in Canada* predicted that "if these represent the best of her hundreds of still uncollected stories, Montgomery fans probably won't have to make much room on their bookshelves for future volumes" (Smith 22). The editing of Montgomery's early stories, often based on a great deal of sleuthing on the part of researchers, failed to impress reviewers.

In contrast, the next posthumous Montgomery publication during this period, *My Dear Mr. M: Letters to G.B. MacMillan from L.M. Montgomery*, published by McGraw-Hill Ryerson in 1980, received far more positive coverage: *Atlantis* declared that "readers will discover a more sophisticated and multi-faceted Montgomery than the one usually evident in her novels" (Joyce-Jones 144), whereas *Canadian Literature* announced that "the editors [Francis W.P. Bolger and Elizabeth R. Epperly] ... are to be commended. Every selection is of interest" (Whitaker, "Literary" 143). What is apparent, then, is a disjunction in the reception at this time of Montgomery's magazine work, which is deemed uninteresting or inferior to her best novels, and her private life writing, which contains a depth of personality and intellect that is presumed not to be present in her popular fiction.

This pattern was repeated in the two decades that followed: the five volumes of Montgomery's *Selected Journals*, published by Oxford University Press between 1985 and 2004, received rave reviews in popular and scholarly periodicals, but the eight collections of Montgomery's rediscovered short stories, edited by Rea Wilmshurst and published by McClelland and Stewart between 1988 and 1995, received rather tepid reviews, particularly Wilmshurst's decision to organize each volume by theme, which reviewers found too repetitive. Similarly, *The Poetry of Lucy Maud Montgomery*, selected by John Ferns and Kevin McCabe and published by Fitzhenry and Whiteside in 1987, received a stridently critical review in *Canadian Literature* (Whitaker, "Women"). Although popular adaptations of her work for television during the 1980s and 1990s boosted Montgomery's visibility in Canada and beyond and have received sustained scholarly attention, her short stories and poems have so far been met with almost total indifference, a marked contrast to the eager reception of her journals. Certainly, the auspicious timing of the journals' publication underscores the importance of the central question that must be asked about each edition: Why this particular edition now?

As Mary Rubio notes in her essay "'A Dusting Off': An Anecdotal Account of Editing the L.M. Montgomery Journals," her stated editorial goal was to use the journals to establish and elevate the academic reputation denied the author during her lifetime and afterwards, when modernist fiction was preferred by literary critics who never failed to denigrate Montgomery's writing as sentimental and feminine. The timing was right during the 1980s and 1990s, when the editorial project was propelled forward by an expanding wave of feminist, cultural, and life writing theories in the academy. The editing project of Montgomery's journals coincided with the launching of L.M. Montgomery studies as an academic discipline, and since the diary text is radically different from the author's fiction, it presented an excellent tool for changing perceptions about Montgomery.

Nina van Gessel argues that life writing and autobiography are crucial genres for modernist women's expressions, citing the pre-eminent examples of Anderson's *My Thirty Years' War* and Sylvia Beach's *Shakespeare and Company* (1956), both of which situate female editors directly at the forefront of the literary avant-garde, with both women involved in the editing and publishing of James Joyce's *Ulysses*. While Montgomery generally eschewed modernist tropes in her fictional works, with some exceptions (see Lefebvre, "Pigsties"), she astutely understood that life writing (as practised in her personal journals) constituted an act of self-representation that, as van Gessel notes, "is, after all, essentially an act of self-promotion." Strong gendered biases inhere in life writing, often dismissed as a specifically feminine writing, and consequently as "self-effacing and passive" (141). Yet, as we see with Anderson's and Heap's editorial policies, women's writing is anything but a passive activity. The marked responses of Montgomery's readership to the publication of her journals demonstrate that any act of writing or editing—be it of personal journals or of an avant-garde periodical—is an act of agency, and decidedly antagonistic to the conception of women's writing as passive or domesticized.

Indeed, Rubio and Waterston could not have dreamed up a better text to change public perceptions about Montgomery. Highlighting modernist tropes, the journals depict an interior space in which the narrator's subjectivity comes apart as the world around her plunges into the first industrial war in 1914–18. Montgomery's explosive anger and disturbing mental and physical illnesses were so powerful that they proved disturbing to "Anne fans." This tension is evocative of the explosive tagline that Anderson attached to *The Little Review*: "making no compromise with the public taste" (qtd in Marek 86). Talking about the difficulty of editing the journals for a readership of "fans [who] had an incredibly passionate attachment to [Montgomery]," Rubio asserts: "To shatter her fans' sense of who she was would engender a sense of loss in them" ("'A Dusting Off'" 71). As Rubio details the anger unleashed by the publication of the first volume of the journals, she notes that many fans turned that anger against the editors, resentful that their view of the cherished author behind the text had been taken away from them. Yet readers came back for more.

The prestige of Oxford University Press helped bolster the editors' goal of elevating Montgomery's academic reputation. The format the editors had chosen in collaboration with their publisher was the "selected" edition, as they proposed to tackle the extraordinary task of editing ten handwritten ledgers of five hundred pages apiece. The main complexity consisted in the publisher's insistence on a low word count; this forced the editors to forgo almost half the content in the Prince Edward Island years, which describe the author's formation and apprenticeship. As Rubio notes: "Generally speaking, our goal in editing was to speed up the movement of her narrative; 1980s readers had much less time for leisure reading than did readers of her era, and the book had to march along at a brisk pace" ("'A Dusting Off'" 58). Selections were made judiciously, reflecting the portrait of the author as she appeared throughout her work in all her complexity, but still, the format of the selected edition necessarily meant that the editors had to leave their editorial fingerprints on the published text—a point that gains poignancy within recent editorial theory linking editing to biography.

In a chapter titled "The Scholarly Editor as Biographer," James L.W. West III posits that "scholarly editing is an exercise in biography" (81)—in other words, editors construct an image of an author that determines all decisions they will make after. West discusses how prior biographers and critics tend to influence such images, how editors decide ahead of time how to revise and edit these pre-existing portraits, and how this decision alters how they edit the text. Since West's subject, American novelist Theodore Dreiser, had been characterized as clumsy, hasty, and indifferent by other scholars, West's methodology for editing Dreiser's fiction was designed to counter such claims, using editing to intervene into a scholarly discussion. These insights apply to Rubio and Waterston's editing of the journals in that their intent was to show the serious and dark side of Montgomery's life in order to counteract the one-dimensional view of the author as a romance writer. The level of editing was impressively high, modelling exemplary textual scholarship that included impeccably researched annotations set apart in notes at the end (a boon for scholarly readers). Each detailed edition contained scrupulous tracking of their omissions, an index, and an introduction outlining Montgomery's writing habits. Yet selections inevitably reveal an interpretation, and their superb editions also reflected the portrait of the author as she would eventually appear in Rubio's remarkable biography, *Lucy Maud Montgomery: The Gift of Wings*: talented, disciplined, neurotic, and angry, locked in a deadening marriage but nonetheless firmly heterosexual in her romantic desire across her entire lifespan. The selections seem to privilege, if ever so subtly, scenes of courtships with male partners and relegate into a more secondary position the romantic effusions of female friendships, perhaps because these expressions were perceived as less important or serious, or perhaps because the editors wanted to "protect" their subject against charges of homoerotic desire. In Volume 4, covering the years 1929 to 1935, the photograph of Isabel (Isobel) Anderson (an Ontario fan and teacher who had a crush on Montgomery, whom Montgomery depicted uncharitably as a sex pervert) was blurred to veil the face, the photograph intentionally marred in reproduction, ostensibly in a gesture of sensitivity towards her family (Montgomery, *Selected Journals* 4: 33); in addition, the editors note that, "for legal reasons, we have excised one surname"—Anderson's ("Note" xxix). These heavy editorial interventions reveal just how sensitive the editors and the publisher were to the fans' perceived strong emotional responses.

Ultimately, the editing of the selected journals illustrates that readers are a powerful social force in determining the shape of editions. Due not to a shift in editorial principles but as a result of the unexpected sales success of the first volume, Oxford University Press agreed to a greater range of selections in later volumes. The *Selected Journals* also had a notable impact on a number of social institutions: they have been featured in a number of university courses, incorporated into Kevin Sullivan's television adaptations of *Anne of Green Gables* and the episodic series *Road to Avonlea*, and used on signage at heritage sites. In 2008, the University of Guelph library launched a website for the Lucy Maud Montgomery Research Centre, which features a searchable database of Montgomery's photographs, including those appearing in her journals (see also *Picturing*). Moreover, the continued demand by readers for Montgomery's unabridged PEI journals prompted Rubio and Waterston eventually to revisit their editorial project, publishing *The Complete Journals of L.M. Montgomery: The PEI Years, 1889–1900* in 2012, with a second volume covering entries from 1901 to 1911 appearing the following year. Not only do these editions reproduce the full text of her handwritten record, but they also approximate her original layout, with several hundred photographs, newspaper clippings, and ephemeral images appearing alongside her text.

## EDITING AS A NETWORK OF IDEAS AND PUBLIC CONVERSATIONS

In reflecting on the dynamics of editing *The Little Review*, Margaret Anderson celebrates the power of talk. "Jane and I began talking. We talked for days, months, years." She continues: "I made up quarrels of opinion so that Jane could show her powers" (107). As Marek observes, "the 'conversation' embodied in *The Little Review* became one of the forces that moved modernism" (61). The avant-garde periodical offered a forum for a rigorous exchange of ideas about avant-garde concerns, in which a variety of foreign editors including Ezra Pound, John Rodker, and Francis Picabia further added to the exchange of ideas and international conversation. Likewise, the editing of the scholarly volume of critical essays perhaps best exemplifies this use of editing as a vehicle for sparking public conversations that create networks of discussion that expand from the local to the international. *The Little Review* created clusters of themes, which allowed the periodical to advance new ideas, ideologies, and movements (such as anarchism, feminism, and Dada) and to promote a new, networked group force, reflected in the titles of the issues (such as the programmatically titled "American" issue, which involved numerous alien writers, and the "Exile" issue, in which Anderson and Heap presented a number of American expatriate writers in Paris to their international audience). Just so, a variety of thematic foci in edited scholarly volumes of essays have vigorously expanded the field and the conversation surrounding Montgomery studies, both nationally and internationally. For example, Gammel and Epperly's *L.M. Montgomery and Canadian Culture* has helped consolidate the role of Montgomery as a Canadian icon by highlighting the ways in which the author and her work are rooted in Canada; this text has also dialectically prompted the exploration of the complementary perspective, namely, the American content deeply embedded in Montgomery's works, particularly the early novels. Gammel's *Making Avonlea: L.M. Montgomery and Popular Culture* engages Montgomery studies with larger conversations about popular culture, deliberately collapsing the divide between high and low literature and firmly anchoring Montgomery within cultural spheres such as business, tourism, and entertainment. More recently, Bode and Clement's *L.M. Montgomery's Rainbow Valleys: The Ontario Years, 1911–1942* reorients Montgomery scholarship in terms of place, given that Montgomery, whose life and work are so firmly linked in people's minds to Prince Edward Island, lived and wrote in Ontario throughout the three decades of her married life.

In this context, editors do more than work behind the scenes as passive barometers of cultural reputations. By marshalling theories and methodologies that engage new networks of conversations, the editors of volumes of critical essays actively shape the field and its readership. By displaying controversies rather than glossing them over, editors of critical volumes demonstrate the relationship between canonized texts and texts that have been relegated to the background. Editors inevitably cultivate a style of criticism; Marek remarks on the strength of Jane Heap's opinions and "her willingness to manipulate public discomfiture" (77). And just as the editing of *The Little Review* has an expansive transatlantic dimension (Chicago, New York, London, and Paris), so the editing of Montgomery has advanced scholarly conversation to an international level, involving critics from countries such as Australia, China, England, Finland,

Germany, Ireland, Italy, Japan, Poland, Scotland, Sweden, and the United States, with the public conversation reflecting increasingly complex cultural values and ideological tensions. Likewise, the centenary anniversary of *Anne of Green Gables* engendered several collections of essays, including Blackford's *Anne with an 'e': The Centennial Study of Anne of Green Gables*, Gammel and Lefebvre's *Anne's World: A New Century of Anne of Green Gables*, and Ledwell and Mitchell's *Anne around the World: L.M. Montgomery and Her Classic*. More than marking an editorial and publishing milestone, these volumes of critical essays extend backward and forward to locate Anne at home in a twenty-first-century world. Similarly, Lefebvre's recent three-volume critical anthology, *The L.M. Montgomery Reader*, joins a selection of Montgomery's essays and interviews to the work of a range of commentators working in scholarly, middlebrow, and mainstream venues, as a way to revisit existing narratives of her critical legacy since the publication of *Anne of Green Gables*.

Consequently, the editing and academic theorizing of Montgomery's work has operated in tandem, reinforcing and complementing each other, as seen in the case of the editorial treatment of the "secret" diary, a fun and bantering text that Montgomery co-wrote at the age of twenty-eight in 1903 with her close friend Nora Lefurgey, and that is found in the typescript version of her journals (the same distilled typescript that Rubio and Waterston decided not to publish, opting instead for the monumental manuscript project). An annotated and illustrated critical edition of this diary was published by Gammel in *The Intimate Life of L.M. Montgomery*, prefacing a collection of scholarly essays that analyze Montgomery's personal writings through the context of life writing theories, essays that attended carefully to the rhetoric of Montgomery's journals, correspondence, and photographs. The editorial intention was to showcase that the diary's tone—bantering, flirtatious, youthful, happy—presents an extreme contrast to that which is employed in the journal entries of the same year. Such a deliberately contrapuntal arrangement was designed to illuminate the compartmentalized and contradictory manner in which Montgomery operated through multiple textual versions or genres, at one and the same time, inhabiting the tone of each to perfection. Such editing is meant to showcase the performative aspect of life writing, which asks us to interpret identity as multiple and contradictory.

## EDITING THE "RESTORED" TEXT

Since the 1980s, publishers of literary texts have encouraged so-called restored or uncensored editions; that is, they have presented new variant editions of books where there has been documented evidence that earlier editors or literary executors imposed a final text that did not fully respect the author's wishes. Restored editions are not without controversy, as seen in the recent example of the Simon and Schuster republication of Ernest Hemingway's beloved Paris memoir, *A Moveable Feast* (1964), which had been published posthumously with the editorial help of his last wife, Mary. Edited by Seán Hemingway, Hemingway's grandson via his second, estranged wife, Pauline, the restored version claims to be closer to the author's final intents, documenting that Mary had intervened in Hemingway's prose much more heavily than by inserting the occasional comma as she had claimed. Yet the dramatic way in which the restored text departs from the memoir known by generations of readers as *A Moveable Feast* has shocked literary scholars such as A.E. Hotchner, who charged the publishers of the new edition with bowdlerizing *A Moveable Feast* and questioned their editorial ethics (Gammel, "Papa's").

Underlying this kind of restoration is the Anglo-American Fredson Bowers and G. Thomas Tanselle's "intentionalist" tradition of editing, in which the author's intent, as articulated at a specific point in time, is declared to be the ultimate authority. In *The Textual Condition*, McGann queries such an approach, arguing instead that "the textual condition is a scene of contest and interaction, a scene where specific textual decisions are made (or unmade) in a context that involves many people," many of which are non-authorial (60). Precisely because of such an origin, McGann argues that authors' intentions are socially constructed and historically conditional. Given this context, the case of Montgomery's *The Blythes Are Quoted*, edited by Benjamin Lefebvre, is an interesting one. Marketed as the final Anne novel by Viking Canada (an imprint of Penguin Canada), it is technically a restored edition that aims to supplant an earlier abridged work.

Lefebvre had first worked on editing the manuscript as part of his graduate studies at the University of Guelph and hoped to publish a critical edition. However, as is frequently the case with restored editions, a complicating factor resided in the fact that large parts of the book had been published in 1974 as *The Road to Yesterday*, though its success had been admittedly modest with both fans and scholars. After many rejections of a proposed critical edition of the book, an offer of publication eventually came from Penguin Canada following the Anne centenary that had allowed a number of publishers to capitalize on the Canada-wide celebrations of the icon. But the question remained: How to package the idiosyncratic book for a trade audience?

Not only had three different typescripts of the book survived, each prepared by Montgomery herself, but the format of the manuscript was entirely unlike anything that Montgomery had ever written: she rewrote fourteen unrelated short stories to include Anne and Gilbert Blythe and their growing family, and between each story inserted forty-one of her own poems, now attributed to Anne and to her son Walter, who dies in the Great War, followed by commentary by the family members in the form of dialogue, complete with stage directions. Not only does the structure of this final book suggest a form of fragmentation that surpassed that of Montgomery's journals, but unlike the cheery optimism that Montgomery infused into *Anne of Green Gables* and many of its sequels, this final book takes a seemingly drastic turn in its tone and subject matter: three short stories include prolonged deathbed scenes, and the deaths of sixty-odd additional characters are mentioned throughout the rest of the book. Additionally, in a book composed in the midst of the Second World War, Montgomery was clearly compelled to reconsider the cultural meanings of the First World War that she had traced two decades earlier in the 1921 novel *Rilla of Ingleside* with patriotic fervour. During the editorial process, Lefebvre came to see this final book as evidence of Montgomery's "late style," a style described by Edward Said whereby authors sensing the ends of their lives or their creative careers reconsider both their medium and their message (see Lefebvre, "'That Abominable War!'"). Lefebvre eventually discovered that Montgomery had submitted the final manuscript of *The Blythes Are Quoted* to her publishers on the very day of her death in April 1942, according to a *Globe and Mail* obituary (see "Noted Author"). This was corroborated by the presence of carbon copies of the final typescript in the McClelland and Stewart archives at McMaster University (Lefebvre, "'That Abominable War!'" 116).

Working with a trade publisher meant compromising the scholarly and critical scope of the editorial project. Thus Lefebvre was unable to include the detailed introduction and notes he had prepared, as the publisher feared that too much commentary would alienate trade readers and have an adverse effect on sales. Beyond this restriction, however, the publisher was supportive of printing a readable version of the text that was as close to Montgomery's typescript as possible along with an afterword and note on the text that summarized the kinds of minor editorial interventions made. The 2009 book was praised for its scholarship in a review by Calgary novelist Aritha van Herk, who describes Montgomery's dismantling of "Victorian felicity" in this book as "a multifaceted ghost story" (F12). Despite the adult topics in the book, large bookstores shelved it in the section devoted to "9–12 Classics," a confusion of readership that also reflects its status as a crossover novel.

In the context of the concerns raised in this essay, the question of editing is ultimately one of ethical and social interest: "Why do we need this particular text at this particular moment?" is the question an editor must pose. Likewise, editors need to ask themselves "whether a critical edition is being proposed, and whether the edition is being imagined as a complete edition, or a selection—and why?" (McGann, *Textual* 23–24). The proliferation of published editions may be the result of the advent of a new digital medium, which is dramatically speeding up and improving access to archival materials, including Montgomery's. The open access provided by digital media presents a revolutionary advantage for scholars, who can access manuscripts in multiple versions and variants where formerly they had to travel to archives and rely on photocopies. Montgomery's novels are now available as e-books, in addition to a number of e-texts available on Project Gutenberg and digital editions available through Google, the Internet Archive, and the Hathi Trust Digital Library. Nonetheless, some caveats remain. Toronto antiquarian bookseller David Mason, who has sold many rare first editions of Montgomery's work to collectors, has voiced concerns that funding formerly invested in collecting and preserving rare editions is increasingly being diverted into the digitizing projects undertaken by libraries, with the result that editions as material objects have become increasingly vulnerable, even while digitizing is making more editions available.

Meanwhile, the editing of Montgomery's texts is an ongoing process that involves readers, librarians, collectors, and institutions, as seen in the release of a facsimile edition of Montgomery's serial "Una of the Garden" by the L.M. Montgomery Institute at the University of Prince Edward Island. Unlike the restored edition of *Blythes*, here the variant edition is meant not to supplant an earlier version but to put into relief the story of how this short serial evolved into the novel *Kilmeny of the Orchard*. In juxtaposing this rich multiplicity of texts and editorial decisions and evolutions, we are ultimately reminded of McGann's observation that "to study texts and textualities, then, we have to study these complex (and open-ended) histories of textual change and variance." Variations allow the text to interact with readers in new ways, encouraging textual and interpretive discoveries. Perhaps McGann sums it up best when he asserts that "every text has variants of itself screaming to get out.... Various readers and audiences are hidden in our texts, and the traces of their multiple presence are scripted at the most material levels" (9, 10).

# The Material and Cultural Transformation of Scholarly Editing in Canada

Zailig Pollock

I have been involved in scholarly editing for almost three decades, a period that has probably seen more radical transformations in editorial theory and practice than at any time since the basis of our profession was first laid down by Zenodotus in Alexandria over 2,000 years ago. The best account of the theoretical underpinnings of editing in Canada over this period is Dean Irvine's "Editing Canadian Modernism" (2007). It is my hope that the following, somewhat anecdotal, report from the trenches in which I have laboured as an editor over the years will complement Irvine's account of the changing cultural and material context in which the work of editing in Canada has been done.

The transitional and contentious nature of the period I will be discussing was brought home to me last summer when I taught the course on Textual Editing and Modernism in Canada, which forms part of the larger training initiatives promoted and sustained by the Editing Modernism in Canada (EMiC) project. As we worked our way through the daunting reading list I had assigned, one word that seemed to come up again and again was "polemical." Virtually all the pieces we read, even ones that purported to focus on issues of theory or praxis, had a polemical edge to them, and I am sure I don't need to remind you that "polemic" comes from the Greek word for war. This was strikingly and amusingly brought home to us by an essay by Kenneth M. Price, "Edition, Project, Database, Archive, Thematic Research Collection: What's in a Name?" (2009), in which, after a sober and sensible survey of the various terms used to describe large-scale digital editorial projects, he proposes the term "arsenal," while acknowledging, as he puts it, that "it seems militaristic" (40). I personally reject the idea of editing as kind of warfare, but I do agree with Price that "we are, for better or worse, always entangled with force and power" (40). It is this entanglement that I will be exploring.

In 2003 I presented a paper at "The Canadian Modernists Meet" symposium in Ottawa, somewhat bombastically titled "Genesis, Exodus, Apocalypse: A Modern Editor's Journey" in line with its triumphalistic account of my own development as an editor in response to the rapidly developing and coalescing digital technology and editorial theory of the time. I stand by the general lines of my account but I now acknowledge that though this development has been to the good, much of it was imposed on me by forces over which I had no control. As the title of my paper suggested, it has been quite a journey for me over the last decades, a journey of perhaps biblical proportions. But the ride, at times, has been a rough one.

In the account that follows, the University of Toronto Press (UTP) is going to loom very large, if only because until recently it published all of my editorial work. In fact, one way of thinking about this account is as the story of how UTP and I came to a parting of the ways. I have tried to be as objective as possible, but I suspect some bitterness will inevitably make its way to the surface. In fairness to UTP, though, I acknowledge that it is responding as best it can to pressures that are making themselves felt everywhere in the world of scholarly publishing. As Kathleen Fitzpatrick points out in *Planned Obsolescence: Publishing, Technology, and the Future of the Academy* (2011), which goes more deeply into the social and technological transformations underlying the current crisis in scholarly publishing than I can in this essay,

> library cutbacks have resulted in vastly reduced sales for university presses, at precisely the moment when severe reductions in the percentage of university press budgets subsidized by their institutions have made those presses dependent on income from sales for their survival.... The results, of course, are that many presses have reduced the number of titles that they publish, and that marketing concerns have come at times, and of necessity, to outweigh scholarly merit in making publication decisions. (3–4)

My work as an editor began with A.M. Klein. Like most, if not all, Canadian editors of my generation, I came to editing with no prior knowledge or expertise in the field. My plan was to write a critical study of Klein's work, but I soon realized that the state of Klein's texts made such a study impossible. By the time I had begun my work on Klein, the A.M. Klein Research and Publication Committee had undertaken its mammoth task of publishing Klein's *Collected Works*, a task that has only now come to an end with the publication of the final volume in the series, the letters, edited by Elizabeth Popham (2012). However, at that time, none of the volumes had yet appeared, and most importantly, no reliable text of the poems was available. The recently published *Collected Poems* edited by Miriam Waddington (1974) was far from complete; moreover, it contained no scholarly apparatus that would enable the user to work out the order of composition of the works; and there was no way of knowing to what extent, if at all, the various poems had been collated and emended. But perhaps most seriously, the volume contained numerous errors, some of major proportions, and after being bitten by basing a key argument in one of my articles ("Sunflower Seeds") on a typo in the Waddington edition, I decided that I needed to do some textual investigation before I could in all honesty begin my critical work on Klein. The first fruits of my editorial work was an article listing the errors I had discovered in the *Collected* ("Errors"), a publication that did not endear me to Waddington but that I felt was necessary as a stopgap pending the appearance of a more dependable edition. About this time, Usher Caplan and Seymour Mayne became aware of my work on Klein and invited me to join the Klein committee, an invitation that happily coincided with my first sabbatical. I eventually became chair of the committee, editor of the *Complete Poems*, and co-editor of a couple of other volumes in the series (*Notebooks*; *The Second Scroll*).

There are a few points that I would like to emphasize about this stage of my career as a textual editor. The first is that I had absolutely no training in editing and only the vaguest sense of what textual editors actually do. This was not perhaps, entirely bad since my editorial practice was driven by my needs as a critic, not by some preconception of the right way to edit a text. In other words, I was actually using my edition as I was creating it. One of the most gratifying comments about my edition that I have heard over the years is that it is "user friendly"—and that is why. To educate myself as an editor, I read fairly widely in editorial theory and quickly realized that in light of my own critical concerns, the approach to editing that I found most congenial was genetic editing, as it had been developing initially in France and Germany (see Deppman, Ferrer, and Groden; Gabler) and was beginning to get a toehold in the still largely intentionalist-dominated landscape of Anglo-American—and Canadian—editing. I also took certain editions as useful models, among them Jack Stillinger's edition of Keats's poetry (1978).

The second point I would make about my Klein years is that I was working in an entirely print-dominated environment. In fact, the poetry volume was the first of the *Collected Works* to be word-processed. I had some difficulties convincing my colleagues of the advantage of working from electronic files, a task that was made somewhat more difficult when our copy editor at the University of Toronto mentioned that they had just received a word-processed text in which all the spaces between words had gone missing.

And this brings me to my third point, namely our relationship with UTP. When I joined the Klein Committee its relationship with UTP had already been in place for several years. The press had expressed an interest in publishing the *Collected Works*, though there was no binding commitment on either side. The understanding was that each volume would be assessed on its own merits without a prior commitment to publish and without an advance, and that the editors were free to take their work elsewhere if they wished. There was no consistency in layout or design or titling for volumes in the series, nor were these matters ever discussed with the press. This did strike me as a bit casual, though in retrospect, this casualness seems a lot more attractive than it did at the time.

My own direct involvement in editing Klein came to an end with *The Second Scroll* (2000), on which I collaborated with Elizabeth Popham, the senior editor of that volume. By this time, I was becoming increasingly uneasy with the limitations of print editing, as I think is evident in the apparatus to *The Second Scroll*, especially the section on "Gloss Gimel" (159–73), which is clearly straining towards hypermedia in its attempt to synthesize several levels of text as well as photographs and diagrams. Like many editors at this time, I had been swept away by enthusiasm for Jerome McGann's utopian and now somewhat dated "Rationale of Hypertext" (1995) and was eager to get involved in a hyper-linked multimedia edition in which I could more fully present the results of my editorial research and do so in a much more convenient manner than the codex allowed. However, it was not clear to me at this time how I would have the opportunity to put into practice my new editorial ambitions.

At this point Sandra Djwa got in touch with me concerning difficulties that had arisen with the *Collected Works of E.J. Pratt*, a second multi-volume project that UTP was publishing simultaneously with the *Collected Works of A.M. Klein*, something that is simply inconceivable nowadays. The two-volume critical edition of Pratt's *Complete Poems* (1989) had just appeared to devastating reviews. Professor Djwa had been involved in this edition along with Gordon Moyles, but her responsibility had been limited to the critical introduction and explanatory notes. The actual textual editing had been the responsibility of Moyles, and, for whatever reasons, it had not gone well. There were numerous errors in the volume, including typos, inconsistent choices of copy texts, and unexplained conflations of readings from different versions, most notably in what is perhaps Pratt's major work, *Brébeuf and His Brethren*. These problems were so serious that a planned *Selected* would need to be done from scratch. At this point, Moyles withdrew from the project and Djwa invited me to Vancouver to discuss how the situation might be salvaged. An added concern was that there were two more volumes in the series pending (*Pursuits* and *Letters*), and Djwa wanted to make sure the problems that had arisen with the poems would not recur. As a result of our discussions I agreed to join the editorial board with the aim of producing a revised version of the poems and an accompanying *Selected* based on it, but in digital format. I also agreed to look over the two Pratt volumes in progress. Before turning to the digital project that resulted I would like to comment briefly on these two volumes, to give some sense of where textual editing stood in the early 1990s compared to now. The first of these, *Pursuits Amateur and Academic: The Selected Prose of E.J. Pratt* (1995), was being copy edited when I joined the project. Susan Gingell had done a very good job of annotating the texts and, as far as I could tell, the texts seemed free of the textual corruption and contamination from which the *Complete Poems* suffered. However, the copy editor had indicated numerous stylistic changes to Pratt's own writing, including correcting gender references that were no longer politically correct—clearly unaware that this was totally inappropriate for a scholarly edition. I made this point very strongly and, as a result of my intervention, Pratt's own readings were restored. The second volume, of Pratt's letters, had been prepared by David Pitt, Pratt's biographer, and was in the form of a manuscript about to be submitted to UTP. I asked to see photocopies of some of the letters so that I could get a sense of the procedures followed in transcription and presentation. On the basis of examining several dozen letters, I estimated that the manuscript contained at least 5,000 errors, some of them very major, involving deletions, transpositions, and errors of transcription. Pitt was not willing to redo the work, so it was agreed that a second editor, Elizabeth Popham, would join the project as co-editor and redo all of the transcriptions. I have gone through this saga in perhaps excessive detail to make the point that an edition of the collected works of E.J. Pratt, one of Canada's major authors, had been undertaken by a group of scholars who—whatever their combined expertise on Pratt's life and work—had absolutely no experience as textual editors; and there was no one at UTP, or at SSHRC, which had funded the edition, who seemed to be concerned about this. If EMiC accomplishes nothing else by the end of its lifespan, I hope it makes it highly unlikely that such a situation will ever arise again.

During the next few years, with the support of a SSHRC grant, I was occupied with retranscribing and collating Pratt's poems and preparing a *Selected* (2000), along with Djwa and W.J. Keith, who had also joined the editorial board; and, most importantly, working with Popham on an interlinked hypertext edition of the poetry and letters of E.J. Pratt (1994). Thinking through the structure of such an edition with Popham was a very valuable experience that has since stood me in good stead; however, we never got beyond the edition of a single long poem, *Behind the Log*, and of a selection of letters, including those from the period of the poem's composition and publication. One reason was funding: the development stage of this project was much more challenging than I had expected, and we had simply run out of money. But another reason was technological. The hypertext Pratt edition was HTML-based, but while we were working on it, it became clear that the future of digital editing was not going to be in HTML. HTML (Hypertext Markup Language) is a presentation-oriented subset of XML (Extensible Markup Language) that focuses on how your text appears on the Web. But XML allows structural and semantic markup as well; it uses stylesheets to transform this structural and semantic information into various presentation formats, including HTML. In 1987, a consortium was established to develop a version of XML designed for the digital humanities, known as TEI, or the Text Encoding Initiative. In 1994, the year I began my work on Pratt, the consortium published its first set of guidelines, since repeatedly and very substantially revised. But at this time there were no reliable editors for XML (oXygen, the most widely used editor, came out in 2002); nor were there Web browsers that could properly render XML files. So all of the HTML encoding I had done was now obsolete—and the time did not yet seem right to make a commitment to TEI. I had experienced for the first time what it means to be on the bleeding edge of technological development. For years, I looked back on my sample edition of Pratt as the great failure of my career, the one instance in which I did not complete a job I undertook and did not give SSHRC value for their money. However, in retrospect—and in light of John Unsworth's argument that "if an electronic scholarly project can't fail and doesn't produce new ignorance, then it isn't worth a damn" (n.pag.)—I now look back on it differently—as a prototype that helped me develop a conceptual model for a digital edition that is still valid and useful for me in the work I have continued to pursue. As Galey and Ruecker put it, prototypes "are also theories" (n.pag.).

Now that I had arrived again at something of an impasse in my career, Sandra Djwa once more came to my aid. She had been working on her biography of P.K. Page and had become aware—as I had when I began my work on Klein—of the unsatisfactory textual situation. The only edition of Page's collected poems, *The Hidden Room* (1997), edited by Stan Dragland, was a fine work in its own right, without the textual errors that marred Waddington's edition of Klein's *Collected*. Dragland had worked very closely with Page to design a carefully crafted thematic presentation of her work, with which I know Page was very pleased. This volume performed its main task very well, providing an accessible and beautifully designed presentation of the bulk of Page's finest work up to that time. But, apart from the fact that Page had continued to be prodigiously productive after the appearance of *The Hidden Room*, the edition did not meet the needs of the scholarly community or of the classroom. There was no chronology, no index, no indication of the source of the texts—no editorial material at all. Page had an enormously long and varied career, in which she and her art went through some stunning transformations. But because of the thematic arrangement of the poems in *The Hidden Room*, this fascinating story was not accessible the reader. So while *The Hidden Room* is a valuable contribution to Page's oeuvre, it simply is not a scholarly edition, nor was it intended to be. It is a different genre altogether, an example of what Dean Irvine describes as the "second stage in the editing of modernist poetry in Canada, one that typically takes place during the lifetimes of the poets and marks definitive moments in their careers, occasionally at their height and, more often, near their end" (54). What was needed, if the study of Page's work was to be put on a firm scholarly basis, was a "third stage" edition, "usually undertaken after the publication of collected editions … and consisting of comprehensive volumes of complete poems" (54).

Page had read my critical study on Klein, *The Story of the Poet* (1994) and had written a very kind of review of it; and, at Djwa's suggestion, she agreed to my editing her poetry if I wished to do so. I first checked out her manuscripts in the Page Fonds at Library and Archives Canada to decide if her handwriting was legible. In this I was following the principle of the elderly Shakespearean actor who, when asked what is the most important thing about playing Lear, said, "a light Cordelia." On determining that Page's handwriting was in fact quite legible, compared to the challenging chicken scratches of Klein and, even more formidably, of Pratt, I agreed, and thus began by far the most interesting, stimulating, and difficult period of my career.

The first difficulty that arose, and nearly sidelined the edition altogether, was copyright. Page, Djwa, and I signed an agreement dated 29 July 2002, drawn up by Page's literary agent at the time, Kathryn Mulders, giving us "the right to assemble and create" the *Collected Works of P.K. Page* on the understanding that Page "retain[ed] copyright" in any of the work included in the edition. Unfortunately, Page had failed to consult her publisher, Tim Inkster at the Porcupine's Quill, who, according to the contract for *The Hidden Room*, shared rights to all of the poems included in that volume. Inkster was not happy, to put it mildly, when he discovered that I was working on an edition of the poems without his knowledge, which he saw as being in direct competition with *The Hidden Room*. For some time, as a result, Inkster and I were not friends, a situation exacerbated by the fact that he had not realized that it was Page who had approached me to do the edition in the first place, not the other way around. Inkster and I eventually survived this chapter of accidents, with the help of the wise mediation of Constance Rooke, and are now close collaborators. But the struggle to get there was not a pretty one, and this is where UTP re-enters the picture.

As is clear from the preceding account, I had been working with UTP for many years when Djwa and I began to plan an edition of Page's *Collected Works*, one that would make full use of the technological resources I had developed since my initial Pratt prototype. It was as a result of this long relationship that I was asked by Bill Harnum, senior vice-president of scholarly publishing at UTP, to help Page edit a collection of her prose writings, which she had put together and which was eventually published in 2006 under the title *The Filled Pen*. Although I undertook this edition purely as a favour to Page and UTP, and it was much more limited in its aims than the planned *Collected Works*, I saw it as a useful first step in a future collaboration with the press on the *Collected*

*Works.* I was wrong. It turned out to be not the beginning of a new phase in my relationship with UTP but the end of that relationship, at least as far as textual editing is concerned.

This is not how things appeared at first. Soon after Djwa and I began planning the *Collected Works,* I received an email from Siobhan McMenemy (3 December 2001), acquisitions editor for Canadian literature at UTP, expressing keen interest in having the press publish the edition. A similar interest had been expressed by Bill Harnum in an email of 3 October 2000 (though with no actual commitment by either of them, it should be noted). As a result of protracted negotiations involving Harnum, Inkster, and myself, we eventually arrived at an agreement whereby Inkster would agree to have UTP publish scholarly print editions of the *Collected Works* to be accompanied by an online edition, in return for the Porcupine's Quill retaining subsidiary rights for all works it had published. After a somewhat stormy beginning, all seemed to be well with the *Collected Works.* But this forecast turned out to be false.

My first sense that the climate at UTP had changed was when I was informed by McMenemy that that I would be required to put together a proposal for the *Collected Works* as a whole, specifying in considerable detail the structure, contents, and length of each volume, the editors responsible for each, and the proposed dates of publication. I was taken aback by this request. No such documentation had been required for the Pratt or Klein editions. For these editions there was a general expression of interest on the part of UTP, which was given right of first refusal, but volumes were submitted for evaluation on a case-by-case basis as they were completed. Moreover, as I tried to explain to McMenemy, the edition was a research project in progress. A substantial portion of Page's writings had not yet been made available in her fonds at Library and Archives Canada—less than half, as it turned out—and much of the information required by the press could be only speculative. I was informed that, notwithstanding, this was now policy and that the press would not consider undertaking the edition without a full proposal. I was further concerned to learn that even if the press approved of the proposal, this did not mean that they were in any way committed to publishing the *Collected Works.* It just meant that we were given permission to submit the volumes to the press, and, as in the past, they would decide on a case-by-case basis on each volume as it was submitted. So I was expected to devote considerable energy to producing a document, which I realized was largely fictional, without any commitment from the press in return. There was no budging the press on this matter, so I prepared the required proposal, which ran to some ten single-spaced, highly imaginative pages.

After submitting the proposal I heard back from Ryan Van Huijstee, with whom Djwa and I had been dealing while McMenemy had been on leave, that UTP would agree to consider publishing the *Collected Works* (again with no prior commitment to any of the individual volumes) only on the condition that the editors provide $8,000 for each volume—this being in addition to the usual subsidies from the Aid to Scholarly Publishing Program. Moreover, the press insisted on retaining exclusive subsidiary electronic rights to all the volumes. Van Huijstee, who had always been highly encouraging and enthusiastic about the project, was clearly as dismayed as we were at this response. I wrote to him expressing my unwillingness to proceed with the press under these conditions. He was very sympathetic and wrote back that he was seeking expressions of support from the scholarly community for the edition in the hopes that this would lead to a revaluation of the proposal (22 April 2009). Soon after (7 May 2009), he reported that he had received a large number of enthusiastic letters of support from leading Canadianists. However, it quickly became clear that, even if the committee were to relent on their insistence that the editors subsidize the project (which was unlikely), they certainly were not going to yield on the issue of electronic subsidiary rights—and there was no way that Inkster was going to surrender his subsidiary rights, electronic or otherwise. In this matter I was in complete agreement with Inkster.

This was perhaps the lowest point in my career as an editor. However, in discussing the UTP fiasco with Dean Irvine, who had joined Professor Djwa and me as one of the general editors of the proposed *Collected Works*, I gradually came to realize that perhaps it was not such a bad thing after all. UTP's lack of interest in supporting another major print edition, except under the impossible conditions it had imposed, had made it clear not only that the model for such editions was no longer economically viable, but also that, from the point of view of editorial practice and theory in a digital age, it was no longer desirable. Instead, Irvine and I reconceived the *Collected Works* as *The Digital Page*, a comprehensive digital edition, which would be supplemented by print volumes for readers and students, with minimal editorial commentary. We broached this subject with Inkster, and he enthusiastically agreed to join us in this multi-year project. I think it is fair to say that Page was very pleased at the prospect—"Actually Zailig, I think some kind of miracle has occurred!" she wrote to me (10 August 2009)—and actively participated in the production of the first print volume of the series, *Kaleidoscope: The Selected Poems of P.K. Page* (2010), right up until the time that death cut our collaboration short. She would certainly have been pleased with the result. *Kaleidoscope* is a beautifully designed and produced volume consisting of a substantial selection of Page's poems from all periods of her career, some previously unpublished, all edited to the highest scholarly standards of which I am capable. The poems are dated and arranged chronologically; there are explanatory notes for references that absolutely require glossing; and there is a brief statement of editorial principles, with the fuller textual apparatus, including the textual history of each poem, and a list of variants, emendations, and regularizations reserved for the digital edition. Moreover it is cheap. At $24.95 it probably costs about one tenth of what a scholarly print edition with full apparatus, along the lines of the Klein and Page volumes, would cost in today's market. And the e-book is only $4.99.

In "Respect des fonds and the Digital Page" (2011) Emily Ballantyne and I discuss in some detail the theory and practice behind *The Digital Page*, by far the most exciting project in my career as an editor. Rather than rehashing our discussion of the theoretical and practical aspects this particular project, I would now like to turn to a different aspect of editing that has changed drastically since I first began my work, and very much for the better—the cultural aspect.

From the account of my earlier years as an editor, it should be clear that editing in Canada has been up until fairly recently the province of amateurs, working more or less in isolation from one another. This is not an entirely bad thing, perhaps, when the amateurs are such figures as Northrop Frye or A.J.M. Smith or Stan Dragland. The enthusiasm, broad general culture, and personal knowledge that such individuals bring to their task is all to the good. But there are drawbacks as well. For one thing the default position for such editors is the authorial intention copy-text model—that is, you find the last edition published with input from the author, clean up any typos, and publish. When, in 1989, Moyles states, "this edition of *E.J. Pratt: Complete Poems* presents a critical text prepared in accordance with modem editorial theory and procedure" (xlix), this is what he has in mind, not the theories and procedures discussed, for example, in McGann's *Critique of Modern Textual Criticism* (1983) or McKenzie's *Bibliography and the Sociology of Texts* (1986); and not the work on genetic editing in France and Germany that was well developed by this stage. Another example of the limited concept of "modern editorial theory and procedure" that dominated Canadian textual editing at this time is provided by the Centre for Editing Early Canadian Texts, which in 1979 adopted the authorial intention copy-text model, as promulgated by the Modern Language Association's Committee on Scholarly Editions, as the basis of its series of editions of nineteenth-century Canadian fiction. Whatever the arguments for this approach to editing, there are obvious disadvantages to having all of the texts in our literature run through the same editorial sieve.

This unquestioning acceptance by editors of Canadian texts that their job is to put into practice a theory of editing that had already been settled did not leave much room for debate: there was hardly anyone in Canada with whom I felt I could discuss the theoretical and, latterly, technological developments that were shaping my own editorial practice. Things began to improve as the century turned, but for me, the really important turning point was the establishment of EMiC. EMiC has allowed me to discover a cohort of dedicated fellow editors, and, to some extent, to create this cohort through the Textual Editing and

Modernism in Canada summer institute with which I have been involved, along with Dean Irvine, since it began in 2008. The guest speakers in this course—including established scholars (such as Alan Filewod, Michael Groden, Catherine Hobbs, Carole Gerson, Ruth Panofsky, and Paul Tiessen), as well as ones at the beginning of their careers (such as Bart Vautour, Marc Fortin, Emily Ballantyne, and Hannah McGregor)—have given me a real sense of participating in a shared and growing enterprise. Perhaps even more important is the close contact I have had with an amazing group of young scholars who are incomparably more sophisticated about the challenges and possibilities of editing than I was at their age. And in many cases this contact has continued and, I hope, will continue as long as I continue to be actively engaged in textual editing. To give an example of how things have changed: while working on this essay I have been interrupted by emails from Dean Irvine, Neil Besner, Melissa Dalgleish, Chris Doody, Michael di Santo, Eric Schultz, Shannon McGuire, Matt Huculak, and Martin Holmes—I hope I haven't left anyone out—all fellow scholars involved in editing whom I would never have met except through EMiC.

I would like to conclude with some brief comments on one final aspect of the material and cultural transformation of scholarly editing in Canada in my time, which may, in the end, prove to be the most important of all. Although I am not in the habit of romanticizing or envying the way scientists do things, I have always admired the collaborative way in which scientists work together towards larger goals beyond the capacity of any one researcher. One obvious advantage of this approach is epistemic, to use K. Brad Wray's term:

> Collaborative research is becoming more popular in the natural sciences, and to a lesser degree in the social sciences, because contemporary research in these fields frequently requires access to abundant resources, for which there is great competition. Scientists involved in collaborative research have been very successful in accessing these resources, which has in turn enabled them to realize the epistemic goals of science more effectively than other scientists, thus creating a research environment in which collaboration is now the norm. (150)

In recent years the advantages of collaborative research have been more widely recognized, both in the social sciences and in the humanities. Paul Thagard's comments on "collaborative knowledge," although they focus primarily on his own field of philosophy, clearly have a wider application:

> Student/apprentice collaborations can also benefit from the fact that graduate students in philosophy often have backgrounds that complement the knowledge of their professors. Working collaboratively with graduate students in philosophy at the University of Waterloo, I have benefited from students' knowledge on topics with which I was comparatively unfamiliar,

> such as the history of mathematics, mythology, dynamic systems theory, and empathy. Hence a student/apprentice collaboration can take on the characteristics of a peer-different one. (259)

The growing appreciation of the relevance of a collaborative approach in the digital humanities in particular is signalled by a forthcoming collection of essays edited by Marilyn Deegan and Willard McCarty, *Collaborative Research in the Digital Humanities*. EMiC, with its heavy emphasis on training and collaboration, has made a major contribution to this development and, to speak personally for one last time, I am beginning to undertake joint projects, presentations, and publications with former students who have made a major contribution to my thinking and to my work, something that I had never done in the past. Several volumes of *The Digital Page* will be edited by well-established senior scholars but others by scholars at the very beginnings of their careers—in this way, we will be encouraging the continuation into the next generation of a genuine community of scholars fully aware of and adequate to the challenges of contemporary textual editing. For editors committed to the model of scholarly editions that Fitzpatrick rightly characterizes as obsolescent, it may be the worst of times; but for the rest of us it is the best.

# Editing without Author(ity): Martha Ostenso, Periodical Studies, and the Digital Turn

Hannah McGregor

## 1. MARTHA OSTENSO: A SHORT HISTORY

Martha Ostenso (1900–1963) is best known as the author of *Wild Geese*, originally published in 1925 by Dodd, Mead and Company, a New York publishing company. The publisher, along with *The Pictorial Review* (a popular magazine) and Famous Players–Lasky (an American motion picture and distribution company), sponsored an annual Best North American Novel of the Year Award, which Ostenso won in 1925. The event launched a literary career that would include a first-refusal deal with Dodd Mead, a film adaptation of *Wild Geese*,[1] and enough financial success for her to support herself, her husband Douglas Durkin, and both their families through the worst years of the Depression (Atherton 214).

*Wild Geese* marked the beginning of a long and financially lucrative writing career for Ostenso. A look at the scholarship on her work, however, will reveal a near total silence on the topic of the fourteen novels and as of yet uncounted short stories that followed *Wild Geese*. Indeed, while Ostenso was once a central enough figure in Canadian literature to warrant her own entry in the ECW *Canadian Writers and Their Works* series, in recent years she has fallen almost entirely off the academic radar, with the notable exception of Faye Hammill's excellent scholarship on Ostenso as an example of literary celebrity and middlebrow authorship. My assertion, in this essay and in my work on Ostenso in general, is that Ostenso's critical dismissal is a result of her fluidity and instability as a literary figure, and calls out for an editorial intervention.[2]

This fluidity exists at various levels. Ostenso was born in Norway, lived and taught briefly in Manitoba, published her first novel in New York, and spent much of her career living and writing from a cabin in Minnesota. She published in Canadian and American venues while identifying strongly as a member of the Scandinavian diaspora. Her work thus refuses to be reduced to national literary narratives.

To paraphrase Hammill, nationality and citizenship were not the only boundaries that Ostenso challenged ("Martha" 19). On 11 February 1958, Ostenso and her husband Douglas Durkin signed a legal agreement in the presence of their attorney, stating that "all of the literary works of Martha Ostenso commencing with the publication of 'Wild Geese' in 1925, were the results of the combined efforts of Douglas Leader Durkin and Martha Ostenso" (Durkin and Durkin 1). This agreement, coming at the end of the couple's long literary career, retroactively declared the collaborative nature of the fifteen novels published under the name "Martha Ostenso" between 1925 and 1958. Most troubling for the reputation of the authors, it suggested that Ostenso received the 1925 award, reserved for first-time novelists, fraudulently, if the more experienced Durkin (who had published at least three novels prior to 1925) collaborated on *Wild Geese*. This legal agreement not only throws into doubt the entire narrative of Ostenso's career; it also destabilizes the notion of singular authorship that lies at the heart of this narrative, and raises the question of how collaborative authorship can and should be handled by literary critics and, more pertinently for this collection, scholarly editors.

Ostenso's work refuses to fit into a simplistic notion of the highbrow/lowbrow binary. To paraphrase Hammill again, the large and variegated body of Ostenso's work, especially if we read it alongside Durkin's, undermines the divide that so much evaluative criticism relies on, between serious literature and "potboilers" or cheap commercial literary production. Her work instead falls into what Hammill calls "the troublesome realm of the middlebrow," in which work "depend[s] ... on the conventional structures of popular fiction" while "diverg[ing] from such models in interesting ways, thereby disrupting cultural hierarchies" ("Martha" 21–22). It is arguably the middlebrow-ness of her work that has led to its critical dismissal, for a variety of reasons.

Literary history, in the case of Ostenso, has become a tool with which to domesticate these messy problematics, to narrativize them in ways that write the mess out of existence. Thus the standard narrative runs as follows: as a young prodigy Ostenso produced a single masterpiece, *Wild Geese*, which qualifies as a legitimate work of Canadian literature because it was inspired directly by her experience of the Canadian landscape and people and because it fits nicely into the timeline of the development of prairie realism, alongside Grove's *Settlers of the Marsh* (1925).[3] *The Western Home Monthly*, the Winnipeg-based magazine that serialized *Wild Geese* in Canada, certainly emphasized this connection by promoting Ostenso as "a Manitoba girl, educated in the schools of Brandon,

Winnipeg, and Manitoba University" ("Wild Geese" 27). Early commercial success, however, lured her into the larger and more lucrative American literary
marketplace, where she sacrificed artistic quality for financial reward and began
to produce inferior novels and short stories with American settings. What gets
left out of this narrative? Ostenso's other prairie novels, like *The Young May
Moon* (1929), set either explicitly in southern Manitoba or in a prairie landscape
with no clear national affiliations; the two novels set in British Columbia (*Pro-
logue to Love* [1931] and *The White Reef* [1934]); the aesthetic and thematic continuities between her earlier and later fiction that belie this narrative of rupture;
and the entire body of magazine publications that demonstrate a remarkable
fluidity of style, setting, content, and audience. As for the collaboration, the prevailing critical attitude is summed up fairly well by David Arnason's comment
in his 1980 dissertation on prairie realism: "It would be a hopeless task to try
to sort out Ostenso's and Durkin's individual contributions to the collaboration
and it would also be almost fruitless"; thus, in Arnason's opinion, Durkin's novels
should be read in isolation, while Durkin and Ostenso's collaboration should be
treated "as a separate and quite distinct unity to be discussed as if Ostenso had,
in fact, quite independently written the work attributed to her" (102).

What stands between Ostenso's body of work and a more active critical
interest is a strong editorial intervention. This paper will begin to outline the
possibilities of such an intervention by focusing on Ostenso's short stories as a
fruitful starting point. As short, discreet works of fiction published in a variety of popular Canadian and American magazines, the stories constitute an
ideal microcosm for considering the possibilities of a digital editorial approach
to Ostenso's work. Between 1924 and 1946, Ostenso published at least thirty
short stories. The only existing bibliography of Ostenso's work, compiled by
Joan Buckley as an appendix to her 1976 PhD dissertation, is an important but
incomplete record.[4] Even a sample survey of these stories immediately suggests
the enormous range of Ostenso's writing style, and the flexibility with which
these stories were adapted to their publication venues. The stories published in
*Country Gentleman*, for example, tend to focus on rural settings and the social
values of prairie farmers, particularly those of Scandinavian extraction. Stories
in Canadian periodicals such as *Chatelaine* and *Canadian Home Journal* often
include explicitly Canadian content, with references to the fur trade and loca-
tions like Winnipeg. While some stories are generically conservative, following
the patterns of the sentimental romance, others are more stylistically innovative
and broach taboo subjects like female sexuality and divorce. "Good Morning,
Son," which I will discuss in some detail, is an example of the latter, characteristics suiting its publication in *McCall's* at a time when the magazine's editor, Otis
Wiese, was trying to shape it into a venue for serious, realistic fiction for women.

"Good Morning, Son" serves as a useful example of how an editorial intervention might allow for a revitalized approach to Ostenso's work from the perspectives of collaborative authorship, periodical studies, and middlebrow studies. I hope to illustrate how a text-based and author-centric editorial approach elides much of what makes Ostenso an interesting literary figure, whereas a digital social-text edition—or archive, or database, or arsenal[5]—provides a variety of lenses through which her work can be productively revisited or, in the case of the short stories, encountered for the first time.

The context in which I first encountered Ostenso and her periodical publications was as a member of EMiC UA, a collaborative team of researchers and tool developers based out of the University of Alberta, under the direction of Paul Hjartarson, and part of the Editing Modernism in Canada project. For this reason I immediately conceived of Ostenso's relation to literary history as an editorial problem, and one that could best be addressed by a collaborative and interdisciplinary team of scholars, coders, digitization specialists, librarians, and archivists. This kind of collaboration—particularly from the perspective of an emerging scholar—rejects the model of independent scholarship and the authority over one's work that accompanies it. Furthermore, digital knowledge and research production entails a further destabilization of authority, with scholars and editors unable to predict or control how their work will be used or understood (Folsom 1577–78). My interest in destabilizing the ossified literary-critical and -historical narratives that have turned "Martha Ostenso" into an overdetermined authorial signifier is no coincidence considering the impossibility of author(ity)—by which I mean the complex of author-function and discursively generated textual authority—that accompanies most aspects of my work. To refuse author(ity) is to enter into a tentative and exploratory relationship to a body of texts, the process of research and editing itself, and the "finished" product that emerges from that research.[6] This paper pursues such a tentative and exploratory path, suggesting possibilities but evading the reinscription of author(ity) wherever possible.

## 2. SOCIAL-TEXT EDITING AND THE PROBLEM OF THE AUTHOR

Emerging from the work of D.F. McKenzie and Jerome McGann, the practice of social-text editing emphasizes the sociality of text and the influence of literary historical narratives through which "the signifying processes of the work become increasingly collaborative and socialized" (McGann, *Textual* 58). McGann reminds us that "texts are produced and reproduced under specific social and institutional conditions"; thus "a 'text' is not a 'material thing' but a material event or set of events, a point in time (or a moment in space) where certain communicative interchanges are being practiced" (*Textual* 21). Because of my abiding interest in interrogating the literary historical narratives that have so curtailed critical engagement with Ostenso's work, my editorial perspective "maps its particular investigations along the double helix of [Ostenso's] reception history and [her work's] production history" (16) in order to examine the "material event" of her work, in all its permutations.

Dean Irvine states, in response to McGann's claim that "an author is a plural identity" (*Textual* 75), that "if an author's identity is plural ... it is so because his [or her] identity is socially—and multiply—constituted" (74). "Martha Ostenso" is a perfect example of the multiple social constitutions of authorial identity. Social-text editing makes space for an understanding of both author and text as collaborative and fluid, effectively divorcing the text from notions of authorial intention. Furthermore, McGann makes it clear that the digital environment is the ideal medium for social-text editions, making it possible to highlight the complex, multimedia, collaborative nature of most texts. A rigorous social-text edition requires a quantity of space that would make a print edition technically and financially unfeasible; it also allows, in McGann's conception, for an environment in which narrative is less dominant, in which a variety of tools "facilitate critical reorganizations and reconceptions of the underlying data" ("From Text" par. 39). In fact, McGann's conception of the digital archive is strikingly similar to Ed Folsom's description of the database: both prefer networks of interconnection over narratives, complexity over decisiveness, and place value on the open-ended and user-shaped edition.

There is no Ostenso archive, and for the moment there are no manuscripts. My task as an editor thus involves bringing together information that is currently uncollected, including texts, images, documents, and contextual information, to create a digital edition that does not privilege any single author, medium, document, or interpretation of the material at hand.[7] In imagining what this kind of edition might look like, I am particularly drawn to Folsom's metaphorical articulation of the database as a non-narrative rhizomatic construct suggesting "virtuality, endless ordering and reordering, and wholeness" (1575). By making possible endless links between discreet units of information, the database destabilizes familiar, sometimes calcified narratives and allows new and unexpected connections to emerge, displacing the messianic centrality of the author-figure and instead creating a portrait of authorship that is messy, fluid, and inevitably collaborative (1576). Price echoes Folsom's interest in undermining the narrative of author-as-isolated-genius by drawing out the fundamentally collaborative nature of Walt Whitman's work (para. 13). Neither Price nor Folsom, however, seems particularly interested in the power disparities that inform and shape collaborative relationships, and that a digital database may have to *actively work against*. I worry, in fact, that the "database" or "arsenal" has taken on a messianic role in their scholarship, with genre becoming a panacea for all editorial ills, especially the narratives that surround an author like Ostenso. Thus, while social-text editing is the starting point for my editorial intervention, my own work will have to go further, highlighting not only the collaborative nature of authorship but also the gendered narratives often attached to collaboration.

## 3. COLLABORATION AND GENDER

Scholarship on collaborative or multiple authorship points out the ubiquity of the notion of authorship as singular, describing it as "so widespread as to be nearly universal" (Stillinger 183). The image of the creative genius composing a work in isolation is both iconic and highly gender- and class-specific, and has been interrogated by a variety of recent critical turns. After Barthes famously declared the death of the author, Foucault challenged the notion of authorship through his concept of the "author-function," which works to rationalize a text using an author's biography, to unify a body of writing despite its discrepancies through narratives of maturation and influence, and to "neutralize the contradictions that are found in a series of texts" ("What" 128). This is the kind of work that literary-historical narratives do in turning the author-function into the author. Other areas of scholarship, from "research on the history of copyright" to "studies of contemporary compositional practices," have contributed to the destabilization of the singular author (Stone and Thompson 9).

The death of the author, however, has not been decisive. For Harold Love, it is not the notion of authorship that has died, but a very particular model of it: "What is happening is closer to 'The author is dead: long live the author' with the nature and lineaments of the new successor still fully to reveal themselves" (9–10). The author that has died is the solitary genius; the author that lives is a point of considerable debate in the fields mentioned above, as well as in attribution studies, linguistics, and cognitive science. Jack Stillinger argues convincingly for not eliminating the author altogether, but for multiplying it: "Real multiple authors are more difficult to banish than mythical ones, and they are unquestionably, given the theological model, more difficult to apotheosize or deify as an ideal for validity in interpretation or textual purity. The better theories may turn out to be those that cover not only more facts but more authors" (24). The development of a "better theory," however, relies upon meticulous literary-historical work and an extensive archive through which scholars can reconstruct the details of particular collaborations. Creative relationships, Marjorie Stone and Judith Thompson point out, come in various forms and are understood in different ways depending on the relationship in question (5). These scholars concur on the importance and pervasiveness of multiple authorship but warn against turning collaboration into a new myth of authorship.

This is precisely the pitfall into which Ostenso scholars have fallen. In the absence of textual evidence, the nature of the Ostenso–Durkin collaboration can be ascertained only from unreliable second-hand sources that tend to rely on gendered stereotypes where real data are lacking. This specifically gendered aspect of collaboration turns me to Joanna Russ's *How to Suppress Women's Writing*, a survey of the strategies through which literary criticism and history erase women writers. Russ sums up the problem of gender and collaboration quite succinctly: "Since women cannot write, someone else (a man) must have written it" (20). A remarkable number of the strategies that Russ describes align with the history of Ostenso reception and criticism, including the assignment of the label "regionalist" (53) (Ostenso is primarily studied for her contribution to prairie realism); "*the myth of isolated achievement*" (62; her emphasis) (critical consensus has generally asserted that *Wild Geese* is the only Ostenso novel worthy of critical attention); and the propensity of women to write in vernacular or popular forms (128–29) (the bulk of the Ostenso corpus has been labelled as middlebrow "potboilers"). The patriarchal undertones of Ostenso criticism come through in Arnason's description of the Ostenso-Durkin collaboration, based on an interview with Ostenso's younger brother Barney. Ostenso, Arnason summarizes, did most of the actual drafting of the writing, while Durkin charted out detailed plots, "revise[d] and polish[ed]" Ostenso's prose, and "handle[d] the business details of contracts and sales. Martha ... would contribute the poetry of the novel. Durkin, who was interested in D.H. Lawrence, would handle the 'grit'" (Afterword 305). In the context of Russ's claims about the suppression of women's writing, this account of the collaboration emerges in a different light. Above all, it suggests that the collaborative dimensions of authorship should not be simplistically lauded without considering the power differentials at work in most collaborative partnerships.

The narrative that Ostenso wrote *Wild Geese* with the assistance of her husband suggests an attempt to account for an unlikely achievement, thus constructing Ostenso's career in terms of a gendered and hierarchical model of mentor and ingenue. This is clearly the narrative that scholar Peter E. Rider has constructed out of the limited evidence of the Ostenso–Durkin collaboration: "Flamboyant, vibrant, and imaginative, Martha had a creative literary ability which was to become the source of many fine novels. Douglas, on the other hand, had the technical skills and experience to give her ideas shape and strength" (xvii). The source of Rider's particular version of the collaboration is unclear, and thus it is difficult to say whether he is drawing upon primary materials currently unavailable to other critics, or speculating based upon preconceived notions of how a collaborative writing relationship *must* function in the context of a heterosexual relationship between a younger woman and an older man. Rider's subsequent discussion emphasizes Durkin's lack of crit-ical acclaim for their joint work, implying that the presence of Ostenso's name on their co-written novels in some way threatens familiar notions of gendered authorship, especially because, within husband–wife collaborations, the hus-band is more likely to be the declared author (Stillinger 50). Furthermore, the patriarchal implications of Durkin's contribution to the Ostenso novels may account for why the collaboration often goes unaddressed in feminist work on Ostenso.

Why, then, should the response to this unaddressed and undertheorized col-laboration be an editorial rather than an exclusively critical intervention? The goal of editorial work is to provide a textual and historical environment in which other scholars can perform more rigorous scholarly work. To demonstrate the heuristic possibilities that might be generated by a social-text digital edition, I will turn to one story, "Good Morning, Son," which I will discuss in terms of production, print, and reception history. Through this reading, I will gesture toward the potential of particular editorial strategies and the critical interven-tions they make possible.

## 4. COLLABORATION, SOCIAL-TEXT EDITING, AND CRITICAL READING STRATEGIES

"Good Morning, Son" was published in the September 1938 issue of *McCall's* magazine. *McCall's* began in 1870 as an advertising supplement for McCall's sewing patterns called *The Queen: Illustrating McCall's Bazaar Glove-Fitting Patterns*. Over time it was extended to include information on homemaking and handiwork, then children's issues, health, beauty, and foreign travel. In the 1920s, with the advent of Harry Payne Burton as editor, it began to publish popular fiction by authors such as Zane Grey and Kathleen Norris. Perhaps the most significant shift in the magazine's editorial policy occurred in 1928, when Otis Wiese was promoted to editor. Between 1928 and 1947, Wiese increased the circulation from 2 million to 3.6 million. It was also Wiese who, in 1932, created the "Three Magazines in One" format, in which *McCall's* was separated explicitly into three sections: News and Fiction, Homemaking, and Style and Beauty. Each section "had its own cover, and ads appropriate to it inside" ("The Press" para. 4). Wiese also worked on associating *McCall's* with more serious or quality fiction. In a 1947 *Time Magazine* article titled "The Press: Man in a Woman's World," Wiese is quoted as saying that "women were ready for more significant fiction than Gene Stratton Porter and articles more serious than the featherweight stuff they were getting" (para. 3). He privileged "realistic" writers and "went after the taboos that governed the sweetness & light fiction of women's magazines" (para. 4). Taboos Wiese was interested in breaking included adultery, homosexuality, and—in the story I will be discussing—divorce.

This masculine editing of a women's fiction magazine gives us another opportunity to consider the power dynamics at work within collaboration between men and women. According to the *Time* article, Wiese was "certain that women need men to edit their magazines. Says he: 'A woman has the courage to think for herself but not for other women. It takes a man to do that'" (para. 6). Compare this to Arnason's and Rider's descriptions of the Ostenso–Durkin collaboration. These narratives do a similar kind of work. Neither silences the contribution of women, but both subsume that contribution within a literary world dominated by the mastery of men. Women, these narratives tell us, can write for themselves, but it takes a man to turn that private writing into something public. These are old gender roles, and not all that surprising. And Arnason is correct: without archival evidence, scholars have very little hope of coming up with anything more *accurate*.

A different editorial approach, however, opens up a space in which to critique these narratives. More specifically, a social-text editorial approach that situates all textual production as part of a complex collaborative network provides readers of this text with information that plain text—in, say, a print anthology of Ostenso's short stories—could not duplicate.

"Good Morning, Son" can thus serve as a case study. The story is reminiscent of radio drama, narrated entirely in the distinctive voice of a woman identified as the mother of Jerry, the grown son to whom the story is addressed. More than halfway through the story Jerry's mother is named as Josephine, just in time for that same name to be given to Jerry's first-born daughter. Josephine discusses her son's recent marriage while attempting to come to terms with his divorce from his previous wife, Anna. As the story progresses, it becomes increasingly apparent that a major cause of the breakdown of Anna and Jerry's marriage, as well as Anna's emotional collapse, was Josephine's perverse emotional manipulations and her determination to turn her daughter-in-law into a mirror image of herself. The voice of the story is entirely that of the mother; her son is completely silenced, made present to the reader only through traces: an ellipsis, a hasty response, a cup of coffee going cold, an ashtray full of cigarette butts. In fact, as Jerry's new wife worries, he is effectively "pinched" out by the women in the story (13), particularly his manipulative mother and his ex-wife Anna. But while Jerry is silent, he is also the centre of the story and the unspeaking mover of all these women's worlds. How do we read a woman's voice in relation to a male voice that is silent but everywhere felt? Such is the voice of Wiese, declaring Ostenso's work adequately "realistic," subdividing a woman's proper life into definable and differentiated areas, deciding which products should be advertised where. This is collaboration—in many ways Wiese is as much an author of this text as Ostenso—but it may be a troubling collaboration, one that suggests the limited contexts in which women could publish in the early twentieth century.

The context of the magazine and its editorial policy, as proclaimed by Wiese, sheds further light on gender and collaboration. The goal of the magazine was to provide women with serious, taboo-breaking literature. The audience, as evinced by the advertisements and the editorial policy, is clearly gendered. This is "gritty" work written by women, for women. It is a space in which the familiar narratives of motherhood and wifehood at least seem to be interrogated. The figure of Anna is key to such a reading; she rejects society's ownership of her body and the old-fashioned notions of femininity espoused by her mother-in-law but is ultimately destroyed by her failure to evade those norms, a failure both evidenced by her representational containment within her mother-in-law's speech and undermined by the ways in which she constantly erupts through that containment. Like the new wife Betty, Anna proves "a little difficult to understand" (13). This story, then, stands as a counter-narrative to the gendered roles of the Ostenso–Durkin collaboration: Ostenso providing the poetry, Durkin the grit. That is, grit is cast in the feminine here.

There is another layer of narrative available to the story's readers, however, depending on the editorial approach, which allows for a radically different reading of the story. To make such a reading possible, an editor must incorporate information about circulation as well as production history, paying heed to the story's print format—a context that is central to the methodologies of periodical studies.

## 5. PERIODICAL STUDIES AND THE POSSIBILITIES OF THE DIGITAL ARCHIVE

Modern periodical studies, with its investment in interdisciplinarity and digital humanities methods, emerges in part from the social-text school of editorial theory, in which the material contexts of publication are considered paramount to a critically rigorous reading of a text. However, unlike social-text editing, with its roots in Romantic studies, modern periodical studies has been articulated by scholars of modernism including Sean Latham, Robert Scholes, and Clifford Wulfman, and piloted in the *Modernist Journals Project*, an online database of early-twentieth-century periodicals of cultural significance, particularly modernist literary magazines.[8]

The basic premise of modern periodical studies is, in brief, as follows. Modernity marked the emergence of an unprecedented mass literary culture made possible by several technological advancements in printing—including the rotary press, lithography, and offset printing—as well as the emergence of new cheap sources of pulp for paper. At the same time, editors of periodicals came to a realization: they could achieve wider circulation by selling magazines at less than the cost of production and making a profit instead through the advertising they attracted via circulation. This important production shift led both to the emergence of mass culture magazines and to the modernist little magazine as a space of resistance to the popularism and celebrity culture of the mass magazines. Contrary to the high/low cultural binary that has often characterized modernist studies, however, canonical modernist authors published across the cultural spectrum, and all of these periodicals, from the little magazines to pulp sensationals, included advertisements as a fundamental component of their circulation and appeal, and thus of their content. Unfortunately, librarians have long followed the practice, based on economy of space, of stripping the advertisements from periodicals when binding them into larger volumes, thus "suppress[ing] the cultural context in which our literary monuments first saw the light of day" and depriving readers and scholars of the function of periodicals as "a priceless window into [another] world" (Scholes and Wulfman 42). From the perspective of modern periodical studies, the solution involves high-quality digital editions of periodicals that re-create the original reader experience by including full advertisements as well as adequate contextual information to make the texts meaningful to present-day readers and scholars.[9]

Editing, from the perspective of periodical studies, is no longer the painstaking comparison of textual variations to a copy text in pursuit of a definitive version. Instead it includes the exhaustive archival research necessary to find full, unstripped runs of these magazines, the creation of coherent markup and metadata to make them searchable and usable, an explanatory introduction, and adequate historical and contextual data (Scholes and Wulfman 150). This is the sort of editorial approach suitable to, and possible with, Ostenso's work. Uncollected, scattered across uncounted libraries and archives, in need of order and context to make it meaningful to a new generation of scholars, her oeuvre demands the same editorial intervention as periodicals in general.

"Good Morning, Son" can once again serve as a testing ground for investigating the general claims of periodical studies and the heuristic value of advertisements. The pages I have been working with come from the *McCall's* microfilms at the University of Alberta, black-and-white images that obscure the detail of the magazine's many illustrations and advertisements. Despite much progress on this front, there is no existing standard for how magazines are scanned, photocopied, or otherwise preserved, and much information is lost as a result. Nevertheless, a rich variety of contextual information is still provided by the microfilm of the September 1938 issue. First, it demonstrates Wiese's division of the magazine into three parts, each with its own title, cover photograph, and distinctive content. At the same time, it complicates this seemingly neat division: single stories span across the three sections, defying these purported boundaries and suggesting similarly non-linear reading patterns. The other fiction contributors—Helen Hull, Josephine Bentham, Sarah-Elizabeth Rodger, Charles Bonner, and Norma Patterson—are invaluable in providing a sense of literary context. Hull's story, for example, begins with a note from the editor that emphasizes its "gritty" content: "Here begins the strongest story ever to appear in a woman's magazine. It is certain to excite controversy because—with warmth and wisdom—the author explores a woman's fundamental emotions, evaluates the code of marriage and examines intricate relationships in the searching light of honesty" (Hull 7). The controversial content of this story contrasts with the generic familiarity of romances like Rodger's "'Doctor Wyatt Speaking'" and Bentham's "Wedding Cake Is to Dream Upon." Ostenso's work enters into a network that includes her other publication venues as well as those of these other authors. A database would make it possible to create visualizations of these interconnections, representing the complexity of early-twentieth-century periodical publications and middlebrow cultural production. Plotting those periodicals and authors against a map might give us an equally strong sense of the transnational networks of publication in this period that would certainly belie the assignation of the "regional author" label to Ostenso.

The context of the magazine as a whole raises an important question about the object of study and anthologization. If the origin of editorial and scholarly interest is Ostenso herself, should an edition of her short stories include only the magazine pages on which her actual work appears or the entirety of every periodical issue? Sean Latham has suggested the aleatory dimension of magazine reading: readers are more likely to flip through the whole magazine, glancing at this and that, perusing the advertisements and illustrations, before turning back to a particular story to read it all the way through.[10] As an editor, I cannot know what productive connections another scholar might find in Marian Corey's "Interview with a College Girl" or Elizabeth Woody's "Now Let's Plan Meals"—but to exclude this material would pre-emptively eliminate the possibility. As an example of one such productive connection, I might look at the issue's letter to the editor. This sentimental narrative of a mother adopting a baby boy reveals a certain anxiety over the definition of motherhood and its basis within blood relation and patriarchal reproduction. "I have been told," writes the woman who identifies herself only as "Jan's Mother," "that I could not know the feelings of a real mother unless I suffered the pangs of childbirth. Maybe not, but being my kind of mother is pretty grand" ("As" 2). Read against Ostenso's story of two mothers, one defined wholly by her maternal role and the other resisting it, this anxiety over reproduction and the assertion of sentimental rather than biological motherhood offers an increasingly complex look at the politics of women's reproductive bodies in the period between the wars.

Turning to the pages on which "Good Morning, Son" appears, I encounter one of the primary paratextual focuses of periodical scholars: advertisements. The fourth page of this story features an advertisement for Lux soap that demands of the reader: "Are you as *dainty* at night as you are by day?"

(fig. 1). Accompanied by a large photograph of a woman brushing her hair, it also features several small graphic illustrations with captions explaining that "dainty wives" take care of "perspiration odor" by washing their nighties "after each wearing" (81). The advertisement aggressively associates the female body with dirt and the necessity of hygiene, and is moved by the unseen and unnamed husband who is grammatically exempted from the logic of the text when we are told that "Charming wives **never** risk offending" and that "She is always adored … the wife who is exquisitely dainty in every way!" (81). If the argument stands that advertisements are in conversation with the stories with which they share the page, what new readings might emerge from this page? In this pivotal moment in the story, Anna (Jerry's first wife) has become pregnant and, according to her mother-in-law, "the better side of her nature showed itself for the first time" (81). After the child is born, however, she proves an unsatisfactory mother, treating little Jo—short for Josephine—"almost as if Jo didn't belong to her at all" (81). This maternal

**Figure 1**  *McCall's Magazine,* September 1938

failure leads to Anna's first "violent outbreak" when Josephine (senior) suggests that Anna might have another child: "It must have been one of Anna's nervous days, because she said something about an old belief that women had no souls of their own, but that women were well known to have bodies and they should have something to say in what they did with them—even if it came to keeping them under lock and key" (81).

How might these two narratives—the dainty wife versus a woman demanding the right to control her own body—be read against each other? I suggested above that the story interrogates familiar constructions of motherhood. Anna's resistant voice penetrates the narrative control of her mother-in-law and seems to exist *in excess* of Josephine's representational boundaries. Her deliberate failure to understand Anna's resistance serves to heighten the emphasis allotted to it; what the story will not tell becomes what the story tells most urgently. But read in the context of the mass magazines, deliberately orchestrated by a male editor to sell more copies to housewives looking for a little titillation, does the story signal resistance to the magazine's metanarratives of femininity? Or does the advertisement signal the complicity of this resistance within the metanarrative itself, suggesting an industry of feminine identity so powerful that it can absorb and depoliticize female resistance as part of its larger economy of commercialized femininity? These are questions that can only be asked of the text as it stands: story and advertisement put into dialogue within the original print context of the magazine.

Perhaps the most exciting prospect of digital editing is its facilitation of lateral connections between unlikely texts and contexts via databases that allow for complex searches across large, variegated bodies of material. Digital editing, I am trying to argue, attempts to maintain something of the serendipity that often accompanies the reading process. To demonstrate where such serendipity might lead, I followed the conspicuous word "dainty" to the "How Not to Offend" chapter of Marshall McLuhan's *The Mechanical Bride*, in which he examines the cult of personal hygiene in the first half of the twentieth century. The advertisement he discusses in this chapter is for Lysol, specifically in its feminine hygiene applications. Like the Lux ad, it links the unhygienic female body to failed marriage via the trope of daintiness and the presence of a never-named husband: "Too late, when love has gone, for a wife to plead that no one warned her of danger. Because a wise, considerate wife makes it her business to *find out* how to safeguard her daintiness in order to protect precious married love and happiness" (61). In his accompanying commentary, McLuhan links anxiety over hygiene with industrialization and modernity:

> Implied in the cult of hygiene is a disgust with the human organism which is linked with our treating it as a chemical factory. D.H. Lawrence, rebelling against the puritan culture in which he was reared, insisted all his life that industrialization was linked to the puritan hatred of the body and detestation of bodily tasks. This, he claimed, not only was reflected in our hatred of housework and physical tasks but in our dislike of having servants smelling up our houses while helping with that work. So that the small, hygienic family unit of our cities and suburbs is, from this viewpoint, the realization of a Calvinist dream. (*Mechanical* 61)

McLuhan's arguments illuminate my discussion of Ostenso in two ways. First, his politicized reading of the "small, hygienic family unit" recalls the failure of that unit to cohere in "Good Morning, Son," which suggests the possibility of reading that story as a Lawrencian critique of industrialization. It also, however, recalls the Ostenso–Durkin collaboration via the figure of D.H. Lawrence. Arnason uses Lawrence as a metonymic figure for the type of "grit" that Durkin contributed to the novels in contrast to the "poetry" of Ostenso's contributions. However, as I argued before, insofar as this story is gritty or even Lawrencian, it is firmly ensconced in the world of stories for and by women. The binary ascribed to the Ostenso–Durkin collaboration cannot hold up in this context.

The lines between serious "gritty" modernist fiction and frothy middlebrow romance fiction are thoroughly blurred. In his work on pulp publication and modernism, David M. Earle argues against the divisions of highbrow, middlebrow, and lowbrow. These cultural productions, he argues, are not opposed to one another, but are necessarily interrelated dynamics of what he calls the Paper Age (6). Thus when we incorporate the material print histories and contexts of Ostenso's stories into scholarship on her work, via a social-text editorial approach, the old gendered narratives of collaboration begin to topple without the necessity of (unavailable) manuscript evidence.

## 6. MIDDLEBROW STUDIES AND THE DIGITAL TURN

From print and production history, Earle's problematization of "brows" leads to the question of reception history. Critics have tended to approach Ostenso's work from an evaluative framework. Atherton's assertion that some of Ostenso's novels "deserve to be more widely known" but that most "should be left to gather dust on library shelves" (241) is paradigmatic of her reception, as is his argument that "instant access to large amounts of money was at the root of her inability to develop as a serious novelist" (244). Hammill, as I mentioned earlier, has discussed Ostenso in the context of the middlebrow and argued convincingly for a more holistic approach to her body of work that reads it in relation rather than subdividing it into worthy and unworthy texts. Such an approach is made difficult by the unavailability of the texts that seem to lend themselves most clearly to an examination of middlebrow culture: the short stories. Even a single story such as "Good Morning, Son" provides a variety of ways in which to interrogate the clash of high and low culture, the dialogue between advertising and literature, and the gendered dynamics at work throughout. A corpus of stories ranging across publication venues and genres would only increase the possibility for this sort of critical engagement.

Modern periodical studies, because of the central position of the *Modernist Journals Project*, has been dominated by a relatively highbrow aesthetic in which scholarly interest in advertising emerges from the already-established canonicity of modernist authors and critical investment in little magazines. The time is ripe to complicate this scene. Earle has done so with lowbrow or pulp magazines through his excellent *Re-Covering Modernism: Pulps, Paperbacks, and the Prejudice of Form*. Scholes and Wulfman point to the importance of similarly engaging the "often excluded middle range of literature," which they describe as "a rich mixture of the new and the traditional, of art and advertising, of the poetic and the rhetorical—a mixture that allowed new writers to reach a wider audience" (128). Hammill and Michelle Smith dedicate sustained critical attention to these questions in *Magazines, Travel, and Middlebrow Culture: Canadian*

*Periodicals in English and French 1925–1960*. It is in this liminal space between the avant-garde little magazine and the pulp magazine that most of Ostenso's stories and serialized novels are to be found.

Susan Brown argues that the ways in which "digital media and methods" is rapidly and profoundly "retool[ing]" the humanities calls for new and increasingly self-critical methodologies (203). In the context of scholarly editing, this digital turn demands a reconceived notion of what it means to be an editor and of the relation between scholarly editing and research. As Brown points out, the highly experimental nature of digital scholarly production means that "working at the interface of the digital-humanities divide constitutes, in itself, research" (218). Digitization is an enormous and accelerating phenomenon, and the task of the digital humanist is to render the sheer mass of information meaningful and usable for scholars via contextualization and metadata that will allow for navigation and searching (211–13). In some ways the advent of large-scale digitization and digital editorial projects recalls the canon debates and their encouragement of a self-reflexive relation to our objects of study. But the context of these debates has shifted dramatically with the technologies—a reminder that research and tools are mutually interdependent. Critical attention to digital modes of dissemination and their impact on textuality has only increased scholarly engagement with the material and technological contexts of print culture, while the "crisis" of an overflowing digital archive exponentially greater than the sum of print production (203) demands reconsideration of how cultural production is hierarchized and why.

Ultimately, I view Ostenso as less extraordinary than exemplary. She exists within a complex network of early-twentieth-century cultural production that includes novels, periodicals, and films. While she is a fascinating figure, and much of her work has been unjustly neglected for the reasons I have outlined, the critical questions her work opens up—on collaboration, middlebrow magazines, authorial fluidity, transnationalism, and so on—are not limited to her work. Thus the devising of a theoretically rigorous digital editorial practice, using Ostenso's work as a blueprint, will have outcomes that extend beyond a single author, a single archive, or a single scholar, and thus beyond author(ity) itself.

# Editing the Letters of Wilfred and Sheila Watson, 1956–1961: Scholarly Edition as Digital Practice

Paul Hjartarson, Harvey Quamen, and EMiC UA

"In the past, an archive has referred to a collection of material objects rather than digital surrogates. This type of archive may be described in finding aids but its materials are rarely edited and annotated as a whole. In a digital environment, archive has gradually come to mean a purposeful collection of surrogates. As we know, meanings change over time, and archive in a digital context has come to suggest something that åblends features of editing and archiving. To meld features of both—to have the care of treatment and annotation of an edition and the inclusiveness of an archive—is one of the tendencies of recent work in electronic editing."

Kenneth M. Price, "Edition, Project, Database, Archive, Thematic Research Collection: What's in a Name?" (para. 22)

## INTRODUCTION

In this essay members of the Editing Modernism in Canada collaboratory at the University of Alberta (EMiC UA) examine scholarly editing as a digital practice and focus that examination on our lead project, a joint initiative with the University of Alberta Libraries (UAL) and the John M. Kelly Library at St. Michael's College, University of Toronto, to digitize and edit the letters Wilfred and Sheila Watson wrote each other between 1956 and 1961. For those five years, Sheila Watson was a graduate student in Toronto studying for her doctorate under the supervision of Marshall McLuhan while Wilfred Watson, a recently appointed professor of English at the University of Alberta, was in Edmonton seeking to build on his reputation as an internationally recognized poet and to establish himself as an avant-garde playwright. The Watsons maintained separate residences during this period not just so Sheila could study for her doctorate but also because they had become estranged through Wilfred's marital infidelity. Even in this period of estrangement, however, they wrote each other several times each week, sometimes several letters in a single day. As F.T. Flahiff observes in his life of Sheila Watson,

> Letters made possible the continuation of what in their relationship survived separation, their intense intellectual capability. Each became so immersed in the interests of the other that it is sometimes difficult to determine where an interest [that] has become associated with one or the other had its origins.... Even when relations between them were most strained, they did not lose interest in each other's interests. This was the stuff of their letters during these years, the glue that sealed them. (179)

Although we are digitizing and editing all the letters Wilfred and Sheila Watson wrote each other, the letters from this five-year period constitute the single largest and most important group; what is more, this correspondence dates from arguably the key decade in the life of each writer. The correspondence will be published both in print and digitally. Since our work on the letters is in its early stages, this essay is necessarily a report from the field.

For Wilfred and Sheila Watson, and for Marshall McLuhan, a significant figure in the lives of both Watsons, the 1950s proved a decisive decade. In the five years covered by the letters alone, Sheila Watson published *The Double Hook* (1959) and the third of her Oedipus stories, "Antigone" (1959); Wilfred Watson began a decade-long dialogue with Marshall McLuhan that would not only lead to their collaboration on *From Cliché to Archetype* (1970) but also transform Wilfred's thinking as a playwright. McLuhan himself was completing work on *The Gutenberg Galaxy: The Making of Typographic Man* (1962) and laying the ground for *Understanding Media: The Extensions of Man* (1964). In these years, all three writers sought to understand how new media—photography, film, radio, television, and computing—were not only remediating established art forms but also altering day-to-day life in the postwar era. Even at this early stage in the development of computing, McLuhan was intrigued by the change it might bring: "A computer as a research and communications instrument," he wrote in 1962, "could enhance retrieval, obsolesce mass library organization, retrieve the individual's encyclopedic function and flip it into a private line to speedily tailored data of a saleable kind" (qtd in Coupland 10; cf. Iyer). Fifty years after McLuhan speculated on the computer's potential as a "research and communications instrument," it seems fitting to examine how computing is changing scholarly editing and to focus that examination on the letters Wilfred and Sheila Watson wrote each other during this period.

Although Shirley Neuman and Paul Hjartarson are co-editing the letters, the print and digital editions are not the work of two people but of the collaboratory as a whole, an interdisciplinary team that includes Harvey Quamen, digital lead on the Watsons projects, archivist Raymond Frogner, and graduate students Rebecca Blakey, Matt Bouchard, Kristin Fast, Joseph MacKinnon, and Nick van Orden. The letters project is part of a larger initiative: EMiC UA is engaged in digitizing and editing the Wilfred Watson Fonds. The members of the EMiC UA collaboratory are not only digitizing the archived papers but also seeking to understand how the digital turn is altering our practice as researchers and editors.

"If one of the primary aims of the humanities is to make sense of the human record and human experience," Susan Brown argues in "Don't Mind the Gap: Evolving Digital Modes of Scholarly Production Across the Digital-Humanities Divide,"

> the rapid shift to digital media for recording, interpreting, preserving, and engaging in human activity is of profound significance. Furthermore, access to digital primary sources as the basis of future humanities scholarship will depend as much on how material is digitized and archived, and by whom, and its ability to be sorted, searched and to interact with other materials, as it will on what is being digitized. The tools developed for archiving, teaching, researching, communication, and dissemination will transform the humanities beyond what we can imagine. (203)

Brown's comments raise at least two issues: one concerns the nature and extent of changes currently under way in the humanities; the other, the role of digital technology in these changes. That the shift to digital media is transforming not only how humanities scholars study the human record but also what gets preserved as part of that record cannot effectively be denied. Digital technology is enabling researchers in the humanities to frame new objects of study and to pose new questions even as digital tools themselves alter scholarly practices. Whether the digital turn will ultimately transform what it means to be human and, as part of that transformation, the meaning and aim of the humanities, is much less clear. Although some scholars speak of a "digital revolution" and assume that digital tools are spearheading that revolution, new media are, as Lisa Gitelman argues, "complicated historical subjects" and need to be understood less as agents of change than as "socially embedded site[s] for the negotiation of meaning as such" (6). Change occurs when people interact with the new digital technologies and begin, individually and collectively, to develop the social and cultural practices that inform those interactions.

"Don't Mind the Gap" was published in *Retooling the Humanities: The Culture of Research in Canadian Universities* (2011), a collection of essays in which scholars examine the changing "culture of research" and its import for the humanities. To read Brown's essay in this context is to situate the digital turn in

relation to other economic, social, and cultural factors reshaping the humanities. These include not only globalization and commodification but also the
changing valuation of the humanities in relation to the sciences; of solitary,
curiosity-driven scholarship in relation to large, team-based research focused
on patent or policy-oriented issues; and of government and government funding in relation to the marketplace and private sector funding and involvement.
Certainly scholarly editing as a digital practice cannot be understood apart from
the interdisciplinary research group in which that work takes place. Research in
the humanities, particularly research grounded in English as a discipline, has
traditionally been conceived as both solitary and collaborative: solitary because
the scholar normally works alone; collaborative, in that each solitary scholar
is in dialogue with, and contributing to, work in the field. Although humanities scholarship has traditionally been conceived as solitary, editorial projects,
particularly larger-scale editorial projects, have frequently been undertaken by
teams of scholars. In many ways, the Watson letters project fits the older, editorial team model; however, whereas earlier editorial teams might consist entirely
of English scholars, digital humanities teams are necessarily interdisciplinary,
working not just across humanities or humanities–social sciences disciplines but
at what Brown terms "the interface of the digital-humanities divide" (218). To
work at that interface is to edit in an environment in which the humanities and
digital technologies are inextricably related: virtually every editorial decision
has a technological component; every digital decision, an editorial consequence.

The challenges to collaborating across the digital humanities divide are for-
midable. Collaboration is not for everyone and, in the humanities as presently
constituted, invariably not the sole mode of research. The need is to create a
space in which those inclined to collaborate can settle into the work. If the
project is intent on moving beyond "proof of concept" to build working tools
and environments—as the Canadian Writing Research Collaboratory (CWRC),
EMiC, and the Watsons projects are—the stakes involved in successful collaboration are even higher. The impediments to digital humanities collaboration
prompted Stan Ruecker and Milena Radzikowska to develop the concept of an
iterative "project charter," a contract team that members develop in the early
stages of their work together and revise as the project evolves, as digital humanities projects invariably do. The charter articulates the principles and policies
governing collaboration. The practice of jointly developing a project charter has
been adopted by a number of digital humanities groups, including EMiC UA.
Stan Ruecker himself refers to successive iterations of charters for the projects
in which he has participated as "the history of his mistakes" and states that
he aspires "to make only new mistakes" (personal communication). However
self-deprecating his comments, they suggest something of the difficulties. Since
collaborating within a post-secondary environment almost invariably involves

both mentoring and the completion of degree requirements in the various disciplines represented on the project, there is the added challenge of integrating that work into digital humanities projects so that graduate students, postdoctoral fellows, and untenured faculty from each discipline can participate fully in the project and receive appropriate credit for the work they do. Collaboration across the digital divide, collaboration that integrates mentoring into the work, is vital not just for the Wilfred and Sheila Watson letters project but also for digital humanities projects generally.

## EDITING THE ARCHIVE

> *Tuesday. Dear Wilfred … Today I took M.M. the outline of the thesis. I'm glad he insisted. He has given me his blessing—He also glanced at some of the first pages of the new draft and said the prose would do.*
> (Wilfred Watson Fonds, 95-131, box 13, folder 235)

In *Merchants of Culture: The Publishing Business in the Twenty-First Century* (2010), John B. Thompson examines the many challenges Anglo-American trade publishers have faced since the 1960s. In an earlier study, *Books in the Digital Age* (2005), Thompson analyzes the problems the digital turn has posed for the academic and higher education sectors of book publishing in the United States and the United Kingdom since the 1980s. In *Merchants of Culture* he not only shifts sectors but also broadens the timeline: the "digital revolution" becomes one of many changes large trade publishers have confronted since the 1960s. (Others include the growth of retail chains, the rise of literary agents, and the emergence of media corporations.) To understand rapid technological change, he argues in the closing pages of *Books in the Digital Age*,

> we have to look beyond the digital revolution as such; we have to go back and reconstruct the structure and evolution of the fields within which these industries operate, for only then will we understand the distinctive interplay of economics, technology and culture which defines the logic of each field and the conditions of success or failure within it. (438)

In *Merchants of Culture* he undertakes that broader study, returning in the closing chapters to rethink his analysis of the digital revolution.

"The transformation of the field of trade publishing," Thompson argues in *Merchants of Culture*,

> was a process driven above all by social and economic factors, by actors and organizations pursuing their aims, responding to changing circumstances and taking advantage of new opportunities in the competitive field of Anglo-American book publishing. But interlaced with this transformation and contributing to it was a technological revolution that first began to make

itself felt in the book publishing industry in the mid-1980s and became a source of increasing speculation and concern from the early 1990s on. By then the digital revolution had already convulsed the music industry and seemed set to cause similar disruption in other sectors of the creative industries. The rapid growth of the internet from the mid 1990s on served only to heighten speculation. By the late 1990s many publishers were pouring millions of dollars into electronic publishing projects of various kinds and venture capitalists were launching new companies aimed at digitizing book content and making it available in a variety of formats. (312)

In rethinking his analysis of the "digital revolution," Thompson examines the rise of e-book sales, particularly since the release of Sony's e-book reader in the United States in 2006 and of Amazon's Kindle in 2007. (The launch of Apple's iPad in April 2010 occurred too late for Thompson to factor it into his analysis.) Although Thompson acknowledges that the future of Anglo-American trade publishing is uncertain, he argues that much of the concern about the e-book itself is misplaced. In his view, whether the e-book replaces or simply displaces the codex is beside the point: computing has, in fact, already remediated virtually all aspects of publishing, from operating and content management systems to digital workflows, sales, and marketing. While the issue of content delivery is significant, he argues, e-books are not the harbinger of change in the publishing business but a sign that change is already well advanced.

Thompson's approach is a good place to begin analyzing technological change in the humanities in general and in the field of Canadian literature in particular. The shift to digital media in the humanities, as in publishing itself, is not a new development but part of a historical process that dates back to at least mid-century.[1] As Thompson argues, these technological changes are inextricably bound up in other economic and cultural forces; together they define the logic of Canadian literature as a field and the conditions of success or failure within it. The essays in *Retooling the Humanities* analyze the interplay of the economic, technological, and cultural forces that have created the contemporary culture of research; some recognize the need to ground that analysis in an understanding of the structure and history of Canadian literature as a field. In the opening pages of *Retooling the Humanities*, co-editors Daniel Coleman and Smaro Kamboureli describe that book as "a direct outcome of the TransCanada project and the three conferences that have animated it (Vancouver 2005, Guelph 2007, Sackville 2009)" (x). In the TransCanada project, Roy Miki and Smaro Kamboureli set themselves, and Canadian literature researchers generally, an ambitious, twofold task: "to undertake a major rethinking of the assumptions that had governed the field of CanLit studies and to rejuvenate the field through a renewed sense of collective purpose" (Kamboureli, Preface xiii). To rethink the field, it is necessary to understand its history.

In the Preface to *Trans.Can.Lit: ReSituating the Study of Canadian Litera-ture*, the first book to emerge from this large, collective project, Kamboureli articulates critical assumptions governing the field in the first decade of the twenty-first century:

> Canadian literature: a construct bounded by the nation, a cultural byproduct of the Cold War era, a nationalist discourse with its roots in colonial legacies, a literature that has assumed transnational and global currency, a tradi-tion often marked by uncertainty about its value and relevance, a corpus of texts in which, albeit not without anxiety and resistance, spaces have been made for First Nations and diasporic voices. These are some of the critical assumptions scholars have brought to the study of CanLit, as we have come to call it for the sake of brevity, but also affectionately, and often ironically as we recognize the dissonances inscribed in the economy of this term. (vii)

As Kamboureli's brief summary suggests, post–Second World War Canadian literature was shaped by many forces, including the cultural nationalism of the early postwar decades, the Cold War, and Canada's deeply troubled relationship both to the First Nations and to immigrant communities. Although Miki and Kamboureli conceived the TransCanada Project in the first decade of World Wide Web, technological change did not originally factor in their thinking; it is, however, inextricably linked to several components of their analysis, including globalization, interdisciplinarity, and collaboration. Technological change may seem a new force shaping the field of Canadian literature, but it too has a history. Concern over the introduction and rapid growth of television in the United States, for example, played a significant role in the work and recommendations of the Massey Commission (1949–51) and fed on earlier concerns about radio broadcasting. Similarly, the military integration of North America fed by the Cold War, and the rapid growth of computing technology fuelled by the US/Soviet race for space, helped foster postwar cultural nationalism in Canada, including institutional support of Canadian literature. The "Editing as Cultural Practice" workshop, a joint initiative of the TransCanada Institute and the Edit-ing Modernism in Canada project, is one step in analyzing not just modernism or scholarly editing in Canada but digital tools themselves as factors in shaping CanLit as a field.

If, following Lisa Gitelman, new media are conceived less as agents of change than as "socially embedded site[s] for the negotiation of meaning as such," they become particularly interesting, if complex, lenses through which to study his-torical change (6). In the opening pages of *Always Already New: Media, History and the Data of Culture*, Gitelman offers the following definition of media:

> I define media as socially realized structures of communication, where structures include both technological forms and their associated protocols,

and where communication is a cultural practice, a ritualized collocation of different people on the same mental map, sharing or engaged with popular ontologies of representation. As such, media are unique and complicated historical subjects. Their histories must be social and cultural, not the stories of how one technology leads to another, or of isolated geniuses working their magic in the world. Any full accounting will require, as William Uricchio (2003, 24) puts it, "an embrace of multiplicity, complexity and even contradiction if sense is to be made of such" pervasive and dynamic cultural phenomena. (7)

Note that Gitelman includes in her definition of media not just "technological forms" but "their associated protocols." As both Thompson and Gitelman argue, the history of computing—whether it is in the field of publishing or Canadian literature or scholarly editing—is necessarily social and cultural. It is the study of the ongoing negotiation of meaning via changing cultural practices.

Following Thompson, could one not argue that concern about the impact of the e-book on the humanities in general and on Canadian literature and Canadian literary criticism in particular is also misplaced? Whether a scholarly edition is published in print, via e-book, or online—or by some combination of these—the editing is undertaken on computers, will involve some use of editing tools, and will be delivered to the publisher, if not to the reader, electronically. The question is not whether this will happen—it is already happening—but what role Canadian literature scholars and editors want to play in that work or in the analysis of changing protocols and practices. As Jerome McGann, Johanna Drucker, Susan Brown, and Dean Irvine (among others) have argued, humanities scholars need to address what Drucker terms "the methods and implications of the migration of our cultural legacy into digital form" (Drucker xii; cf. McGann, "Electronic" 41). The Watsons letters project is involved not only in digitizing literary papers but also in addressing the methods and implications of that work. That Wilfred Watson, Sheila Watson, and Marshall McLuhan were themselves concerned with new media as factors shaping both contemporary life and literature, and wrote about these subjects in their letters, makes this archival and editorial work particularly interesting.

Even a brief examination of the finding aids—available online—reveals that the Wilfred Watson and Sheila Watson Fonds are both large and relatively comprehensive (Pomahac; St. Onge). In addition to published and unpublished manuscripts, the archives include journals and notebooks, personal and professional correspondence, personal and professional records, and photographs of family, colleagues, and friends. In a forthcoming essay, "Editing the Wilfred Watson and Sheila Watson Archives: Scholarly Editions ↔ Digital Projects," Paul Hjartason, Harvey Quamen, and Kristin Fast offer a rationale for digitizing the Wilfred and Sheila Watson archives and outline plans for the first phase of that work. Editing the letters Wilfred and Sheila Watson wrote each other is foundational to that work. Why? The letters are invaluable for what they reveal about the writers themselves, and about the creative exchange between them, in this pivotal decade of their lives. In 1956, Wilfred and Sheila Watson had just returned from a year in Paris, and each was working through ideas and manuscripts they had written or revised there. In the five years from 1956 to 1961, they wrote each other about the events shaping their lives and careers in this formative period. The letters are also invaluable for what they reveal about the Edmonton and Toronto communities in which each writer lived and worked during this period. Wilfred's letters tell us about the community of directors, actors, and set designers involved in the University of Alberta's Studio Theatre; about the community of writers and professors, including Henry Kreisel, Eli Mandel, and F.M. Salter, centred on the English Department; about writers and artists, such as Dorothy Livesay and Jack Shadbolt, passing through the city; and about the university itself in this expansive period of development. Sheila's letters tell about life as a doctoral student at the University of Toronto, a life centred on St. Michael's College and increasingly on her study, with Marshall McLuhan, of the writing and painting of Wyndham Lewis, but also about her life as a writer in Toronto, and about lectures, exhibitions, plays, and concerts she attended. This body of correspondence thus offers insights into the cultural life of two universities and two cities in the late 1950s, and into the national writing community in a formative period of postwar development.

An edition of the letters is foundational for another reason as well. In examining the Wilfred Watson and Sheila Watson Fonds, EMiC UA researchers identified the long and complex genesis of the published work as the distinguishing characteristic of both archives. That the manuscripts themselves are, for the most part, undated complicates study of both the published and unpublished texts. Although many of the letters Wilfred and Sheila Watson wrote each other between 1956 and 1961 are dated only by the day or the week—"Sunday evening," for example—most can be dated either through references within the letters or by cross-referencing the letters with the journals or other documents in their own archives or in the archives of other writers and colleagues (such as Marshall McLuhan). While editing the letters will leave some letters and manuscripts undated, it should establish a chronological frame of reference for study of published and unpublished texts.

F.T. Flahiff's inclusion of a lengthy selection of Sheila Watson's Paris journals in *Always Someone to Kill the Doves* renewed interest in her writing and focused that interest on her life in the mid-1950s. Publication of the letters Wilfred and Sheila Watson wrote each other between 1956 and 1961 is predicated on Flahiff's publication of Sheila Watson's journals, a project in which he is engaged with the help of Shirley Neuman. The letters complement—and complicate—the journals in at least two ways: first, they provide a different perspective on the relation-ship between Wilfred and Sheila Watson in these crucial years; and second, they constitute a different kind of writing—a different audience certainly—and catch the writer in different moments and moods than in the journal writing. Approximately 1,527 Wilfred and Sheila Watson letters are extant in the two archives: 1,142 in the Wilfred Watson Fonds; 385 in the Sheila Watson Fonds.[2] The vast majority of these letters are from Wilfred to Sheila: 1,193 letters from Wilfred versus 334 from Sheila. Why so many letters from Wilfred Watson or so few from Sheila? Not because he wrote far more letters than she did but because at one point Sheila Watson began destroying her letters, and Wilfred, dismayed, hid what he could from destruction. These letters came to light when Shirley Neuman was sorting through Wilfred Watson's papers prior to depositing them in the archive at the University of Alberta. According to her account, Sheila was made aware of the extant letters and agreed that they be deposited in the archive. The relative paucity of extant letters from Sheila to Wilfred Watson creates obvi-ous editorial difficulties: there are enough letters extant to reveal the nature, depth, and range of the exchanges between them, including frequency, playful-ness, and shifts in tone and mood over time; and, since Wilfred routinely notes and responds to letters from Sheila, we also have a good idea of the number of letters she wrote and some idea of their content. We can surmise more from letters to friends and from journal and notebook entries. Ultimately, however, there is no papering over the relative absence of letters from Sheila Watson. The paucity of extant letters from Sheila to Wilfred Watson presents the single biggest problem we face as editors of the correspondence.

The letters Wilfred and Sheila Watson wrote each other are deposited in two different archives. In *Always Someone to Kill the Doves*, F.T. Flahiff states that Sheila Watson did not want her papers deposited either in the University of Alberta archive alongside the papers of her husband, Wilfred, or with Library and Archives Canada, which holds the papers of her doctoral supervisor and friend, Marshall McLuhan. Biographers and critics will undoubtedly debate Sheila Watson's reasons for years to come. Our focus here is on the difficulties researchers face as a result of the inevitable division of their papers and the deci-sion to deposit the two collections in repositories more than 3,500 kilometres apart. Other than the periods of separation we have noted, the two writers lived and wrote side by side for more than fifty years; together they built a library of over 8,000 books and an art collection that included work by, among others, Michael Ayerton, David Blackwood, Molly Lamb Bobak, Emily Carr, A.Y. Jack-son, Wyndham Lewis, Henry Moore, Jack Shadbolt, and Norman Yates. Divid-ing their papers for deposit in two separate fonds must have proved a difficult, occasionally problematic, sometimes painful, task. Not surprisingly, perhaps, signs of that difficulty are apparent in the finding aids for the two fonds. The letters Wilfred and Sheila Watson wrote each other are spread across the two collections with little discernible rationale for that distribution. One might, for example, expect the letters from Wilfred to Sheila would be held in the Sheila Watson Fonds; Sheila's letters, in the Wilfred Watson Fonds. That is certainly not the distribution here. A page missing from a letter in one collection—perhaps left in a book, notebook, or journal—might appear amidst papers in the other collection. What is true of the letters is arguably also true of drawings, photographs, a manuscript or typescript page or poetry or prose. In editing the correspondence, the first task is to gather together the letters themselves, and related documents, from two archives geographically remote from each other.

## DIGITIZING THE LETTERS

> *Dear Swp. I've not written you very good letters over the weekend, for I've been seething inwardly with the Cockcrow ms. business. One point is clear: the end needs considerable revision. But I don't despair—the first ¾ are achieved.*
>
> (Wilfred Watson, letter to Sheila Watson, undated)

The epigraph for this essay is taken from Kenneth M. Price's "Edition, Project, Database, Archive, Thematic Research Collection: What's in a Name?" (With Ed Folsom, Price co-edits the online Walt Whitman Archive). Price begins his essay with a series of questions:

> What are the implications of the terms we use to describe large-scale text-based electronic scholarship, especially undertakings that share some of the ambitions and methods of the traditional multi-volume scholarly edition? What genre or genres are we now working in? And how do the conceptions inherent in these choices of language frame and perhaps limit what we attempt? How do terms such as *edition, project, database, archive,* and *thematic research collection* relate to the past, present, and future of textual studies? (para. 1; emphasis in original)

In the essay Price attempts to chart changing institutional formations and practices through shifts in the meaning and use of keywords. The epigraph occurs at the outset of his discussion of "archive" and raises at least two issues: one indirectly, the other directly. The issue Price raises indirectly concerns the relationship between the material archive—that is, the boxes of documents stored in a repository—and digital scans of those documents stored on a server and accessible online. The issue he raises directly focuses on the relationship between archiving and editing. In digitizing Wilfred Watson's papers, and in digitizing and editing the letters Wilfred and Sheila Watson wrote each other, the members of EMiC UA have confronted both issues.

Because Wilfred and Sheila Watson created most of their artwork before personal computers were widely used, and certainly before the advent of the World Wide Web, neither archive includes born-digital materials or computer files of any kind. Both writers typically wrote longhand and then had typists transcribe their texts. As "collections of material objects," Wilfred and Sheila Watson's archives consist primarily of handwritten and typed documents (although both also include artwork and some multimedia). Will online digital archives make what Price terms "collection[s] of material objects" redundant? If not, how will the existence of "purposeful collection[s] of surrogates" alter the scholarly use and understanding of the material archive? Answers to these questions are neither clear nor simple. In digitizing the Wilfred and Sheila Watson papers, EMiC UA researchers have chosen to align the digital archive with the material archive and to adopt the file-naming conventions used in organizing the material archive. In "Editing the Wilfred Watson and Sheila Watson Archives: Scholarly Editions ↔ Digital Projects," we explain why we chose to develop the Wilfred Watson digital archive as a hybrid database, why we parsed the existing Encoded Archival Description (EAD) into a database, and how we are extending the existing Wilfred Watson finding aid from file to item level. As we explain in the essay, our research group is using this database to develop metadata for each digital object, to establish relationships among the documents that enable us to date each text more accurately, and to collaborate with one another in that work. Because we are aligning the digital collection with the material archive, a researcher who accesses Wilfred Watson documents online can visit the material archive and use the digital file name to request the material object. We have adopted this practice in the belief that digital archives complement existing material collections rather than making them redundant. If, as Kenneth Price argues, the digital turn is blending features of archiving and editing, it is important that digital humanists collaborate with archivists in that work.

Because the digitization of literary fonds blends archiving and editing, the ultimate objective of such projects might seem to be a scholarly edition of the collected works. There are at least two problems with this assumption. First, for the archives of most Canadian modernists, a scholarly edition of the collected works is, at best, a distant ambition. In most cases, bibliographical, biographical, and editorial work is in its early stages; in many, the archives themselves have only recently been opened for study. If a biography has been published, it is usually a first assessment; often, the documents required for a more definitive biography of the writer—letters and journals, for example—have not themselves been published in a scholarly edition. This is certainly the case for both Sheila and Wilfred Watson. Although F.T. Flahiff published a life of Sheila Watson—he resists using the term "biography"—neither her letters nor her journals have appeared in print; indeed, the archive itself has only recently opened for study. Although Wilfred Watson's archive was opened for study a decade earlier, critical studies of his writing (Tiessen; Betts; Betts, Hjartarson, and Smitka, eds.) are only now beginning to appear. The other problem with the idea that editing an archive of literary papers involves producing a scholarly (digital) edition of the collected work is that this goal is derived from print culture. The shift to digital media is also a shift in objectives; instead of producing a definitive edition, the goal of a digital archive might be to create the digital infrastructure scholars and teachers need to access and study texts and to produce the editions they want and need for their work. The edition might be for use in a classroom or in a stage production, for inclusion in an anthology of poems, short stories, or plays, or in support of a biographical or historical project; it might be a reading text with minimal scholarly apparatus or a genetic edition with full apparatus; the edition might be a previously unpublished text or an earlier, previously unpublished version of a published text.

Whatever the researchers' stated objective, the immediate need is to build infrastructure and, one would hope, to build for the long term. Digitizing a literary archive involves not just assembling an interdisciplinary team of researchers but also partnering with other projects, organizations, and institutions, beginning with the libraries that hold the papers themselves and the literary executors who act in the best interests of the estates. The Editing the Wilfred Watson Archive Project is grounded in our partnership with the University of Alberta Libraries (UAL) and with the literary executors; our work on the Wilfred and Sheila Watson letters project, on partnerships with both the University of Alberta and the John M. Kelly Libraries. That the two large digital initiatives within which the Watson projects are nested, the Editing Modernism in Canada research cluster and the Canadian Writing Research Collaboratory, are themselves centred on partnerships with libraries is no accident. Building a sustainable digital archive demands such partnerships and the long-term commitment they involve.

The database-driven website we use to gather metadata for each archival document is a key component of the Watsons projects' infrastructure. Watsons project researchers use the database not only as a repository for accumulating, correcting, and updating metadata but to communicate with other members of the group. As we explain in "Editing the Wilfred Watson and Sheila Watson Archives: Scholarly Editions ↔ Digital Projects," using a database as a repository enables the Watsons projects to maintain a "schema agnostic" version of the metadata and gives us flexibility in the future to output that data in a variety of formats and thus to adapt more readily to technological change. EMiC UA members are also using the website to compile the information we need in order to date the letters between Wilfred and Sheila Watson. As already noted, the letters they wrote each other are frequently undated; that is, they are dated only by the day of the week "Thursday," sometimes also by the time of day ("Sunday evening"). Sometimes we can date letters from the postmark on the accompanying envelope, but only if an envelope survives. Of the 1,193 letters held by the University of Alberta Archives, for example, fully 488 are undated. Since Wilfred and Sheila wrote each other almost daily, and since they engage in dialogue on many issues, including local and national events, we are frequently able to date the letters from contextual evidence or by cross-referencing the letters with one another or with other dated material in the archives; indeed, we are confident that we can date most of the undated letters in this way. Watsons project members use the website to gather information, to record the evidence on which we base the dates and any problems or follow-up work needed. Accurately dating the Wilfred–Sheila correspondence is crucial to our work on the letters but will also assist us in establishing the composition history of published and unpublished writing. Transcribing the letters enables us to make them accessible to searches and queries early in our editorial work.

Two other digital components of the Watsons projects' infrastructure work thus far merit comment. First, as F.T. Flahiff notes, together Wilfred and Sheila Watson built a library of over 8,000 books. In *Always Someone to Kill the Doves*, Flahiff reports that Sheila shipped some of them to him with her papers and that the remaining 7,280 arrived by truck following her death. Although the John M. Kelly Library agreed to house Sheila Watson's papers, the library retained and catalogued only 952 of the books. With the assistance of Michael Bramah at the Kelly Library, Harvey Quamen pulled the cataloguing data for the 952 books from the University of Toronto Library system. He is using those records to build a database of the Wilfred and Sheila Watson library holdings. Fortunately Flahiff himself catalogued the Watson library holdings, recording on index cards not only the basic bibliographical data but also notes regarding inscriptions. In annotating Sheila Watson's journals, Shirley Neuman made significant use of the index cards; indeed, she began transcribing the information from the cards into a Word document. Following discussions with her, we took over the work of transcription. Joseph MacKinnon, a University of Alberta graduate and the EMiC UA member who took the lead in scanning the Wilfred Watson letters in 2010–11, completed the work of transcription.

Joseph MacKinnon also took the early lead in transcribing Wilfred Watson's letters. Although at this stage of project work, our top priority is necessarily scanning and metadata entry, we have begun thinking through the task of transcribing and annotating the letters. As part of that work, EMiC UA is developing a prosopography, that is, a database of the people—family members, fellow writers and professors, artists, directors, set designers, actors, students, etc.—who are mentioned in the letters, journals, and notebooks or who enter into the archived papers in one way or another. While the database will allow us to collect significant amounts of data on these people—birthdates, death dates, occupations, places of residence, business and personal relationships of any duration between any of them—we can also collect from the database a simple list of names of the type that would be familiar to many editors and digital humanists as an "authority list." To scan and transcribe the letters, notebooks, and journals is to begin gathering that information. Given that our object of study finally is not just Wilfred and Sheila Watson but also the communities in which they lived and worked—communities centred on the Studio Theatre, on the journal *White Pelican*, and on the English departments at the University of Alberta, St. Michael's College, and elsewhere—and the relationships they developed, the use of a prosopographic database seems a good strategy to follow. That database will be used and developed not only by the editors of the letters but also by Kristin Fast in her work on Sheila Watson's short stories, by Vanessa Lent in her work on Wilfred Watson's *Cockcrow and the Gulls*, and by other projects currently in development. Here, as with metadata generally, we need to work closely with EMiC, CWRC, and our institutional partners to ensure interoperability.

Clearly, then, an important part of our infrastructure work thus far has been to build a series of databases. These digital infrastructure tools will help us, in the end, to produce a variety of editions of the letters. The digital aspects of our work remain—and need to remain—agnostic about metadata standards, markup schemas, and editorial theories. As Jerome McGann has written: "One can build editorial machines capable of generating on demand multiple textual formations—eclectic, facsimile, reading, genetic—that can all be subjected to multiple kinds of transformational analyses" ("From Text to Work"). Our decision to store information (metadata, for example) in databases rather than in a series of documents (which may or may not be marked up in XML according to some schema) gives us the long-term flexibility to which McGann refers.

These databases provide other opportunities as well. We can track workflow progress as we scan and transcribe our way through the archive, and team members can make notes on, and register problems concerning, any given archival object. In the Watsons project's home-brewed parlance, a "note" is an observation that properly ought to become part of the permanent record of an item (e.g., noting damaged or missing pages); a "problem" is an issue that needs to be examined more closely and solved by the EMiC UA team (e.g., correcting transcription mistakes or rescanning poor images). Moreover, the use of a database means that we can generate a prioritized to-do list simply by querying the "problems" field of all records and sorting that list by the dates on which the problems were first logged. At any given time in the future, we can export other relevant fields of our database to produce, for example, an up-to-the-minute finding aid for the archive, perhaps as a plain text document or as a Web page or automatically encoded in XML according to any schema we choose, regardless of whether the schema needed is EAD or MODS or something else entirely.

One of the guiding principles behind this strategy has been drawn from recent developments in software design. In "agile development" or so-called "extreme programming" (XP), the design of a system is constantly revisited throughout the project's development phase. Consequently, any decision—even a major one—is delayed as long as possible to incorporate as much new information and as much team experience as possible. As author Kent Beck writes: "XP-style design is a shift in the timing of design decisions. Design is deferred until it can be made in the light of experience and the decisions can be used immediately" (69). Although Beck is a computer programmer, he was trained in a manner probably not unlike most humanists: "I was taught exactly the opposite of this strategy in school: 'Put in all the design you can before you begin implementation because you'll never get another chance'" (32). That old-fashioned "design first and build later" strategy oftentimes turns out to be wholly wrongheaded for digital projects. By adopting some of the tenets of extreme programming, we feel we can create a more robust, more adaptable, and ultimately more useful digital archive.

Susan Brown has argued that working at the interface between the digital and the humanities is possible only insofar as "the two aspects of the research seriously engage with one another" (218). For the Watsons project, this means taking seriously the concerns of editors, archivists, and computer programmers. We have not treated the "best practices" developed by experienced computer professionals as simply a digital add-on to an otherwise routine editorial project: incorporating XP-style decision-making into our project has shaped how we define our editorial practices; similarly, our discussions about editorial practices have, in turn, shaped the ways in which we design our databases and other digital infrastructure tools.

## CONCLUSION

The fields of Canadian literature and scholarly editing have undergone significant change in the post–Second World War period. What John B. Thompson says of the field of Anglo-American publishing is no less true here: Canadian literature and scholarly editing have been transformed by a multitude of social and economic factors, by actors and organizations taking advantage of opportunities that develop. As both Thompson and Gitelman argue, digital tools are less agents of change than "socially embedded site[s]" for the ongoing negotiation of meaning (Gitelman 6). Wilfred and Sheila Watson's engagement with new media fifty years ago, and Marshall McLuhan's interest in computing as "a research and communications instrument," serves as a reminder that computing, including humanities computing, is not new; the fact that participants in the "Editing as Cultural Practice" workshop wrote and submitted essays electronically, and that we read the papers submitted by others via a wiki, indicates that technological forms and associated protocols have changed and continue to change. If, as Brown argues, the shift to digital media is transforming the humanities, that transformation begins at the level of the research group itself. Digital humanities projects are necessarily interdisciplinary; what is more, they need to work at what she terms "the interface of the digital-humanities divide." To work in a serious and sustained way at the interface, team members need clearly articulated principles and policies concerning both collaboration and mentoring. This essay is our report from the field on the Watsons letter project: the challenges faced and strategies developed to digitize the archive and edit the letters.

# The Politics of Recovery and the Recovery of Politics: Editing Canadian Writing on the Spanish Civil War

Bart Vautour

> "You cannot say a poem is ever ended
> or catalogued once for all"
>
> Kenneth Leslie, "No Poem Is Ever Ended,"
> *O'Malley to the Reds & Other Poems (35)*

## PART I

The following chapter presents a rejoinder, in the form of an editorial consideration, to a mode of cultural selection that would discharge political protest from the production of literary history in Canada. While using the example of literature written by Canadians about the Spanish Civil War, I explore and (re)invigorate the literary-critical category of occasional literature—*pièces d'occasion*—in the contexts of contemporary scholarly editing and the recovery of political literature. In considering how occasional, event-based literature is often subject to editorial erasure, I mean to highlight how literary-historical effacement through editorial practice can result in a silent transvaluation into restrictive conceptions of both citizenship and political commentary in literature. Counter to the editorial erasure of politicized occasional literature, I suggest a development of an event-based editorial practice that highlights possibilities for a re-evaluation of occasional literature. Beyond initiating a reconsideration of ways to edit Canadian literary history, this theoretical framework, when applied to Canadian literature written about the Spanish Civil War, is also capable of pointing scholarly inquiry toward rethinking conceptions of contemporary citizenship beyond restrictive national or neoliberal formulations by emphasizing an underrepresented moment of transnational political engagement. Emerging out of overriding tropological concerns of the writing itself, this framework understands Canadian literary expressions about the Spanish Civil War to be deeply interactive, reactive, and responsive to transnational and cosmopolitan literary and political networks. Before proposing an event-based editorial practice, it is important to get a sharper sense of occasional literature and the ways in which such literature is often conceptualized.

An early theorist of event-based literature, Hegel noticed an undervaluing of occasional literature by the literary-critical establishment in his *Aesthetics*:

> Poetry's living connection with the real world and its occurrences in public and private affairs is revealed most amply in the so-called *pièces d'occasion*. If this description were given a wider sense, we could use it as a name for nearly all poetic works: but if we take it in the proper and narrower sense we have to restrict it to productions owing their origin to some single present event and expressly devoted to its exaltation, embellishment, commemoration, etc. But by such entanglement with life poetry seems again to fall into a position of dependence, and for this reason it has often been proposed to assign to the whole sphere of *pièces d'occasion* an inferior value. (995–96)

Hegel understood the role of poetry in communicating the conditions of an event to be different from that of historiography: poetry creates a different material reality of an event than does historiography. In that creation, Hegel suggests that poetry *seems* to depend on the external event but that poetry can avoid this dependence by not trying to become the occasion (996). He seems to suggest that when poetry presents itself *as* the event or occasion, or when readers seek to replace the event with the poem, Western literary-critical traditions often assign an ephemerality to the work as it categorically moves from literature to history or historiography. Occasional literature, then, must not be taken up as direct mimetic reproduction of a non-literary event if it is to hold literary value under traditional rubrics. Instead, under these traditional parameters a text must be framed in such a way as to animate an augmentation of the event rather than an emptying of the text's literary value and assignment to literary ephemerality.[1] This traditional rubric for assigning literary value has its corollary in the perennial undervaluing and (often) expunction of occasional literature by editors. Editorial rationales often fail to recognize the importance of works of occasional literature to the oeuvres of individual authors and the ways in which certain historical events capture the global literary imagination and cause a sea change in the prevailing modes of literary production. These events often foster new literary forms and experimentations that disappear from critical view when a given text is editorially discharged from posterity based on its event-based content. Sustained scrutiny from literary critics and scholarly editors is needed when such historical events captivate large numbers of writers from around the globe. The Spanish Civil War is such an event, a "matrix-event." It changed the structures of political formations and, more importantly here, it changed the structuring logic of cultural production. As Valentine Cunningham suggests in *British Writers of the Thirties*, if there is "one decisive event which focuses the hopes and fears of the literary '30s, a moment that seems to summarize and test the period's myths and dreams, to enact and encapsulate its dominant themes and images, the Spanish Civil War is it" (419). Indeed, as I have argued elsewhere, the anti-fascist cause in Spain helped reorganize some of the prevailing aesthetic principles circulating throughout Canada.[2]

The conflict in Spain began when a group of fascists attempted a *coup d'état* in July of 1936, which turned into a full-scale conflict lasting until the spring of 1939. The fight against fascism in Spain was central to the writing of many well-known authors such as W.H. Auden, Nancy Cunard, Ernest Hemingway, Langston Hughes, Pablo Neruda, George Orwell, Dorothy Parker, Stephen Spender, and Genevieve Taggard, among many others, and a large body of Canadian writing likewise responded to the event both during and after the conflict.[3] Before turning to two examples of Canadian texts about the Spanish Civil War that enable critical analysis of Canadian editorial history (the work of Kenneth Leslie and Sir Charles G.D. Roberts), it is important to explain what I mean by suggesting that the Spanish Civil War is a matrix-event.

Not every event has the same gravity in the world. For example, birthdays or marriages—for which we have the occasional literary modes of the genethliacon and epithalamion—rarely, on their own, cause a large-scale shift in modes of literary and social production. Rather, important here is the type of event around which a body of social, political, and cultural discourse grows and how we set to work arranging the textual, literary products that emerge out of that discourse. Recent editorial theory and practice have worked to displace the "authority" of "intent" in order to oust long-standing hierarchies that have ordered and shaped sites of literary dissemination. Anglo-American eclectic editing, associated with W.W. Greg and Fredson Bowers, survives but is no longer the default practice in the preparation of critical or scholarly editions of English-language texts. Looking at more than moments of textual origin or final intentions, scholars such as Jerome McGann and George Bornstein shift precedence to all of the "textual constitutions which the work undergoes in its historical passages" (McGann, *Textual* 62). This shifting focus in recent editorial theory to the historical passages of texts has continued to give primacy to texts as they get coded over time and space. While materialist conceptions of a text already prompt editors to think historically so as to make history explicit in linguistic and bibliographic code, additional possibilities, problems, and recalibrations arise when a historical event is given structural primacy over the subsequent literary texts that the event occasions.

To explore event-based editorial practice, the work of the French *Annales* school proves useful in making a distinction between types of events and, as a result, modes of occasional literature. It might seem odd to turn to a scholarly group that was actually founded on a critique of the methodological reliance on political and diplomatic events for the writing of history. In the early years of the *Annales* school, the scholars involved aimed to shift focus from the telling of history as one event after the next, to a focus, perhaps echoing Bergson, on the *longue durée* or broad, long-term persistence of structures within society. Over time, the *Annales* group of historians and social scientists came to pinpoint types of events that they found necessary to address when looking at the emergence and persistence of structures within society. Events of this kind have been termed "matrix-events"—moments that reshape hegemonic structures at an ideological and conscious level. As the Canadian historian, Ian McKay points out, "wars and matrix-events often go together. In wartime the [very] language of politics is transformed" (*Rebels* 101). Matrix-events are contradictory moments that demand a new or transformed framework of understanding—a new or transformed discourse. While, as McKay points out, the "craven failure of the liberal state to defend democracy in Spain in the 1930s stank in the nostrils of [the] left" (*Rebels* 101), I suggest it also changed the ways the proponents of liberal democracy could smell themselves. In other words, the state-sanctioned disavowal of Spanish democracy by the majority of Western democracies was at odds with the popular support the cause received from within those self-same states.[4] People's idea of what democracy would stand for was shaken and, as a result of this contradiction, many people found alternative ways of expressing citizenship—in both words and actions. While close to 1,700 Canadians volunteered in Spain to fight for the anti-fascist government in contravention of Canadian law, other Canadians articulated a transnational citizenship based on the political solidarity of anti-fascist beliefs through artistic innovation: Spain became their political and artistic "homeland." A literary-historical establishment that often dismisses occasional literature and operates strictly within a framework of "national literatures" will miss the complexities and alternatives articulated over time in response to a wide-reaching matrix-event such as the Spanish Civil War. For one feature of a matrix-event is that its gravitas can live on, often to be recalled at strategic moments, even after other structure-changing events have superseded the first. The Spanish Civil War, for example, continues to be evoked by writers as a political and literary resource. As such, literature written about the conflict in the years following the fascist victory remains occasional literature. While Canadian writers, in the past eight decades, have continued to draw on the Spanish Civil War and its attendant politics to write *pièces d'occasion*, the scholarly community has not sought to collate the material for public consumption in any systematic way.[5]

Adjoined to the technical and theoretical project of editing Canadian writing on the Spanish Civil War—it is important to admit—is an activist impulse toward recovery akin to, but separate from, the project of literary protest taken up by many Canadian writers against fascism and in solidarity with Spanish anti-fascists. Recovery through editorial production heeds Raymond Williams's familiar proposal to "search out and counterpoise an alternative tradition taken from the neglected works left in the wide margin of the [twentieth] century" (*Politics* 35). My own editorial work on Canadian writing about the Spanish Civil War aims to recover an alternative vocabulary for talking about transnational citizenship and cultural expression. This work of recovery is a project undertaken with the knowledge that, as Cary Nelson notes in his introduction to *Repression and Recovery*, "one never actually 'recovers' the thing itself. Literary history can never have in view, can never hold within its intellectual grasp or even merely in its gaze, some level of sheer, unmediated textual facticity, let alone any stable system of signification. History and its artifacts are always reconstructed, mediated, and narrativized" (8). Further, my critical approach to the act of recovery works from the assumption that all literature has political investments and that political organization always utilizes narrative strategies. In this sense, then, the moment of a transnational matrix-event affords the opportunity to recover and re-present a conjuncture of literature and politics that troubles easy notions of Canadian literature as a solely national project while at the same time questioning the sovereignty of Canada's liberal order framework across the decades.

## PART II

The introductory remarks to *The Poems of Kenneth Leslie* (1971) betray an antimodernist editorial approach that, despite his broad and sustained engagement with cosmopolitan networks of Christian humanism, socialist politics, and poetic modernism, situates Leslie—foremost—as a "Maritimer, with a close awareness of the landscape and heritage of early Canada" (n.pag.). What is more, the editors of the collection provide an editorial rationale that actively excludes texts that explicitly offer evidence of engagement in the above-mentioned networks: "This collection includes almost all of Kenneth Leslie's poems, but a few have been omitted (even *The Shanachie Man*, one of the better known poems) because they seem not to have worn as well with the passage of time, or because they were light verse, or political verse, which fulfilled a temporal need" (n. pag.). So disappointed was Leslie in the erasure of politics from a volume supposing to represent his poetic oeuvre that he edited his own collected poems and self-published the volume the very next year under the title *O'Malley to the Reds & Other Poems* (1972). In his self-edited collection Leslie foregrounds the political nature of his poems by opening with texts that respond to particular events and historical contexts such as "O'Malley to the Reds," "Moscow's Measure,"

"Mao Cooks a Dish," and "Poetry and Propaganda," among others. One of the poems that was excluded from the edition published by Ladysmith Press in 1971, but included in his own edited collection, is "The Censored Editor," a poem that Dorothy Livesay, in her retrospective article on Canadian poetry and the Spanish Civil War, identified as the "most ambitious of any poems written in Canada about Spain" (16).[6] When Ladysmith Press produced its collection of Leslie's poems the editors (consciously or unconsciously) participated in a process of cultural selection that silences instances of political protest that inform Canadian cultural history and that evoke alternative models of citizenship.

The Ladysmith edition posits literary value as a temporal concern. In the above-quoted rationale, the editors subject Leslie's work to the all-too-familiar "test of time." Indeed, the rationale for the Ladysmith edition of Leslie's poems signals a conjunction of evaluative measures that rely on two different configurations of time. The editorial statement situates literary value as, on the one hand, reliant on the prolonged, undiminished temporal duration of criteria that the editors have neglected to name in (generically unidentified) poems, and on the other hand, reliant on the evacuation of those same unidentified criteria in (generically identified) "light" and "political" verse, causing a diminished temporal duration of literary value. In other words, two different conceptions of "literary time" are given importance in the process of editorial evaluation in order to conceal the non-acknowledgement of other, elusive criteria. What is more, the editorial rationale suggests that the "temporal need" of politics is not the "temporal need" of poetry without explaining why this might be the case; this editorial valuation happens without explicitly laying bare the institutional and ideological implications of where the line between literary time and political time is drawn. This type of editing of literary value, I argue, is part of a larger critical disregard for politicized occasional literature. Under literary-editorial rubrics such as that put forth in the Ladysmith edition, occasional literature is consigned to the ephemeral and kept beyond the ken of an editorially legitimized oeuvre. This is not unique to Ladysmith press. Rather, it is a particular example of a long-standing problem of literary valuation in editorial practice.

While the Ladysmith edition of Leslie's poems illustrates a common problem for the collation of individual oeuvres, what editorial possibilities arise when the scholarly editor assembles a collection wherein there is a prioritization of the event in editorial practice? The potential abounds as editorial possibilities shift under the conditions of emerging digital environments, but it is useful to start with a very basic example familiar to the concerns of textual studies.

In February of 1937, Sir Charles G.D. Roberts composed a poem that appeared in the *Dalhousie Review* under the title "Those Perish, These Endure." It was published the same year it was composed. It then appeared in *Twilight*

*Over Shaugamauk*, which was published later in 1937. It was also published in *Canada Speaks of Britain*, in 1941. "Those Perish, These Endure" is a twenty-eight-line poem, with four stanzas and an ABCB rhyming scheme. Not much of a modernist experiment in form, to be sure, but the poem does work through a dialectical process that sees Roberts engage with the horrors of modernity in an effort to construct a nostalgic, antimodernist poetic subject.

Two holograph manuscripts and seven typescripts of the poem survive. Typescripts ONE through FIVE all appear to be earlier than any printed text. Typescripts SIX and SEVEN appear to have been made after the publication of *Twilight Over Shaugamauk*, but before the publication of *Canada Speaks of Britain*. What makes all this relevant is that typescripts six and seven contain the never-printed subtitle "Spain, 1937." There is nothing explicit in the first two published versions of the poem, or the first five typescripts, that signal that the poem was written in response to the Spanish Civil War. In the first two published versions the third stanza begins with the line, "In troubled lands afar" (9). In its next printing, in *Canada Speaks of Britain* of 1941, the same line is changed to "In war-torn lands afar," signalling the specificity of a violent conflict. Noticing the poem's published revision in 1941, in a collection of poems directed in some way to Britain, would lead a reader to surmise, I think, that the poem was revised to address the escalation to the global, mass conflict of the Second World War. The change from "troubled" to "war-torn," though, occurred in a holograph manuscript a mere ten days after the poem's initial composition began on 14 February 1937. Roberts was thinking of a specific "war-torn" land when he was in the initial stages of composition, but the actual change from "troubled" to "war-torn" does not appear in typescript form until Typescript SIX. Typescripts SIX and SEVEN, then, contain the most evidence out of all the textual variants that the poem was a response to the Spanish Civil War. One result of the editorial principles adopted by Desmond Pacey and Graham Adams in their edition of *The Collected Poems of Sir Charles G.D. Roberts* is that this heightened evidence of the poem's direct response to the conflict in Spain is obscured. This is not to say that Pacey and Adams committed some sort of error in their his adoption of those principles. Rather, I mean to suggest that when constructing editorial principles for an event-based edition or collection, our traditional editorial theorizations may fall short. If, for example, the editorial goal is to adopt a copy-text policy for a print collection that best represents the cultural response to a matrix-event such as the Spanish Civil War, we need to come up with an editorial rationale that affords the ability to choose the SIXTH or SEVENTH typescript of Roberts's poem instead of a version based on final intention or even first publication. This editorial principle would necessarily privilege the event itself over traditional modes of literary valuation. The poem, then, would appear under the title, "Those Perish, These Endure: Spain, 1937."

One of the chief aims of scholarly editing is to provide literary historians with a narrative with which to construct an informed literary-critical reading.[7] What consequence, then, might the presentation of "Those Perish, These Endure: Spain, 1937" have on existing literary-critical accounts of Roberts or, say, the assumption (indeed, often my own) that the emergence of a leftist politics of transnationalism in Canadian literature was largely developed alongside the experimentations of Canada's modernists? We are not often afforded this type of critical perspective because event-based collections of literature are rarely scholarly editions. The vast majority of event-based collections do not undertake the work of collating variants and, moreover, are not explicit about their process of editorial arrangement and presentation. While some of these collections give historical context through general introductions (fewer through explanatory notes), it is rare to find textual notes in event-based collections. Through *seeming* prioritization of the event over textual history, event-based collections that are not accompanied by a scholarly apparatus actually work to obscure the historicity of the event by presenting texts inspired by the event as static rather than by making clear the "textual constitutions which the work undergoes in its historical passages" (McGann, *Textual* 62). As the material production of the matrix-event continues across space and time, so do the literary texts the event occasioned; texts about events go through as many historical passages as do texts not explicitly inspired by an event.

While there may be any number of reasons why event-based collections are rarely accompanied by a scholarly apparatus, I suspect the reason rests most often on added production costs as well as the large amount of labour involved and the dispersed availability of resources. In other words, the enormity of a matrix-event has often proved too difficult to account for in comprehensive ways. Texts about matrix-events (in both manuscript and published form) are not generally gathered in one space and rarely in the same *type* of space. For instance, research must go beyond literary archives to search out texts with varied accession histories, such as the archives of social or political organizations or governments. These conditions often restrict the ability of individual scholars to be comprehensive. I would like to suggest that a scholarly approach to the editing of literary responses to matrix-events requires two key components: collaboration, and remediation of more than just literary texts. Matrix-events deserve matrix-editions: a matrix-edition acts the part of a resource hub or research environment. Under current cultural conditions, this hub requires a productive mix of technologies—both print and digital—as well as multi-use tools for research and dissemination. Again, a matrix-edition, research hub, or research environment requires a coming together of multidisciplinary expertise that invites collaboration.

A project of this scale that attempts to address the enormity of a matrix-event cannot be confined to traditional editorial modes; it requires the remediation of more than just literary texts themselves (all those texts that normally contribute to the production of a scholarly edition such as manuscripts, letters, journals, and of course published versions of literary texts). That is, a scholarly approach to literary texts that responds to matrix-events demands remediation of a diverse set of scholarly modes of documentation—gathering versions not just of texts but also gathering divergent modes of documenting bibliographic and historiographic codes in order to lay bare the multiple ways these texts have been taken up across disciplinary divides and prevent readers from collapsing the event and the literary text. As suggested above, the possibilities for recovery through comprehensive approaches to scholarly editing have expanded with emergent methodologies in Digital Humanities scholarship. One of the key features I want to highlight about these emergent possibilities is that they afford the ability to mobilize a combination of recognized literary-critical editorial practices and non-scholarly editorial practices within traditional print and emergent digital environments.

Until recently, editors have been forced to choose between types of editorial practice—between, for example, fully annotated scholarly print editions and affordable reading/classroom print editions without a scholarly apparatus. But the necessity for making this choice is fading, and the number of hats worn by a scholarly editor—or, importantly, a collaborative team of scholars—is expanding. Under the conditions of emergent digital technologies, a scholarly edition can easily have the in-built tools to at once enable an enumerative bibliography, a pedagogical resource centre, and productive and sustainable collaboration with print technologies, among other things. We are at a moment in technological history when we can start to process the enormity of matrix-events and their attendant literary products in a networked environment. In other words, we are starting to be able to recover and remediate event-based literature in such a way as to enable the matrix-event to continue gaining a rich literary history while also telling the story of how much literary history has already been produced.

# Keeping the Code: Narrative and Nation in Donna Bennett and Russell Brown's *An Anthology of Canadian Literature in English*

Robert Lecker

This chapter has two parts. In Part I, I offer some background thoughts about the nature of anthology formation, while in Part II, I look at a specific example of this formation: Russell Brown and Donna Bennett's *An Anthology of Canadian Literature in English*, first published in 1982. My interests emerge from a recent study I completed on the history of English-Canadian literary anthologies from 1837 to the present, titled *Keepers of the Code*.

## I

To date, no one has provided a sustained history of anthology formation in English Canada, although several articles have examined the relationship between anthologies and the canon, or anthologies and the idea of nation in different periods.[1] The absence of such a history seems odd to me, simply because anthologies play such an important role in canon formation, institutionalization, and pedagogy. Although my broad intention is to treat these anthologies in the context of questions related to literary value, national ideals, and the material forces that have allowed Canadian literature to be published and disseminated, I also consider these works as narratives that embody the tensions and anxieties felt by their editors when faced with the challenge of constructing or rejecting various models of a national literature. My aim is to examine the figures, tropes, and archetypes associated with a quest for national self-definition as it is expressed through the tension between anthological desire and anthological doubt. I want to show that these anthologies are never innocent collections; they are intensely self-conscious literary constructions with their own discursive mechanisms and architecture. Every anthology tells a story about how it came into being, and about how it means to be.

The dream of effectively collecting the best of the nation's literature has been shared by influential anthologists in English Canada from the mid-nineteenth century to the present. I argue that these editors share a complex code that translates their literary nationalism into archetypes, symbols, and metaphors that appear again and again in anthologies of English-Canadian literature. These anthologies are anxious expressions of the desire for place, cohesion, identity. Their editors imagine themselves as figurative wanderers looking for a new place to call home. I call this group of editors the keepers of the code.

At one level, this code is easy to describe. Because the valorization of nation rests on the idea of wholeness and continuity, the most influential anthologies of English-Canadian literature implicitly support the kinds of poetry and fiction that are best suited to reinforcing the concreteness of nation—they are conservative works that tend toward the mimetic and the realistic, rather than toward the expressive and the experimental.

It seems redundant to assert that English-Canadian anthologists are nationalists. However, many editors, preferring to see themselves involved in the act of selecting "the best," or "the representative," studiously avoid the nationalist badge. In fact, the apparent trajectory of anthological discourse in Canada is toward an increasing rejection of overt claims to nationalism. One would be hard-pressed to find a modern editor blatantly supporting the assertion made by Edward Hartley Dewart in his 1864 anthology that "a national literature is an essential element in the formation of national character" (ix). If it is true that nationalism lies at the heart of these anthologies, but that open expressions of this fundamental nationalism have increasingly been silenced in modern and contemporary works, the question becomes: Where is this controlling vision of nationalism hiding?

In my initial foray into the canonization of English-Canadian literature, I argued that Canadian literature exhibits a number of features that point to its fundamental conservatism: "a valorization of the cautious, democratic, moral imagination before the liberal, inventive one; a hegemonic identification with texts that are ordered, orderable, safe" ("Canonization" 658). I argued further that this conservatism is a reflection of the institution that reinforces the canon. The canon functions reflectively, much like the literature it values, which tends to be mimetic because "mimetic discourse is the appropriate instrument of power in an institution that seeks to verify its solidity and authority over time" (666). I proposed that mimesis is a displaced formal equivalent of nationalism. It is a mode of bearing witness to the country. It is also the mode that allows people to see themselves as members of a community: the literature reflects them to themselves. Mimesis is the means by which critics affirm that the subject of their inquiry is real. One answer to the question "Where is nationalism hiding in Canadian literature?" is that it is not hiding; it has only been displaced into mimesis.

In attempting to explain the mimetic bias of the Canadian canon and the majority of its critics I made no mention of Canadian anthologists, arguably the most influential group of all when it comes to defining the English-Canadian canon. I also did not discuss the relationship between anthologies and literary institutions in Canada. As Jeffrey R. Di Leo observes, "[a]nthologies are considered to be reflective of the laws of their domain" ("Analyzing" 1). They write back to the institutions that empower them, working with those institutions to further their values. They influence the ways in which students understand literature, and, particularly when it comes to courses devoted to national literatures, they provide a particular rendition of the country, not only through the content of anthology selections, but also through the style and techniques employed by the writers who are brought together into a quasi-community that speaks on behalf of the country they have chosen to serve.

Most discussions of anthology formation scarcely mention the ways in which anthologies manufacture and transmit cultural capital (to use Pierre Bourdieu's term). Commentary on anthology formation usually focuses on what Barbara Benedict calls "the 'demand' or consumer side of the literary culture of anthologies, the way they were received and read," while bypassing "the 'supply' side—the story of the material connections informing the construction of value and cultural currency in anthologies" (*Making* 31). Even more surprising is the absence of commentary on the narrative dimension of anthologies, for surely these collections bring together stories or poems to create a narrative of nation. A few commentators have begun to explore this narrative dimension in anthologies of American and British literature. Jim Egan argues that different anthologies "begin the narrative of American literature" in different ways and put forward a "notion of America each anthology wants its audience to learn and, no doubt, reproduce" (106). Anne Ferry maintains that "the anthologist as author of the book supplants the author of the poem in choosing how it should be presented, with interpretive consequences" (2). For Christopher Kuipers, the selection, arrangement, and presentation of the works in an anthology are all essential elements of literary creativity. Like Ferry, he asks: "Can the anthologist be considered an author of some kind?" ("Anthology as a Literary Creation" 123). It may be that the anthologist actually supplants the author of the works he or she collects.

While anthologies are often discussed in the context of canon formation, studies of the creative representation of nation by the editors of these anthologies are comparatively rare. The process of forming these anthologies involves imagining the country, imagining a community, imagining an identity. Through this kind of imagining the anthology editor promotes a form of what Edward Said calls "affiliation." For Said, "affiliation" is a "kind of compensatory order that, whether it is a party, an institution, a culture, a set of beliefs, or even a world-vision, provides men and women with a new form of relationship" (19). This kind of anthological affiliation is not restricted to the twentieth century. In *Discourse Networks,* Friedrich A. Kittler observes that "anthologies in late eighteenth-century Germany replaced the Bible as the book that unified a culture" (Di Leo, "Analyzing" 7). Barbara Benedict explains why anthologies can be seen in this way: "because of their cooperative means of production and multiple author-ship, anthologies are material expressions of a kind of community, and their format also directs readers to understand them as vessels of a common enter-prise, even while registering the independence of each author" ("Paradox" 242).

Although the relationship between reader and anthology obviously does not enact a direct correlation between citizen and nation, the conversation between audience and anthology remains highly figurative, a symbolic means of experi-encing the country through the always conflicted pages of the text. Of course, there is no such thing as the accurate representation of nation through a national literature anthology. Paradoxically, national literature anthologies underline the fact that nations are plural and unstable, unmappable in any form. As edited collections, they are necessarily self-defeating. What we learn from such anthol-ogies is that the nation they purport to represent cannot exist. At best, the nation is inevitably undermined by the anthological act. National literature anthologies are naturally conflicted and in doubt. So they should be; nations are naturally conflicted and in doubt. The challenge is to read these anthologies through the anxieties that haunt them. This can be a mobilizing cultural experience for students, who are encouraged to explore the nature of these anxieties as they emerge in the anthologies they are required to use.

Just as the national literature anthology implicitly supports a code that reifies and verifies the nation, so does it establish a relationship with a reading com-munity that is also committed to the code. The professionalization of Canadian literature was in many respects founded on the assumption that the nation was knowable, that one means of knowing it was through its literature, and that teachers explaining that literature were implicitly explaining the country. Real-istic literature served this function much more effectively than experimental writing, which is often more concerned with the nature of language than with the ability of language to truthfully represent external reality.

One of my aims in discussing anthologies of English-Canadian literature is to test the idea that their editors are fundamentally Romantic nationalists who have gradually displaced the value of nationalism into the value of mimesis. Nationalist discourse fades into language about how the Canadian writer is dis-tinguished by his or her attention to the details and beauty of place. The pursuit of these details becomes a sign of quality, mainly because capturing the "essence" of a place is a form of bearing witness to it, of proving it exists. Anthologists in the 1940s, 1950s, and 1960s were all drawn to various elements of realism: its scientific bias, its faithfulness to details and everyday events, its grounding in the here and now, its emphasis on measurability, location, exactness. This focus on time and place is also a means of affirming community, for those who participate in the process of bearing witness to a place are also configuring themselves as members of a community who are giving collective voice to a shared vision.

The unstated pact between teachers and anthologizers rests on the tacit sharing of the canon as an epistemological base. Literature becomes a means of knowing the country. Anthologists deliver the means of accessing this knowledge. The canon supports the conviction that what is known has been tested by others in the past, and has met the standards of those whose function it is to police the canon in the present. The users of the canon understand that there will be disruptions—incursions, rejections, exclusions, faddism—but they also understand deeply that the anthologists they trust will know the limits, that they will not allow the canon to be so truncated as to become unrecognizable, any more than they would assume that Canada was unknowable or divisible.

Historically, the promoters of the canon have been invested in the literature and the country because their jobs depended on transmitting and extending the model. The training of their successors also depended on the presence of a describable tradition, a sense of heritage that made the idea of a national literature tangible, teachable, and real. The professionals could object to constructions of the nation, but they could never abandon their belief that Canadian literature was worth understanding. The anthologists were conduits to this understanding. They provided the means to access what was essentially a conversion experience in the guise of pedagogy. This is not surprising, because many of the professors of Canadian literature who emerged in the 1970s and after were inevitably touched by the literary evangelicalism that characterized the post-Centennial years. And the next generation of Canadian literary scholars could hardly ignore this evangelical past. The keepers of the canon had to promote a literary model based on mimetic ideals, for only the mimetic model would allow for self-recognition and the potential for existential awakening that came with such recognition.

An anthological focus on realism calls upon readers to pay tribute to the country, to join the editor in affirming the presence of the place. Although this process of framing the country is initially an editorial activity, the ritual of reading Canada in this way—of joining others in a group devoted to a central text that affirms the national object of their study—has obvious religious implications. Canons originated in the church; therefore, studying canonical texts is historically aligned with acts of faith. The construction and maintenance of canons has ecclesiastical roots. This is another aspect of displacement. If nationalism morphs into realism, it can also be argued that a religiously based canon must have a modern and secular form. Canonical texts in the secular world are still documents attesting to faith.

The group of believers who place their collective faith in those documents form a distinct community—a modern-day congregation. The act of bearing witness to the country, of partaking in the realistic act, is simultaneously a religious experience in secular guise. The congregation has moved from the church to the classroom; the preacher has become the teacher. Yet what is happening in the classroom still centres on questions of belief. Anthologists provide teachers with a form of proof concerning the presence of the nation. Realism helps them with this testimony, catalyzes the act of faith. Their job through successive generations is to pass down the Romantic nationalist mythology, to sustain the discourse of nation, to promote its archetypes and language, to uphold the canon as a vital transubstantiation of Canadian culture.

This portrayal of Canadian anthologists as culture keepers, as secular agents vested with the responsibility of transmitting national archetypes and tropes, allows us to conceive of them as storytellers in their own right. Some are merely dilettantes, but the vast majority of editors who have devoted themselves to anthologizing English-Canadian literature create powerful narratives through the processes of selection and representation. Although there is scattered commentary on the values or biases connected with various Canadian anthologists, and although we can find analyses of their role in constructing national value, there is practically no scholarship on how these editors emerge as characters in their own right or on how they create tension-ridden narratives about their own role as literary creators. In *Keepers of the Code*, I focus on these narratives as they are revealed by the tropes, strategies, and structures employed by editors to frame and explain their books. While I am concerned to a certain extent with the specific poems and stories contained in various anthologies, my central aim is to show how the editors of English-Canadian anthologies from 1837 to the present share a set of beliefs and practices that make them keepers of the code. Not all anthologists endorse this code. Some work against it, even unintentionally. Some are false prophets—they think they are transmitting the code, but they are simply using the language without understanding its symbolic potential. The most influential anthologists are those who inherit the code, struggle with the implications of their guardianship, and end up creating powerful narratives about the nature of human choice.

It would be inaccurate to claim that each of these editors follows the same path or explores identical archetypes. That would make their anthologies static documents. By and large, they're not. They are dynamic texts precisely because their editors try to negotiate between a stable and cohesive view of literary history and the desire to destabilize this cohesion in pursuit of material that challenges established norms. These anthologies are interesting subjects of study because they do not propose a unified vision and because they do not necessarily agree on canonical values. However, beneath their varied exteriors, they struggle with the same issues and display a similar range of metaphors and archetypes related to that struggle. I don't think of these anthologists first as editors. I think of them as narrators putting together a story, creators of what Eli Mandel suggests are long poems that meditate on the nature of nation. Like all long poems, they display the anxieties of their creators, their uncertainty about their historical position, their desire to impose order, their fear that order is an illusion, their endless and restless search for an impossible ending to their multi-vocal accounts.

Anthologies are little worlds: they contain their own creation stories, their own narratives of progress, their own distinctive landscapes rendered by the editor's hand. Frequently in Canadian anthologies the editor frames her collection as an existential journey waiting to be experienced by the reader. Or the editor figures himself as our guide into a promised land. The rhetoric is consistently related to travel, discovery, self-improvement, and heightened experience. Canadian anthology makers often see their activities in quasi-religious or biblical terms. For many of them, the acts of selection and election are related. (Many early Canadian anthologists were Methodists.) Their anthologies provided the reader with the means of achieving a conversion experience: to discover the nation was to discover oneself. To read Canadian literature was to find identity and the means to salvation in a promised land. In this sense, the nationalist fervour and commitment that mobilized Canadian editors, publishers, and academics in the 1960s and 1970s linked their interests with those that had driven the earliest anthology makers, as far back as Edward Hartley Dewart and William Douw Lighthall. The anthology became an existential and quasi-religious symbol of "home."

## II

Donna Bennett and Russell Brown's *An Anthology of Canadian Literature in English* was first published as a two-volume set in 1982–83. The anthology was revised in 1990, 2002, and 2010. In constructing this anthology Brown and Bennett were partaking in a concept shared by their anthological predecessors: the idea that producing a Canadian national literature anthology was a means of validating the nation. The predominant tropes in these volumes are mimesis, community, and union. My central argument is that the canonical currency of this anthology (in its different editions) is based on the editors' reinforcement of an equation between mimesis and community first enunciated by Canada's early anthologists and transmitted as a binding canonical principle from 1864 to the present.

With a combined weight of just over 2 kilograms and containing 1,314 pages, the dual volumes comprising Brown and Bennett's *An Anthology of Canadian Literature in English* are the heaviest anthology of Canadian literature ever produced. The sheer size of this collection provides ample evidence of how commercially viable the anthologizing of Canadian literature had become by the early 1980s. It also points to the solidification of a Canadian literary canon that was established in the years following the 1978 Calgary Conference on the Canadian Novel. While some of the critics attending the conference challenged its canon-making orientation, including its list of "the most important one hundred works of fiction," no sustained attack on the canon or its underlying ideological assumptions appeared in the 1980s. The proceedings of the Calgary Conference were not published until 1982, a fact which suggests that the articulation of Canadian canonical models was still in a very early stage. While it is true that numerous small presses and alternative magazines encouraged anti-canonical aesthetics throughout the 1960s and 1970s, the dominant movement was toward the consolidation of canonical norms as an expression of national identity. The dissenting voices served the important function of reinforcing the idea that a canon existed, and that it was worthy of dispute.

In earlier decades, anthologists had imagined a popular audience for their collections, underlining their assumption that an appreciation for Canadian literature was something that could be gained by the reading public at large. But now an important change had set in: anthologists understood that the main readers of their books would be students and that in order to reach those students they had to appeal to the professors and teachers who had become canonical gatekeepers, professionals responsible for determining how the Canadian canon would be represented, and according to what terms. The anthologies edited by academics were made to *serve* the needs of pedagogy, not to challenge those needs.

Brown and Bennett's anthology entered the market with excellent timing. Volume I came out the same year as the Canadian constitution was patriated, an event that drew increasing attention to the nature of Canadian identity and its expression in the nation's literature. There had not been a major new anthology of English-Canadian poetry and fiction since Klinck and Watters published the third edition of their *Canadian Anthology* in 1974 (and it was seriously out of date). Brown and Bennett had a wealthy and committed publisher in Oxford University Press, they had no serious competition except from other Oxford anthologies that focused strictly on poetry or fiction, and they were tied into the academic network through their connection with the University of Toronto, where both of them taught.

Brown and Bennett both grew up in the United States. They met in Houston, where Bennett was in high school and Brown was in his third year at Rice University. In correspondence with me, Brown described the circumstances surrounding their move to Canada in 1969. He was completing his PhD at SUNY Binghamton, where he was a teaching assistant for Robert Kroetsch. He says that

> Donna and I were both deeply affected by the [Vietnam] war and the social climate and politics surrounding it—and especially by the 1968 Democratic Convention, which we watched on TV pretty much from morning to night for four days. That one event (which included watching the National Guardsmen push their rifles into the car windows of individuals driving through Chicago) and all that surrounded it (eventually including the Chicago Seven Trial) was possibly the most significant factor in our decision to emigrate to Canada—though the election of Richard Nixon in the fall certainly confirmed it. (Brown, Letter n.pag.)

Brown got a job teaching at Lakehead University in the summer of 1969. In a letter to me, he explained that even after more than thirty years in Canada, he still felt "moved" by the words of broadcaster Andy Barrie, who said (in John Hagan's *Northern Passage*):

> When I came to Canada I'd never been here, and I thought I had arrived home. In fact, all these years I might have imagined I was being socialized as an American in the States—it seems like I was in fact, in some way I couldn't know, being socialized as a Canadian—like what transsexuals say, "I'm a male trapped in a female body," I was a Canadian trapped in the body of an American. (Brown n.pag.)

Brown explains that "my experience of crossing the border was like an early version of what came to be thought of as social deconstruction, because I discovered that a lot I had taken as 'natural' was actually cultural (the need to rebel against authority, for example)" (Brown n.pag.). An important context for this border-crossing experience is provided by Robert Kroetsch's fiction. Kroetsch was himself a border-crosser, and his work with the postmodern journal *boundary 2* at SUNY Binghamton was one means of extending his own border consciousness.

Brown's first publication was a review of Kroetsch's *The Studhorse Man*. The novel prompted him to read more Canadian literature (he says, "I was deep into Laurence, Davies, Grove, etc.") because "those books were telling me about the place to which I'd come." In 1974 he taught the Canadian survey course at Lakehead. He began to think about a career move that would enable him to become involved in Canadian literature full-time. To this end, he gave up his post at Lakehead to take a limited term appointment at the University of Toronto. In 1979 he taught a small class on Canadian poetry and realized that the students were not bothering to look up allusions or the meanings of obscure words ("a great deal of class time therefore had to be given over to explanation"). When a representative from Oxford showed up at Brown's office, he pitched her the idea of creating an anthology similar to the *Norton Anthology of American Literature,* one that would include critical introductions to each author as well as detailed footnotes. It was this "highly pragmatic concern about teaching Canadian texts" that led to his and Bennett's contract with Oxford, and to the first edition of their anthology (Brown n.pag.).

Although Bennett and Brown undertook their editorial work with practical aims in mind, the anthology provided them with a symbolic means of confirming their identity as Canadians. In embracing this project, they were partaking in a concept shared by their predecessors: the idea that editing a Canadian national literature anthology was a means of validating the nation (and, by extension, the editor's role as a participant in and maker of that nation). It is therefore not surprising to find them equating their pursuit of Canadian literature and identity with a movement north, for, like many other anthology editors, they saw nordicity and Canadian identity as interwoven. Kroetsch gave voice to this quest for the north in several of his novels and poems. Brown says that his leaving the United States to teach in Canada while still a graduate student at Binghamton may have been one of the sources of inspiration for Kroetsch's *Gone Indian*, with its story of Jeremy Sadness searching for his true identity in the North. In this context, and perhaps from Kroetsch's point of view, Brown becomes the iconic traveller, the figure who goes "Indian" by travelling north, demythologizing and remythologizing himself in terms of a consciousness that is northern, new, unknown.

As Aritha van Herk observes, "Jeremy Sadness, named after Jeremy Bentham, wants to be Grey Owl, the fake Indian Archie Belaney invented himself to be" ("Robert Kroetsch" n.pag.). I don't think Brown and Bennett wanted to be Grey Owl, but the connection between "going Indian" and transforming one's identity is hard to ignore. Canadian anthology-making becomes a means of "going Indian," of embracing metamorphosis and transubstantiation.

In an article titled "Crossing Borders," Brown meditates on what it means to move between countries. Inevitably, he ends up considering Kroetsch's novel. His comments might well be directed at himself:

> In *Gone Indian* a young American graduate student named Jeremy Sadness comes to Canada, ostensibly in search of a job, though really seeking several less tangible, if more valuable, things. As it did for many young Americans at the end of the sixties, the northern border has a special appeal for Jeremy: he believes he is crossing into a land where existence will be freer, simpler, more natural, renewing. In fact, since Jeremy thinks of that border as a substitute for the frontier which long ago vanished from the American West,

his journey into Canada is also a search for a lost American dream. He is a
man who had come to believe that his whole life was shaped and governed
by some deep American need to seek out the frontier. (159–60)

Sadness and these two editors are voyagers; their journey north is existential, a
means of re-creating themselves in the context of a new landscape that is open,
new, "natural." Brown casts himself in the role of the wanderer/explorer who
approaches a new country and its literature as an excursion into identity. In this
way, he participates in the quest motif that figures so prominently in anthologies
of English-Canadian literature, which consistently frames the editor as a traveller whose editorial activities will bring him or her to a new world, a metaphoric
promised land. Consciously or not, Brown and Bennett join those keepers of
the code whose anthologies are symbolic expressions of a rebirth narrative organized around motifs associated with travelling North.

To what extent is this voyage into a new world reflected in the anthology
itself? In the introduction to Volume I, Brown and Bennett point to several
aspects of their selections that are of particular interest to them. Perhaps the
most important feature they identify is the idea of community expressed by
many of the writers, mainly because that idea of community ultimately leads
the editors back to their own place in it. They begin by holding it at a distance,
but as the idea of community unfolds it gradually morphs into a mythology
that is articulated by the writers they have brought together. In a final step, the
editors who unite these writers become myth-makers themselves, participants
in the community their collection has created. It is an assertion of identity that
sets up a correspondence between writer and editor. Brown and Bennett start
out by noting that their critical introductions to each author's work locate "their
place in the Canadian literary community" (1982, xi).[2] Canada, they write, has
a "close community of writers" (xii). This community forms what Northrop
Frye calls a "milieu" that is the product of an "imaginative continuum" in which
"writers are conditioned by the attitudes of their predecessors" (xii). Affirming
this continuum is crucial, because it is part and parcel of a "literary mythology"
that "has been emerging for some time" (xii). In this mythology, the writers
"become myth-makers and even mythic figures" (xii). At the same time, the
editors who capture this mythology write themselves into it, becoming part of
the imaginative continuum.

These words energize the editors. We begin to realize that what Brown and
Bennett are saying about the writers could equally be said about themselves as
Americans who have come to Canada in search of a new order. In writing about
the community these writers have created, they are implicitly writing about
the community they have found. In writing about the indigenous mythology
these writers have constructed, they are also talking about their embrace of a

new mythology. And in identifying the "three large movements" that characterize "the development of Canadian literature" (xii), they could just as easily be describing their own immigrant experience.

In the first movement, "pre-Confederation writers initiated the struggle to find suitable language and forms to describe new experiences in a new landscape" (xii). Brown and Bennett arrive in Canada and find themselves in a new landscape, surrounded by a new literature.

In the second movement ("the emergence of a national literature"), Canadian writers continued to investigate the themes "that had been of concern to Canadians since the first days of settlement: a consciousness of exile and isolation; a sense of inchoate identity; ambivalent feelings about nature that sometimes led them to question their place in a universe that seemed hostile or (even worse) indifferent" (xii). Brown and Bennett understand that they have chosen exile from their homeland. Their exile and displacement is existential, forcing them to question their own place in a universe that is either "indifferent" (the word comes from the French existentialists, especially Camus) or "hostile" (with this word we see the influence of Margaret Atwood and Northrop Frye).

In the third movement ("the initial stage of literary modernism in Canada"), the Canadian modernists displayed "a distaste for revolt, the revolutionary character of European and American modernism—which manifested itself in a desire to shock or astound and in a tendency to break sharply with the past" (xii). Brown and Bennett may have left the United States behind them, but they are no revolutionaries who want to dismiss the past. Rather, the challenge for them is to find a *new* past, a *new* history they can embrace, and that is exactly why the idea of finding a community of writers who are anchored in "historical contexts" and an "imaginative continuum" is of such interest to them. They are editorial pilgrims in search of stability and order.

Although the first volume of Brown and Bennett's anthology appeared in 1982, it makes no mention of a fourth movement, which would encompass the initial stages of postmodernism in Canada. Perhaps they felt that this fourth movement would best be described in Volume II, which is devoted to writers born after 1914. In that volume they note that "in all parts of the world today we hear statements about the end of modernism and about the beginning of a 'postmodern' era characterized by literary forms that are self-conscious and self-reflexive, but that also express considerable ironic doubt about the self as an object of inquiry" (1983, xv). If Canadian writers are interested in postmodernism, Bennett and Brown argue, it is because "its concerns are strikingly congruent with preoccupations—such as the Canadian anxiety about self-identity—that already existed in the country" (xv).

The editors' approach to postmodernism provides a good indication of the extent to which its Canadian appearance lagged. Brown and Bennett were talking about the "beginning" of a postmodern era in 1983 and putting the term in quotation marks, but postmodern writing had dominated American literature throughout the 1970s and had entered Canada in the mid-1970s and early 1980s in the work of Frank Davey, Robert Kroetsch, and Linda Hutcheon. Their own selections indicate that Brown and Bennett knew the origins of postmodernism in Canada were earlier than their introduction claims: they included Kroetsch's "Unhiding the Hidden: Recent Canadian Fiction," originally published in 1974.

However, this is not an anthology that celebrates postmodern theory or innovation. Its central alignment is with more conventional ideas of community, tradition, and realism associated with earlier models of Canadian literary history. This is not surprising to find in an anthology created by two editors who had found a new home in Canada, and who had articulated their respect for community and coherence in the first volume of their work. At its heart, postmodernism challenged the mimetic structures on which the idea of coherent and recognizable communities was founded; at the same time, postmodernism undermined monolithic assumptions about national identity that had dominated anthological discourse since the nineteenth century.

Despite its claim to currency, and the fact that in most respects its selections were quite up to date, a lingering sense of nostalgia informs Brown and Bennett's collection. The marble paper cover motif, designed by Bill Toye, harks back to an earlier era. The even weighting of both volumes spells stability, as does the equal weight given to the two editors, whose names are reversed for the separate volumes, which mirror each other (Brown and Bennett are married). This is a reflective world, not a self-reflexive one. The predominant tropes of these coupled volumes are reflection (mimesis) and union, which is fitting for a book that celebrates the coherence of a country.

Although it appears in what the editors recognize as a postmodern age, Bennett and Brown's anthology wants to calm its readers, to assure them that this will be a guided, pragmatic voyage onto established canonical terrain. On the first page of the introduction to Volume I we find ten consecutive lines that include the word "important" (two times), "importance" (once), "significant" (twice), "substantial" (once), and "major" (once) (1982, xi). That is seven canonical terms in ten lines, a clear indication of the extent to which Brown and Bennett value canonical language. At the same time, they emphasize ease of access to the canon. We are told that the anthology is "a convenient starting point," that its footnotes are designed to be "useful," that its technical apparatus "has been kept as simple as possible," that the aim is to provide "reliable and readable texts" (1982, xiii), and that when in doubt about the need for annotation the editors "consulted students in Canadian-literature and in first-year English courses and have been guided by their responses" (1983, xvi). In offering these assurances, the editors demystify the process of canonical initiation while validating the status of the canonical novitiates, those students whose responses guide the editors in their technical endeavours. Implicit in this stance is the value of creating an anthological community in which all members are empowered, a kind of mini-model of the ideal democratic state. The rhetoric is inclusive and user-friendly. In this sense, Brown and Bennett distinguish themselves from earlier editors, who often saw themselves as elitists making educated selections for the literary unwashed. For Brown and Bennett, the anthology is the print version of the classroom. And, as Brown indicated to me, they often thought about the order of their selections in terms of the kinds of connections with other works that teachers and students might make during the discussion of a particular poem or story in class.

When we study the contents of these two volumes, it soon becomes apparent that Brown and Bennett's anthology is much more geographically representative of Canadian poetry and fiction than its predecessors. They also filled in some of the earlier gaps left by Klinck and Watters. For example, they added material by Mavis Gallant, Henry Kreisel, Phyllis Webb, Robert Kroetsch, and Clark Blaise. In terms of new fiction, they included stories by Leon Rooke, W.D. Valgardson, Rudy Wiebe, Audrey Thomas, and Alistair MacLeod. And they made the poetry selections more contemporary by adding Patrick Lane, Frank Davey, Dennis Lee, and bpNichol, and by including a special twenty-seven-page section called "Poets for Further Reading," representing work by David Donnell, Gary Geddes, Daphne Marlatt, Andrew Suknaski, Robert Bringhurst, Mary di Michele, Roo Borson, and Erin Mouré. In one sense, this brief addition, devoted to relatively undiscovered poets, was a gesture toward contemporaneity. But it is significant that this contemporaneity is cordoned off, as if these younger writers inhabited a realm distinctly apart from the unbounded space enjoyed by the more established writers in the rest of the volume, who get an expansive 606 pages. By placing the younger writers together, at the end of the anthology, Brown and Bennett marginalize the contemporary and exclude it from what had become mainstream and canonical.

Nevertheless, by bringing in new writers and including poets and short story writers from east to west, Brown and Bennett created a much more inclusive anthology than had been realized by earlier editors. They did this at a time when regional interests were displacing the centralist values that had defined the Canadian canon. There is an increased consciousness of prairie writing, an attention to voices from the west coast, a nod to Atlantic Canada with the material by MacLeod, and even a return to new writing from Montreal (Geddes, di Michele, Mouré), which had been displaced by Toronto over the preceding decade. By constructing their anthology in this way, Brown and Bennett demonstrated their recognition of different regions; they also showed themselves to be shrewd in their understanding that the professors teaching Canadian literature courses in different parts of the country wanted to be able to use material that was geographically related to where they lived. Bennett and Brown had created a winner. Brown indicated to me that their anthology has been Oxford's best-selling book since its publication.

For the 1990 revision of their 1982–83 anthology, Brown and Bennett were joined by Nathalie Cooke, who had recently completed her doctoral dissertation and was awaiting her thesis defence. She took no hand in making the overall selections, but she did write the biocritical introductions for the new writers included in this revised edition, thus freshening the overall tone of the collection. However, the anthology remained very much the editorial product of Bennett and Brown. The two original volumes were reduced to one. Literary criticism was dropped. The shift in selections was characterized by a movement away from some of the modernist poets associated with Contact Press: Louis Dudek and Raymond Souster were deleted, along with another modernist, Anne Wilkinson. Raymond Knister's and W.W.E. Ross's imagist poems are nowhere to be found. The editors also distanced themselves from writers of short fiction in Montreal, cutting Hugh Hood and omitting John Metcalf. Although the anthology appeared after a seven-year period during which some of the most prominent experimental writers emerged, little of that experimentation is reflected here. The major change is the addition of twelve female and four male authors.[3] Brown, Bennett, and Cooke acknowledge "the present expressions of a more confident post-colonial self-awareness" (1990, xvi), yet they still draw attention to the promise of mimesis, to the belief that in Canada, writers have "sought a reality based in or made accessible through daily experience and have therefore made their relationship to place an important element of their writing" (xvi). This is "everyday realism that responds to the need for self-definition" (xvi). For the editors, "the Canadian literary tradition seems to be chiefly made up of 'realistic' writing, a literature that, in its tendency to focus on the events of everyday existence, has been shaped by a need for chronicling the Canadian experience and developing a sense of self-identity" (xv).

Brown, Bennett, and Cooke recognize that Canadian writing sometimes rejects this realist model: "The general move away from modernism that begins around the middle of the twentieth century and gains impetus after the sixties is characterized by an emphasis on literary forms that are self-conscious and self-reflexive, and that express ironic doubt about the reality of both the self and the external world as objects of inquiry" (xvii). However, the anthology does little to represent this shift, choosing instead to remain faithful to an overall emphasis on mimetic values and their relation to "Canadian experience" and "self-identity" (xv). As the editors say, "the question of what constitutes reality, reconceived … is central to the creation of a national identity and literature, because the sense of what is 'real' grounds any definition of self" (xv). The links between realism, national identity, self-identity, and national literature remain firm, even if they are starting to rust. The editors recognize that new theories of language have challenged many of the assumptions behind realist aesthetics, but they want to hold on to the idea of a realistic continuum in Canadian writing:

> It would be misleading, however, to suggest that contemporary writing in English Canada has made a radical break with older techniques and aesthetics: a wide range of work that has been affected by these concerns nevertheless remains continuous with the literature that has come before. And, even in this recent work, the longstanding interest in mapping out the nature of the Canadian experience and the reality of the Canadian identity often remains visible. (xvii)

This statement is deeply tautological, for the way in which contemporary writing is represented is largely a function of the editors' selections. If that writing is marginalized in favour of literature that is involved in "mapping out the nature of the Canadian experience," then it will appear that experimental writing is not central to "Canadian experience" or "Canadian identity." The simple invocation of these terms ties the editors' discourse to the prevailing anthological tradition, which has been predominantly concerned with the national-realist literary "mapping" that is essential to the construction of a story called "the English-Canadian literary tradition" (xvii). However, even in the process of affirming this tradition, one central concept has been lost: community. The introduction to the second edition never mentions it. Gradually, the very underpinnings of a national literature anthology—the idea of a coherent literary community—are beginning to dissolve. Yet if that idea disappears entirely, what, then, is the task of national literature anthologists, who can no longer make any valid claims about the unity of a particular collection? On behalf of whom do the editors speak? In relation to what kind of national consciousness? And how is the editorial act that pretends to bind these authors together in this transient anthological community open to doubt? Perhaps the business of putting together a national literature anthology does a disservice to the nation by organizing its literature into patterns or themes that ultimately turn something that is plural and dissonant into something that is ordered, explicable, and safe.

In 2002, Brown and Bennett (now working without Nathalie Cooke) published the third edition of their anthology. The back cover copy indicates their awareness of the challenges to the canon that appeared over the previous decade. They speak of the way in which the anthology embraces both the canon and the new voices outside it: "Balancing the canon as it has traditionally been presented with the broader perspectives that have emerged in recent years, it highlights the connections between various authors and their works, setting tradition and innovation in dialogue" (2002, 1182). From this perspective, the editors become the balancers, mediators in a productive dialogue between the old and the new. The anthology is predicated on the idea that a Canadian canon does indeed exist, that it is a civilized meeting place, and that the way to deal with works outside it is simply to add them. It is the canon, plus.

Brown and Bennett argue that one way the reader may understand Canadian literature "would be to focus on the issue of representation" (xvi). Another way would be to understand Canadian literature in terms of a search for myth, "a numinous world within or beneath the quotidian one" (xvii). They understand realism and mythopoeia as central aesthetics informing Canadian writing, but they also acknowledge here, as they did in 1990, that "today, many hold some version of one of these earlier views, but a pervasive wariness has arisen about the limitations of human abilities to describe, generalize, or judge with acuity; a belief in Truth has been challenged by a sense that truths must be plural and may be contingent" (xvii).

These seem to be the "broader perspectives" mentioned earlier. But if it is true that contingency and pluralism are credible forces in 2002, how is it possible to put together a book that embraces the plural, the contingent, the representational, and the mythic, all under the rubric "English-Canadian"? The editor who attempts this task must understand him or herself as a mediator among possible worlds rather than the packager of a specific world. This offers little comfort to the national literature anthologist, who needs to find connections that unite the selections in order to rationalize the existence of the anthology in the first place. Like other successful anthologists, Brown and Bennett could not completely reposition the canon. Had they done that, all the instructors who relied on their work would find themselves at a loss.

This forced them to make some hard choices. The 2002 edition of the anthology added a number of Native writers.[4] More women writers were added as well.[5] Regional and ethnic representation was broadened. If one looks back to the first edition of this successful anthology, it is clear that Brown and Bennett were committed to expanding the canon and were not not afraid to exclude some heavily anthologized names (gone were William Wilfred Campbell, Charles G.D. Roberts, Bliss Carman, John Newlove, and Clark Blaise). Brown and Bennett were clear about the changes they had made:

> Some of the writers who appear for the first time in this edition of our anthology come out of new writing by individuals of Native descent; some are here as a result of the increased impact of Maritime and Western writers beyond their regions; some are shaped by the continued urbanization of Canada, some by the increased presence of immigrants who trace their descent from areas other than Europe; some have found their voice because of the acknowledgement of greater sexual diversity; and some would previously have been visible only in minority communities. (xiii)

The anthology is presented as an equalizer: it brings together minorities, ethnicities, regional affiliations, and sexual differences. Now, more than ever, the country can be celebrated as a true mosaic. Brown and Bennett emphasize the celebratory nature of their enterprise: "Although we are acutely conscious of the serious problems now facing Canadian literary publishing and concerned about the future implications of the current inadequacy of arts funding, we can also say that there has never been a better time for Canadian literature" (xiii). The new writers added to the anthology contribute further to the growth of the Canadian tradition, even though the idea of community—and indeed, the word "community" itself—is no longer used. Like the idealized country it celebrates, the anthology is meant to reflect diverse interests and identities, which are melded into an organically "flowering" entity, a greenhouse that displays its diverse vegetation in an orderly array. In this sense, its function remains mimetic, a means of gathering together those voices that bear witness to the country. By doing so, it also civilizes them, draws them into the fold, makes them part of a vibrant tradition, and so neutralizes a central aspect of the power they had obtained by being outside that tradition.

In the most recent edition of their anthology (2010), Brown and Bennett note that after the Centennial, as critical assessments of Canadian writers began to proliferate, "the function of anthologies" was "to capture these assessments and reassessments of Canadian writing and to provide the material for critical narratives of the development of a Canadian literary tradition" (2010, xiv). Although they recognize that the canon attached to this tradition is always in flux, they seem comforted by the idea that signs of stability remain: "The fact that fifty-five writers who were in the first edition of this anthology reappear in this one and that forty-nine authors have been in all four versions does suggest that the Canadian canon, while changing and expanding over the last twenty-five years, now has a stable core" (xiv).

These comments are not directed toward the student users of the collection, most of whom would have little stake in the canon or in the question of whether or not it is stable. The communication here is designed to assure instructors that the fundamental contract between editor and teacher has not changed. The editors point to the ongoing stability of their choices and suggest an equation between the anthology and the country itself: although both exist in a time of change and challenges to authority, a basic core of values remains unaltered, even after close to thirty years. Their anthology becomes an ark in a sea of change, a testament to "wholeness," unity, and the permanence associated with canonical order.

In affirming the existence and continuity of an English-Canadian literary canon Brown and Bennett are not alone: they join other Canadian anthologists in creating what Smaro Kamboureli calls "normalizing instruments"—texts that disseminate and consolidate existing values even while they act as "instruments of modernization" that ostensibly question such values. In this sense, they serve a "*disciplinary* function" (*Making* xi) by reinforcing a narrative of "belatedness" that makes editors and critics anxious about the process of challenging the canon: "This belatedness signals at once the ideology of liberalism that permeates Canadian society and culture and the institutional limits of Canadian postcolonial practice today" (xiv). However, even this belatedness is coming to an end.

In 2005, participants in the TransCanada: Literature, Institutions, Citizenship conference in Vancouver were arguing that Canadian literature occupied a field of "occlusion and repression" superimposed on a "troubled trajectory" that contests the country itself (Kamboureli, Preface ix). In Kamboureli's words, "Canada is an unimaginable community, that is, a community constituted in excess of the knowledge of itself, always transitioning" (x). Given the widespread attraction to course packs designed by individual instructors for their courses, the traditional authority of national literature anthologies is bound to dwindle, especially once online anthologies begin to proliferate, as they inevitably will. Today, every teacher can become an anthologist and the "transitioning" of the canon is a matter of personal choice. Furthermore, that plural canon, and all that it implies about Canada, will no longer shift slowly over the years as new national literature anthologies come into print. It will shift rapidly from institution to institution and from instructor to instructor every single year. In this way, future anthologists of Canadian literature may find that they are unable or unwilling to be keepers of the code, simply because they will be operating in a world devoid of the sense of permanence, community, and archetypal direction embraced by their predecessors, who saw themselves as protectors and directors of literary faith.

# Performing Editors: Juggling Pedagogies in the Production of *Canadian Literature in English: Texts and Contexts*

Laura Moss and Cynthia Sugars

> "Never again will a single story be told as though it were the only one."
> John Berger, via Michael Ondaatje, *In the Skin of a Lion*

> "To bring postcolonialism into the Canadian literature classroom is to ignite controversies seldom generated by a focus on generic conventions or prosody."
> Diana Brydon, "Cross-Talk" (57–58)

**B**ecause an anthology is implicitly a pedagogical project—in some cases literally so in its capacity as a teaching text for college and university classes—the project of editing such a work involves a juggling of pedagogical imperatives. In this essay we consider the different pedagogical concerns that informed our discussions, and decisions, in editing the two-volume *Canadian Literature in English: Texts and Contexts*, published by Pearson/Penguin Canada in 2009. The anthology entailed a good deal of juggling, as our aim was to produce a book that would facilitate different kinds of pedagogical approaches, teaching philosophies, critical interests, and textual preferences. We also wanted to create a book that would appeal to students, researchers, and faculty as it traced the extensive literary history of Canada. At the outset, it is important to note that there are different kinds of anthology projects, just as there are different kinds of editorial endeavours. Carole Gerson provides a very good outline of the "imprecise nature" of these editorial distinctions in the introduction to her contribution to this collection ("Project Editing"). While a literary anthology governed by a unified topical focus might aim to present the "best" literature of a particular kind, the editors of a teaching anthology must negotiate a number of vying priorities. For these editors, the selection of the "best" covers such considerations as the "best" in the sense of having pedagogical value (from the perspective of both teachers and students, which is not necessarily the same), the "best" in the sense of being historically representative, the "best" in the sense of reflecting regional and cultural diversity, and the "best" in the sense of having literary merit. A national-historical anthology of the kind we were undertaking, in other words, is a combination of many internal "anthologies" that work in productive conjunction (or, sometimes, disjunction) with one another.

The institutionalized study of Canadian literature as an organized university discipline is a relatively recent phenomenon, which had its beginnings in the 1960s and early 1970s (see Sugars, "Postcolonial" and Fee, "Canadian"). The post-1950s cultural-nationalist imperative made the CanLit pedagogical project appear relatively straightforward, though hardly uncontentious. As Margaret Atwood famously stated in her 1972 manifesto for Canadian literature teachers, "we need to know about here, because here is where we live" (*Survival* 19). It is not so much that this question is irrelevant today, but rather that its terms of reference need to be unpacked, as indeed Canadian literature specialists have been doing for the past forty years. One cannot apply Atwood's "here" to contemporary Canadian national and transnational contexts without specifying whose "here" is being invoked. The version of national identity that dominated when Atwood wrote *Survival* was displaced in the late 1980s and early 1990s by concerns over who was included and excluded in such a conception of the nation. In essence, critics were interrogating the implied "we" of Atwood's formulation. Furthermore, an expansion of "here" needs to include not only diverse regional and demographic perspectives, but also shifting conceptualizations of place. Such shifts range from questions of Aboriginal land title to experiences of global mobility, illegality, and invisibility, and from the effects of changing citizenship and immigration policies to privileged notions of inheritance and rights. Even the word "live" in Atwood's formulation brings to the fore issues of migration, social disempowerment, environmental crisis, health, safety, community, and invisibility in discussions of Canada's cultural heritage. Certainly a post-Atwoodian anthology of national literature is committed to articulating the "here," but as a generation of scholars has shown, the concept of here as an overarching and encompassing term, linked by a notion of Canadian "identity," is untenable today.[1] Our goal in editing *Canadian Literature in English* was to facilitate an engagement with the complexity of the Canadian literary past in order to help augment critical literacy in the present.

A contemporary anthology of Canadian literature, especially one designed for the classroom, must therefore embed within it, as both impetus and intent, a recognition of the potential for "unpacking" as unlearning, or "un-learning our privilege as our loss," as Gayatri Spivak put it in *The Post-Colonial Critic* (9). From the outset, it is necessary to unlearn what has been taken for granted as academic, social, and cultural inheritance. It is also vital to try to learn what was previously not available to be known. In creating our anthology, we realized that our first task was to pinpoint what it was that we might have inherited, not only as teachers/students, but also as *editors* of Canadian literature. We asked ourselves a series of questions: What have we been taught to assume is acceptable "literary" knowledge? What texts have been passed down as foundational? What invisibilities and omissions have been inherited in this encoding as well? Are some texts "paper shadows" that carry with them a legacy of what John Willinsky describes as "the learned forgetfulness and complacency displayed in the face of history" (263)? Or do some have the opposite purpose, functioning almost as purloined letters, which seem so obvious yet which have been forgotten alongside some of the other documents and literary texts of the period? We are not suggesting that all inheritance must be pitched overboard, just that it is an editor's imperative to approach the literary-cultural inheritance with renewed incredulity. This method takes at least two forms: first, subjecting historical material to the kinds of cultural-political questions that concern us in the present; and second, considering—and respecting—the historical moment in which these works were produced, and hence listening closely to what a given author in the past was trying to say without oversimplifying a writer's position by subjecting it to presentist preconceptions. These two modes sometimes come in conflict, and it is vital in a teaching anthology to be open about where such clashes in pedagogy take place. Nevertheless, it is important to keep both processes in operation.

Editors take something from the past and organize it in the present so that the material (not only the individual selections, but the stories their conjunctions relay) may be read in the future. One of the tasks of the editors of a teaching anthology, for us at least, is to select on the basis of a pedagogical sensibility that is trying to open doors not close them, to open conversations in the classroom and not shut them down. This approach is indebted to a conception of inclusivity and difference, but it is also grounded in historical principles. The anthology format enabled us to present a continuum of literature and competing ideas from five centuries in Canada, allowing us to (re)introduce some important ongoing conversations about art, culture, and politics that might otherwise be unfamiliar to contemporary readers unaware of the historical complexity of past artistic practices and intellectual debates—readers who might sometimes end up reinventing creative and critical wheels. It makes a difference to contemporary discussions about national literatures to know that Thomas D'Arcy McGee was arguing the need for "Protection for Canadian Literature" in 1858, for instance. Yet a commitment to historical principles draws the anthologist/editor into a quandary, since a faithfulness to historical conditions is not necessarily equivalent to historical completeness. To what extent does a faithfulness to historical conditions entail a renewed silencing of voices that were already silenced in the past? Should the contemporary anthologist be committed to providing formerly silenced voices some space from which they might be heard? We want, and need, to hear these voices today. But we need to hear the established voices of the past as well.

At the outset, our anthology was designed to attend to what Diana Brydon identifies as a mutually informing cultural and critical literacy ("Cross-Talk" 61): the first including literary works that one might say constitute part of Canadian cultural literacy (e.g., canonical figures such as Charles G.D. Roberts and Michael Ondaatje); the other including both literary works and non-literary pieces that encourage a critical response of some kind (e.g., feminist writing by Agnes Maule Machar and anti-racist writing by Sui Sin Far). These two kinds of literacy are not mutually exclusive. Our goal was to represent both canonical and non-canonical works within the same volume, in addition to less often anthologized non-literary pieces (essays and acts of legislation) that could be brought to bear on the other materials in the book or read as significant discursive constructions in their own right. Furthermore, our intent was to present a multiplicity of perspectives, aesthetics, ideologies, and documentary materials. It is within this kind of voluminous heterogeneity that the "sanctioned ignorance"—which Brydon defines as "those forms of ignorance we feel no need to remedy, and indeed may wish to protect" ("Cross-Talk" 68)—that infiltrates pedagogical scenarios may be ruffled and unsettled: unsettled not in terms of what is not yet known, but in terms of what is presumed to be already known and evident. As Paulo Freire puts it (citing Marcio Moreira Alves), the central problem in such knowledge-imparting contexts is "'an absence of doubt'" (23), which is echoed by Henry Giroux and Roger Simon's notion of critical pedagogy as a mode of "uncertainty" ("Popular" 252).

As we have stated, there are different kinds of anthologies and different motivations and methodologies for anthologization. An anthology of the best nature poems or experimental fiction, for example, will not be guided by the same selection principles as a historical teaching anthology of Canadian literature. Because we were producing a teaching anthology, many of our criteria for selection and organization were determined with material pedagogical concerns in mind. In our case, the process of selection for anthologization was integrally bound up with an anticipation of the uses to which the anthology might be put within a variety of pedagogical situations. It is impossible to anticipate all of the ways one's text will be used, but it is important to consider ways in which the usefulness of the anthology might be expanded. This, too, entailed a lot of uncertain juggling, but in a productive sense, as we hope to show.

The value of uncertainty informs what are often referred to as "teaching moments," when intellectual ambiguity is transformed into a productive hurdle that can be worked through with often unexpected and illuminating results.

But how can the selective, and in our case attempted comprehensive, drive of anthologization be made to serve the interests of a desired doubtfulness? And is it one thing for the users of an anthology to court the myriad manifestations of invigorating doubtfulness, but another thing for the editors of a text to be directed by it? Can one even embed or insert "doubt" into a pedagogical enterprise, or is this something that has to emerge spontaneously? Is this element embedded in texts or does it cause doubt to emerge within a reader? Can one *inscribe* (let alone *prescribe*) this form of constructive doubting? There may be no concrete answers to these questions, except to insist that a teaching anthology must, at the very least, make the production of such doubtfulness a possibility.

Stephen Greenblatt famously said that he undertook the study of English out of a "desire to speak with the dead" (1). This is an apt way of articulating what may lie behind the construction and reception of a historical anthology. Greenblatt's phrase is echoed, of course, in Jacques Derrida's exhortation that people learn to talk with ghosts. In our view, pedagogy extends beyond the classroom context, not only because readers often undertake their reading of the text outside of the classroom, but also because they carry what occurs within the classroom into the world outside. Derrida's phrasing implies two pedagogical situations—communing with ghosts and using ghosts in order to converse. The result is a two-stage pedagogical process enacted by the readers of an anthology as well as its creators. On the one hand, communing with ghosts might involve listening to conflicting voices from the past and the present, as a way of learning from them. On the other hand, using the ghosts to talk might be a way of thinking about what happens when readers leave the classroom or close the anthology, since these are the voices they carry with them in their encounters in everyday life. And how does this reflect on what we mean by "literacy"?

Undoubtedly, we need to consider which of the dead we are talking about, which are the ones that we choose to become possessed by. Does an anthology remember the writerly, the silenced, the radical, or the sanctioned voices? Those who are famous or those who have been relegated to the wings? The historically representative or the vocally wilful? Whose voices are given the honour of haunting the national cultural framework? Or rather, which writers, by the very fact of having their words reprinted in a national anthology, are given the privilege of *no longer haunting*? What about writers who are still active? How do the living interact with the dead? We raise these questions as a way of grappling with the priorities, in terms of representation, that an editor must continually juggle in a literary pedagogical enterprise of this scope.

A part of our own pedagogical juggling act was a desire not to be too prescriptive in the ways the anthology might be used. One of the readers' reports we received in response to our original proposal for the anthology stated that we needed to ensure that the book was not too political or, in the words of the report, too "directive."[2] Our goal, then, was somewhat broad: to open up the field of Canadian literature to a wider purview. We hoped to provide the potential for something new to be brought to the study of texts from the past and the present, not only to subject them to critique, but also to elicit renewed discussion and interest in these works. In this sense, we saw ourselves to be making a range of material available that could be put to different uses, depending on an instructor's theoretical or pedagogical interests. While we sought to avoid what Brydon has termed "pedagogies of coercion" ("Cross-Talk" 64), we nevertheless saw ourselves to be generating the potential for pedagogical innovation. So a tangled question emerges: How do you construct a text that is at once pedagogically responsible (both to the past and to the needs/interests of the present), historically committed, and postcolonially informed without being prescriptive? How does one keep different pedagogical possibilities open? The selection of "case studies" that comes later in this essay will explore this question.

## CANADIAN LITERATURE IN ENGLISH: TEXTS AND CONTEXTS

As the editors of *Canadian Literature in English*, then, we were faced with a series of conflicting editorial and pedagogical priorities when deciding which texts from the past five centuries we should include. The question of audience needed to be answered before we could begin. We initially undertook this project because we wanted a textbook for our own university classrooms that matched our contextual approach to teaching. We envisioned an anthology that would take into account many of the postcolonial concerns that had entered into contemporary discussions of Canadian writing, but also one that would not dismiss the contributions of Canadian literary predecessors as the work of outmoded reactionaries. It would aim to be historically situated, without being either naively celebratory or righteously dismissive of the past. Because the publisher sought only national marketing rights, we knew that the primary audience for the books would be teachers and students within Canadian institutions. As we were working on the project between 2003 and 2009, we also knew that the student readership for the books would be multicultural, multiethnic, multiracial, and multilinguistic, and that our books needed, as far as possible, to in some way recognize the demographics of our audience.

In *Canadian Literature in English* we orchestrated over two hundred voices by placing five centuries of Canadian literature in social, political, and historical contexts. We included historical documents that also stand as cultural documents, signalling important moments in Canadian life that have been taken up by poets, playwrights, and fiction writers since the events themselves. We set stories beside maps, and poems beside Acts of Parliament, all the while tracking shifting conceptualizations of Canada as colony, nation, colonizer, post-colony, and global space. We wanted our anthology to provide some sense of the trajectory of the institutionalization of Canadian literature, so we decided to write detailed introductions to each of the seven sections that could provide a literary and cultural history of the period and to include lengthy headnotes for each writer that could act as biographical entries as well as explain their specific works' relationship with the cultural contexts of their day. We could show, for example, that many nineteenth-century cultural critics and writers overtly tied their commitment to the construction of a Canadian literature to a political motive. This means that early cultural configurations of the "idea" of Canadian literature never easily meshed with the seemingly apolitical and universalist literary criteria of other area studies for which these were the prevailing norms. This dilemma of (post)colonial emplacement was a predicament that A.J.M. Smith grappled with throughout his critical writings on Canadian literature, a dilemma he had inherited from his nineteenth-century Canadian predecessors (see Sugars, "Can"). Indeed, overtly nationalist concerns ("What is CanLit?") have always met head on with primarily aesthetic ones ("What is *good* CanLit?"), and this "cross-talk," as Brydon terms it, continues to inform contemporary processes of anthology making.

Up to this point, we have been discussing the choices we made and the questions we asked ourselves as editors. However, an important part of the process of selection related to the ways we digested the information that arrived in the series of readers' reports solicited by our editors at Pearson (editors, of course, often have to work with editors themselves). Over the course of creating the anthology, we had over fifty readers respond to our work. These readers remain anonymous to us even now. Their reports were immensely helpful as each reader suggested improvements to the collection, including suggestions for inclusions and exclusions based on their own classroom needs and experiences. The reports were solicited at three stages: first, in response to the preliminary Table of Contents for the book as a whole; second, in response to the individual Tables of Contents for the chapters as we developed them. Then, finally, after each chapter was complete—including the introductions and the headnotes— readers provided detailed feedback on the specifics of each entry and on the section as a whole.

When our editors at Pearson did the first page estimation, they found that our original wish list/Table of Contents would take up exactly double the space (an extra thousand pages) that we had been given, so we were asked to cut our originally conceived book in half at the outset! At many points along the way (including two months before final publication, when we had to trim a very painful final eight pages), we were asked to cut back the selections to fit the page limit. Even after we begged for (and received 100) more pages, we were forced to make cuts. We often turned to the readers' reports, particularly those from the second stage, to listen to what our colleagues teaching Canadian literature across Canada had said. Because of the sheer volume of responses, we could never follow the advice of all the reports, but we did take their ideas into careful consideration. For this reason, we consider the anthology to be a broadly collaborative enterprise. The readers' reports proved to be valuable indicators of the success of our attempts to provide a fair and balanced selection of writing as well as fruitful commentary on that writing.

The rounds of readers' reports also sometimes left our heads spinning, informed, as they were, by divergent pedagogical needs and priorities. One reader asked for fewer political poems but more "literary" ones that were "compelling as poetry," while another raised the opposite critique, regretting that the women in the book were not represented as political enough. Another reader suggested that we "replace some of the women's writings with pieces that focus more on 'the nation' … rather than having much of the female representation focus on gender." We were asked to omit Agnes Maule Machar's patriotic yet imperialist poem "The Canadian Fatherland," but also to include it. The contradictory requests for both more and less political content highlighted the extremely contentious nature of the critical field of Canadian literature. Our editor at Pearson, Suzanne Schaan, hit the nail on the head when she summed up our apparent dilemma this way: "You're trying to do two things at once: present important literary figures but also explore Canadian history and politics." While we do not believe that one position necessarily invalidates the other—indeed, our editorial approach was committed to both of these goals—the reports did reveal the difficulty of producing a teaching text that would fulfill every reader's "idea" of what was pedagogically essential.

In a sense, the anthology attempts to enact what Friedrich Meinecke describes as a "violent" shaking of history by "plunging it into the present" and thus "ensuring that interpretive struggles about the historical past would henceforth 'always go hand in hand with all the controversies about the shape of things to come'" (qtd in Klancher 29). Anthology editors are engaged in a cultural-historical project that merges the microscopic art of textual editing and the macroscopic act of balancing narratives across multiple spaces, times, and genres. A historical literary anthology thus initiates a meeting of multiple and often competing discourses. By placing texts side by side, editors allow them to speak to each other, in agreement or dissent. Anthologists make difficult choices at all levels: choosing texts, determining copy-texts, deciding on variations, composing annotations, structuring juxtapositions, addressing issues of representation, and creating intellectual montages. Editing an anthology produces a variation of extant texts with an emphasis on juxtaposition. It is through the act of juxtaposition that the sociality of the texts becomes most evident. As Jerome McGann reminds us in his discussion of "the socialization of texts" ("Socialization" 42), books are artifacts travelling from private to public spaces. This sentiment is echoed in Joseph Bryant's conception of textual fluidity. As he puts it, "we need to inquire into the ways in which a fluid text is a confluence of public event and private intention" (18). Furthermore, Bryant notes that "textual scholarship and editing occur when people recognize that a particular document is so artistically compelling, historically important, critically relevant, or even financially promising that they want to see it reproduced" (18). Our aim in the anthology was to convey a sense of the multiple environments within and against which particular texts were written by attending to a number of contexts: issues of relevance or contention at the time a text was created; the contexts of aesthetic tradition and innovation; the material and cultural economies in which a text was sold and read; and the socio-cultural frameworks in which it was embedded. This was a tall order for a text that had to cover five centuries in a mere 1,400 pages!

In order to illustrate some of the points of productive "uncertainty" we experienced in compiling *Canadian Literature in English*, we offer for discussion a series of pedagogical "case studies" that address particular decisions or jugglings that occurred in the course of our development of the anthology's contents and final structure.

## CASE STUDIES

### Early Indigenous Voices

Deciding where to "begin" an anthology of Canadian literature was particularly difficult. We realized, of course, that beginning with the period of European exploration was problematic, since such a perspective seems to take the arrival of Europeans as the starting point of North American culture, and therefore, implicitly, as a privileged cultural reference point. At one moment in our juggling act, we opened the anthology with a series of "creation stories" from a range of Indigenous cultures: Inuit, Anishnaabe, Cree, Haida, Mi'kmaq, Mohawk. Readers' responses to this idea were very mixed. Some saw it as a "sell-out" to political correctness and wondered what "literature" had been sacrificed to create space for these narratives, while others criticized the texts from a different perspective, suggesting that to open the anthology with creation tales implicitly relegated Aboriginal cultures to the distant "past," and hence seemed to signal that this was not a literature with a lively contemporary presence. A further criticism was that we did not represent creation stories from Christian, Islamic, or Judaic traditions so that we were foregrounding some cosmologies over others. Although we did include a large number of early and contemporary Indigenous-authored texts throughout the rest of the anthology, these comments caused us to rethink our approach. We finally opted to open the book with some "first words" as told by contemporary Mohawk writer, teacher, and storyteller Brian Maracle. The prefacing story, "The First Words" (2004), opens the collection by retelling the story of the creation of "Turtle Island" (North America) and by invoking the ceremonial "first words" that preface any instance of storytelling (and hence, we thought, of anthology "telling/reading" as well). Because it was important not to relegate writing by Aboriginal peoples to a moment that is somehow outside history or culture, we attempted to represent the active role Indigenous people have played, and continue to play, in shaping the development of modern-day Canada, Canadian writing, and intellectual debates about cultural history. Canada's own double history as a colony that was responsible for the subjugation and colonization of the First Nations, Métis, and Inuit peoples highlights the complicated nature of postcolonialism in Canada (as a colony that colonized intranationally). This approach is clearly "political," possibly even "directive," but is it prescriptive?

## Duncan Campbell Scott: Aesthetics Meets Politics

Perhaps the most controversial figure in our collection, Duncan Campbell Scott sparked a great deal of response from readers. One reader's report took issue with our initial selection of Scott's work, recommending that we provide "a fairer selection" that would demonstrate "a willingness to admit that aesthetic matters are as important as political matters." By contrast, another reader suggested that the anthology was too laudatory towards mainstream writers from the past and was in need of a "major de-colonizing." We took both sets of comments seriously as we juggled competing pedagogical and ideological priorities in the ways Scott's legacy was to be relayed and interpreted. What does it mean, for instance, to have a "fairer selection," when "fairness" itself is subjective? Is fairness to Scott equivalent to fairness to contemporary readers? Or even contemporary *Aboriginal* readers? There are two (supposedly) competing interests here: Scott was a significant and accomplished writer whose work should be remembered *and* his actions as a senior civil servant in the Department of Indian Affairs were detrimental for generations of First Nations people in Canada. For decades, these two aspects of Scott's life and work remained separate. Was it not "directive" to ignore this context? Is either approach any more or less coercive?

In our headnote to the Scott section, we cited some of his commentary on Aboriginal peoples, namely his own professed official mandate as part of his work for the Department of Indian Affairs, to "continue until there is not a single Indian in Canada that has not been absorbed into the body politic" and "Indians ... finally disappear as a separate and distinct people" (1: 423–24). We also tried to convey some of the nuances of Scott's own position: he was both aware of and troubled by the contradictions inherent in the government policy he was instituting. We also listened to the first reader who suggested that, because a relatively small percentage of Scott's writings involved Indigenous topics, we should provide a wider selection from his work. "That doesn't deny that some of Scott's poems present uncomfortable attitudes," the reader noted, "but it does reveal that he is more than a mere racist or bureaucrat." The reader suggested that we include "The Piper of Arll" in our selection of Scott's writings. In response to this comment, we tried to show the complexity of the poet by placing poems about Indigenous issues beside others, including "The Piper of Arll," and by setting Scott's non-fiction piece about his own role in government, "The Last of the Indian Treaties," beside a short story from much later in his career. We didn't ignore Scott's role in the Department of Indian Affairs, white-wash his role in Canadian history, or exclude his poetry about the "vanishing race." Whether this editorial practice was "decolonizing" enough to satisfy our second reader, we don't know; that reader might have preferred that we omit Scott altogether. Yet we do consider Scott's work to be of aesthetic and intellec-tual merit. And we do regard "aesthetic matters [to be] as important as political matters," as the first reader insisted—but this reminds us that politics, too, are important.

A driving force behind our decision to contextualize literary works comes from the postcolonial insistence on addressing the disjunction between what is studied in a classroom and readers' experiences and environment outside the educational space. In his essay on being taught Joseph Conrad's *Heart of Dark-ness* as a "great" novel and seeing himself and other African readers reflected only in the grunting disembodied figures of the African characters, Chinua Achebe convincingly argues how a context-free presentation of literature as civ-ilized art can have a damaging effect on the reader who is rendered as Other within the text. Achebe says, "I am talking about a book which parades in the most vulgar fashion prejudices and insults from which a section of mankind has suffered untold agonies and atrocities in the past and continues to do so in many ways and in many places today" (10). He continues, "I am talking about a story in which the very humanity of black people is called into ques-tion" (10). Taking issue with the argument that rests on the assumption that an author reflects a specific time and place and so is not responsible for expressing sexist, racist, or anti-Semitic views in his/her literary output, Achebe takes up the role of pedagogy. Even if a text reflects the attitudes of its day, it cannot be taught unapologetically without context when received in a different time and place. Correspondingly, when Scott's poetry was taught for many years without reference to his role at Indian Affairs, generations of readers who suffered the effects of the policies he helped implement were also taught that their people's experiences could serve as topics of consumption in aesthetically accomplished poetry without being contested or defended. Consider being an Indigenous student being taught about the "weird and waning race" of "The Onondaga Madonna," for instance. This is where an awareness of audience comes to the fore. As *Canadian Literature in English* is primarily a teaching anthology, the principal audience is a young and diverse group. We think these readers should see this diversity reflected in the literary history of their country. By not creating space for multiple aesthetic and ideological frameworks, the anthology would have been doing a disservice to its contemporary readership, instructors and students alike.

### Louis Riel and the Northwest Rebellion: Representing History Accurately?

We are indebted to our colleague at the University of Alberta, Albert Braz, for a few sleepless nights.[3] Over drinks at the "Rediscovering Early Canadian Literature Symposium" in Ottawa in May 2010, Braz asked a question that has since proved central to our thinking about the ongoing pedagogical juggling act involved in anthology selection. Because of his long-standing research interests in literary and cultural representations of Louis Riel and Thomas Scott, Braz was interested in the published anthology's representation of Louis Riel and the Northwest Rebellion. Pointedly, he asked why we had chosen to include two poems roughly contemporaneous with the Northwest Rebellion in 1885 that expressed a position in favour of Louis Riel: Pauline Johnson's "A Cry from an Indian Wife" (1885) and Agnes Maule Machar's "Quebec to Ontario, A Plea for the Life of Riel" (1899). In actual fact, Braz noted, the majority of Anglo-Canadians were publicly anti-Riel, so wasn't our anthology misrepresenting the historical "reality" of responses to the event (in terms of averages, if nothing else)? Indeed, we know that most of the Anglo-intellectuals, politicians, and writers of the period were adamantly opposed to Riel and the Saskatchewan Métis. Braz's point was all the more important because we recognized that his question was not inspired by a reactionary sympathy with less progressive ideas, but quite the opposite—it emerged from an ethically responsible and theoretical sense that emphasizing voices from the past which one agrees with is less important than acknowledging that history didn't always happen the way we might have liked. It is important to clarify, as well, that Braz's point was not about what texts became canonized in the Canadian literary tradition, in which case we might have argued that we were merely correcting canonical biases that had not preserved oppositional voices or, from another perspective, that some poems were aesthetically "better" than others. Braz's concern was that we were misrepresenting the period in the interests of contemporary political correctness. His point raised the question of what it is that the editors of an anthology such as ours see themselves to be accomplishing. Is the anthology primarily committed to historical representation, or is it also a pedagogical intervention (in the sense of trying to draw attention to those whom we, in the present, now think should be heard or should have been heard)? In other words, at what point does historical representation give way to an awareness of the politics of representation? If we are committed to historical representation, do we then commit ourselves to duplicating the absences and silencings of the past? Surely this is not what we want to uphold in the production of a contemporary Canadian literature anthology, when the goal is to present diverse perspectives about what was happening in the past.

In fact, we did originally have an anti-Riel poem included in the book. Isabella Valancy Crawford's "The Rose of a Nation's Thanks," published in the *Toronto Evening Telegram* in June 1885, is a tribute to the Canadian troops returning victorious following the North-West Rebellion. We had a photograph of Sparks Street in Ottawa, decorated with the victory ribbons at the conclusion of the battle, to accompany the poem. At some stage along the way, when we were told by the press that we had to cut another two hundred pages from the manuscript, we decided to cut it in favour of other poems by Crawford. So, at first, we were trying to give some sense of the "poetic" responses to both sides of this debate. In the end, we had to make a choice, and we decided on a selection that echoed the generally pro-Riel position of our present day, in part because these literary voices from the past (Johnson's, but even more so Machar's), particularly as instances of early women's publicly engaged civic activism, are not often heard.[4] However, Braz also felt that the works by Johnson and Machar held back from a full engagement with the history and exhibited a form of evasiveness by approaching the North-West Rebellion indirectly. As he subsequently put it, "it's striking that while both poems are supposed to be about the Northwest Rebellion, neither one has much to say about the Métis and Riel ... as if they aren't positive what Riel stands for and how they feel about him, which results in a certain disingenuousness" (Braz n.pag.). This is certainly a question worth considering, and one that might usefully be posed in a pedagogical context when the works are read in the classroom as examples of ostensibly pro-Riel literature. Machar's poem, for example, frames its "plea for the life of Riel" in the context of French colonial history, aligning French-Canadian losses alongside those of the Métis and, as Braz notes, implying that the failure of Riel's "wild scheme" was inevitable. Braz's point offers a good example of the different ways similar materials in the book can be addressed in the classroom, even works that appear to be supporting an overall postcolonial ethos within the anthology as a whole.

Historically, voices expressing opposition to Riel and the Métis, not to mention racist accounts of Indigenous peoples generally, have been heard loud and clear. The contextual materials in the anthology presented the widespread opposition to Métis land claims on the prairies, as did other kinds of texts, such as excerpts from the Indian Act and, decades later, Maria Campbell's short poemstory "Jacob" from her collection, *Stories of the Road Allowance People* (1995). But Braz's question challenged us to reconsider our editorial prerogative. Do editors perform as "trustees" of a *silenced* legacy instead of an *inherited* legacy?

Is it the editors' responsibility to represent history "accurately" by providing a proportionate representation of texts in adherence to statistical mimesis? Or, might this be one instance of unlearning our learned forgetfulness? This is not to invent voices from the past, but perhaps to "move over" to give them a chance, at least, to be remembered.[5] And, taking Braz's point above, might part of this process of "unlearning" involve being willing to question even the progressive writings of the past? It may be the editors' job to investigate the voices and documents that were part of the discourse of the period but that may not have formed part of the publicly conscious literary-historical record that dominates our cultural inheritance. One goal of a teaching anthology is to provide access to the kinds of cultural documents that inform cultural *and* critical literacy today. Of course, a given instructor is not bound to teach these materials. But the opportunity is there, just as there are similar opportunities for other, perhaps divergent, pedagogical interests.

### Stephen Leacock and the "Woman Question"

A related, though opposite, question to that raised by Braz arose with respect to the anthology's representation of Stephen Leacock. If Braz wished for a greater adherence to cultural-historical realities, one of the press's readers objected to the fact that Stephen Leacock's commentaries on the "Woman Question" presented him in a poor light. In this case, we were accused of being too attentive to the historical record.

The anthology's selections from the writings of Leacock include "The Marine Excursion of the Knights of Pythias" (one of the best-known stories from *Sunshine Sketches of a Little Town*), an excerpt from one of Leacock's political lectures in support of Canadian imperial ties with Britain ("Greater Canada: An Appeal"), and an essay published in the October 1915 issue of *Maclean's Magazine* titled "The Woman Question" that was a direct response to Nellie McClung's bestselling collection of essays in support of suffrage, *In Times Like These* (1915). Leacock provides a useful case study for illustrating the balancing act of editors trying to juggle literary-historical significance, aesthetic merit, and contemporary politics. "The Marine Excursion" illustrates Leacock's wit, satirical edge, critique of small-town pretensions, and flair for characterization. It shows why he is still one of Canada's favourite humorists and why his name is on the premier literary award for Canadian humorous writing to this day. The other two pieces showcase two of the central issues in the opening years of the twentieth century: the changing nature of Canada's relationship with Britain, and the "Woman Question." That Leacock was intensely engaged with both these issues is not surprising, given his intellectual stature and political interests. In the early 1900s, Leacock had established a reputation as an internationally acclaimed lecturer. "Greater Canada: An Appeal" was one of these lectures, delivered during an around-the-world tour in 1907 that was sponsored by the Cecil Rhodes Trust. His pro-imperialist and anti-suffrage position might seem outdated and troublingly conservative to a contemporary audience, but they do give an accurate sense of the kinds of positions that were prominent at the time. That such an erudite and well-respected figure as Leacock should so adamantly oppose women's suffrage gives a very clear sense of what Canadian feminists in the early twentieth century were up against.

Our reader's objection in part revolved around the implicit question of whether such public texts should be read as reflective of a time and place (i.e., early-twentieth-century Canada), or whether they are an example of individual idiosyncrasy. The reader took issue with our decision to include "The Woman Question," arguing that it would cause the short story to "sink under the ideological weight of the evidence of the author's sexism." Indeed, s/he added, to include "The Woman Question" would "devalue Leacock" and thus would be a "self-afflicting move for any anthology." This comment certainly gave us pause. This reviewer went on to clarify that s/he was not suggesting that the "author is beyond criticism" but rather that it was difficult to show an author in a positive light when one was also worried about showing his limitations. Arguing that race and gender concerns came across in the selections from Emily Murphy, L.M. Montgomery, Nellie McClung, and Deskaheh, s/he suggested that it was not necessary to raise these issues with Leacock. However, it was precisely the weight of the selections by Murphy, Montgomery, McClung, and Deskaheh that made us want to provide other responses to the central issues of the period. The position was not forced on Leacock, since Leacock made no attempts to be silent about his stand against women's suffrage. This was not a private document, but an essay published in one of the foremost cultural and political affairs magazines of the day. Leacock's position, in other words, was accepted at the time as a legitimate and laudable one, and hence echoed the thoughts of many others of the time. Were we suggesting that Leacock was the only man of his time to voice such a view? Obviously not; on the contrary, the excerpt (and its appearance in *Maclean's*) suggested the broadly accepted nature of these attitudes.

The reader was right to point out that Leacock's views would not find widespread support in Canada today. But is the purpose of an anthology to represent authors in only their best light? Were we not showing how attitudes we might now find distasteful were ingrained in even the best thinkers and writers, which effectively is why the women's movement had to mobilize with the force that it did? Leacock's essay tells us something about the depth of the entrenched sexism of the early twentieth century. As a historical as well as a literary document, it provides some common ground for the pieces by McClung and Murphy. If we presented only the feminist position, how could we discuss what it was, precisely, that these women were reacting against? Without this range of voices debating the "Woman Question," students today who take basic feminist gains for granted would have no sense of the widely accepted and vociferous attitudes that the women of this period were confronting. By moving from Leacock to McClung (as these were positioned in the anthology), the reader would be able to follow an argumentative thread. Following the Leacock section, the anthology includes an excerpt from McClung's novel *Purple Springs*, as well as one from "Speaking of Women," an article she wrote in direct response to Leacock's piece and also published in *Maclean's* (in May 1916). The pairing of the two essays gives a very good sense of the social and cultural investments of these two notable writers. From a pedagogical perspective, there is much to be gleaned from the arguments rallied by both authors. Part of the "unlearning" process might involve students recognizing that writers don't exist in a vacuum, that they engage with the issues of their day, and that creative ability does not decline in proportion to a writer's politics.

## The Present: How to Choose?

Finally, just as we had struggled with how to begin the anthology, we also wrestled with how to close it. When we were choosing selections for the historical sections, we knew that we were invested in presenting canonical figures beside non-canonical ones and that we were committed to presenting some contextual documents that we knew had an impact on Canadian cultural life. When it came to the contemporary period, however, it was more challenging to decide which versions of the thriving Canadian literary and contemporary cultural scene we wanted to represent. We asked ourselves what role literary prizes and institutional backing have on the nascent contemporary canon and how much anthologists have to take such public recognition into account when choosing what to include. How do you narrow the field to a handful of the hundreds of writers producing strong work today and squeeze their writing into two hundred pages?

While creating this anthology we struggled with issues of balance, genre, artistic merit, historical import, gender, regional representation, racial and cultural diversity, and space. In the final chapter we were also fully aware that we were dealing with living writers who might be materially impacted by having been included in the book, particularly if it was used in university classrooms as we hoped it would be. We had agonized over cutting the poetry of Bronwen Wallace and Rita Joe, and the short fiction of Timothy Findley and Mordecai Richler. We regretted cutting the work of such fine living writers as Erín Moure, Lee Maracle, David Adams Richards, M.G. Vassanji, Shani Mootoo, Lynn Coady, and Anne Michaels. This is when we became most aware that we, too, were contributing to the creation of a canon whether that was our intention or not. Such a responsibility weighed heavily on us. Our governing questions seemed even more pertinent here. First, which texts stood out as timely and in conversation with the macro-stories in the anthology? To put it another way, which pieces engaged with the debates of the past centuries and which pieces contested predominant literary-cultural inheritances? Second, who was forging new technical or intellectual ground? How were genre, form, language, and aesthetic modes of presentation being innovated? Finally, how many versions of *here* could we include?

On our original wish list for the contemporary period we included the work of fifty authors, though we compiled this list knowing that some pieces would have to be cut. To help us decide on the final selection, our publisher sent out the preliminary Table of Contents for this section to a group of six readers. These readers were asked to tick boxes in a column indicating whether they would or would not teach a particular author/text. One must keep in mind that a "no" indicator did not necessarily mean that a given reader had an aesthetic or political antipathy to a particular author; rather, the question was whether a given author was regularly taught in their classroom or whether they might see that person's work forming part of future syllabi. As a hypothetical example, one might say "no" to a figure such as Ann-Marie MacDonald, not because one objects to her work but because her novels are too long to be pedagogically workable in the short time span of a CanLit survey teaching term. The process reminded us just how much we were creating a teaching anthology with a specific market in mind. This was a form of product testing, after all. Once again, we had to grapple with myriad contradictions, and this time there was even less consensus than in the reviews of the earlier chapters. For instance, one reviewer noted that s/he was "delighted to see an extended section" on Anne Carson while another stated that s/he did not regularly teach her work. Someone commented on our "conservative" poetry selection, and another complimented us on the strong range of poetic forms represented. Without letting the readers overturn our belief in our selections, we paid attention because the readers were expressing their own pedagogical needs. If we were going to produce a text that would be useful and challenging for people working in the field, we had to take into account their articulations of what they wanted to see in a new CanLit teaching anthology.

While anthologies do participate in shaping a literature, it is important to note that our anthology is first and foremost a teaching text. We knew that teachers and professors were the people who were (or were not) going to order this text. So if they said they found the book less useful because it included an author whom they did not teach, we thought we should listen. In other words, we did not feel that this book should be about only what *we* liked. We had to consider what other Canadian literature professors might want in the book we were producing for them to use. This does not mean that we accepted every suggestion that was expressed in the reports (the case studies reveal otherwise);

rather, if the reviewers' work was not to be completely pointless, it certainly merited our attention. If the textbook was to be useful for a body of professors working in the field of Canadian literature today, we had to give their assessments some credit, particularly as they expressed their preferences both in terms of literary content and in terms of pedagogical needs. Ultimately, the final composition of the book represents our own decisions, which combined our own preferences (often debated between the two of us) with some of the feedback provided in the reports. We were also guided by our own experience teaching Canadian literature in the classroom (what worked, what did not) and by countless conversations with our peers about their experiences teaching CanLit. Inevitably, then, the book emerged as a collective enterprise. All of this was part of the difficult juggling act we performed as editors of *Canadian Literature in English*.

▼

One of the primary goals of the anthology was to provide a sense of the shifting debates about literary culture in Canada from its inception through to the present, particularly debates about the links between literary production and national identities. In 1972, Atwood still felt that one could not take the idea of Canadian literature for granted, hence her decision to write a "guide" to the topic. But even she recognized the pedagogical complexities inherent in the project: "Writing Canadian literature has been historically a very private act," she commented. "Teaching it, however, is a political act" (14). Her statement, four decades later, still testifies to the difficulty facing the contemporary Canadian literature anthologist. How does one capture the often conflicting variations of Canadian literature? In the nineteenth century, people weren't sure it existed. According to some, colonialism had killed it before it ever took root—or so thought Goldwin Smith and Sara Jeannette Duncan. "We are still an eminently unliterary people," wrote Duncan in 1886, at the height of what many literary historians consider to be a peak period in Canadian literary nationalism (707). A.J.M. Smith and other modernists bemoaned the prevailing torpor of the preceding era of Canadian literature; in their view the colonialism was deep-rooted and entrenched. This meant that Canadian literature very definitely existed after all, but it required an overhaul. A very young Desmond Pacey wrote an impassioned exploratory essay, "At Last—A Canadian Literature," in 1938. Twenty years later, in "Literature in a New Country," Hugh MacLennan lamented the direction of contemporary Canadian literature and argued that socially relevant writing needed to be revived in Canada. The nationalism of the thematic critics of the 1970s was replaced by the post-nationalism of the *fin de siècle*. Similarly, the long-derided focus on nature stories and regionalism as the heart of Canadian literary expression has been given renewed urgency today in the approach of transnational ecocriticism. In the 1980s, foremothers were rediscovered, although this didn't stop John Metcalf from declaring that there was still no such thing as a Canadian literature. In the 1990s many thought that the nationalist bias of Canadian literature was exclusionary and in need of opening up "thru race."[6] Now, some argue that we are as post-racial as we are post-national. Others vehemently disagree. This ever shifting series of burials and rediscoveries reveals the diverse perspectives among different literary commentators and communities throughout Canadian cultural history, in terms of both the literary tradition itself and the continuously self-reflexive history of the discipline as a whole. "Canadian literature," like the nation, has always been something of an unfinished argument.

Our challenge in creating a Canadian literature anthology was to see if we could juggle a selection of works that balanced a range of contemporary positions on topics such as gender, race, class, citizenship, environment, work, region, and nation, alongside a commitment to historical representation and a passion for literature. In other words, the challenge was to create an anthology "for our times," one that was respectful of the historical realities and ambivalences of the past while remaining attuned to the zeitgeist of the present.

# Labours of Love and Cutting Remarks: The Affective Economies of Editing

Kate Eichhorn and Heather Milne

Editorial work is frequently described as a labour of love. The construction of editorial work as a labour of love recognizes that editorial projects are both essential to fostering and sustaining literary communities and deeply undervalued. Writers who engage in such work do so for little or no monetary compensation, and often at great loss to their own writing and research time. Although academics are compensated for such labour to the extent that editorial work may be understood as research, or at least service to the profession, they still engage in such work at their own loss, since editorial projects are frequently considered less significant than single-authored monographs. Rather than engage in editorial projects for monetary or professional gain, writers and critics take up such projects for other reasons, reasons often deeply entangled in their affective attachments to other writers and literary communities. This is especially true when the writers and communities at the centre of an editorial project include one's contemporaries.

On this basis, we maintain that editorial projects may be better understood through the framework of affective rather than monetary economies. We borrow the concept of "affective economies" from Sara Ahmed. Emotions, Ahmed maintains, "*do things* ... they align individuals with communities—or bodily space with social space—through the very intensity of their attachments" ("Affective Economies" 119). Ahmed further emphasizes that the "economic model of emotions suggests that while emotions do not positively reside in a subject or figure, they still work to bind subjects together. Indeed, to put it more strongly, the nonresidence of emotions is what makes them 'binding'" (119). Ahmed's understanding of affective economies resonates with other contemporary theories of affect, including Eve Kosofsky Sedgwick's model, which maintains that "affects can be, and are, attached to things, people, ideas, sensations, relations, activities, ambitions, institutions, and any number of other things, including other affects" (Sedgwick 19). Notably, for both Ahmed and Sedgwick, affects are about attachment (how things are bound together and how things get "stuck"), but this is not to imply that affects are necessarily synonymous with permanence or residing. Affects, after all, are not owned but rather felt, enabling them to have powerfully binding effects at specific sites while remaining in circulation. As such, affects are integral to the building of communities, both political and aesthetic, but as a result, they are also integral to how such communities frequently come irreparably undone.

Significantly, our focus on the affective economics of editing both extends and seeks to complicate the assumptions embedded in discussions of literary production as a "gift economy." Following Steve McCaffery, we recognize that economy is a productive way to understand writing—and, more generally, literary production—to the extent that the concept is "concerned with the distribution and circulation of the numerous forces and intensities" (201). Our concern, however, is not only with what is in circulation but also with the nature of these "intensities," bearing in mind, as Brian Massumi observes, that emotion itself may be understood as "qualified intensity" (28).[1] Our concern, then, is both with the emotions that are generated within gift economies and with the emotions placed under erasure when the gift economy's promise of operating as a field of cultural production without "any structurally necessitated reciprocality" is overdetermined (McCaffery 219). After all, gift economies rest on the assumption that goods and services still circulate but not necessarily with an expectation of a direct return (e.g., as in a barter economy) or any promise of material accumulation. Beyond the fact that this model frequently fails to account for the extent to which, in the field of cultural production, producing "art for art's sake" has different effects depending on the producers' social status and political allegiances, we maintain that this model's focus on the excess or surplus produced through one's labour may be inadequate to fully understand the work of editing, which is less concerned with meaning and its exhaustion than with relationships and proximities. Moreover, when we imagine ourselves, be it as writers, critics, or editors, operating within a gift economy (a model that has been widely embraced by both the experimental and feminist writing communities at the centre of our editorial work), which affects are generated and which ones obscured? How do we account for the "ugly feelings" (Ngai) invariably generated in gift-giving economies? As literary editors, especially if our work involves anthologizing previously published texts, we are ultimately engaged in the work of keeping things in movement, but due to the constraints of the codex form, we are also always already engaged in the work of breaking things apart. What feelings of gratitude but also resentment, jealousy, and anger are generated by such acts?

Without necessarily proposing to replace one model with another, then, we argue that also understanding editorial work within the framework of affective economies is important because these economies can exist without the direct exchange of goods and services and thereby more easily account for the actual losses (temporal, monetary, professional) that editorial work sometimes entails. In an affective economy, what matters is not what is in circulation but circulation itself. Applied to questions of editing, a focus on affective economies brings into relief how people, works, and practices become attached to one another, how things get entrenched and even stuck, and how people, works, and practices sometimes come apart.

This essay explores several interrelated questions: (1) Are editorial projects undervalued precisely because they operate as "labours of love" or forms of affective labour that privilege collaboration and personal relationships over monetary or professional gain? (2) How might an affective economy of editing enable us to theorize the frequently unacknowledged dynamics of working on editorial projects with living subjects? And (3) to what extent might an affective economics of editorial practice enable us to better understand the differential treatment of editorial projects that reify canonical texts, writers, and traditions versus those that are staged as interruptions to established literary canons? And to what extent is this important to understanding the affects that structure intergenerational dynamics in editorial relationships? After all, as Ahmed suggests, "emotions are 'sticky,'" (*Cultural Politics* 16) in the sense that they hold the potential to create vital bonds between subjects and subjects, subjects and objects, but also at times lead us to become dangerously stuck (e.g., to solidify a position). Our exploration of these questions is informed by the collaborative editorial projects we have worked on together or with other writers and critics since 2008. These projects, all focusing on feminist poetics or the work of contemporary avant-garde writers, include our co-edited anthology *Prismatic Publics: Innovative Canadian Women's Poetry and Poetics*, published by Coach House Books in 2009; two issues of *Open Letter* (*Beyond Stasis: Feminist Poetics Today*, edited by Kate Eichhorn and Barbara Godard, and a special issue on the work of Lisa Robertson, edited by Heather Milne and Angela Carr); and *Belladonna Elders Series,* vol. 6 (a collection of interviews and experimental prose by Kate Eichhorn, M. NourbeSe Philip, and Gail Scott produced by invitation for the New York–based avant-garde feminist press, Belladonna Books, in 2009). For brevity, and because it's the project we worked on together, we pay specific attention to *Prismatic Publics*.

## EDITORIAL WORK AS AFFECTIVE LABOUR

In an ideal world, there would be no need to measure the value of editorial work at all, but as literary scholars face increased pressure to publish single-authored monographs and creative writers increasingly find themselves working full-time in the academy, where they are subjected to its specific demands and hierarchies, it is impossible to ignore the question of value. If one has any doubt about the low value attached to editorial work, consider the late Barbara Godard as a case in point.

Godard's participation as a member of the editorial collectives of *Tessera* and *Open Letter*, as well as her work editing key volumes of essays, including *Collaboration in the Feminine*, were integral to the development of feminist writing and theory in Canada. Indeed, largely through these editorial projects, Godard became one of the most influential figures in this field. However, as those of us who worked closely with Godard know, her decision to engage in collaborative editorial work did little to support her status within official academic hierarchies. When she was nominated for a distinguished research professorship at York University, where she taught for nearly forty years, she was denied the designation on the basis that she had not authored a scholarly monograph. The university's response implied that no number of articles, reviews, book chapters, art catalogue essays, and collaborative editorial projects—no matter how great their impact in the field—is equal to the apparent value of the single-authored monograph. However, as was evident at the symposium held in her honour in December 2008 and in the posthumous editorial projects we have seen emerge since her passing, the impact of Godard's work was far-reaching, transforming the landscape of Canadian women's writing, translation studies, literary studies, and cultural studies. What is important about what she produced during her tireless lifetime of scholarship, teaching, and cultural activism, however, is not simply what she published but rather what so many of these publications *did* through their process of coming into the world and through their subsequent circulation. After all, ultimately, Godard was in the "business" of generating social networks, multiple and intersecting communities, long-standing friendships, and, in some cases, also long-standing rivalries. Those of us who knew her as a colleague, collaborator, teacher, and mentor appreciate that much of her labour was about making connections between people and across communities separated by disciplinary divides and artistic practices as well as geography and generations. She carried out this work compulsively, often awkwardly, and sometimes at a professional loss. We maintain that the work Godard carried out—work that would prove so very undervalued by the institution she called home for so many years—may be understood as a form of affective labour.

Affective labour, sometimes referred to as "emotional labour," describes labour carried out with the intention of evoking specific emotions or sentiments. The spectrum of affective labour is vast but also largely feminized, most often referring to sex work, mother work, and domestic work and occasionally to the work of therapists, teachers, and caregivers. Michael Hardt and Antonio Negri suggest that the workings of affective labour can be understood "by beginning from what feminist analyses of 'women's work' have called 'labour in the bodily mode'" insofar as it is a form of labour that is "immersed in the corporeal, the somatic" (293). In spite of its rootedness in the physical, affective labour produces "immaterial" effects: "What affective labor produces are social networks, forms of community, biopower" (293).

To be clear, it is not our intention to create a false analogy between sex work or domestic work and editorial work. Such a comparison would, to say the very least, be grossly misleading, even if, as editors, we frequently feel like we are simply gratifying another's needs. However, we do maintain that understanding editing not as work that first and foremost leads to the production of texts but rather as work that produces social networks and forms of community is one way to further an analysis of the value, effects, and, of course, affects generated when we choose to engage in such work. As explored throughout this paper, the affective labour of editing is instrumental to the formation of canons, counter-canons, and movements, as well as, perhaps most importantly, to the facilitation of social relations. Editorial labour creates proximities across space and time, including relationships across generations. It is frequently the catalyst for establishing new social networks, new communities, and sometimes simply what makes existing social networks and communities visible to people working beyond their borders. Significantly, this is something that Godard appeared well aware of. In her 2002 article "Feminist Periodicals and Their Cultural Value," she writes, "As gift, [editing work] links culture to the social processes of life giving, of creating, rather than to the commodification and appropriation of the living" (211). While she notably retains the "gift" discourse, she also explicitly aligns feminist cultural production—specifically, editorial work in this context—with "the social processes of life giving, of creating," thereby alluding to both the physical and affective dimensions of this work. It is precisely this analysis that we seek to extend.

## GENERATIONAL ENVY AND THE PRODUCTION AND RECEPTION OF *PRISMATIC PUBLICS*

*Prismatic Publics* was initiated in May 2007 in an email sent from Kate Eichhorn—at the time, travelling in the United States—to Heather Milne. By June, a prospectus for a collection focusing on the relationship between Canadian and

American contemporary innovative women writers, tentatively titled *Peripatetic Lines*, had been sent to Coach House Books. Although both the title and the proposed focus of the anthology would shift over time, by September a contract had been signed for the production of an anthology on innovative Canadian women's poetry and poetics, and Alana Wilcox, Senior Editor at Coach House Books, was warning us that we were "not going to make any friends" editing an anthology of this nature.

*Prismatic Publics* was produced in approximately twenty-four months; it was, however, the result of a long-standing dialogue on the subject of innovative women's writing. In many respects, it was a public manifestation of a conversation in which we had been engaged since at least the mid-1990s. Both of us had started reading innovative women's writing in the late 1980s to early 1990s—an era of heightened visibility for experimental feminist writers in Canada (or at least, this was our perception). By the late 1990s, we had observed that venues for critically engaging with innovative women's writing were in decline (in part due to the collapse of several key feminist journals and presses); we also realized that we knew very little about the writers of our own generation (women born since the mid-1960s), who were publishing but not necessarily yet receiving the attention they presumably deserved. At the centre of our concerns, then, were a series of questions about the visibility of different generations of innovative women writers. In the end, these concerns motivated us to edit *Prismatic Publics*; they also would prove integral to the affective relationships done and undone through the anthology's making. Indeed, our editor's warning that we would not make any friends editing this anthology would prove most true precisely in the context of these generational concerns and tensions.

In the beginning, we were intent on including a generation of writers, at the time in their late thirties to late forties, who we felt had not yet received adequate critical attention. We wanted to bring these writers into proximity with more established writers, now in their fifties and sixties. In the end, our attempt would result in a complex set of generational tensions that we continue to untangle and even regret. Immediately after the anthology's publication, we received an email from a writer who felt excluded from the "public" we had apparently cemented through the making of the anthology. The writer, a contemporary of the most established writers included in the anthology, demanded to know our selection criteria. As she pointed out, some of the poets included in *Prismatic Publics* do not identify as poets or identify as women and several do not live in Canada or do live in Canada but have little regard for national identifications. Since she was definitely a poet, a woman, and a Canadian, on what basis had we chosen to exclude her? Despite various efforts—emails, phone calls, interventions made through mutual friends—nothing would quell this writer's anger and disappointment. In the end, she would hold us accountable for something she considered to be a brutal excommunication from a literary community she had once helped to define. Despite best intentions, we were apparently very bad "daughters of the movement," guilty of, among other things, a symbolic matricide for which no apology would be adequate.

As *Prismatic Publics* continues to circulate, however, we have been forced to come to terms with other critiques—in this case, from a younger generation of writers. As it turned out, while some of the mid-career writers included in the anthology appeared to be suffering from underexposure when we initiated our editorial project, by the time the anthology appeared, several of these writers had been nominated for major awards and begun to enjoy considerable attention in Canada and abroad. In the years following the publication of *Prismatic Publics*, younger writers, in their late twenties to mid-thirties, would wonder why we systematically excluded anyone younger than ourselves from the anthology. While we had, at the time, decided only to include writers with at least two books who had been active as writers for over a decade, in retrospect, we had to face the consequences of this arbitrary and admittedly misguided decision. If, as we claim in the introduction to *Prismatic Publics*, "nation and gender are politically saturated concepts, and when adopted as selection criteria or frameworks for analysis, linguistic innovation is often eclipsed" (9), why did we assume that generation was any less problematic, and at what cost did we make this decision? Every anthology reflects the moment in which it was produced, but its effects linger long beyond these moments of inception. What responsibility did we have to writers both established and emerging who had been excluded from our act of community building and canon formation? If our anthology produced feelings of envy, resentment, and jealousy, to what extent were we/are we responsible as editors for managing these affects?

Coming of age and to theory and writing in the afterlife of another generation's revolutions and innovations, it took us well over a decade to appreciate that we could intervene by developing our own critical apparatus, something we attempted to do through the creation of *Prismatic Publics*. Both our belatedness and some critics' responses to our anthology, however, may be read through a complex circuit of generational affects, which include but are by no means limited to envy. In an issue of *Women's Studies Quarterly* devoted to the topic of envy, Astrid Henry theorizes the feeling of belatedness among third-wave feminists in relation to Melanie Klein's formulation of envy and gratitude. Henry detects a tone of "generational envy" among third-wave feminists due to "the sense that the second wave already lived through the big battles, making us merely the beneficiaries of their efforts" (147). However, as Henry notes, envy flows in both directions: younger feminists deploy their differences from their feminist foremothers to position themselves as enviable by breaking away from second-wave feminism and charting new ground (150). Such divisions are not necessarily destructive but rather productive:

> But generations are also, after all, generative, and it is precisely in its hostility to the "mother" that the third wave has generated its own "creative," read enviable, position. When younger feminists assert themselves as a new wave with a distinctly generational perspective, we should rightly view this as a creative expression, an attempt to generate our own feminism. And so envy does not necessarily "destroy creativeness" but is itself creative. (150)

Sianne Ngai similarly argues that the dynamic of envy and its attendant antagonisms and aggressions may in fact be constitutive agents for the formation of "homosocial group formations" like feminism (135). Acts of disidentification, of asserting generational, political, or aesthetic differences within feminism, "can play as active a role as identification in facilitating the transition from single to group femaleness," which can in turn underscore "the primary and ... even constitutive importance of antagonism to collective political formations such as feminism" (161). Ngai is referring not to a collective antagonism that feminists might hold in relation to patriarchal forms of oppression, but rather to the divisiveness that often characterizes relations among women, and especially between feminists. Such divisions, Ngai claims, enact a transformation from the singular to the compound female subject.

However, envy, in this case, arguably does much more than produce identifications and disidentifications among different generations of feminists. As Elizabeth Freeman suggests in *Time Binds*, the complex dynamics that separate different generations of women, especially in queer and feminist contexts, have also informed our generation's cultural production on many levels. For those of us born during and after the rise of the second-wave feminist movement, for example, "the 1970s emerge as a scene of mass socialist, feminist, and gay-liberationist projects retrospectively loved or hated but also used as placeholders for thinking beyond the status quo of the 1990s and early years of the twenty-first century" (xiv). In other words, the past is not simply a scene of identification or disidentification, envy or gratitude; it is also something we might strategically mine to move forward in the present. Our decision to edit an anthology that traced cross-generational lines of continuity rather than edit one that simply reproduced the work of established feminist writers or that just "introduced" our own generation of writers might be read as a manifestation of this somewhat contradictory impulse to express our gratitude for the work of an earlier generation while enacting a turn or movement forward; we sought both to install a younger generation of writers as objects of inquiry, if not of envy, and to locate these seemingly less-established writers in relation to a tradition of innovative feminist poetics. In many respects, like the visual artists at the center of Freeman's study, who frequently mine "the present for signs of undetonated energy from the past" (xvi), our anthology reflects our own complex relationship to another generation's revolutions and innovations.

The reactions we have received—which have indeed run the gamut from resentment to appreciation and envy to gratitude—speak not only to our own affective investments but also to those of the anthology's audience and contributors; further, they speak to the centrality of these dynamics to feminist editorial scholarship. Also apparent, however, is that our intervention will continue to produce positive and negative affects as long as it stays in circulation. Ironically, as editors, we can only hope that sooner rather than later a younger poet or critic is moved, even if by negative affects, to produce a much more current and relevant anthology, because again, as Henry maintains, envy is a destructive but also creative and generative force (150).

## THE AFFECTIVE ECONOMIES OF CANON FORMATION

By default, since our own editorial projects have invariably been feminist, queer, and in some respects post-national projects, in this essay, we have run the risk of perpetuating the assumption that affects reside primarily in these kinds of projects. This is by no means the case. Affective economies are often associated with queer, feminist, and anti-racist work that seeks to question canons and challenge social and cultural inequality. Emotions are seen to run high in discussions of political and politicized scholarship and identities. Sara Ahmed, for example, has theorized the "feminist killjoy," the "unhappy queer," and the "melancholic migrant" (*Promise* 17) as three examples of the tendency to associate affect with oppressed identities. However, affective economies inform and structure all kinds of editorial projects, even more traditional or canonical ones. Like projects that deliberately introduce diversity into the canon, editorial projects that reassert established and traditional patterns of power and privilege might be read in relation to affects such as envy, love, nostalgia, pride, or fear.

"Emotions," Ahmed maintains, "create the very effect of the surfaces and boundaries that allow us to distinguish an inside and an outside in the first place" (*Cultural Politics* 10). She further maintains that they "are not simply something 'I' or 'we' have. Rather, it is through emotions, or how we respond to objects and others, that surfaces or boundaries are made: the 'I' and the 'we' are shaped by, and even take the shape of, contact with others" (10). On this level, emotions are integral to understanding nationalism, but here, some emotions figure more prominently than others.

Pride, as Silvan Tomkins emphasizes, goes hand in hand with shame, because both pride and shame are invariably about identification (136–37). One can only experience shame in the face of the other. Shame requires an audience or imagined audience. Similarly, pride is not experienced in private. Pride is about a collective identification. For this reason, Ahmed observes that pride and shame are deeply bound up in nationalism. She writes: "Shame and pride have a similar affective role in judging the success or failure of subjects to live up to ideals, though they make different judgements. The possession of an ideal in feelings of pride or shame involves a performance, which gives the subject or group 'value' and 'character'" (*Cultural Politics* 109). She further observes: "We 'show' ourselves to be this way or that, a showing which is always addressed to others. It is the relation of having as being—of having ideals as a sign of being an ideal subject—that allows the 'I' and the 'we' to be aligned" (109). To such an extent, editorial projects that are directly engaged in establishing, contesting, and re-visioning a national literature are, in every respect, also projects that can never be fully untangled from affective economies. Where the nation is present in editorial projects, so too is a desire to "show ourselves to be this way or that" to some "others," and to simultaneously forge alliances with one another in the face of some other.

Whether one's editorial project seeks to define the literature of a specific community or a nation, then, turning our attention to affective economies enables us to account not only for why we engage in editorial work but also for the sometimes "sticky" situations that arise as a result of such literary interventions. Moreover, thinking about editorial work through the lens of affective economies allows us to locate and identify value precisely where affects "stick." To the extent that affects bind subjects together, they function to create communities, conversations, dissent, and debate, all of which are vital to the labour of editing.

# bpNichol, Editor

Frank Davey

In his early teens, future poet bpNichol edited and glued together for him-self one-copy anthologies of news and magazine stories about long-distance runners—Vladimir Kuts, Roger Bannister, Emil Zatopek, John Landy. These "books" still exist in his wife's basement. He then—at the 1958 Pan-American Games trials in Winnipeg—became the record-holding two-mile junior cham-pion of Manitoba.

Like many writer-editors, Nichol was an amateur, unpaid and self-trained. Never being an academic or an employee of a publisher, he benefited from his editorial work only indirectly, gaining more knowledge of whatever he was edit-ing and greater possible range for his own writing, and enlarging and altering the literary contexts in which his writing was to be received. He had only two years of post-secondary education, the first a senior matriculation year at Van-couver's King Edward High School, and the second a teacher-training year at the University of British Columbia in 1962–63. During the latter he audited UBC's introductory Creative Writing course, in which *Tish* editor Jamie Reid was a stu-dent, along with future *Tish* editors Robert Hogg and David Cull—but although he recorded some of their conversations in the journal he was keeping, none of them recalls his presence. In this relative invisibility he became accustomed to the notion of young writers editing their own magazines rather than trying to get work accepted by established ones, and to the way in which writer-edited magazines could create a city-wide milieu within which other literary happen-ings—readings, workshops, spontaneous seminars—might occur.

Two small events during this period appear to have influenced much of his later editorial activity. One was that he had difficulty finding a copy of Sheila Watson's *The Double Hook*—a novel he perceived as so good that it made writ-ing a better novel almost impossible,[1] yet was already out of print although first published in 1959. The other was the difficulty he had in finding any example of Dadaism, which he was often hearing loosely referred to by other young Vancouver writers as an extreme avant-garde practice. All that he could find in the available libraries and bookstores were descriptions of it, not the work itself (Miki 238–39). Almost twenty years later he would note in a 27 February 1982 letter to Louis Dudek that the "less popular" forms of modernism seem subject to a kind of cultural "amnesia" that causes them to be neither widely taught nor widely republished, and thus when later generations discover them they hail them as new when they are not. To say this, he continued, wasn't the same as dismissing some modernisms as things all done and finished "in Berlin in the 1920s"; it was to urge that artistic continuities not be lost or denied. He would much rather "reclaim" the past than "overthrow" it, he wrote, because of the importance to him of the "craft" it might teach, and "possible techniques."[2]

On moving to Toronto in the spring of 1964 to seek help from a lay psycho-analyst for recurrent bouts of depression, he had taken a job at the University of Toronto's Sigmund Samuel Library and begun to encounter there the work of many of the central figures of Dadaism, including Alfred Jarry, Hugo Ball, Tristan Tzara, and Kurt Schwitters. But as his letter to Dudek indicates, his positive view of them was not exactly Dadaist. These artists who had opposed high art and the sacralizing of the art object were for Nichol major figures whose artworks were worthy of preservation and celebration. He would be attracted not by their activist anti-war politics, or by their iconoclasm, such as in Duchamp's *Fountain* or *L.H.O.O.Q.*, but rather by their "craft" and "techniques"—including their editorial practices. This emphasis on craft, with what writers anywhere could do with words, would differentiate him from many later Canadian writer-editors. His engagement would be with literary culture and civilization overall rather than with a national literature, or with an individual's pain, or with the social welfare and access to literary expression of particular constituencies within a nation. There are hints of this also in a 1985 interview with Geoff Hancock:

> The umpteenth poem on me & mom, the home scene, or me and the lyric impulse, which is the bulk of Canadian poetry, doesn't give me any *news* ... it's okay poetry, well written, competent, but not very exciting ... how many poems can I read about two people fighting in a darkened room? I've heard that beat. I've been criticized for my formalism. You can see the bones in my pieces. When I look at the traditional poem or story, that's an exoskeletal structure. I can see the beats, the pegs they hang their narrative on. (Hancock 36)

His planning of his first editorial venture began in 1964, before he had published his first poem. Seemingly influenced by Charles Olson's injunctions against lyrical self-expression,[3] as well by his increasing awareness of the psychological disturbances that he was indulging in his lyrics (see Niechoda 135), he had given up trying to write discursive poems and was focusing instead on writing visual poems, which that summer he had begun sending to Canadian little magazines such as *Island*, *Imago*, and *Blew Ointment*. Concurrently he had persuaded poet David Aylward, one of his co-workers at the Sigmund Samuel, to help him found a magazine, which they called *Ganglia*, and which published its first issue late that year. It was to be a relatively conventional, eclectic poetry magazine, published to subscribers on a regular schedule—possibly a compromise between his ideas and those of Aylward, who at the time disliked visual poetry. Nichol later said that one of his hopes for *Ganglia* was that it would give Vancouver poets he had known or come to know access to Toronto publication (Hancock 32)—David Phillips, Judith Copithorne, and others whom he had known while at King Edward, and bill bissett, who had recently accepted for *Blew Ointment* what would be Nichol's first published poem. All three poets were in *Ganglia*'s first issue.

The second issue of *Ganglia* was a book, by the late British Columbia poet Red Lane, *The 1962 Poems of R.S. (Red) Lane*, which Nichol had solicited through George Bowering; he was already signalling that he wanted to be a book editor as much as a magazine one. This was the first of his several editorial efforts to preserve the historical record. He was also attempting unsuccessfully, mostly through bissett, to obtain a book manuscript from Jamie Reid, and working on a bissett manuscript, *We Sleep Inside Each Other All*, to be the fourth issue of *Ganglia*. This project would cause Nichol to publish his first literary essay, which appeared as the book's afterword. Editing was now not just publishing; it was also mediation—recommending and explaining what one was publishing.

Nichol and Aylward were financing *Ganglia* themselves. Nichol would go on to finance all of his personal editing himself—the later issues of *Ganglia* and his various grOnk and Underwhich chapbooks. He deliberately refrained from applying for arts council funding in order to keep himself free of jury suggestions and fixed production schedules—from the kinds of actual and imagined obligations that Darren Wershler in this collection argues lead to a condition of "ethical incompleteness." But he would encounter such feelings of conflict and guilt numerous times when he began editing in 1975 for the Arts Council–funded Coach House Press.[4]

By the third issue of *Ganglia*, published in May 1966, Nichol had been in contact with the visual poetry movements in the United States and Britain, and the contributors included not only British Columbia poets Bowering, Copithorne, Martina Clinton, Jim Alexander, Pat Lane, Scott Lawrance, Wayne Nyberg, and Pat Lowther, but also the American d.a. levy and Ian Hamilton Finlay of Britain. Thus began an internationalism that would also be characteristic of his editing. He now understood some of the links between 1960s European visual poetry and sound poetry and the earlier Dadaists. But the overall concept of such a magazine—its regularity and eclecticism—was beginning to bore him. He wrote in the 1972 Ganglia Press index that "we were discouraged with the whole business of subscribers (who kept (rightfully we had to admit) demanding where our paid for copies were as our publishing schedule regularly fell behind) of poems & the endless stream of self-addressed stamped envelopes in fact the whole business aspect of it … more fun really were the small pamphlets that we did & ended up giving away to friends" (*Ganglia* n.pag.). Nichol told interviewer Geoff Hancock that the example of *Tish* was also influencing him: "*Tish* was an inspiration for one notion: you didn't have to have subscribers. It could just be something you sent out if you thought the writing was interesting to people" (Hancock 32). Nichol and Aylward, who was at this point much more a financier of *Ganglia* than an editor, mischievously converted Issue 6 of *Ganglia* into a press called grOnk that over approximately fifteen years published more than seventy small-print-run pamphlets and chapbooks, some sold in Toronto bookstores or at readings, and others given away. These included Earle Birney's *Pnomes Jukollages & other Stunzas*, with another short essay by Nichol, Czech visual poet Jiri Valoch's *Unlucky Number*, Copithorne's *Rain*, and American poet D.r. Wagner's *Sprouds & Vigables*. Nichol's explanation to Hancock linked the wave of ephemera he was producing, and his haste in producing it, to the ephemerality he sensed in his own life. His reference here to having thought he "would die at 16" alluded to his frequent irrational impulses to kill himself, impulses that he was hoping to overcome through psychotherapy and that he would describe in lines toward the end of *The Martyrology* Book Two, published in 1971, as "the one thing always i have feared / my own rashness / killing myself on whim." He told Hancock that he thought he might not have enough time to revise or reconsider:

> *Ganglia* was more like a newspaper in my thinking about it. A lot of my editing was news edited. "I like this line, the rest of it is just okay" and "what's happening in this line is goddamn exciting, let's develop it and get it out right away!" … In my thinking I was not trying to preserve immortal works in magazine form. (34)

> I'd simply say "Here's what's new." Someone else can collect them, if they want, on a "timeless basis." I was interested in the half-life of the poem, the decay, the fact things faded away. The model for me was Keats, dead at 26. All that bullshit about making it wait, make it the considered thing, was not for me. I could be dead. I thought I would die at 16. (35–36)

> My impulse had nothing to do with preserving in that sense. To get it on the record, yes. But even that was a later thought. Earlier on the thought was to get the news out. I published tons & tons. (36)

Nichol could have also told Hancock, however, that his editing model was—perhaps inadvertently—now Dada, particularly its disdain for regular publication schedules or financial goals. The conversion of one scheduled *Ganglia* issue into approximately seventy irregularly published pamphlets, most of which might be given away (and not necessarily to the magazine's paid subscribers), was an act of Dadaist mischief—particularly toward librarians and bookstores. The pamphlets' design and production were, like his thoughts of suicide, whimsical—some, like his *The Langwage The Langwedge* (1966) might be published in twenty copies or less, with their covers individually hand-drawn. Others, such as his *cold mountain* (also 1966), were printed in editions of two hundred (although Nichol bibliographer John Curry notes that 120 copies of *cold mountain* "were accidentally destroyed" [250]). In size they could be as small as 3.5" x 4.5" (Nichol's *Lament*, in 1969) or as large as 8.5" x 14" (his *Captain Poetry Poems*, co-published with bill bissett's Blewointment Press in 1971). Also seemingly Dadaist in inspiration was the frequent use of photocopy-collage techniques in these pamphlets and in the occasional promotional sheets he called "grOnk mailouts."

Nichol's idea of publishing quickly and irregularly just "to get the news out" largely matched his poetics at the time. By 1967 he had returned to writing discursive poetry, but with what he was calling, after Charles Olson, a "processual" poetics—a poetics in which the poem could not be consciously shaped but had to generate its own content. That is, each line had to imply in its syntax, phonemes, and semantics the content of subsequent lines. He could not allow himself to write concurrently two parts of the same poem, since one part had to lead to another. These poetics, besides leading him to arrange his poems in the sequence in which they were written, also led him to try to avoid sequencing his visual poems—unless they were alphabet based, as in 1971 in *ABC: The Aleph-Beth Book*. So when he published visual poems in his first Canadian book publication, the box-book *bp* in 1967, he placed them loose in an envelope. When he edited his only anthology, Oberon Press's *The Cosmic Chef* in 1970, he arranged all the pages loose in a box, without page numbers, as he also did with his own visual poem collection, *Still Water*, published by Talonbooks in 1970. In all three of these early box books—with their echoes not only of Olson but also of Marcel Duchamp's *Boîte-en-valise*—Nichol, as conceiver of the project, was effectively the primary editor.

His processual poetics were also derived in part from Freudian psychotherapy and his new employment, beginning in 1969, as a lay psychoanalyst. He would become the only major poet in English to have been a practising psychoanalyst. Moreover, Nichol was not merely a psychoanalyst who also wrote poetry. He was a poet who had chosen to take up psychoanalysis in part to continue living and in part to be a better, less restricted poet. In psychoanalysis he found not only personal insights that allowed him to transcend the petty narcissistic complaints about love affairs that—to his increasing dismay in 1964–65—his early lyrics had been mostly limited to, but also an understanding of language as multilayered, rich with secrets or partly signalled meanings—language as an ongoing human dream. Freudian analysis is founded on suspicious readings of dreams, speech, and actions—on the sense that such events are not always what they seem. Sometimes a cigar is only a cigar, Freud eventually had to say. As both poet and therapist, Nichol looked for the times the cigar wasn't one, ultimately founding his poetics on the second look that psychotherapy teaches one to give every sentence and gesture. "Did I really say that?" This is likely why there appears to be so little revision, so little editing, in most of Nichol's poetry—each line is already a kind of editing or revision or qualification of the one before. The poems foreground an ongoing suspicious reading of what has just been written. The first version of a passage of poetry that he writes in his notebook is often identical to the version published in the resulting book. But there is also more conventional editing (entire passages are crossed out in the notebooks and in the manuscripts)—the very engagement or focus that caused that moment in writing is refused as a false start or a mistaken interpretation, much like books such as his mock biography "bpNichol by John Cannyside"[5] or his early long poem "The Plunkett Papers" were repeatedly rewritten, refused, and sometimes abandoned. Editors who approach Nichol's manuscripts the way editors have approached Lucy Maud Montgomery's incomplete or unpublished work will have to include Nichol's own jaundiced editorial view of these texts, however they choose to deal with them.

These two major modernist influences, Dada and Freudian psychotherapy, were at times uneasily interwoven in Nichol's work. Dada had variously aspired to create rupture, shock, accident, meaninglessness, parody, hypothesis, art "events," and the readymade, to emphasize the materiality of art while refusing it mystery or "aura," and this had led Nichol toward improvisational sound poetry, his 'pataphysical writings, his "probable systems" poems, his computer-programmed "kinetic" visual poems *First Screening*, and his conceptual pieces such as the leaflet and acetate sheet titled *Critical Frame of Reference* (in an edition of four) or the bag of talcum powder titled *Plaster de Paris* (in an edition of 100), with its allusion to Duchamp's vial of *Air de Paris*. Freud had led him to value autobiography, family history, and the continuities required to understand the present by understanding the past, and thus to writing *Familiar, Continental Trance*, and the ever-continuing long poem *The Martyrology*, and toward believing that all facets of his writing were part of a single, large, difficult-to-perceive text. His critics and editors have often tended to view him primarily as either the Freudian humanist of *The Martyrology*, who seeks an ontological certainty that he knows impossible, or the Canadian inheritor of

Dada, who wittily demonstrates the constructedness of being. The relationship between the two views has at times been bitter, as when Nichol editor Darren Wershler ridiculed many readings of *The Martytology* as the work of "disciples and exegetes, mystics and sycophants" (Wershler-Henry 43).

Nichol would publish pamphlets under the grOnk imprint intermittently into the 1980s, independently of Aylward and of other co-editors who had assisted them in the late 1960s. Impatience continued to be a factor—impatience particularly with how long it took for poems to appear in magazines. He wanted specific readers to see his new work *now*. He wanted to be able to sell *today's* work to those he was encountering at his numerous public readings. In 1976 he would print a full draft of the still-being-written *Martyrology* Book IV to give away at a reading in Edmonton. But his main editorial efforts shifted to my journal *Open Letter* around 1972, to Coach House Press in 1975, and to the writer-collective Underwhich Editions in 1978.

His *Open Letter* and Coach House work were the first where he, or he and Aylward, were not themselves paying all production and distribution costs. The first *Open Letter* issue to be mostly his initiative was the Winter 1974–75 "Sheila Watson: A Collection," which republished almost every essay and short story Watson had published between 1954 and 1973, and published for the first time the story "The Rumble Seat." His second was the 1978 "Between Poetry and Painting" issue, edited by British art writer Kevin Power, but acquired for the magazine by Nichol. The issue featured essays on the work of three British artists, Ian Tyson, Joe Tilson, and Tom Phillips, who like Nichol worked with words and letters as well as colour and drawing. His third was the 1979 "R. Murray Schafer" issue, co-edited with Steve McCaffery, which presented the writings of someone primarily known as a music composer and opera creator. The fourth, co-edited with McCaffery as the somewhat less than 'pataphysical "TRG," the "Toronto Research Group," was the 1980 "Canadian 'Pataphysics" issue, in which they argued for "not a 'pataphysics at all but rather a superinducement of the superinducement, nothing less than a Canadian 'Pataphysics."[6] The sixth was the 1983 collection "Robert Kroetsch: Essays," which he and I co-edited, and which Oxford University Press republished, minus the photos, and with an additional essay as well as all of our editing, two years later as *The Lovely Treachery of Words*. Evident here was not only the anti-amnesia recovery of texts likely to drop from view, such as Watson's or Schafer's (but evidently not Kroetsch's), but also an attempt to direct attention away from the popular and toward the kinds of intergenre and intermedia work pioneered by Dada and likely to escape literary notice—writing in which the bones showed.

He made similar attempts in urging *Open Letter's* publication of "Louis Dudek: Texts and Essays" in 1981, which he also co-edited with me, and the

Barbara Caruso issue, which he edited in 1986. The Dudek issue gathered essays not included in Michael Gnarowski's previous Dudek collection, plus eight conference papers previously unpublished. With photographs of manuscripts and quotations from his epigrams, the collection emphasized much more than Gnarowski's the materiality and historical contexts of Dudek's critical engagements, and their close relationship to his own poetry—a kind of "unification" that Nichol was now often speaking about for his own work, as in his prefatory note in 1976 to *A Draft of Book IV of The Martyrology*.[7] To Nichol's amusement, no university press sought to republish the Dudek collection. Nichol's Caruso issue focused once more on an artist who worked between media, one known as a painter but who not only worked with language elements in her painting but also frequently collaborated with writers. In the 1980s Nichol was almost single-handledly responsible for the five *Open Letter* "Notation" issues, which focused on material questions in the visual representation of various kinds of poetries. Again his eyes were on the bones. He was not at all interested in what Bart Vautour in this collection calls "occasional poetry." For Nichol, the form and language of any poem had to be sufficiently intriguing that the poem stood a chance of being read long after any event that might have occasioned it had been forgotten. A writer can't trust the intensity of the occasion to give power to his text. In fact, for Nichol, it was only riskily innovative writing that could make possible the continuing remembrance of events. Memorability is created by the writer, not by the occasion.

At Coach House Press his substantial editorial work—approximately one-quarter of all Coach House publications between 1976 and 1982—was largely with assisting younger or less-established writers or with getting British avant-garde poets more visibility in Canada. At editorial meetings he would frequently propose a covertly Freudian rational for publishing a problematic manuscript—that its non-publication would "block" the author from further and better writing. The books by British poets—Bob Cobbing's *Bill Jubobe*, Ian Hamilton Finlay's *The Boys Alphabet Book*, Thomas A. Clark's *Madder Lake*, and Bill Griffith's *A Tract Against the Giants*—all took unpleasantly long amounts of time to produce because they had to be printed without government subsidy. Of his work with younger or beginning writers, who included John Riddell, Lola Lemire Tostevin, Stephen Morrissey, Ken Norris, Ann Rosenberg, Gerald Lampert, Sean O'Huigin, David Phillips, Maxine Gadd, Paul Dutton, Richard Truhlar, and Gerry Shikatani, Nichol told Hancock—echoing his remarks about how he had edited *Ganglia*—"I tend to take the text as it is, make my suggestions, and they [the authors] take it or leave it. I take it as it is because it already interests me" (36). But Ken Norris, being interviewed by Keven Spenst about the hours Nichol spent with him on the manuscript of his *The Better Part of Heaven*, recalls his editing quite differently: "His imagination was so vast, his skill level so accomplished, that he would help you to completely reimagine what you had written in multiple ways, so that it suddenly dawned on you that you had infinite choices, abundant options, as opposed to the one way you thought the poem inevitably had to be written" (Spenst, "Ken Norris").

Norris's recollection of spending numerous hours with Nichol, including five discussing the implications of the book's half-title, title, acknowledgements, and other preliminary pages, was probably typical of the experience of authors who met with bpNichol in person. Again Nichol was emphasizing, as he was doing in his own writing, the materiality of the book object, or as he and McCaffery were calling it in their Toronto Research Group articles in *Open Letter*, "the book as machine." Norris told Spenst in a second interview, "Looking back now, I feel like he was preparing me for the rest of my writing life, getting me interested in all aspects of the book, right down to the texture of the paper" (Spenst, "Kevin Spenst").

At Coach House, Nichol was also one of the initiators of the late 1970s "Manuscript Editions" project—a project that had become possible because of the 1975–76 computerizing of Coach House Press typesetting. The press invited writers to submit successive drafts of works in process, which would be keyed into the press computer, with printouts being made publicly available "on demand." Most of the writers who submitted a draft moved so quickly to a conventional finished draft that the potential of the idea of a succession of working drafts was seldom realized. Also, there was much more money to be made by the press—in terms of both sales and Arts Council subsidies—in encouraging the writer to proceed quickly to a print edition. But the project reflected once again Nichol's view that the process of creating a text was as interesting as the end product, and that both editing and reading should acknowledge that process, as does the "genetic" editing mode discussed in this collection by Christl Verduyn and Zailig Pollock.

Nichol's editing with the Underwhich Editions collective was similar in content to that with Coach House, except that he, like the other Underwhich owners/editors, personally financed the production of each title he edited. This was a press that Nichol initiated, having noted that several of his writer friends at this time were publishing small books under their own small press imprints—Michael Dean (Wild Press), Richard Truhlar (Phenomenon Press & Kontakte), Steve McCaffery (Anonbeyond Press)—much as he had been intermittently publishing under the grOnk imprint. He persuaded them that by combining these into one imprimatur they could at the very least improve distribution, be able to help one another with design and production, and have an annual catalogue. Each "editor" would continue to finance whatever he published. The resulting press went on, between 1978 and 2000, to publish almost ninety titles, mostly by writers who saw themselves, as original collective member Paul Dutton has written, not as "amateurs waiting in the wings for fame, but proponents of an alternative esthetics"; not as in "a stage to be outgrown but [one] to grow through" (Dutton n.pag.). Two of the press's first titles were Rafael Barretto-Rivera's *Here It Has Rained*, financed by Nichol, and *Sound Poetry: A Catalogue*, edited and financed by Nichol and McCaffery. The latter, with its frequent allusions to Alfred Jarry, Kurt Schwitters, and Hugo Ball, underlined the importance of Dada in the literary community that Nichol's editing was helping to develop, much as his co-editing of *Canadian 'Pataphysics* would two years later. The existence of Underwhich would, in the case of his commitment to publish Bill Griffith's *A Tract Against the Giants* through Coach House, enable Nichol to get the book produced without the personally embarrassing multi-year delays that he had encountered when editing the Finlay, Clark, and Cobbing Coach House titles. He arranged co-publication by Underwhich and paid half the production costs himself.[8] Overall, Nichol's editing emphasized, as much as it was possible to do during the strongly nationalist 1970s and their aftermath, the international character of modernism. In *Ganglia* he published British, American, Belgian, and Czech visual poets, and the French spatialistes j.f. bory and Pierre Garnier, alongside the Canadians. That editorial field reflected the post-Dada field of inquiry in the Toronto Research Group essays on poetics that he later co-wrote with McCaffery. It also reflected an impatience with academic editors. Once he realized he had lived longer than Keats, the impatience that had characterized his early editing of *Ganglia* waned, along with some of his haste to get his own writing into print. He would take six leisurely years to write and publish *The Martyrology* Book 5 (although publishing two "chains" of it as booklets along the way). But his sense that academic and commercial priorities were not a writer's priorities, that thematic questions might eclipse for most literary academics the material questions of both book and text construction, and that the academy might leave the essays of Watson, Schafer, or Kroetsch, or the papers of Dudek, uncollected, or intermedia work such as that of Schafer, Tom Phillips, or Caruso unacknowledged, was strong and quite possibly justified. Of course his own understanding of a writer's editorial and critical responsibilities was also rooted in international modernism and its early history of artists who made their own events, wrote literary theory, edited anthologies, or otherwise intervened to help shape the cultural contexts in which they worked—not waiting for anyone. They could be dead—and in 1988 Nichol was, leaving numerous boxes of his writing for other editors.

To date there have been seven: Jack David, who edited Nichol's 1980 *As Elected: Selected Writing*, collaborating with him on the selections, and collaging quotations from Nichol with his own remarks to create his introduction; Irene Niechoda, who edited *The Martyrology Book(s) 7&: Gifts* in 1990 and the 'pataphysical *Truth: A Book of Fictions* in 1993; George Bowering and Michael Ondaatje, who edited *An H in the Heart: A Reader* in 1994; Carl Peters, who edited *bpNichol Comics* in 2002; and Lori Emerson and Darren Wershler, who edited *The Alphabet Game: A bpNichol Reader* in 2007.

David was the most self-effacing of the editors, allowing Nichol the freedom to present himself only as "an explorer in language" (9). The titles of the two posthumous "readers" explicitly marked Bowering–Ondaatje as perceiving a humanist Nichol and Emerson–Wershler as arguing for Nichol the neo-Dadaist— although interestingly, the former included only a few pages from *The Martyrology*. Niechoda's editing of *The Martyrology Book(s) 7&* was controversial because of Nichol's long-announced intention to publish it as a "shuffle text" of loose pages in a box—an intention he had discarded in his latest manuscript—and because of his instructions to "interleave" his final five poems randomly as loose sheets of paper within the volume. Niechoda and the publisher, concerned that the poems not quickly fall out the book and become lost, possibly before a bookstore had sold it, chose the compromise of placing the 4.75″ x 5.25″ slips of paper in an envelope secured to the inside back cover. The Bowering–Ondaatje *Reader* was controversial for being published by a commercial press with which Nichol had repeatedly said he would never publish—as recently as three days before his fatal surgery (see Jaeger 84). Of course, commerce- and high-art-scorning Dadaists have had major exhibitions at numerous prestigious high-culture galleries—MOMA, the Guggenheim Bilbao, the Washington National Gallery, the Kunsthaus in Zurich—and several at the Pompidou. One could wish Nichol's drawings, comics, and book objects to have had such presentation. Peters's edition, *bpNichol Comics,* was notable for its misidentification of a lengthy text and for its long commentaries, one on each selection, often repetitively arguing for the humanist Nichol.

By contrast, the editing of the Bowering–Ondaatje and Emerson–Wershler readers appeared unintrusive, although both volumes not so subtly proclaimed their positions. *An H in the Heart* carried two expressive photos of Nichol on the cover and a third facing the title page, and began and ended with reminiscences of him by the editors. The "H" that the cover photos formed was largely obscured by the photos. *The Alphabet Game* dramatically displayed variously sized letters of the alphabet on the cover—the materials of his work—and a small, almost unidentifiable photo of Nichol from behind, dwarfed but ready to play. At the back there was another small and somewhat blurred photo of him along with a statement about the editing that noted how texts are materially altered by being removed from their original fonts and formats and placed in a uniformly formatted collection, and then several pages of "Notes on the Poems," which are largely descriptions of those original formats. McCaffery and Nichol's understanding of "the book as machine" (McCaffery and Nichol 59–96) was being taken into account.

Nichol's last big editorial project, undertaken for Coach House in 1985 and released in 1987, reflected his 1964 difficulty in locating examples of Dadaism. It was Lee Harwood's edition of Tristan Tzara's selected poems, *Chanson Dada*.

## Air, Water, Land, Light, and Language: Reflections on the Commons and Its Contents

Robert Bringhurst

I

**A**ir, water, land, light, language. We have all been taught that these precious substances are compounds. We can break them into components. They may still form a periodic table of sorts. They are (to us) essential, if not quite elemental. Some very good Indo-Europeanists, however, hold that the word *element* is related to *elephant* and to ἐλέφας, the old Greek word for ivory[1]—in which case preciousness, not irreducibility, may have been the point all along.

These five essential substances share some other properties too, including their relative ubiquity, receptivity to pollutants, and remarkable fluidity and consequent resistance to permanent partitioning. In short, they are not just precious and destructible; they are fragile, and they are slippery. Attempts to lock them up or hold them down lead readily to arguments, lawsuits, or worse. We might begin by eavesdropping on one such dispute by putting our ears against the border.

In 2002, Barbara Boxer, one of the two federal senators from California, introduced a bill to protect several million acres of public land in the northern part of the state by creating a number of new wilderness areas and enlarging some existing ones. It took a few years and a good deal of horse-trading to move the bill forward, but a reduced version did finally pass both House and Senate. It was signed into law in 2006. As finally enacted, the bill transferred a little over a thousand square kilometres or 266,000 acres of land to wilderness status and so protected it from what is politely called development. Six months after the bill was passed, Professor Tibor Machan, who is a research fellow at the Hoover Institution, undertook to explain what a terrible mistake it was. I will quote Professor Machan at some length, so you can get a feel for his style of argument as well as his point of view. (I have made some corrections to his grammar and punctuation, but I have not interfered with his phrasing or vocabulary.)

> The idea of collective ownership, by the way, is totally anti-American. It belongs within the political-economic framework of socialism in which, as Karl Marx and Frederick Engels made clear in their book, *The Communist Manifesto*, the right to private property must be abolished. In its place the incoherent idea of public or collective ownership is introduced, [an] idea that ultimately means that some very few people in society actually own what is called "public property." Of course, these few people will allow others to make some use of their lands because, well, they need to in order to remain in power. But what they allow, and [to] whom, is for them to decide.
>
> The American idea, laid out in the political theory of John Locke, is the right to private property. It is this right that makes possible, if property [is] defended in the legal system, the freedom of diverse uses of lands and other property, uses that will serve the purposes of a highly diverse population....
>
> The idea that some kind of fair, general, universal use can be made of public lands is a myth, one identified by, among others, Thucydides. As he observed, when people own things in common, "each fancies that no harm will come [of] his neglect, that it is the business of somebody else to look after this or that for him; and so, by the same notion being entertained by all separately, the common cause imperceptibly decays." (Thucydides, *The History of the Peloponnesian War*, bk. I, sec. 141). (Machan n.pag.)

If I may summarize Professor Machan: Locke is good, Thucydides is good—or at least his central subject, Athenian democracy, is good—while Marx and Engels are bad; and to make sure you know how bad they are, let me remind you that they are the authors of that demonic text, *The Communist Manifesto*. Locke is the architect of American civil and economic liberty, and there is no place in Locke, nor in Thucydides, nor in America for any collective ownership. It is not only un- but anti-American.

Actually, though, John Locke says clearly and repeatedly that he sees collective ownership as the foundation of all relations of humans to property. He says that we convert things from collective to private ownership by mixing them with our individual labour—but we should not, according to Locke, take anything more from the commons by this means than we actually have use for. (This is all laid out quite clearly in a single chapter of the *Second Treatise of Government*.)

As for Thucydides, I suppose it was lack of space that prevented Professor Machan from revealing that he was not exactly quoting Thucydides himself. He is quoting, in Richard Crawley's translation, the first of the three war speeches of Pericles as Thucydides remembered them. In this particular speech, delivered just before Athens entered the Peloponnesian War, Pericles is rallying his fellow citizens, urging them to commit themselves to the conflict. The war will be short, and we are going to win decisively, he says (as so many others have said so many times since). The reason we Athenians will defeat them so quickly, Pericles says, is that the Peloponnesians are just a bunch of farmers, each concerned with his own affairs. "They devote a very small fraction of their time to the consideration of any public object, most of it to the prosecution of their own objects" (Crawley 70).[2] Athens, according to Pericles, is a wholly different place, where people do know how to form a common cause and how to stand behind it. There is no mention here of common *property* or collective ownership, but only of common *cause* and public spirit. Pericles merely claims that the Peloponnesians are selfish and disorganized, and in consequence incapable of keeping up the fight. Writing this, 2,400 years ago, Thucydides knew that Pericles was wrong. He knew that Pericles had overestimated his friends and underestimated his enemies, and that the flaws in his analysis were so deep that the war lasted 28 years and yielded no victory even then. Professor Machan should know all these things too. He is after all a senior professor and a research fellow of an institution that claims to stand on guard for American democracy, protecting his fellow citizens from such manifest dangers as the public ownership of land.

I have lived for most of the last forty years on the southern and central coast of British Columbia, often described as part of the same geophysical and ethnographic province as Northern California. And indeed, I often hear in my own back yard the kind of fruitlessly aggressive political debate in which Professor Machan is here engaged. Still, I notice a slight rhetorical and dialectical difference. I haven't yet heard anyone claim that "the idea of collective ownership is totally anti-Canadian."

Professor Machan is wrong about Locke and Thucydides, but if he is right about Americanism and ownership, then he has handily explained a durable conundrum. He has explained why artists and writers from Henry James to the present have encountered what William Everson called "the innate American hostility to the artist."[3] For without some form of collective ownership, there is no culture at all. Culture, like language, cannot be successfully privatized. Culture, like language, only functions where it is shared. And culture isn't something confined to the library, art museum, and concert hall. Rivers, mountains, forests, grasslands, and the wild plants and animals who inhabit them are the real foundation of culture. When they are gone, the books and paintings and string quartets will blow away like so much chaff in a dry breeze.

I am not suggesting that we abolish private property. My house is lined with books that I have bought, and I insist that they are mine for as long as I need them. I also guard my copyrights as zealously as anyone. At the same time, I relish the thought that the books I own are beyond my capacity to exhaust, and the copyrights will expire soon after my death. If a misguided government insists upon extending those rights to preposterous lengths, I will do what I can to ensure that the work gets into the public domain one way or another as soon as my immediate family and I no longer need the income it provides.

Public domain is another name for collective ownership, or the commons. The works of Locke and Thucydides—and of Marx and Engels too—are now in that sphere. Their term of private ownership has expired, and that is why Professor Machan and I are both free to quote them, and even to misinterpret them if we choose to, without fear of being sued. The physical books that he and I have been consulting all our lives, in public and university libraries, and the buildings in which we have consulted them, are also collectively owned. Without such resources, Professor Machan would have no knowledge to abuse, no education to betray, no one such as the Hoover Institution to subsidize and sponsor his activities.

Thucydides himself, in the opening chapter of his big, unfinished book, tells us that he wrote it "more as a treasure for all time than as a competition piece to be listened to right now" (κτῆμά τε ἐς αἰεὶ μᾶλλον ἀγώνισμα ἐς τὸ παραχρῆμα ἀκούειν). It is too late to pay Thucydides in cash for his years of patient labour, but we can still continue to pay him in the currency of attention and respect. One of the ways we do this is to keep pulling his work out of the commons, into the realm of the privately owned, then letting it slip back again. This process works exactly as Locke described. Someone takes an old work from the public domain, mixes it with his labour by making a new edition or translation, and then, for a little while, he owns *that version* of the work, though he never gets to own, and should never get to control, the ancient original.

## II

I still have the immigration card I was issued in Coutts, Alberta, when my parents brought me to Canada in 1953. I was six years old and had little idea of where I was bound. School did not help much. I remember learning some didactic little stories, like windup toys made out of words, that featured Champlain and Cartier, Wolfe and Montcalm, Alexander Mackenzie, John Macdonald, and Louis Riel, and memorizing, along with the multiplication table, the names of all the provinces and their capitals. That is useful knowledge, to be sure, but not what it takes to make a house a home or turn a landscape into a cultural identity. School was a stone building named for King Edward, and I had to ask a friendly teacher who King Edward was. The male students of King Edward School played two games I had never seen or heard of, soccer and hockey. And there were biweekly classes in French, taught by an Irishman named Kennedy, who had a small fictitious dog he called Hypothesis. Kennedy had a withered right arm but played the piano with great energy, leaving out most of the notes in the treble clef. He made up for this partly by singing the melody and partly by reaching down from time to time with his bass-clef arm to fondle the imaginary dog, while saying, "Good Hypothesis! Good Hypothesis!" French lessons consisted mostly of learning chansons, their attenuated melodies punctuated by this 6/8 benediction, which was always uttered in English. The dog we couldn't see was evidently monolingual, though many of the rest of us were not. The first friend I made in Canada was Polish, the girl I fell in love with was Estonian, her best friend was Latvian, and so on. In time I made some friends who were Blackfoot and Cree, but in many respects they seemed as disoriented as I was. I had the feeling that Canada too was a kind of imaginary dog.

In 1961, my parents took me back to the USA, and the exercise of cultural reorientation and catch-up started all over again. Three years later I left home, moving to Lebanon, then back to the USA, to the Middle East again, then to Central America, and back once more to the USA. In 1973, I moved to the British Columbia coast, which has been my home for almost all of the forty years since. I mention these details to make it clear just how ignorant I was of Canadian literature and tradition when I returned here under my own steam in 1973, despite the fact that I was twenty-six years old—old enough, in other words, that I should have been fit for work.

I had published, by 1973, a couple of flimsy books of poems, the best parts of which had more to do with Palestine, Mexico, Greece, and the Sinai Peninsula than with anything in North America. I had strong, if childish, memories of the Athabasca River country, but I am not sure I had read a Canadian book. I had probably never seen a Canadian painting, and except for the national anthem and a couple of Gordon Lightfoot songs, I had probably never heard Canadian music. I knew a few words of Blackfoot and Cree but had no context—neither songs nor stories—into which these words might fit. This brings me to a central point: culture is necessarily common property, but not all common property is culture. A language, for example, in and of itself, is not a culture. And a lot of what we do these days with language doesn't seem to be culture either. Culture is like vegetables, fruit, and eggwhite: it has nutritional value. Things that do not have nutritional value—and a lot of such things are common property nowadays—may fill up cultural space, but I wouldn't call them culture. Culture is food; the other stuff is partly straw and partly drugs. It's not always easy to tell the difference. That's where editing comes in. You could say, I think, that the primary function of editing is to distinguish food from straw and food from drugs.

Editing is work, and to use Locke's language again for a moment, what we do when we edit a text is to mix our labour with a portion of the commons. In doing so, we make it temporarily our own. It is true, of course, that a lot of what gets edited is newly written and therefore not in the commons *yet*, but if it is any good, it is headed there. When we privatize some part of the common heritage anew, by mixing our labour with it, we do so on the implicit understanding that it will revert to common property in due time. Editing in this sense is just value-added packaging. Or that is what it ought to be. Sometimes, as we all know, editing turns out to be value-subtracted packaging instead. (Professor Machan's miscast quotation from Thucydides is a pretty clear example.)

Anyone as ignorant of his circumstances as I was, coming to Canada in 1953, or coming back again twenty years later, is at the mercy of teachers and editors, and hardly fit to join or help them in their work. The words edit, editor, and edition are from the Latin verb *dare,* to give. What there is to edit is what there is to give to other people. But what there is to give is primarily given already: it is the commons—along with the accumulating pile of new work that is the commons-in-waiting. A person who does no editing of any kind is failing to pull his weight. A person who does no editing has also abdicated control of his own life, and his proper share of control over his connections to the lives of others. You have to do some of the editing, just as you have to do some of the cooking and washing up, if you are going to be a citizen.

Cooking itself, of course, is a kind of editing. Hunting and gathering and gardening are editing. Doing the laundry and making the beds are editing. Rearranging the deck chairs is editing. So is washing up. Except for the deck chairs, these in fact are some pretty important kinds of editing, and they exemplify the normal spectrum of editorial activity, from the potentially very creative and highly skilled to the highly repetitive, conventional, and plain. There is a hierarchy, in other words—and many people think that the least creative tasks should always be left to the juniormost, least experienced members of the team. Since I usually work, like the hypothetical Peloponnesians, in a team of one—or a team of two, in which neither one has any seniority over the other—I see the issue differently. The analytic approach to management, in which tasks are broken up into specialized pieces, is universally understood to be the only way of dealing with very large projects, but I have a hunch that many such projects might be better left undone. Breaking projects up into discreet, repetitive pieces seems to me to frustrate and inhibit the intelligence to a dangerous degree. In the Buddhist monastery where I once spent some time, cleanliness was considered very important, but no one worked full-time at a menial task such as washing the dishes, sweeping the floors, or cleaning the toilets. Indeed, it was only the senior monks who were permitted to clean the toilets, on the theory that only they knew how to find real value in the experience. I would not have an inexperienced editor correcting grammar and punctuation for exactly the same reason.

One of the ways to think about this is to ask what "labour" really means. Does it include pointless fiddling or busy work? Does it include the mindless imposition of arbitrary conventions? Does it include "making one's mark" by defacing an object or scrambling a sequence, making a change for the sake of change? In our time, there are countless attempts to stake private claims on parts of the commons by just such means. We see the results in the form of logotypes and trademarked names and phrases, as if one could take ownership of words by changing the typeface or the spelling, or by eccentric use of capitals and spaces. Responsible editors encourage creative work and resist linguistic vandalism, but how do they tell the difference? Real writers and speakers make language their own through the vivacity of their thinking and the vitality of their style, not through superficial orthographic changes. Real typographers make language more resonant by tuning its visible form, adding historical and architectural overtones that enlarge and colour meaning. Real editors encourage this kind of work and nudge it along, tuning, shaping, and cross-checking as they go.

In 1973, I knew something, but not very much, about the geography, flora, and fauna of western North America. I had a rudimentary knowledge of linguistics and a little bit of experience working with ancient texts—mostly Greek and Arabic. I also had a weak and tentative knowledge of European literature and art. But I was not a European, so literarily and intellectually I was almost entirely homeless. This was (and still is) the normal and usual North American condition. It is, in fact, the general condition of all those societies that V.S. Naipaul calls cultures of conversion. I have found this a very useful term, in which the similarities among Canada, the United States, Afghanistan, Nigeria, and Pakistan are manifest. But in Vancouver in the 1970s, none of us would have said that poetry drew its energy from cultural conversion. Nearly all of us, on the contrary, said that poetry was a manifestation of place. Place entered the heart of a writer through the soles of his feet and blossomed out of his mouth. This sounded as good to me as it did to anyone else—I thought of myself as a landscape writer, after all, and not a portraitist or dramatist or purveyor of historical tableaux—but I was also well aware that I had almost no Canadian knowledge, and very little Canadian experience, in spite of my Canadian address. How was the place going to find me?

Two things happened over the next several years that helped me understand that question. First, through a mutual friend, the novelist George Payerle, I met Dennis Lee. He was an ardent crusader for Canadian literature and Canadian cultural identity, and his principal weapon in this campaign was an editorial pencil. Lee was a cofounder, and for years the de facto director, of the House of Anansi Press, where he published essays by his teachers George Grant and Northrop Frye, and the poems and novels of dozens of his colleagues. This work was intertwined with the role he played at the highly idealistic and short-lived Rochdale College. I saw none of this at first hand and had scarcely worked with Dennis until we both became involved in McClelland and Stewart's Modern Canadian Poets series in 1982. But six or seven years before that I had started reading his poems, then his essays, and had grasped, I thought, the force of his editorial example. Canada was overrun, in his view, by American ideas. The solution to this was to publish more and better Canadian books. Immigrants, however—even immigrants like me, who had come from the USA—were not to be shut out. The force of the land was such that we too, unless we were deaf and blind to our surroundings, could be Canadian writers. This view has very obvious political ramifications, but it seemed to me to rely for its energy and direction on something more primary than politics, and to have no inherently jingoistic or racist presumptions, in spite of the nationalist stance.

Gary Geddes observed thirty years ago that for Lee poetry, criticism, and editing formed a trinitarian calling.[4] This is still the case, I think, and the vision that fuels this nexus is expressed very well in Lee's long poem called *The Death of Harold Ladoo*. It was published in 1976 by the Kanchenjunga Press, a tiny binational outfit I was running in those days. Kanchenjunga was not only tiny, it was fast, because Payerle and I controlled the means of production. But Lee, who edits himself as compulsively and relentlessly as he edits anyone else, had nevertheless altered his poem considerably between the time it was typeset and the time it was printed and bound. When he came to Vancouver to launch the book, the text he read and the text we sold had grown markedly different. Every published version since has embodied further changes. Not all of us edit ourselves with such persistence, but the principle invoked here is still sound: it is that editing is never really finished.

According to Lee's poem, editing means, among other things, calling one's friends to account. It means insisting that as much sense as possible be made by those who are given time and space in the commons to speak. That is the commons, with small *c*, and not the House with capital *H*. A higher standard of behaviour is required, and yet more freedom is permitted, in the small-c commons than in the House of the same name. There is no speaker, no whip, no caucus, no recess, and no clock; there is an ecology instead. I am not asserting that poets are legislators, unacknowledged or otherwise; I am asserting that ecologies are real and self-policing in a way that legislatures are not, and that poetry is ecological in a way that legislation is usually not. (Legislation is usually managerial, and while management and ecology can converge in a thoughtful society, with us they are routinely poles apart.)

As a typographer, I have to say that the Anansi books of the 1960s and 1970s left a lot to be desired. No one then at Anansi had any typographic knowledge or printing experience, and the aim—very sensible under the circumstances— was to make the money go as far as possible. Typographically, things were more exciting a few blocks away, at the Coach House Press, where my late friend Glenn Goluska[5] became the unofficial and anonymous chief designer in 1975.

Some very fine Canadian literature was published by Coach House in those days, but the editorial philosophy was more inward-looking, urban, and self-indulgent. It was also far more indulgent of language itself, as if language and the self were the fountains of meaning. Editorially, then, Coach House was no help to a person in my predicament. But it was a fine typographic exemplar, and a fine exemplar in other ways as well. More than any other Canadian publishing house I knew of in those days, it sustained an atmosphere of friendliness, technical competence, and good cheer. These are not necessarily indicators of wisdom, but they are at least, I think, signs of spiritual health.

### III

I was saying (rather too long ago) that two important things happened to me after coming back to Canada in 1973, and I turn now to the second and more important of those two. I didn't know where I was, so I went to the library to find out. I went to the big library, where there is only one book on the shelf—earth, sea, and sky: a three-volume set—and I went to the littler libraries where the printed books are kept. I spent a lot of time climbing and hiking in the Coast Range, and kayaking the coast between Vancouver and Glacier Bay. I also spent a lot of time reading field guides and monographs on the local plants and animals. I made friends at the university herbarium who could help me identify specimens I brought in from the field, and I eventually met the legendary dean of British Columbia lichenologists, Trevor Goward, whose knowledge of natural history I have been sponging off ever since. Besides that, I started visiting native communities, meeting some of the people who lived there, and reading, in English translation, the texts that their forebears had dictated to Franz Boas, John Swanton, and Edward Sapir, the three great linguistic anthropologists, or anthropological linguists, who worked in British Columbia in the late nineteenth and early twentieth centuries.

While I was reading John Swanton's translations of the texts that he transcribed in southern Haida between the fall of 1900 and the summer of 1901, something happened to me that had happened rarely before and has happened rarely since. I began to feel quite sure that, lurking in the dark on the other side of these translations, there were great works of literature that I needed to get closer to, no matter what the price. I felt morally obliged to learn the language of those texts well enough to read them in the original. That seemed to me the requisite act of respect for the major Haida authors—Skaay, Ghandl, and Kilxhawgins—that Swanton had introduced me to. I learned that Swanton's southern Haida typescripts—almost all of them unpublished—were in the American Philosophical Society Library in Philadelphia, and that I could buy a microfilm copy of this manuscript for the price of a normal hardcover book. So I sat down with the Haida originals, Swanton's translation, and his rudimentary Haida grammar (now more than a century old), and began what has become a lifelong task.

Doing the laundry does, I repeat, seem to me an important kind of editing. But it is trivial compared to the significance of editing in the arts. The conservation and restoration of old texts, old paintings and sculptures, old musical instruments and scores, opens the gates of the prison of time and the prison of social conditioning. I like clean underwear quite a lot, but I'd be happy to wear dirty rags for the rest of my life if that were the price of getting sprung from the cramped and raucous cage of North American pop culture. Fortunately, the keys are not hard to get hold of, though they're not always left in plain sight. In the meantime, however, more and more of the natural world keeps falling under the saw and the paving machine, and more and more humans are spending their time in an electronic landscape, where there is nothing to be seen or heard or touched that is not the fruit of human engineering: not so much as a single cut flower or potted plant or even a piece of bone or leather or wood. In a world where nature doesn't exist, there are no implicit benchmarks of beauty or truth. In that sort of world, postmodernism comes true with a vengeance: everything turns into advertising and fantasy, because nothing is better or truer than anything else. That part of the jail is constantly growing, and it is now redecorated daily, making it brighter and louder and worse. So the presence of those keys— the ones that will open the gates—becomes ever more important.

The familiar and still quite accessible keys are the treasures of Western and Eastern culture. Some of these can be found in public and school libraries even in small towns, and in music and book shops even in airports and strip malls. From there you can find your way to the national park or the university, and in the national park or the university, despite the increasingly corporate style of management, you can still find more of the keys that will let you into more-than-human and more-than-present space. More-than-present space means the space of historical and geological time. More-than-human space means the space of natural history, in which time is polyphonic, because different species run on different clocks.[6]

I have just suggested that you can find the keys only in the university or the national park, and this may seem an exaggeration—as if there were no residual forest or tundra or grassland: no middle ground between the parking lot and the park. I concede that I am exaggerating here. There is plenty of "nature" not yet confined to the park. I exaggerate on purpose, to emphasize my sense that we are headed in that direction. There is an increasingly sharp division between "protected lands" on the one side and, on the other side, lands that have been "developed" or are slated for or available for "development." Development, whatever it once meant, now more often than not means degradation, which is the antithesis of good editing.

I have also, perhaps, just implied that if you get hold of some of the keys to the prison and let yourself out of the jail of mindlessness, all will be well after that. This is not necessarily true, especially if you live in North America. Here in particular, you can get out of jail and still find yourself locked in an old colonial mindset. You can make yourself into an artist or an intellectual and nevertheless find that you are condemned to live as an intellectual tourist or voyeur in the land where you were born. This is because of the walls we have built, in Canada, the United States, and Mexico, between indigenous and colonial traditions. They resemble the wall that used to run between East and West Berlin less than they do the wall that used to run between black and white districts in South Africa. They are usually not physical walls; they exist only because people believe in them.

I began to study the Haida language around 1980 and have been learning it ever since. My method of doing so has disturbed a few people, and I am sorry for their distress, but I make no apology for my approach. What I had in front of me were manuscripts from a culture that had vanished. That statement too will irritate some people, but it is true, and I will stick with it. The Haida people have most certainly not vanished, and the effort now under way among the Haida to reclaim their lands and their right to self-determination is to me a very moving and promising event. But the texts dictated to John Swanton in 1900 and 1901 by Skaay, Ghandl, Kilxhawgins, and other Haida poets and historians, are for all practical purposes testimonia from pre-contact Haida culture. That culture, like the culture of Renaissance Florence or ancient Athens, has, as a living entity, ceased to exist. This does not mean that the Haida have no future, and it does not mean they have no past. It means that their past, present, and future are different—as indeed they always are, for all of us.

The Haida texts appeared to me to be cultural treasures, and I treated them as such—very much as I would treat ancient Greek texts written on papyrus or ancient Arabic written on paper. They needed, in my opinion, retranslation. I needed retranslation too, and the best method available to me for retranslating myself seemed to be to retranslate those texts. I admired Swanton's translations, but I could see right away that there were things he had deliberately left out and things he had inadvertently overlooked. In time I felt sufficiently sure enough of myself to say there were also things he had misunderstood. I presented these findings to some of the Haida I knew and got a wide range of reactions. In fact, the reactions are still coming in, and they will, I expect, be coming in for some while yet. As people have got older and more thoughtful and acquired more information, some of their views have also changed substantially. It is still the case, however, that the warmest response I have had from any Haida reader came from Bill Reid, who read many of my Haida translations in manuscript but who died in 1998, as I was just beginning to publish them.[7] Reid was not a Haida speaker, but he had spent his life learning the graphic language of Haida painting and the glyptic language of Haida sculpture, and he had learned them well enough to bring those great arts back to life. "They were never lost," some people say, "so there was nothing to rekindle. All he did was to capture public attention." But they were in fact lost. There was in fact, and there still is, a Haida renaissance, and Reid was its primary agent. He saw at once what I was doing with Swanton's texts, and why. He also understood at once the differences between my task and his. He was rejuvenating a vivid but silent language—or a pair of closely related languages—by creating new work. I was rejuvenating old work by translating from a language that is, as a living language, still being lost, despite some serious efforts to reclaim it. But literature can be brought back to life through translation, where sculpture cannot. And Reid is the only prominent Haida I have ever known whose view of such questions was entirely nonracist.

The fundamental question here, it seems to me, is whether or not aboriginal literature belongs, or can ever belong, to the commons. If it does, then we are all free to study and edit it—even if our methods and conclusions strike others as peculiar. If it doesn't, then we aren't. If it does belong to the commons, then it doesn't belong to *us*, but in a real sense *we belong to it*—just as we belong to the local land, water, and language.

The arguments against treating aboriginal literature, language and culture as part of the commons are pretty straightforward. Native people have been horribly mistreated since the dawn of the colonization. Their lands have been stolen, their social structures mauled, their civilizations dismantled, their children abducted and forcibly deschooled. In the United States and Canada, up to the end of the nineteenth century, at least six million indigenous people were killed by imported disease; many thousands more were poisoned, shot, or starved. The story is just about as ugly as any story ever told. Surely the descendants of the colonists ought to keep their guilty hands off whatever indigenous people still possess. There are some difficulties here, including the suggestion that whole communities are guilty of crimes committed by individuals, whole populations guilty of crimes committed by governments, and grandchildren guilty of crimes committed by their forebears,[8] but the root fact of severe and sustained and blatant injustice is not in any doubt.

The arguments in favour of treating aboriginal literature, language, and culture as part of the commons seem to me straightforward too. I will mention four that seem to me important.

First, segregation makes things worse instead of better. It has made things worse in Ireland, in Africa, in Palestine, in India and Pakistan, and in North and South America. Catholics and Protestants, black people and white people, Christians and pagans and Hindus and Muslims and Jews, indigenous people and immigrants, have to live together because they do live together, and their traditions have to live together too.

Second, teaching all North Americans at least the fundamentals of indigenous tradition is the only hope we've got. This was the view of Louis Riel; it was the view of my Haida friend and teacher Bill Reid; it is the view of Gary Snyder and of John Ralston Saul,[9] and incidentally it is my view also. Native North American traditions are very numerous and various, but they have some things in common. They all, without exception so far as I know, teach respect for the land, respect for non-human creatures, and the necessity of moderation in the demands that humans place on the environment of which we are a part. Those are precisely the values Europeans forgot to bring with them when they colonized the Americas.

Third, with respect to indigenous art and literature in particular, these are the things that people chose to say for themselves, the things they chose to share. They are not sectarian liturgies, occult secrets, or private rites; they are the stories people chose to tell to others, the songs they chose to sing aloud, the objects they elected to display. The stories John Swanton transcribed in Haida, for example, are the stories people chose to tell to an outsider with a notebook and a pencil, knowing that what he transcribed would be carried away. The work was done openly, payment was made, no one was told any lies about the agenda, and no one was pressured to reveal what they preferred to keep to themselves. Some pretty shady characters have called themselves anthropologists, and some highly untrustworthy people have published "versions" of native stories, from cultures and languages they knew little or nothing about. Physical artworks have also, quite often, been stolen from their rightful indigenous owners, just as Van Goghs and Picassos have been stolen from European and North American collectors and museums. Wherever you go, you can find some unsavoury people who covet beautiful things. But I have been studying Native American languages and their literatures for more than thirty years, and I have yet to encounter a case in which actual texts, in indigenous languages, were extorted from their speakers.

Fourth, quite simply, culture is not genetic—so any legislation that declares culture to be an ethnic possession will, in the long run, probably fail. Can it serve a useful purpose in the meantime, like the imposition of quotas in civil rights campaigns? That is not a question I am qualified to answer.

Swanton was a very gentle, respectful investigator, but some of those who helped him in his work may have sensed a future value in the task that is never mentioned by Swanton himself, in his books or in any surviving private letters. His Haida colleagues may have realized that the stories he carried away might also, later on, in an even more difficult time, be brought back to the very places where they were told, to the descendants of their tellers. And they *have* been brought back, in both in Haida and English. For the Haida themselves, Swanton's work has therefore proven worthwhile, and the trust that his Haida teachers placed in him has been vindicated. That is how literature functions, regardless of whether it's oral or written. It is how art and music function too. You give things away, and a long time later you may find yourself or your children enriched. Not necessarily in money, but in more-than-present, more-than-human space. It was Bill Reid's dream that if everyone in North America, no matter what their ethnic heritage, studied indigenous literature and art, adopting it as part of their own identity, "we could become *North Americans* at last, instead of displaced Europeans" (Reid 30). I believe he was right. And it seems to me, again, our only chance. If so, there is a lot of urgent work for editors, whatever their ethnic heritage, to do.

# The Ethically Incomplete Editor

Darren Wershler

> "Artists are channeled like service providers to manage the social."
> Miller and Yúdice 20–21

The technologies that govern the publication and circulation of books in Canada have much in common with the technologies that govern the training and working lives of professional and scholarly literary editors. Both are part of a larger set of political technologies called "cultural policy," which manage the relationships of individual subjects and institutions to the state. The problem is that Canadian literary studies rarely addresses the topic of cultural policy, and when it does, it usually does so within the limits of its own critical canon.

This lack of scrutiny is worrisome for several reasons. Cultural policy orders and regulates the existence of the very objects that Canadian literary scholars typically study: books, magazines, genres, critical and political movements, authors, presses. Further, Canadian literary research is structured in part by those same technologies, to the extent that academic literary research is government-funded and that scholars participate in the daily operations of Canadian literary presses. And further still, the subjectivity of scholars, editors, and writers is structured by cultural policy as well. This set of relationships is of particular interest to me because I've been a professional literary editor (full-time and freelance at various moments) as well as a scholar. Like many of my academic colleagues, I continue to edit and design books for a number of literary small presses. This process is far from simple. It involves negotiating not just the differences between the academic and literary economies of production, but also a series of relationships with the state which determine the ongoing worthiness of a given press to receive funding to produce books. By implication, this is also an assessment not just of one's ongoing worthiness to edit those books, but also of one's worth as a citizen making contributions to national culture. Yet there's very little writing on the subject of how scholar-editors negotiate these complex and conflicted relationships—professionally, economically, personally, or otherwise.

In his writing on power and subjectivity, Michel Foucault argues that "the political, ethical, social, philosophical problem of our days is not to try to liberate the individual from the state, and from the state's institutions, but to liberate us both from the state and from the type of individualization linked to the state" ("Subject" 337). Closely studying the way that such individualization operates in Canadian cultural policy would be a crucial step in any attempt to imagine new forms of literary production, let alone new modes of subjectivity. I believe that it's time for Canadian literary studies to make a disciplinary turn toward critical cultural policy studies on the scale of the turn toward literary theory that occurred in the 1980s (often associated with the work of critics like Eli Mandel, Frank Davey, Barbara Godard, and E.D. Blodgett).

Some of the scholar-editors who were major contributors to the theoretical moment in Canadian literary studies are the same people who began the call for a closer study of the literary aspects of Canadian cultural policy. In "The Critic, Institutional Culture, and Canadian Literature," Barbara Godard comments to Smaro Kamboureli that the need for academic study of Canadian literary institutions is pressing and persistent (Godard and Kamboureli 33). To date, much of the work on questions of policy has focused on the discourses of feminism and postcolonialism. As Bill Ashcroft, Gareth Griffiths, and Helen Tiffin point out in *The Empire Writes Back*, this is the case because the precondition for recognizing discourses of exclusivity is a study of national literary traditions and the claims they make (17). One example is Alison Beale and Annette Van Den Bosch's 1998 collection *Ghosts in the Machine: Women and Cultural Policy in Canada and Australia*. (Because of the strength of Australian cultural policy studies, and similarities between Australian and Canadian cultural policy due to their common colonial past, it's not surprising to see such a convergence.) Arguments in this volume range from instrumental calls for greater involvement of the private sector in arts funding to a renewed sense of the importance of the public good, but all argue for a greater degree of feminist and anti-racist involvement in cultural policy formation and critique (Fiamengo, 126).

What's currently missing is an explicit bridge between the analysis of the relations between cultural and economic institutions that feminism and postcolonialism exemplify and the projects of textual and discursive analysis. In his 2003 overview of cultural policy studies, Jim McGuigan argues that political economy–based approaches require some sort of "discursive form of analysis which is properly sensitive to the complexity of symbolic process and the meaning and use of cultural products in specific contexts," and that merging political-economic analysis and textual and contextual interpretation would be a laudable project (33). But the complement is also true: literary studies should be interested in political economy and cultural policy to a greater degree than it is currently, because it needs to understand the conditions of its own possibility at a moment when the system that has traditionally sustained it is labouring under new forms of strain.

A handful of essays written over the past two decades, such as Margery Fee's "Canadian Literature and English Studies in the Canadian University," Aritha van Herk's "Publishing and Perishing with No Parachute," Danielle Fuller and DeNel Rehberg Sedo's "A Reading Spectacle for the Nation: The CBC and 'Canada Reads,'" exemplify the sort of work that needs to be done in terms of documenting and critiquing the functions of the institutions that determine what counts as Canadian literature. These authors carefully describe the material and ideological factors that underpin the particular sense of literary value that these institutions promulgate in ways that highlight the value for literary studies of political economy and critical cultural policy theory, and vice versa. But despite the value of these interventions, there still isn't much contact between the worlds of cultural policy studies and literary studies.

As Sophie McCall points out, though, despite frequent invocations of the importance of interdisciplinary work in the contemporary academy, the gap in critical approaches to cultural policy between the humanities and the social scientists may actually be widening (95). McCall bases this observation on the contrast between two critical anthologies published in 2005: Caroline Andrew, Monica Gattinger, M. Sharon Jeannette, and Will Straw's *Accounting for Culture: Thinking Through Cultural Citizenship*, and Chelva Kanaganayakam's *Moveable Margins: The Shifting Spaces of Canadian Literature*. Though McCall sees in Andrew and her colleagues "the potentially reductive imperative to count and itemize cultural difference" (96), her criticism of Kanaganayakam's collection is more pointed, and more apposite for this discussion: "the notion of literature occupying a privileged space outside bureaucracy is also symptomatic of the disciplinary norms in Canadian literary studies whereby critics opportunistically tune out the material constraints within which Canadian culture is produced, packaged, and sold today" (96). But these two modes of analysis need each other very much, because of a particular shell game that governments play with cultural production: "When governments create policy to support funding initiatives, the emphasis is always on 'culture.' Later, when the same bureaucrats design mechanisms of delivery, the emphasis shifts to 'industry'" (Côté 201). Each perspective recognizes something obscure to the other. In an environment where "the Canadian retail book market is shaped by government policy and practice more than any other industry, including banking" (Côté 200), it's incumbent on editors and scholars to consider the conditions of possibility of the spaces they occupy.

Scholars like van Herk, Fuller, Sedo, and McCall, whose object of study is primarily literary but who have a strong sense of the importance of cultural policy issues, can make a difference. Pedagogical shifts are slowly changing the sort of research that students produce. With projects such as *The Book of MPub*, students in the Master of Publishing program at Simon Fraser University are producing original research on the publishing industry and the policy that shapes it. The work coming out of the MPub program is encouraging, but it needs to be articulated to some form of critical analysis to a greater degree than it is at the moment in order to move beyond the instrumental. Recent doctoral dissertations, such as Karis Shearer's "Constructing Canons: Postmodern Cultural Workers and the Canadian Long Poem" (2008) and Owen Percy's "Prize Possession: Literary Awards, the GGs, and the CanLit Nation" (2010), indicate that a shift toward a greater concern with cultural policy is under way, if still a minor tendency.

To recap: The bad news is that even in instances when Canadian literary studies does venture away from literary theory into questions of policy, it rarely considers critical and theoretical work written by scholars outside of its own canon. This is a problem to the extent that without recourse to such writing, literary scholars find themselves in the position of having to reinvent useful concepts and tools that are already available elsewhere. The good news is that there is a growing body of international research into critical cultural policy studies that is extremely pertinent to Canadian literary studies. Some of the primary documents and key essays that would provide a historical groundwork for such study, to which Godard alludes, have been gathered in recent volumes such as Sourayan Mookerjea, Imre Szeman, and Gail Farschou's massive *Canadian Cultural Studies: A Reader*. For a sense of the breadth of this research, Justin Lewis and Toby Miller's *Critical Cultural Policy Studies: A Reader* is a good place to start.

The portion of critical cultural policy studies that I want to focus on for the remainder of this paper has to do with "ethical incompleteness," a key concept that emerges in the work of Toby Miller. He has been developing the notion of ethical incompleteness since its appearance in his first book, *The Well-Tempered Self: Citizenship, Culture, and the Postmodern Subject* (1993), in which he lays the philosophical groundwork for its use. In *Cultural Policy* (with George Yúdice, 2002) and *Critical Cultural Policy Studies: A Reader* (edited with Justin Lewis, 2003), Miller presents a general overview of the role the concept plays in the subjectivity of citizens under liberal democracy. His recent work on the increasing tendency toward substituting the notion of the "creative industries" for "cultural industries" ("Creative" 2008) is edging closer to the subjectivity of Canadian literary and scholarly editors, especially in terms of their relationship to the state, but it's worth doing some conceptual unpacking before proceeding further.

## ETHICAL INCOMPLETENESS

The overall goal of cultural policy in a contemporary democracy, writes Miller, is "to produce loyal citizens who learn to govern themselves in the interests of the cultural-capitalist polity" (*Well-Tempered* ix). In contemporary democracies, this process of constructing citizens occurs more often through cultural means than it does by main force. As Michel Foucault argues, an intricate set of disciplinary systems provides power over contemporary subjects even as it furnishes them with the power to function effectively and autonomously (*Discipine* 222). This is important because for Miller, the techniques for producing civil subjects are the basis for "the discursive tactics of cultural policy" (*Well-Tempered* 40).

Moreover, "there is a continuity and coincidence between cultural policy and textual analysis" in terms of the techniques of self-scrutiny that they employ (Miller, *Well-Tempered* 95). Kathleen Fitzpatrick concurs, and provides an example from the specific milieu of academic publishing. Just as subjects internalize state discipline though micro-techniques of power, disciplinary techniques of academic editing such as peer review transform state censorship into a system of self-policing, producing "the conditions of possibility for the academic disciplines that it authorizes" (21). As each generation of students replaces the previous generation of professors, the former objects of discipline become its subjects, and the system of values and practices reproduces itself (Fitzpatrick 22). The discourses and techniques that produce Canadian citizens and teach us how to behave are also the low-level components of the institutions (ideological state apparatuses, if you like) that manage Canadian publishing, inside and outside of the academy. Both involve copious editing processes, and neither is ever really finished.

The name Miller gives this unending, apprehensive process of self-examination that defines our relationship to the state is "ethical incompleteness" (*Well-Tempered* xii). A scholar-editor's life is largely defined by this relationship, which consists of endless production of budgets, emails, applications, and reports that supplicate various government bodies for the funds to continue operating. Did I complete the copy edits on the manuscripts that go to press this week? Did I sign all of the royalty cheques? Did I file the grant application on time? Did I book the space for next month's book launch? Did I finish cleaning up the raw image scans for the book cover I'm designing? Did I return the latest round of panicked emails from our highest-maintenance author? Did I finish writing the bumph for the sales force? Did I fix the font-matching problem in the Quark document that I'm trying to output to the platemaker that's crashing the PostScript rip? Did I remember about the elementary school that's booked a field trip to the press tomorrow? Did I get the annual reports on our existing grant in on time? Did I write all of those letters of reference? Did I finish reading the slush pile?

Of course not. Get back to work.

Editing is fractal by its very nature, producing more and more versions of texts that can be examined on a bewildering number of levels with increasing degrees of magnitude. As the edits pile up, so do the various administrative and affective tasks necessary to the continued daily operation of a literary press. The more successful the press, the greater the amount of paperwork, especially where the programs that sustain Canadian literary presses are concerned: the Canada Council Block Grant, the Book Publishing Industry Development Program, various provincial and municipal arts council grants. And editors just can't say no to any of it. Not if they want to remain editors.

Dealing with this perceived lack is "self-editing" in a very literal sense. As Miller and McHoul point out, since the writing of Immanuel Kant, it has been far from voluntary:

> The ability to draw on moral codes to order conduct becomes a requirement, an endless exercise of competition between desire, practice, individuality, and the collective. Self-determined subjectivity and broader social needs enter an ongoing struggle.... Originally whole, each person's ethical substance is split by the division of labor, when an aesthetically derived sense of full personhood separates from its social equivalent, and only cultivation (the humanities or therapy) can reconcile them. We can trace an entire series of dialectical investigations from this presumption that industrial society alienates human subjects from themselves, stretching from Hegel to Marx and beyond. (130)

The ethically incomplete editor is someone who is working hard to mend the split in his ethical substance by immersing himself in the making of culture itself. But the notion of "culture" has been ambivalent from the beginning. Not only does this mean that resorting to cultural practices as part of an attempt to become a better person or a better citizen is never a pure or easy solution; it also reasserts the very problems one is trying to escape. "With the emergence of capitalism's division of labor," writes Miller, "culture came both to embody instrumentalism and to abjure it, via the industrialization of farming, on the one hand, and the cultivation of individual taste, on the other hand" ("Creative" 89). Culture was industrial and instrumental before it was individual and aesthetic.

Beyond the agricultural origins of the metaphor of culture in its broadest sense, though, publishing and literature have always been part of the project of cultivating better citizens. The dilemma that ethical incompleteness presents is that, on the one hand, a certain amount of the anxiety it produces is necessary not just for personal growth, but for the ongoing maintenance and upkeep of that nebulous entity we call "the public good." On the other hand, the degree of politesse that ethical incompleteness instills is the best way of ensuring that none of the basic premises that determine the overall structure of the state, and the way that subjects are interpellated into it, are successfully challenged: "As the spread of literacy and printing saw customs and laws passed on, governed, and adjudicated through the written word, cultural texts supplemented and supplanted physical force as guarantors of authority" (Miller, "Creative" 89). Editing inserts the subject further into the snares of government bureaucracy and further into dilemmas of incompleteness. Yes, Canadian editors help make culture, but they also inevitably evaluate and produce it for the state, acting as cultural gatekeepers, determining what is valuable and what isn't, and who has access to it. Moreover, they do it for a pittance.

## EDITING AS OUTSOURCING

The results of a 2009 survey on the Editors Association of Canada (EAC) website provide some starting points for an assessment of what actual working conditions are like for an editor in this country.

The survey respondents were overwhelmingly female (88%) university educated (89%) freelancers (85%).[1] A large majority worked from an urban home office (70%) for local clients (67%). Signs of ethical incompleteness start to manifest themselves with statistics about their education; almost all were university educated (89%), but also regularly participated in continuing education (64%) and EAC workshops and seminars (78%).

Regarding the terms of their employment, 66% of the survey's respondents worked full-time as freelance editors. Only 12% worked exclusively in-house as employees. Another 20% indicated that they worked both in-house and freelance.

There are already warning indicators here that Canadian editors are not particularly well paid for their work. Aritha van Herk bluntly summarizes the situation: "The publishing industry flourishes on the dedication and hard work of mostly economically marginalized people" ("Publishing" 140). Having to work freelance as well as in-house is often an indicator that you need another job to pay for your job. That only 12% of the respondents to the survey worked in-house is perhaps as indicative of who the EAC draws its membership from (freelancers) as anything else, but it does indicate that a tiny fraction of the country's working editors have even a *chance* of receiving any sort of workplace benefits as part of their employment.

The reported salary range is large: 90% of full-time editors earned between $20,000 and $89,000 annually, with 66% earning between $30,000 and $70,000. The average income for this group was approximately $48,500, with at least two weeks' vacation.

It's important to remember that in the case of freelance editors, these salaries would be diminished greatly after taxes and expenses, not to mention niceties like dental, medical, and optical plans, and various forms of insurance. The notion of "at least two weeks' vacation" is freelance code for "no clients."

Being male, I was never a typical editor. But from a personal standpoint, these salaries seem high to me. While I was the Senior Editor (in-house) at Coach House Books (1997–2002), I never made more than $25,000/year before taxes, with no benefits of any sort. During the period before, during, and after my tenure at Coach House, my freelance editorial and consulting work never brought my annual gross over $50,000 (and this says nothing of the difficulties in getting paid when you invoice). Anecdotally, almost none of the literary editors I know are EAC members, so I suspect that the high end of the EAC salary range represents people who work in professional publishing (i.e., PR and advertising).

The preponderance of freelance editors over in-house editors points to something else that's worth considering: the role of outsourcing in large publishing companies. Many of the editors who receive a decent salary don't actually do all that much editing. They acquire titles (if they're lucky), and they manage the circulation of their texts through the company, which is more about logistics and bureaucracy than an assertion of one's aesthetics. The freelance population is as large as it is because most of the bigger publishers contract freelancers to do their copy editing and substantive editing. Editing at the professional level, if it is in-house, *is* bureaucracy.

The only exceptions to this situation that I know of are in the literary small presses. There, in exchange for retaining some degree of control over the editing and design of your books, you often have to place your own money on the line to run your publishing company yourself. Creating the conditions in which one has access to the full spectrum of editorial work requires a substantial degree of financial and personal risk in order to even presume to have one's hand on the levers of culture. One good question is how long the vague promises of eventual rewards (the Order of Canada? A civic Arts Award? Literary prizes for your titles?) will be enough to motivate people to continue to try. Another question is whether the mechanisms of sales reporting that digital culture has produced that are ostensibly there to help Canadian publishing might do more harm than good.

## BEFORE AND AFTER THE *ANNUS HORRIBILIS*

A large part of the reason for the perpetual anxiety that characterizes the life of the literary editor is the peculiar structure of the publishing process. Most book retailers don't actually pay publishers for the books they receive for several months (the standard during the period when I was editing was ninety days, though many booksellers of all sizes habitually took longer than that). Furthermore, unlike almost every other form of industry, publishers usually sell books to retailers on a consignment basis. In other words, most books can be returned by the retailer to the publisher for full credit—in some cases, even before the bills have come due. If the publisher has already been paid for the returned books, booksellers subtract credit from the invoice for the next season's titles.

In *The Perilous Trade: Book Publishing in Canada 1946–2006*, Roy MacSkimming notes that in the late 1990s, the industry standard for the proportion of returns on purchased titles was 20–30%, except at Chapters, the largest book retailer the country had ever seen. Their wholesale operation, Pegasus, habitually returned 50–60% of its purchases—and this after demanding a sales discount of more than 50% of the cover cost, which was also unusually high at the time (*Perilous* 365). The result of this system was a sort of shell game where booksellers filled their stores with titles they didn't actually pay for. Publishers had to hope that the books that they thought they sold actually did sell, or they could and would find themselves in a situation where they owed retailers credit for the previous season's returned books, their warehousers and distributors for restocking fees, and their printers for new books that they thought they had the funds to produce.

Referring to Canadian publishing as an "industry" is a polite neoliberal fiction that ignores the fact that the whole system is held together by the duct tape of government grants in the name of the public good. As Marc Côté has observed: "Whether or not reports and studies from UNESCO say otherwise, the simple truth is that this country does not have the necessary population with a common language to sustain a viable industry. Basic economics work against Canada sustaining four hundred companies producing six thousand titles a year in two official languages" (Côté 200). When any one element of this system encounters difficulties, it threatens to bring the whole mess crashing down with it.

This is exactly what happened during the years I was working at Coach House: a near-collapse of the Canadian literary publishing system. The Chapters chain failed due to overexpansion and was acquired by Trilogy Retail Enterprises (owners of Indigo) in 2001, destroying any remaining illusions of competition in Canadian book retailing by merging the two largest book retailers in the country. At the same time, and in part due to its inability to process the massive returns from Chapters, General Distribution, which managed warehousing and shipping for 62 Canadian publishers and about 140 other publishers, first stopped paying its bills to publishers, then lurched into bankruptcy after a shaky series of refinancing attempts (MacSkimming, *Perilous* 377–78). For these reasons, Aritha van Herk dubbed 2001 Canadian publishing's "*annus horribilis*" (129).

Coach House was one of twenty-five publishers that made it through this period in part due to an emergency bailout from the Book Publishing Industry Development Program (BPDIP). That, and we had just published one of the most successful books of poetry in Canadian history: Christian Bök's *Eunoia*. Alana Wilcox, Jason McBride, and I spent a very hot, sweaty, dirty summer doing all of our own shipping and mailing for *Eunoia* and our other titles, plus fighting with General to get our books and money back, plus all of the "normal" work that editing entails. On the one hand, Coach House very probably survived because of the success of *Eunoia*. On the other, it's teeth-grindingly maddening to think that the supply chain failed at the precise moment of the press's greatest success, because of what we might have accomplished with proper sales and distribution.

Understanding the way that the Canadian publishing industry was restructured after the Chapters/General debacles is necessary for any comprehension of the current, disastrous publishing environment. In response to calls for help from publishers and editors, and with their assistance after extensive consultation and research, the federal government put in place a system that was ostensibly designed to eliminate the problem of excessive returns, but ultimately remade the entire supply chain according to the logic of the Chapters-Indigo and Amazon databases. Ironically, BookNet, the arm's-length agency that was established to bring order to chaos by mediating between publishers and retailers, aided and abetted by data supplied by Canadian publishers themselves, made it more difficult and time-consuming than ever before to sell small press literature in Canada. And all of this occurred not despite but *because of* the good intentions and extra work of all parties involved.

By 2001–2, the Canadian government was well aware of the issues plaguing the publishing industry. Canadian Heritage's announcement in 2001 of the launch of its Supply Chain Initiative (SCI) funding program was the result of a process that began in 1999, at the behest of the Parliamentary Standing Committee on Canadian Heritage (MacLean 20). In 1999–2000, fourteen of the forty-four meetings the Standing Committee held concerned Canadian publishing, with extensive involvement from publishers and industry associations (21). During the same period, the committee also commissioned a group of Library of Parliament researchers and consultants to conduct an extensive background study (27). The SCI was thus part of the government's formal response to the twenty-five recommendations in the Standing Committee's report, *The Challenge of Change: A Consideration of the Canadian Book Industry* (30–34).

The SCI had three components: a new electronic data interchange (EDI) infrastructure for circulating standardized purchase orders and invoices; a protocol for standardized bibliographic data; and a national infrastructure for collecting, aggregating, and analyzing sales data culled from book retailers' point-of-sale systems and information from the publishers themselves. These modernizations were launched under the assurance that Chapters-Indigo, which now held a near-monopoly on physical book retail in Canada, would be mandating such standards for all suppliers in the near future (Maxwell 330–31). All three of these components were shepherded by BookNet Canada, a not-for-profit arm's-length agency established as part of the SCI.

BookNet is part and parcel of the changes that digital media have brought to the way the Canadian publishing supply chain operates. BookNet now tracks 75% of all Canadian book sales ("About BookNet") and conducts extensive, detailed analyses of bibliographic and sales data.

Scholars and scholarly institutions such as libraries have no access to BookNet's live data but may purchase *The Canadian Book Market* (C$109.99 for "non-subscriber" individuals, $399.99 for a company intranet licence). This is a dense collection of charts and graphs pertaining to the top-selling book titles of the year, including information on average weekly sales, peak week, and peak season sales; the market shares of particular publishers and distributors; comparative performance analyses organized by publication date, format, and price; and unit sales by week, median, and average pricing and summary statistics ("The Canadian Book Market").

Where do the raw data behind these statistics come from? It's supplied, voluntarily, by publishers on one end of the supply chain, and retailers on the other. In return for supplying this information, BookNet currently limits the availability of much of its data to subscribing publishers and retailers.

The relationship between literary editors and BookNet is a classic example of ethical incompleteness. Information that editors submit voluntarily (after a substantial amount of work, of course) is processed and handled by the cheerful, competent people at BookNet, who then make it available to the editors who submitted it, so that they can use it to diagnose their own relative successes and failures. However, they also make that information available to other members of the supply chain that editors might not always appreciate having that information, such as wholesalers and literary agents.

The result of the circulation of this information, as Stephen Henighan outlines in *Geist* magazine, is ambiguous at best:

> BookNet figures prevent authors from growing: your previous sales become your ceiling. It used to be common practice for writers to "move up" from smaller to bigger presses. Today, BookNet wisdom will decree that the author who has a track record of more than one or two books with literary presses, where sales are generally measured in the hundreds rather than the thousands, will sell only a predetermined number of copies. Chapters-Indigo, which controls more than 70 percent of book sales in Canada, will order only the copies required for a writer at this level of anticipated sales. The result is to render improbable publication of the author by a large press with a longer print run. Each book the author publishes closes down opportunities by confirming, or even reducing, the upper limit of his potential sales. Not surprisingly, agents, too, are now using BookNet figures to decide which manuscripts to represent. (Henighan n.pag.)

Where I'd part company with Henighan is in his implication that BookNet is a causative force in this relationship when it is actually symptomatic of a larger systemic logic. BookNet, or something like it, became necessary a decade ago, when Chapters-Indigo and Amazon began to demand increased efficiencies in the supply chain, requiring publishers to adapt to their database formats and their terms of service. Whatever their rationale, editors and publishers did the requested work.

BookNet is nothing if not well-meaning and well-liked among editors and publishers. Its annual PubFight game, a sort of fantasy sports league for publishers, is eagerly anticipated and receives a high degree of participation from Canadian publishers. Everyone plays along, without stopping to think too hard about how such a game reimagines the making of culture as part and parcel of the ruthless logic of the marketplace. Detailed sales data analysis is both poison and cure. We can't get rid of the former without losing the latter, so we're left in the difficult situation of having to figure out what to do next. Again, the notion of ethical incompleteness is useful here because it gives us a vocabulary to describe a situation where we have no choice but to begin in a compromised position. The question is what happens next.

## NONE OF THIS WILL BE YOURS

As Slavoj Žižek has insisted repeatedly over the years, the mode of contemporary ideology is no longer "They do not know what they are doing," but "They know exactly what they are doing, and they are still doing it" (28–29). It is at the precise moment that we believe that ideology has left us a little wiggle room and a little autonomy that it has us most firmly in its grasp (49). In his recent work on the applicability of Actor-Network Theory to Cultural Studies, Tony Bennett concurs, observing that many kinds of resistances operate "on the same level and by the same means as the forms of power they counter" (623). In my reading, this doesn't mean that the struggle takes place on even terrain; rather, that it's incapable of effecting systemic change.

The current politesse of relationships between scholar-editors and grant officers needs to be redefined. For Miller, the citizen is simply too polite, always operating within the borders of acceptable behaviour (*Well-Tempered* 223). And who could be more polite than a Canadian literary editor? While the protocols of ethical incompleteness may allow individuals to argue for equal rights as citizens, the imbrication of the notion of citizenship with doctrines of nation and economy places hard limits on what it's possible to accomplish under their sway.

The collective desire for greater efficiency in the publishing supply chain initially looked like it would help booksellers; after all, its first manifestation after the General Publishing collapse was in the form of bailout money that was reasonably easy to obtain. But a decade later, after all of the consulting and all of the meetings and all of the reports written by earnest, serious people trying to make things better, the outlook for Canadian small press literary publishing is much, much worse. The concentration of the field of Canadian book retailing in the hands of a few enormous companies continues; as of this writing, Amazon.com has abruptly pulled more than four thousand e-books from its site after trying to force the Independent Publisher's Group (IPG) to sell to them at a cheaper price. The change in terms Amazon demanded would see publishers and authors lose nearly another 10% of revenue to the retailer on both print and e-books, in the United States and Canada (Streitfield n.pag.). Those titles include books that I have written, and, if you're reading this, likely books that you have written as well. While the revenues that I stand to lose personally are tiny, the effect on my publishers is much greater. And I'd rather have a country where it's still possible for institutions like literary small presses to continue to exist.

Writers, editors, and publishers of small press literature in Canada need to find a way of proceeding that isn't mired in melancholy and nostalgia. The production and analysis of detailed sales data isn't going to go away, nor are the pressures on editors to continue to do more with less going to subside. Every new, potentially helpful development in the world of digital publishing will also have its downside. The current excitement around the efficacy of crowdfunding tools like Kickstarter and Indiegogo for the subvention of avant-garde publishing projects such as Caroline Bergvall, Laynie Brown, Teresa Carmody, and Vanessa Place's anthology *I'll Drown My Book: Conceptual Writing by Women*, for example, has the spectre of neoliberal funding cuts lurking behind it. In the face of *I'll Drown My Book*'s success—180 backers contributed a total of $8,904 when the project only required $4,000 to proceed (Les Figues Press)—an arts-hostile bureaucrat might reason as follows: if a direct appeal to the market can fund such things, then why do we need a Canada Council publishing program at all? Faced with such dilemmas, we need to imagine what it might be like to be editors who are also, improbably, both policy wonks and shit-disturbers. Otherwise, to paraphrase Will Self, one day none of this will be yours (21).

# Notes

## Literary and Editorial Theory and Editing Marian Engel
Christl Verduyn

1 As Hart and Hartman note in their collection, Georges Bataille claimed that while Blanchot was "not one of the most widely read French writers [he was] the most original mind of his age" (1). "Never a visible public presence"—indeed, Foucault described Blanchot as an "invisible presence"—recent "testimonies within France have continued to make Bataille's claim for Blanchot's significance less wild than it once seemed" (8), though it can still seem odd to "the people who, conditioned to the culture of fame, expect great minds to be familiar faces" (9).

2 Shillingsburg usefully identifies several different definitions of editing, from copy-editing, commercial editing, and newspaper editing to scholarly editing, which he breaks down into academic editing, critical editing, and scholarly editing (2).

3 The notion of a "hybrid" practice is not without precedent. For his work on Canadian poetry texts, D.R. Bentley developed a "'middle way' between intentionalist, eclectic-text editions and facsimile or diplomatic-transcript editions" (Irvine, "Editing" 75). This allowed him to "preserve[] not only 'as much as possible of the appearance and spatial dynamics of the original' but also features such as the author's idiosyncractic or irregular spelling and punctuation (Bentley, "Canadian Poetry Press" viii). While these editions still allow for emendation of obvious typographical and typesetting errors, the editor's intervention is reduced to a minimum" (Irvine, "Editing" 75).

4 Shillingsburg conceives of such as "an artifact. The word *artifact* seems especially suitable here because it subsumes the ideas of artistic construct and historic relic" (4). As I explain here, "rescue" or recovery work was part of the impetus behind the two projects on Engel's writing.

5 As Groden notes, though, only in the 1960s and 1970s did New Criticism come to influence editing theory and practice.

6 The parallel here to archival material seems obvious. Indeed, it strikes me that there is much to be gained not only from bringing together literary and textual theory, as Groden urges, but also bringing archival theory and practice to bear on the theory and practice of editing. I agree with Robin Schulze's claim that "the 'editors' of culture are not, for the most part, literary scholars, but archivists, curators, and librarians—the keepers of large collections of material objects who determine each day which pieces of the flotsam and jetsam of culture to save and which to toss out" (122).

7 The issue of "repetitive material" was also the basis on which I set aside a considerable amount of material in another editing project: Edna Staebler's diaries.
8 Detailed in the Introduction to the volume.

## We think differently. We have a different understanding": Editing Indigenous Texts as an Indigenous Editor
Kateri Akiwenzie-Damm

1 By this I mean oral or written stories or other forms of orature and literature. However, though I agree with Neal McLeod that "editing" occurs through mentoring in the oral tradition as well, for the purposes of this essay, I am focusing primarily on written forms.
2 This is not intended to be a comprehensive list; however, it does represent (arguably) the best-known writers published before 1980.
3 There are other less-established publishers, including Inuit publishers.
4 This is the main funding source for Canadian publishers. Its goal is to offset competition within the Canadian market from foreign/US publishers through a funding formula–based method of support. Francophone publishing was given its own funding formula to help "level the playing field" within Canada. Despite this, calls for an Aboriginal-specific formula that took into account our unique circumstances and challenges were rejected.
5 My understanding now is that this may no longer be the case, i.e., that Theytus Books may not be receiving this funding at this point.
6 Both the Circle of Aboriginal Publishers and Aboriginal Publishers of Canada are defunct, having failed to obtain support for the development of an Aboriginal publishing industry. After numerous meetings, and after responding to various calls for information, we were provided with a single joint Aboriginal Publishers catalogue covering the releases of all four publishers. Although we had not asked for such a catalogue, we were then jointly billed for the cost. We were also provided with a single Aboriginal Publishers banner, which the four publishers were expected to share by mailing it to one another. The stand required to display it was not provided—we were expected to rent it. Again, this was not something we had identified as necessary or useful. Not surprisingly, the banner was not used. Shortly after this, Kegedonce Press withdrew from discussions with Heritage Canada.
7 Other areas where development is needed include the following: developing and training Indigenous book designers, establishing Indigenous editing and design conventions, and developing Indigenous-specific distribution and promotions.
8 At Kegedonce Press, we find that activities undertaken to develop Indigenous publishing, such as developing editing practices and principles and a cadre of editors, are generally not taken into consideration by funders, or by their juries, whose members tend to focus almost exclusively on the number of books produced per year. Obviously, this favours publishers within an established industry. We have also been penalized for not using mainstream "professional" editors and book designers, who would, presumably, force us to conform to mainstream conventions and sensibilities. A few years ago, our publishing program was harshly criticized and penalized by a jury for using "non-professional" (i.e., Indigenous) editors and designers. Although it is part of our mandate to work with Indigenous editors, designers, and illustrators whenever possible, we do ensure that they are qualified and experienced professionals. We often do use "professional" non-Indigenous editors and designers as well. Perhaps because these non-Indigenous editors and designers work with us in a respectful way that supports our goals and do not simply try to impose mainstream publishing conventions on us, they are deemed "non-professional." To call Indigenous editors and designers "non-professional" is arrogant in the extreme and colonial in practice.

9 Some of these arise from government and Indian Act definitions such as "Status," "non-Status," "Bill C-31 Indians," "Bill C-3 Indians," "on reserve," "off reserve," and so on.

10 These circumstances would be somewhat rare, but I believe it would be incumbent on the editor to let the writer know, for example, whether certain choices (swearing in a book aimed at a high school audience, for example) might have a substantial negative impact on the sales success of the book so that the writer can make informed decisions about whether or not to make changes and how to make these changes, if desired.

11 I believe it was one of our authors, Richard Van Camp, who first began using this term.

12 For example, when an article or book, or key parts of these, are based on extensive interviews (i.e., the knowledge of an informant), authorship should be shared. As an Anishnaabekwe, it seems counter-intuitive to me that for published interviews, it is usually only the person asking the questions who is credited as the "author." I have advocated for and gotten co-authorship credit for myself in specific cases. Although there is more work to be done in the area of editing and intellectual property in an Indigenous context, editors of Indigenous texts must understand First Nations Principles of OCAP (Ownership, Control, Access, and Possession). Developed through the First Nations Information and Governance Centre, OCAP principles provide a framework for First Nations to assert their jurisdiction over their intellectual property in ways that are meaningful and important to them.

13 For this section I am indebted to the invaluable input of Warren Cariou and Neal McLeod.

14 Here I attempt to link these principles with the Anishinaabe Seven Grandfather teachings/principles in order to show more fully how these principles for editing Indigenous writers align with my Anishinaabe cultural values and beliefs.

## Toward Establishing an—or *the*—"Archive" of African-Canadian Literature
George Elliott Clarke

1 American philosopher of history Hayden White observes that "we require a history that will educate us to discontinuity more than ever before; for discontinuity, disruption, and chaos is our lot" (White 50). Disjuncture is certainly the fate of any narrative of African-Canadian literature.

2 The tyranny of the new is that it pretends that hard-fought victories are "miracles" and that routs are "preordained"—that history is not made, but "born."

3 As Marianne Korn has said in her study of American poet Ezra Pound, "historical truth is not necessarily fact to be received, simple and unchanged, unmediated …: but rather a 'rag-bag' of details whose status is uncertain, whose truths are unclear, and whose causal links have vanished" (Korn 8).

4 I am deliberately jocular here, for I want to normalize the notion of people of African provenance being also, simultaneously, Canadian. So, if there are Canucks, to use the jocular term, so can there be Black Canucks. Of course, African-Canadian is a more "correct" phrase, though Black Canadian is also fine. To refer to the historical black communities of the Maritime provinces, especially Nova Scotia, I do use, occasionally, my neologism, "Africadian[s]," who reside, thus, in "Africadia."

5 What is so scary about the endeavour to recover early African-Canadian texts and writers? What is it that we do not want them to say to us? That *we* are *not* the "first"?

6 See my "Must All Blackness Be American?" (1996).

7 How does our understanding of the history of English-Canadian poetry shift if we include James Madison Bell as a "Confederation Poet"?

8 The Chorale's website provides a photograph of—and rightly laudatory bio for—Dett ("Roots").

9  If one accepts my arguments, Fouché published both the first African/Black-Canadian book of poetry *and* the first African/Black-Canadian play in French, both in Haiti. This fact should make him a francophone African-Canadian writer that we must study.

## Project Editing in Canada: Challenges and Compromises
Carole Gerson

1  See Cowan and Michon for one of the few such discussions.
2  See Campbell, *Both Hands*, Thomas and Lennox, Lennox and Lacombe, Evain, and the discussion of William Toye in Saltman and Edwards.
3  Susanna Moodie's *Roughing It in the Bush*, ed. Michael A. Peterman; L.M. Montgomery's *Anne of Green Gables*, ed. Mary Rubio and Elizabeth Waterston; and Stephen Leacock's *Sunshine Sketches of a Little Town*, ed. D.M.R. Bentley.
4  See Friskney.
5  The first was edited by Halpenny, and the second by Lennox and Paterson; also see Coldwell.
6  For examples of collection editors' accounts of their experiences, see Gustafson, Kroller, and Lecker ("Materialising").
7  The four volumes I have edited or co-edited are *The Prose of Life: Sketches from Victorian Canada* (1981), *Vancouver Short Stories* (1985), *Canadian Poetry: The Beginnings through the First World War* (1994), and *E. Pauline Johnson: Collected Poetry and Selected Prose* (2002).
8  I address these issues in Gerson, "Design and Ideology"; "'The Most Canadian'"; "Sarah Binks"; and "Anthologies."
9  See Piternick, England, and Klinck.
10 See Fleming ("National") and Lamonde ("*L'histoire*").
11 These are the Bibliography of the History of the Book in Canada / Bibliographie d'histoire du livre et de l'imprimé au Canada; Canadian Book Trade and Library Index / Index canadien des métiers du livre et des bibliothèques; Catalogues canadiens relatifs à l'imprimé / Canadian Book Catalogues; Imprimés canadiens avant 1840 / Canadian Imprints to 1840; and Manuels scolaires canadiens / Canadian Textbooks. See MacDonald.
12 Fleming, Gallichan, and Lamonde, eds., *History of the Book in Canada*, Vol. 1: *Beginnings to 1840*. Hereafter referred to as *HBiC* 1.
13 Lamonde, Fleming, and Black, eds., *History of the Book in Canada*. Vol. 2: *1840–1918*. Hereafter referred to as *HBiC* 2.
14 Gerson and Michon, eds., *History of the Book in Canada*, Vol. 3: *1918–80*. Hereafter referred to as *HBiC* 3.
15 The initial price of Volume 1 (540 pages in the English edition, 570 in French) was $75, while Volume 2 (659 pages in English, 694 in French) and Volume 3 (638 pages in English, 671 in French) each cost $85. The three English volumes were also issued as a set for $200.
16 The first volume of the History of the Book in America, *The Colonial Book in the Atlantic World* (2000) deals only with the original thirteen colonies. Hispanic print culture isn't discussed until the fourth volume, *Print in Motion: The Expansion of Publishing and Reading in the United States, 1880–1940* (2009), and all volumes omit Alaska and Hawaii, which became states in 1959.
17 William Barker, "Books and Reading in Newfoundland and Labrador," *HBiC* 1, 361–68.
18 Claudette Hould, "The livre d'artiste," *HBiC* 3, 372–74.
19 Patricia Kennedy, "Scrip: Printing Eighteenth-Century Currency," *HBiC* 1, 227–29; John Hare, "An Election in the Press: Lower Canada, 1792," *HBiC* 1, 219–20; Patricia Lockhart Fleming, "Printing an Election: Upper Canada, 1836," *HBiC* 1, 220–22; Patricia Kennedy,

"Printing for Public and Private Business," *HBiC* 1, 222–27; Eli MacLaren, "*Facies cholerica*: The Record of Cholera in Print," *HBiC* 1, 303–6.

20  John Willis, "Business by the Book: The Mail-Order Catalogue," *HBiC* 2, 412–13; Elizabeth Driver, "Cookbooks," *HBiC* 2, 408–11; Michel Brisebois, "Posters and Handbills," *HBiC* 2, 111–15.

21  Ian Stevenson, "The CPR in Print," *HBiC* 3, 272–75.

22  Oxford University Press set up its Canadian office in 1904, Macmillan in 1905, and both J.M. Dent and Thomas Nelson in 1913; see MacLaren.

23  Cornelius J. Jaenan, "Native, Oral and Inscribed Discourse," *HBiC* 1, 13–18.

24  François-Marc Gagnon, "Conversion through the Printed Image," *HBiC* 1, 18–20; Joyce M. Banks, "'And not hearers only': Books in Native Languages," *HBiC* 1, 278–89; Cornelius J. Jaenen, "Aboriginal Communities," *HBiC* 2, 33–40; Blanca Schorcht, "Intersections between Native Oral Traditions and Print Culture," *HBiC* 3, 29–34; Cheryl Suzack, "Publishing For and By Aboriginal Communities," *HBiC* 3, 293–97; Brendan Edwards, "Reading on the 'Rez,'" *HBiC* 3, 501–5.

25  Yvan Lamonde, Peter F. McNally, and Andrea Rotundo, "Public Libraries and the Emergence of a Public Culture," *HBiC* 2, 256.

26  Paul Hjartarson, "Icelandic Authorship in Canada," *HBiC* 2, 136–39.

27  Lorne Bruce and Elizabeth Hanson, "The Rise of the Public Library in English Canada," *HBiC* 3, 429–35.

28  See Greenwald.

29  Archana Rampure, "'Harlequin Has Built an Empire,'" *HBiC* 3, 185–88.

30  See McCleery and K. Bode and Osborne.

## Editing Without Author(ity): Martha Ostenso, Periodical Studies, and the Digital Turn
Hannah McGregor

1  *Wild Geese* was adapted in 1926 as a silent film. Atherton claims it was adapted a second time in a 1941 version starring Henry Fonda (4, 36n14), but *Wild Geese Calling* was in fact based on a novel of the same name by America author Stewart Edward White. *Wild Geese* was adapted for a second time in 2001 under the title *After the Harvest*.

2  The current critical moment may in fact be ideal for such a revaluation of Ostenso, characterized as it is by the rise of middlebrow studies and increasing interest in the transnational formulations of early print culture (see, for example, Gerson, "Writers without Borders").

3  For more on the twentieth-century concern with establishing the criteria for Canadian literature, see Mount.

4  Most of the gaps seem to lie in Canadian periodicals, an unsurprising omission, as Buckley is an American scholar. Michelle Smith has discovered at least three previously undocumented stories in *Chatelaine* alone (see McGregor and Smith).

5  Scholars Kenneth Price and Ed Folsom have debated adequate terminology for large-scale digital editorial projects such as their own *Walt Whitman Archive*. The fact that they arrive at different conclusions suggests the ongoing problematic of naming new forms of research production.

6  See the Spring 2009 issue of *Digital Humanities Quarterly*, "Done," edited by Matthew G. Kirschenbaum, which engages with the problematic of finishing large-scale digital humanities projects.

7  A version of this work was done when EMiC UA, in collaboration with the University of Alberta Library Digital Initiatives and the Manitoba Legislative Library, facilitated the digitization of *The Western Home Monthly*, including the five-part serialization of *Wild Geese*. For more on this work see modmag.ca.

8   It must be noted that periodical studies in general has its roots in the Victorian period; for more on the field's longer histories, and the problematic discontinuities between Victorian and modern periodical studies, see DiCenzo.

9   This narrative draws on the work of Sean Latham, Robert Scholes, Clifford Wulfman, and David M. Earle, all major scholars in the area of periodical studies.

10   Latham discussed the serendipitous nature of periodical reading during his keynote at the 2010 Conference on Editorial Problems (23 October 2010); see Lathman, "Unpacking."

## Editing the Letters of Wilfred and Sheila Watson, 1956–1961: Scholarly Edition as Digital Practice
Paul Hjartarson, Harvey Quamen, and EMiC UA

We could not have undertaken these projects without the support of Shirley Neuman, literary executor of the Wilfred Watson estate, and F.T. Flahiff, literary executor of the Sheila Watson estate. Thank you. Thanks are also due to Ernie Ingles, Mary-Jo Romaniuk, and Geoffrey Harder at the University of Alberta Libraries, and to Raymond Frogner, archivist at the University of Alberta Archives when we began our work; to Jonathan Bengtson, former Head Librarian, and to Michael Bramah, Gabrielle Earnshaw, Kate Van Dusen, and Jessica Barr at the John M. Kelly Library; to Susan Brown, Mariana Paredes-Olea, and Jeff Antoniuk at CWRC; and to Dean Irvine, Matt Huculak, Zailig Pollock, Vanessa Lent, and Emily Ballantyne at EMiC. Although we have taken the lead in writing this article, we are building on the work of other members of the EMiC UA collaboratory: Matt Bouchard, Kristin Fast, Raymond Frogner, Andrea Hasenbank, Hannah McGregor, Joe MacKinnon, Charlotte Nobles, and Kristine Smitka.

1   As Susan Hockey notes in "The History of Humanities Computing," "unlike many other interdisciplinary experiments, humanities computing has a very well-known beginning" (para. 3). The date is 1949; the project, Father Roberto Busa's decision "to make an *index verborum* of all the words in the works of St Thomas Aquinas and related authors, totaling some 11 million words of medieval Latin" (para. 3).

2   We use "approximately" as a modifier here because our count of the letters is necessarily preliminary.

## The Politics of Recovery and the Recovery of Politics: Editing Canadian Writing on the Spanish Civil War
Bart Vautour

1   There is a branch of recent textual scholarship that understands the ways in which some occasional literature occupies an important position of ephemerality. Textual scholars who study the transitions into print cultures have usefully split the category of occasional literature into texts and performances, based on a separation between print culture and manuscript culture. Under the rubric of manuscript culture, the term "performance" designates more than an oral presentation. The term is used "to designate any unenduring presentation of a text to a necessarily restricted audience" (Pebworth 64–65). Unlike the history of occasional literature in manuscript culture, in which a text is often not pseudo-stabilized in any authorial way through publication, the dominance of public print culture has shifted the value of literary production away from semi-private manuscript culture, though manuscript culture certainly remains important to textual scholars.

2   See Vautour.

3   Even a partial record of poets who have written on the events surrounding the Spanish Civil War reads like an anthology of modern poetry in Canada: Patrick Anderson, Louis Dudek, Ralph Gustafson, Leo Kennedy, A.M. Klein, Irving Layton, Kenneth Leslie,

Dorothy Livesay, P.K. Page, E.J. Pratt, F.R. Scott, Raymond Souster, A.M. Stephen, Miriam Waddington, Patrick Waddington, Joe Wallace, and George Woodcock, among others. During the conflict itself, two novels with strong Canadian connections were published that dealt directly with the events in Spain: Charles Yale Harrison's *Meet Me on the Barricades* (1938) and Ted Allan's *This Time a Better Earth* (1939). Spain plays a big part in post-conflict novels such as Malcolm Lowry's *Under the Volcano* (1947), Hugh Garner's *Cabbagetown* (1950; revised 1968), Hugh MacLennan's *The Watch That Ends the Night* (1959), Mordecai Richler's *Joshua Then and Now* (1980), which was dedicated to Ted Allan, Mark Frutkin's *Slow Lightning* (2001), Dennis Bock's *The Communist's Daughter* (2006), June Hutton's *Underground* (2009), and, most recently, Stephen Collis's *The Red Album* (2013). To consult an ever-expanding bibliography of Canadian texts associated with the Spanish Civil War, see spanishcivilwar.ca

4 The contradiction between popular support for the Spanish government and the lack of support provided by Western democracies, some have argued, was the beginning of the end for the international liberal order as embodied in the League of Nations. In other words, the failure of Western democracies to aid the Spanish government may have played a large part in ushering in the end of liberal political modernity, only to be superseded by neoliberal economic sovereignty.

5 In 1995 Nicola Vulpe edited a non-trade anthology of Canadian poetry about the Spanish Civil War in an edition of 1,000 titled *Sealed in Struggle*.

6 First published in *New Frontier* (July–August 1937) under the title "The Censored Editor," the poem was published in *By Stubborn Stars and Other Poems* (1938) and *Protestant Digest* (1939) as "Fifth Columnist," and in *O'Malley to the Reds and Other Poems* (1972) as "A Kiss for Guido / An Episode in the Franco Rebellion—1961."

7 See Pollock, "The Editor."

## Keeping the Code: Narrative and Nation in Donna Bennett and Russell Brown's *An Anthology of Canadian Literature in English*
Robert Lecker

1 In terms of Canadian literature, I am particularly indebted to the work of Brydon ("Metamorphoses"), Davey, Gerson ("Anthologies," "The Canon," "Cultural Darwinism," *A Purer Taste*), Irvine (*Editing Modernity*), Kamboureli ("Canadian Ethnic Anthologies"), Keith, Kertzer, Knight, MacGillivray, Mackey, Mandel, and Miki. Research on anthology formation outside Canada includes articles and books by Benedict, Churchman, Dike, Di Leo, Fraistat, Johnson, Kuipers, Lauter, Longenbach, Nelson ("Murder in the Cathedral"), Parry, Price, Rasula, and Schrift. An important symposium on anthology formation—including commentary by Leitch, Johnson, Finke, and Williams—appeared in 2003 (see Leitch et al.).

2 Different editions of the anthology will be cited by publication year for the sake of clarity.

3 Anna Jameson, Sara Jeannette Duncan, Pauline Johnson, Marjorie Pickthall, Joy Kogawa, Daphne Marlatt, Sandra Birdsell, Paulette Jiles, Lorna Crozier, and Dionne Brand. Other new additions to this edition include Timothy Findley, Mordecai Richler, Fred Wah, and Rohinton Mistry.

4 These include Saukampee, Maria Campbell, Harry Robinson, Thomas King, and Tomson Highway.

5 J.G. Sime, Emily Carr, Lucy Maud Montgomery, Adele Wiseman, Carol Shields, Anne Carson, Bronwen Wallace, Jan Zwicky, Jane Urquhart, Anne Michaels, and Stephanie Bolster.

### Performing Editors: Juggling Pedagogies in the Production of *Canadian Literature in English: Texts and Contexts*
Laura Moss and Cynthia Sugars

1   Arguably it was partly Dennis Lee's point in his 1972 essay "Cadence, Country, Silence"—and to a certain extent Atwood's in *Survival*—that there was an inherent discomfort in the inherited Canadian concept of here/not-here. But these authors could assume that their readers would share their unease and welcome their intervention in the reclaiming of Canadian colonial space. They assumed that the term "Canadian" could refer to a unified body, even if that body was defined by "spacelessness."

2   We are extremely grateful to the many anonymous readers who reviewed our original proposal and the seven subsequent chapters. We appreciate their many hours of work in providing us with extensive feedback, and we engage with their comments in a spirit of collegiality. Their comments not only helped us make our selections for the anthology but also helped us articulate and work through our pedagogical aims for the book.

3   Many thanks to Albert Braz for prompting us to articulate our editorial and pedagogical principles more explicitly.

4   Both poems were courageous given that they went against the grain of widely held public and state opinion at the time. Indeed, Johnson's "A Cry from an Indian Wife" appeared in the same issue of *The Week* (18 June 1885) that ran an article detailing the hunting down of the "dangerous" Aboriginal "outlaw" Chief Big Bear. That Johnson wrote the piece before she was a renowned public figure says something about her force of will—and her commitment to ideas of Aboriginal land title—that led her to publish the piece. When considered in this context, "A Cry from an Indian Wife" acquires even more resonance in its relation to her other poems, such as "Ojistoh" and "The Corn Husker," which relate the progressive degradation and disenfranchisement of Indigenous peoples on their own land.

5   The phrase "move over" is an allusion to Lee Maracle's statement at the June 1988 Third International Feminist Book Fair that it was time for non-Indigenous writers to step aside and give Indigenous authors a space to tell their own stories. We tried to do this not only by including Johnson's poem about the Northwest Rebellion but also by including an excerpt from Riel's address to the Jury in 1885.

6   This is an allusion to the pivotal "Writing Thru Race" conference that took place in Vancouver in 1994. The conference addressed questions of appropriation and representation, and, controversially, restricted the attendance of its daytime events to writers of colour. It thus posed a challenge to white mainstream authors and the Canadian publishing industry.

### Labours of Love and Cutting Remarks: The Affective Economies of Editing
Kate Eichhorn and Heather Milne

1   Massumi argues that emotions and affects may be distinguished on the basis of the fact that emotions can be "owned and recognized" (28), whereas affect cannot; by contrast, we maintain that neither emotions nor affects are subject to the constraints of ownership.

### bpNichol, Editor
Frank Davey

1   After finding a copy of *The Double Hook* and reading it along with novels by Kerouac, Burroughs, and Trocchi, Nichol wrote in his first notebook, sometime in January 1964, that there is "nothing left for you to do in prose" and that all he could hope to do is write poetry.

2 Nichol wrote this letter on 8 August 1980, as a comment on the interview "Questions (Some Answers)," which he, Steve McCaffery, George Bowering, and I had conducted with Dudek the month before (Dudek et al.).

3 When interviewed in the 1970s about this period, he usually describes his poetry as "arrogant," telling Dwight Gardiner in 1976 that he was not "giving myself up to the process of writing" (Nichol, *Meanwhile* 154), and Caroline Bayard and Jack David later that year that he had been automatically "imposing some sort of preconceived notion of wisdom on the occasion of writing" (Bayard and David 19). The remarks echo Olson's 1954 essay "Against Wisdom as Such" and Olson's injunction against "arrogating" oneself over nature in his 1951 essay "Projective Verse," the latter re-published in Donald Allen's *The New American Poetry, 1945–60* (1961) and both republished in 1965 in Olson's collection *Human Universe*. Nichol seems to have first heard about the "Against Wisdom" essay in 1963, and to have read it in 1964 (Multineddu 34).

4 One instance of such guilt was occasioned by his editing of Ian Hamilton Finlay's *The Boys Alphabet Book* for Coach House. Nichol had accepted the book for the press in January 1973. On 10 December Finlay complains to Nichol that he "never answered my last letter," and on 23 December 1974 he writes that he is "irked" by the project's lack of progress. On 20 February 1975 he writes that he needs more communication from Coach House. On 14 March 1977 the British photographer for the project, Dave Paterson, writes to Nichol "somewhat in despair, over the continued non-appearance" of the book. On 20 April 1977, Finlay's wife Sue writes to Nichol "as a representative of Coach House Press," tells him "the way this project has been treated by Coach House is disgraceful," and demands that he return the manuscript and all photographs. The book is eventually printed, and the Finlays receive copies on 12 November 1977. Finlay sends a brief note, "Many thanks for the copies of the Alphabet Book."

5 Drafts of this work exist under other titles: "The First Book of John Cannyside," *Notebook begun March 13, 1971*, MsC 12.d.13, likely March 1971; "John Cannyside," *Notebook begun March 13, 1971*, MsC 12.d.13, likely May 1971 and July 1971; "John Cannyside," *Notebook "begun July 15, 1971 for working on John Cannyside*," MsC 12.d.13, July 1971; *No Tree Book begun February 18 1983*, MsC12.d.13, May 3, 1985; *The 'Four Years Later ...' Notebook of bpNichol begun July 14 1986*, November 13, 1986; "John Cannyside Part 3," *The Way Notebook begun July 23/1977*, MsC 12.d.13, likely November 1977.

6 Nichol and McCaffery use double closing quotation marks here to create a word that will differentiate a Canadian from a European 'pataphysics. The two poets had collaboratively written and published numerous essays on writing theory as "TRG" during the 1970s. McCaffery edited and published a collection of these in 1992 as *Rational Geomancy: The Kids of the Book Machine: The Collected Research Reports of the Toronto Research Group 1973–1982*.

7 "I have, for a long time, been working toward the unification of what have seemed to many ... as the disparate areas of my concern. The focal point of that unification process remains THE MARTYROLOGY ..." (2).

8 After Nichol's death in 1988 the Underwhich collective published only occasionally, and in many years not at all; by the mid-1990s its membership had fallen to three. It is currently inactive.

## Air, Water, Land, Light, and Language: Reflections on the Commons and Its Contents
Robert Bringhurst

1 The etymology of Latin *elementum* is, as they say, disputed; it is therefore a topic that many conventional dictionaries simply do not touch. But see for instance Klein, s.v. "element."

2   This again is Crawley's translation, and the passage quoted by Machan follows this sentence directly. The original reads as follows: χρόνιοί τε ξυνιόντες ἐν βραχεῖ μὲν μορίῳ σκοποῦσί τι τῶν κοινῶν, τῷ δὲ πλέονι τὰ οἰκεῖα πράσσουσι, καὶ ἕκαστος οὐ παρὰ τὴν ἑαυτοῦ ἀμέλειαν οἴεται βλάψειν, μέλειν δέ τινι καὶ ἄλλῳ ὑπὲρ ἑαυτοῦ τε προϊδεῖν, ὥστε τῷ αὐτῷ ὑπὸ ἁπάντων ἰδίᾳ δοξάσματι λανθάνειν τὸ κοινὸν ἁθρόον φθειρόμενον. Crawley's translation is perfectly sound; so is the older translation of Thomas Hobbes. Here, for comparison, is a third: "They come together reluctantly, devoting little time to public issues and a lot of time to their own domestic affairs; and each supposes his own neglect portends no misdirection [in public affairs], for they are someone else's concern; they fail to see how, through everyone's taking a similar view, the public interest is destroyed."

3   The statement comes from an unpublished interview with Everson, conducted by Ruth Teiser on 13 December 1965. See *Brother Antoninus: Poet, Printer, and Religious* (Mss BANC 67/92c, Bancroft Library, University of California at Berkeley, 1966), 10.

4   This is the opening statement of Geddes's entry on Lee in the old *Oxford Companion to Canadian Literature*, edited by William Toye (1983).

5   There will, I believe, be a book-length study of Goluska's work in due time. Meanwhile, see Bringhurst, "Glenn Goluska."

6   I borrow the term "more-than-human," with gratitude, from my friend David Abram—though I see that in doing so I have skimped on its definition. For a broader view, see Abram.

7   The results form a trilogy consisting of one, rather oversized, introductory volume and two volumes of translation: (1) Bringhurst, *A Story as Sharp as a Knife: The Classical Haida Mythtellers and Their World*; (2) Ghandl of the Qayahl Llaanas, *Nine Visits to the Mythworld*; (3) Skaay of the Qquuna Qiighawaay, *Being in Being: The Collected Works of a Master Haida Mythteller*.

8   Dwight Macdonald published a remarkable essay on this subject in 1945 titled "The Responsibility of Peoples," reprinted in *The Responsibility of Peoples, and Other Essays in Political Criticism*.

9   See for instance Gary Snyder, *A Place in Space: Ethics, Aesthetics, and Watersheds,* and John Ralston Saul, *A Fair Country: Telling Truths about Canada.* For a little more background, see also Snyder, *He Who Hunted Birds in His Father's Village: The Dimensions of a Haida Myth,* 2nd ed., with a foreword by Robert Bringhurst.

## The Ethically Incomplete Editor
Darren Wershler

1   All statistics in this section from Grondahl et al.

# Works Cited

"About BookNet." *BookNet Canada*. BookNet Canada, 2007–9. http://www.booknet canada.ca/index.php?option=com_content&view=article&id=426&Itemid=137

Abram, David. *The Spell of the Sensuous*. New York: Pantheon, 1996.

Achebe, Chinua. "An Image of Africa: Racism in Conrad's *Heart of Darkness*." In *Hopes and Impediments: Selected Essays 1967–1985*. London: Heinemann, 1988. 1–13.

Adams, Thomas R., and Nicholas Barker. "A New Model for the Study of the Book." *A Potencie of Life: Books in Society*. Ed. Nicholas Barker. London: British Library, 1993. 5–43.

Ahmed, Sara. "Affective Economies." *Social Text* 22.2 (2004): 117–39.

———. *The Cultural Politics of Emotion*. Edinburgh: Edinburgh UP, 2004.

———. *The Promise of Happiness*. Durham: Duke UP, 2010.

Akiwenzie-Damm, Kateri. "Daniel Heath Justice: Speaking His Truth." *First Nations House Magazine* 1.2 (2009): 12–14.

———. "Survivance: Talking with Gerald Vizenor." *Rampike* (Spring 2011): 22–28.

Allan, Ted. *This Time a Better Earth*. New York: Morrow, 1939.

Allen, Donald M. *The New American Poetry 1945–60*. New York: Grove, 1961.

Anderson, Benedict. *Imagined Communities: Reflections on the Origin and Spread of Nationalism*. London: Verso, 1991.

Anderson, Margaret. *My Thirty Years' War: An Autobiography*. New York: Covici, Friede, 1930.

Andrew, Caroline, Monica Gattinger, M. Sharon Jeannette, and Will Straw, eds. *Accounting for Culture: Thinking Through Cultural Citizenship*. Ottawa: U of Ottawa P, 2005.

"*Anne of Green Gables* (1908)." In Lefebvre, ed. 3: 51–68.

Armstrong, Jeanette. "The Disempowerment of First North American Native Peoples and Empowerment through Their Writing." In *An Anthology of Canadian Native Literature in English*. Ed. Daniel David Moses and Terry Goldie. 2nd ed. Toronto: Oxford UP, 1998. 239–42.

Arnason, David. Afterword. *Wild Geese*. By Martha Ostenso. Toronto: McClelland and Stewart, 1989. 303–9.

———. "The Development of Prairie Realism: Robert J.C. Stead, Douglas Durkin, Martha Ostenso, and Frederick Philip Grove." Diss. U of New Brunswick, 1980.

"As You Like It." *McCall's Magazine* 65 (September 1938): 2.

Ashcroft, Bill, Gareth Griffiths, and Helen Tiffin. *The Empire Writes Back: Theory and Practice in Post-Colonial Literature*. London and New York: Routledge, 1989.

Atherton, Stanley S. "Martha Ostenso and Her Works." In *Canadian Writers and Their Works: Fiction Series*. Vol. 4. Ed. Robert Lecker, Jack David, and Ellen Quigley. Toronto: ECW, 1991. 211–53.

Atwood, Margaret. *Survival: A Thematic Guide to Canadian Literature*. Toronto: Anansi, 1972.

Austin, Allan D. "Delany, Martin R." *The Oxford Companion to African American Literature*. New York: Oxford UP, 1997. 205–6.

Badaracco, Claire Hoertz. *Trading Words: Poetry, Typography, and Illustrated Books in the Modern Literary Economy*. Baltimore: Johns Hopkins UP, 1995.

Badiou, Alain. *Being and Event*. London: Continuum, 2005.

Ballantyne, Emily, and Zailig Pollock. "Respect des Fonds and the Digital Page." In *Archival Narratives for Canada: Retelling Stories in a Changing Landscape*. Ed. Kathleen Garay and Christl Verduyn. Halifax: Fernwood, 2011. 184–201.

Barber, John. "Where Have All the Book Editors Gone?" *Globe and Mail*, 4 February 2011. http://www.theglobeandmail.com/arts/books-and-media/where -have-all-the-book-editors-gone/article565446

Bayard, Caroline, and Jack David. *Out-Posts/Avant-Postes*. Erin: Porcepic, 1978.

Beale, Alison C.M., and Annette Van Den Bosch, eds. *Ghosts in the Machine: Women and Cultural Policy in Canada and Australia*. Toronto: Garamond, 1998.

Beck, Kent, with Cynthia Andres. *Extreme Programming Explained: Embrace Change*. 2nd ed. New York: Addison-Wesley, 2005.

Bell, Bill, Philip Bennett, and Jonquil Bevan, eds. *Across Boundaries: The Book in Culture and Commerce*. Winchester and New Castle: St. Paul's Bibliographies and Oak Knoll, 2000.

Bell, James Madison. "Modern Moses, or 'My Policy' Man." *African American Poetry of the Nineteenth Century: An Anthology*. Ed. Joan R. Sherman. Urbana: U of Illinois P, 1992. 199–209.

Benedict, Barbara. *Making the Modern Reader: Cultural Mediation in Early Modern Literary Anthologies*. Princeton: Princeton UP, 1996.

———. "The Paradox of the Anthology: Collecting and Différence in Eighteenth-Century Britain." *New Literary History: A Journal of Theory and Interpretation* 34.2 (2003): 231–56.

Benjamin, Walter. "The Storyteller: Reflections on the Works of Nikolai Leskov." In *Illuminations*. Ed. Hannah Arendt. Trans. Harry Zohn. New York: Schocken, 1968. 83–109.

Bennett, Ethel Hume. "Biographical Notes." *New Harvesting: Contemporary Canadian Poetry, 1918–1938*. Ed. Ethel Hume Bennett. Toronto: Macmillan, 1938. 193–99.

Bennett, Tony. "Making Culture, Changing Society." *Cultural Studies* 21.4 (2007): 610–29.

Bentley, D.M.R. "Canadian Poetry Oress Editions." *Canadian Poetry* 27 (Fall/Winter 1990): v–xi.

Berg, A. Scott. *Max Perkins: Editor of Genius*. 1978. New York: Simon and Schuster, 2013.

Betts, Gregory. *Avant-Garde Canadian Literature: The Early Manifestations*. Toronto: U of Toronto P, 2013.

Betts, Gregory, Paul Hjartarson, and Kristina Smitka, eds. *Counterblasting Canada: Marshall McLuhan, Wyndham Lewis, Wilfred Watson, and Sheila Watson*. Edmonton: U of Alberta P, 2016.

Bissett, Bill. *We Sleep Inside Each Other All*. Intro. Sam Perry. Afterword bpNichol. *Ganglia* 4. Toronto: Ganglia, 1966.

Black, Fiona A. "Print Culture History: Geographical Perspectives." http://pchgp .management.dal.ca

Blackford, Holly, ed. *Anne with an "e": The Centennial Study of* Anne of Green Gables. Calgary: U of Calgary P, 2009.

Blanchot, Maurice. *Le Livre à venir*. Paris: Éditions Gallimard, 1959.

——. *The Book to Come*. Trans. Charlotte Mandell. Stanford: Stanford UP, 2003.

Bock, Dennis. *The Communist's Daughter*. Toronto: HarperCollins, 2006.

Bode, Katherine, and Roger Osborne. "Book History from the Archival Record." In *The Cambridge Companion to the History of the Book*. Ed. Leslie Howsam. Cambridge: Cambridge UP, 2015. 219–36.

Bode, Rita, and Lesley D. Clement, eds. *L.M. Montgomery's Rainbow Valleys: The Ontario Years, 1911–1942*. Montreal and Kingston: McGill–Queen's UP, 2015.

Bornstein, George, ed. *Representing Modernist Texts: Editing as Interpretation*. Ann Arbor: U of Michigan P, 1991.

Bower, Gavin James. "The Age of Amazon Still Needs Editors like Max Perkins." *Guardian*, 4 October 2013. http://www.theguardian.com/books/booksblog/2013/oct/04/ age-amazon-editors-max-perkins

Brand, Dionne. *In Another Place, Not Here*. Toronto: A.A. Knopf Canada, 1996.

Braz, Albert. Email message to Laura Moss and Cynthia Sugars. 18 April 2012.

Bringhurst, Robert. "Glenn Goluska (1947–2010)." *Amphora* 159 (2011): 3–8.

——. *A Story as Sharp as a Knife: The Classical Haida Mythtellers and Their World*. 1999. 2nd ed. Vancouver: Douglas and McIntyre, 2011.

——. *The Surface of Meaning: Books and Book Design in Canada*. Vancouver: CCSP, 2008.

Brown, John Lennox. "The Captive: Snow Dark Sunday." Ottawa: Ottawa Little Theatre, 1965.

——. "A Crisis: Black Culture in Canada." *Black Images* 1.1 (1972): 4–8.

Brown, Russell. Letter to Robert Lecker. 2 April 2009.

——. "Crossing Borders." *Essays on Canadian Writing* 22 (1981): 154–68.

Brown, Russell, and Donna Bennett, eds. *An Anthology of Canadian Literature in English*. Vol. 1. Toronto: Oxford UP, 1982.

——. *An Anthology of Canadian Literature in English*. Vol. 2. Toronto: Oxford UP, 1983.

——. *An Anthology of Canadian Literature in English*. Rev. 3rd ed. Toronto: Oxford UP, 2010.

——. *A New Anthology of Canadian Literature in English*. Toronto: Oxford UP, 2002.

Brown, Russell, Donna Bennett, and Nathalie Cooke, eds. *An Anthology of Canadian Literature in English*. Rev. and abr. ed. Toronto: Oxford UP, 1990.

Brown, Susan. "Don't Mind the Gap: Evolving Digital Modes of Scholarly Production across the Digital–Humanities Divide." In Coleman and Kamboureli, eds. 203–31.

Bruns, Gerald L. *Maurice Blanchot: The Refusal of Philosophy*. Baltimore: Johns Hopkins UP, 1997.

Bryant, Joseph. *The Fluid Text: A Theory of Revision and Editing for Book and Screen*. Ann Arbor: U of Michigan P, 2002.

Brydon, Diana. "Cross-Talk, Postcolonial Pedagogy, and Transnational Literacy." In Sugars, ed. 57–74.

———. "Metamorphoses of a Discipline: Rethinking Canadian Literature within Institutional Contexts." In Kamboureli and Miki, eds. 1–16.

Buckley, Joan Naglestad. "Martha Ostenso: A Critical Study of Her Novels." Diss. U of Iowa, 1976.

Bushell, Sally. "Textual Process and the Denial of Origins." *Textual Cultures: Texts, Contexts, Interpretation* 2.2 (2007): 100–17.

Buss, Helen, ed. "Writing and Reading Autobiographically: Introduction to *Prairie Fire*'s 'Life Writing' Issue." *Prairie Fire* 16.3 (1995): 5–15.

Butler, Sharon, and William P. Stoneman, eds. *Editing, Publishing, and Computer Technology*. New York: AMS, 1988.

Campbell, Sandra. *Both Hands: A Life of Lorne Pierce of Ryerson Press*. Montreal and Kingston: McGill–Queen's UP, 2013.

———. Rev. of *HBiC*, vol. 2. *Canadian Historical Review* 89.3 (2008): 407–10.

Canada. Constitution Act 1867 (UK), 30 and 31 Victoria, c. 3. 1867. http://laws.justice .gc.ca/eng/Const/page-1.html

"The Canadian Book Market." *BookNet Canada*. BookNet Canada, 2007–9. http://www.book netcanada.ca/index.php?option=com_content&view=article&id=206&Itemid=323

Cariou, Warren. Letter to Kateri Akiwenzie-Damm. 13 October 2011.

Chan, Vanessa, Cari Ferguson, Kathleen Fraser, Cynara Geissler, Ann-Marie Metten, and Suzette Smith, eds. *The Book of MPub: New Perspectives on Technology and Publishing*. Vancouver: Canadian Centre for Studies in Publishing, 2010.

Chandler, Nahum Dimitri. "The Economy of Desedimentation: W.E.B. DuBois and the Discourses of the Negro." *Callaloo* 19.1 (1996): 78–93.

Churchman, Philip H. "The Use of Anthologies in the Study of Literature." *Modern Language Journal* 7.3 (1922): 149–54.

Clarke, George Elliott, ed. *Eyeing the North Star: Directions in African Canadian Literature*. Toronto: McClelland and Stewart, 1997.

———, ed. *Fire on the Water: An Anthology of Black Nova Scotian Writing*. 2 vols. Lawrencetown Beach: Pottersfield, 1991–92.

———. "Must All Blackness Be American? Locating Canada in Borden's 'Tightrope Time,' or Nationalizing Gilroy's *The Black Atlantic*." *Canadian Ethnic Studies* 28.3 (1996): 56–71.

———. *Odysseys Home: Mapping African Canadian Literature*. Toronto: U of Toronto P, 2002.

Coldwell, Joan. "Walking the Tightrope with Anne Wilkinson." In *Editing Women*. Ed. Ann M. Hutchison. Toronto: U of Toronto P, 1998. 3–25.

Coleman, Daniel, and Smaro Kamboureli. Acknowledgements. In Coleman and Kamboureli, eds. ix–xi.

———, eds. *Retooling the Humanities: The Culture of Research in Canadian Universities*. Edmonton: U of Alberta P, 2011.

Côté, Marc. "Cultural Industries." *Canadian Literature* 177 (2003): 200–201.

Coupland, Douglas. *Marshall McLuhan*. Intro. John Ralston Saul. Toronto: Penguin Canada, 2009.

Cowan, Ann, and Jacques Michon. "Editors and Editing." *Encyclopedia of Literature in Canada*. Ed. W.H. New. Toronto: U of Toronto P, 2002. 326–30.

Creelman, June, and Irene Gammel, curators. *Reflecting on Anne of Green Gables*. Library and Archives Canada, 2008. http://www.collectionscanada.gc.ca/013/013-344-e.html

Cullen, Darcy, ed. *Editors, Scholars, and the Social Text*. Toronto: U of Toronto P, 2012.

Cunningham, Stuart. "Cultural Studies from the Viewpoint of Cultural Policy." In *Critical Cultural Policy Studies: A Reader*. Ed. Justin Lewis and Toby Miller. Malden: Blackwell, 2003. 13–22.

Cunningham, Valentine. *British Writers of the Thirties*. Oxford: Oxford UP, 1988.

Curry, John. "Notes Toward a Beepliography." *Open Letter* 6th ser. 4–5 (1986): 249–70.

Darnton, Robert. "What Is the History of Books?" *Daedelus* (1982): 65–83. Rpt. in *The Book History Reader*. Ed. David Finkelstein and Alistair McCleery. 2nd ed. London: Routledge, 2006. 9–26.

Davey, Frank. "'AND Quebec': Canadian Literature and Its Quebec Questions." *Canadian Poetry: Studies, Documents, Reviews* 40 (1997): 6–26.

———. *Surviving the Paraphrase*. Winnipeg: Turnstone, 1983.

Dawe, Alan. "Scrap from the Barrel." Rev. of *The Alpine Path: The Story of My Career*, by L.M. Montgomery. *Vancouver Sun*, 27 December 1974: 30A.

Deegan, Marilyn, and Willard McCarty, eds. *Collaborative Research in the Digital Humanities*. Farnham: Ashgate, 2012.

Deppman, Jed, Daniel Ferrer, and Michael Groden. "Introduction: A Genesis of French Genetic Criticism." In *Genetic Criticism: Texts and Avant-Texts*. Ed. Jed Deppman, Daniel Ferrer, and Michael Groden. Philadelphia: U of Pennsylvania P, 2004. 1–16.

Delany, Martin Robinson. *Blake; or, The Huts of America*. 1859; 1861–1862. Rpt. in *Violence in the Black Imagination: Essays and Documents*. 1972. Ed. Ronald T. Takaki. Expanded ed. New York: Oxford UP, 1993. 102–214.

Dett, Robert Nathaniel. *Album of a Heart*. Jackson: Mocowat-Mercer/Lane College, 1911.

———. *Religious Folk-Songs of the Negro as Sung at Hampton Institute*. Hampton: Hampton Institute, 1927.

———. *The Dett Collection of Negro Spirituals*. N.p.: Hall and McCrealy, 1936.

Devereux, Cecily. "A Note on the Text." In Montgomery, *Anne of Green Gables*, ed. Devereux 42–50.

———. Introduction. In Montgomery, *Anne of Green Gables*, ed. Devereux 12–38.

Dewart, Edward Hartley. "Introductory Essay." In *Selections from Canadian Poets*. 1864. Toronto: U of Toronto P, 1973. ix–xix.

DiCenzo, Maria. "Remediating the Past: Doing 'Periodical Studies' in the Digital Era." *English Studies in Canada* 41.1 (2015): 19–39.

Dike, E.B. "Improve the Anthologies." *College English* 5.8 (1944): 447.

Di Leo, Jeffrey R. "Analyzing Anthologies." In *On Anthologies: Politics and Pedagogy*. Ed. Di Leo. Lincoln: U of Nebraska P, 2004. 1–27.

———. "On Being and Becoming Affiliated." *symplokē* 7.1–2 (1999): 49–63.

Di Leo, Jeffrey R., and Gerald Graff. "Anthologies, Literary Theory, and the Teaching of Literature: An Exchange." *symplokē* 8.1–2 (2000): 113–28.

Dionne, René. *La Littérature régionale aux confins de l'histoire at de la géographie: Étude*. Sudbury: Prise de parole, 1993.

Drucker, Johanna. *SpecLab: Digital Aesthetics and Projects in Speculative Computing*. Chicago: U of Chicago P, 2009.

Ducharme, Michel. Rev. of *HBiC* vol. 2. *Revue d'histoire de l'Amérique française* 59.4 (2006): 553–54.

Dudek, Louis, George Bowering, Frank Davey, Steve McCaffery, and bpNichol. "Questions (Some Answers)." *Open Letter* 4th ser. 8–9 (1981): 9–38.

Dumbrille, Dorothy. "Early Novelist's Letters." Rev. of *The Green Gables Letters from L.M. Montgomery to Ephraim Weber, 1905–1909*, ed. Wilfrid Eggleston. *Globe and Mail*,

30 April 1960, 21.

Duncan, Sara Jeannette. "Saunterings." *The Week*, 30 September 1886, 707–8.

DuPlessis, Rachel Blau. "Response: Shoptalk – Working Conditions and Marginal Gains." In Loizeaux and Fraistat 85–95.

Durkin, Martha Ostenso, and Douglas Leader Durkin. Agreement. 11 February 1958. Dodd, Mead and Company Fonds. First Accrual, box 1, file 22. William Ready Division of Archives and Research Collections, McMaster U, Hamilton.

Dutton, Paul. "Underwhich Editions and the Radical Tradition." *Descant* 91 (1995): 75–85.

Earle, David M. *Re-Covering Modernism: Pulps, Paperbacks, and the Prejudice of Form.* Farnham: Ashgate, 2009.

Editing Modernism in Canada. "Editing as Cultural Practice: Institutional Formations, Collaboration, and Literatures in Canada." Workshop. http://editingmodernism.ca/events/transcanada-institute

Edwards, Mary Jane. "The Centre for Editing Early Canadian Texts (CEECT) and Cyberspace." In *Cyberidentities: Canadian and European Presence in Cyberspace*. Ed. Leen Haenens and Alan L. Cobb. Ottawa: U of Ottawa P, 1999. 155–61.

––––. "The Peregrinations of Sam Slick, or, Glimpses of Canadian Books in Australia in the Nineteenth Century." In *The Culture of the Book: Essays from Two Hemispheres in Honour of Wallace Kirsop*. Ed. David Garrioch et al. Melbourne: Bibliographical Society of Australia and New Zealand, 1999. 419–29.

––––, ed. *Public Workshop on Editorial Principles and Procedures*. Ottawa: Centre for Editing Early Canadian Texts, 1983.

Egan, Jim. "Analyzing the Apparatus: Teaching American Literature Anthologies as Texts." *Early American Literature* 32.1 (1997): 102–8.

Eichhorn, Kate, and Heather Milne, eds. *Prismatic Publics: Innovative Canadian Women's Poetry and Poetics.* Toronto: Coach House, 2009.

Eistenstein, Elizabeth. *The Printing Press as an Agent of Change: Communications and Cultural Transformations in Early-Modern Europe.* Cambridge: Cambridge UP, 1979.

England, Claire. "The *Dictionary of Canadian Biography*: A Major Bicultural Source." *Reference Services Review* 21.2 (1993): 71–76.

Epperly, Elizabeth Rollins. "L.M. Montgomery's Manuscript Revisions." In Lefebvre, ed. 2: 228–35.

Evain, Christine. *Douglas Gibson Unedited.* Bruxelles and New York: Peter Lang, 2007.

Febvre, Lucien, and Henri-Jean Martin. *L'apparation du livre.* 1958. Trans. David Gerard as *The Coming of the Book.* London: Verso, 1976.

Fee, Margery. "Canadian Literature and English Studies in the Canadian University." *Essays on Canadian Writing* 48 (1992–93): 10–41.

––––. "Canucks between the Covers." Rev. of *HBiC*, vol. 3. *Underhill Review* (Fall 2007): 21–23.

Fee, Margery, and Leslie Monkman. "Teaching Canadian Literature." In *Encyclopedia of Literature in Canada*. Ed. William H. New. Toronto: U of Toronto P, 2002. 1084–89.

Ferry, Anne. *Tradition and the Individual Poem: An Inquiry into Anthologies.* Stanford: Stanford UP, 2001.

Fiamengo, Janice. "Producing Culture." Rev. of *Ghosts in the Machine: Women and Cultural Policy in Canada and Australia*, ed. Alison Beale and Annette Van Den Bosch and *Authors and Audiences: Popular Canadian Fiction in the Early Twentieth Century* by Clarence Carr. *Canadian Literature* 177 (2003): 125–26.

Finkelstein, David. "Cold Type." Rev. of *HBiC*, vols. 1–3. *TLS* (14 September 2007): 22–23.

———. Rev. of *HBiC,* vol. 1. *PBSC* 43.1 (2005): 65–68.

Finlay, Ian Hamilton. Letter to bpNichol. 10 December 1973. bpNichol Fonds, Department of Special Collections, Bennett Library, Simon Fraser U.

———. Letter to bpNichol. 23 December 1974. bpNichol Fonds, Department of Special Collections, Bennett Library, Simon Fraser U.

———. Letter to bpNichol. 20 February 1975. bpNichol Fonds, Department of Special Collections, Bennett Library, Simon Fraser U.

———. Letter to bpNichol. 12 November 1977. bpNichol Fonds, Department of Special Collections, Bennett Library, Simon Fraser U.

Finlay, Sue. Letter to bpNichol. 20 Apr. 1977. bpNichol Fonds, Department of Special Collections, Bennett Library, Simon Fraser U.

Fischman, Sheila. "French and English Texts in Tandem: The Editing of *Ellipse*." In Halpenny, ed. 81–94.

Fitzpatrick, Kathleen. *Planned Obsolescence: Publishing, Technology, and the Future of the Academy*. New York: New York UP, 2011.

Flahiff, F.T. *Always Someone to Kill the Doves: A Life of Sheila Watson*. Edmonton: NeWest, 2005.

Fleming, Patricia Lockhart. "National Book Histories and the Legacy of the *History of the Book in Canada / Histoire du livre et de l'imprimé au Canada*." *PBSC* 46.1 (2008): 35–42

Fleming, Patricia Lockhart, Gilles Gallichan, and Yvan Lamonde, eds. *History of the Book in Canada*: Vol. 1: *Beginnings to 1840*. Toronto: U of Toronto P, 2004.

Folsom, Ed. "Database as Genre: The Epic Transformation of Archives." *PMLA* 122.5 (2007): 1571–79.

Förster, Till, and Sidney Littlefield Kasfir. "Rethinking the Workshop: Work and Agency in African Art." Introduction. In *African Art and Agency in the Workshop*. Ed. Littlefield Kasfir and Förster. Bloomington: Indiana UP, 2013. 1–23.

Foucault, Michel. *Discipline and Punish: The Birth of the Prison*. Trans. Alan Sheridan. New York: Vintage, 1979.

———. *Language, Counter-Memory, Practice: Selected Essays and Interviews*. Ed. Donald F. Bouchard. Trans. Donald F. Bouchard and Sherry Simon. Ithaca: Cornell UP, 1992.

———. "The Subject and Power." *Power*. Ed. James D. Faubion and Paul Rabinow. 3 vols. *Essential Works of Foucault, 1954–1984*. New York: New, 2000. 326–48.

———. "What Is an Author?" *Language, Counter-Memory, Practice: Selected Essays and Interviews*. Ed. Donald F. Bouchard. Ithaca: Cornell UP, 1977. 113–38.

Fouché, Franck. "Un fauteuil dans un crâne." *Optique* 35–36 (1957).

———. *Message*. Port-au-Prince: Nemours Telhomme, 1946.

Fraistat, Neil. "The Place of the Book and the Book as Place." In *Poems in Their Place: The Intertextuality and Order of Poetic Collections*. Ed. Neil Fraistat. Chapel Hill: U of North Carolina P, 1986.

Fraistat, Neil, and Elizabeth Bergmann Loizeaux. "Introduction: Textual Studies in the Late Age of Print." In Loizeaux and Fraistat, eds. 3–16.

Fraser, Robert, and Mary Hammond, eds. *The Cross-National Dimension in Print Culture*. Vol. 1 of *Books without Borders*. Houndmills: Palgrave Macmillan, 2008.

Freeman, Elizabeth. *Time Binds: Queer Temporalities, Queer Histories*. Durham: Duke UP, 2010.

Freire, Paulo. *Pedagogy of the Oppressed*. Trans. Myra Bergman Ramos. New York: Seabury, 1970.

Friskney, Janet B. *New Canadian Library: The Ross–McClelland Years, 1952–1978*. Toronto: U of Toronto P, 2007.

Frutkin, Mark. *Slow Lightning*. Vancouver: Raincoast, 2001.

Fuller, Danielle, and DeNel Rehberg Sedo. "A Reading Spectacle for the Nation: The CBC and 'Canada Reads.'" *Journal of Canadian Studies* 40.1 (2006): 5–36.

Fyfe, Christopher. *"Our Children Free and Happy": Letters from Black Settlers in Africa in the 1790s*. Edinburgh: Edinburgh UP, 1991.

Gabler, Hans Walter. "Introduction: Textual Criticism and Theory in Modern German Editing." *Contemporary German Editorial Theory*. Ed. Gabler, George Bornstein, and Gillian Borland Pierce. Ann Arbor: U of Michigan P, 1995. 1–16.

Galey, Alan, and Stan Ruecker. "How a Prototype Argues." *Literary and Linguistic Computing* 25.4 (2010). http://individual.utoronto.ca/ alangaley/files/publications/Galey _Ruecker_prototypes.pdf

Gammel, Irene, ed. *The Intimate Life of L.M. Montgomery*. Toronto: U of Toronto P, 2005.

———. *Looking for Anne of Green Gables: The Story of L.M. Montgomery and Her Literary Classic*. New York: St. Martin's, 2008.

———, ed. *Making Avonlea: L.M. Montgomery and Popular Culture*. Toronto: U of Toronto P, 2002.

———. "Papa's Changeable Feast." *Globe and Mail*, 22 August 2009, F11.

———. "Staging Personalities in Modernism and Realism." *The Cambridge History of Canadian Literature*. Ed. Coral Ann Howells and Eva-Marie Kröller. Cambridge: Cambridge UP, 2009. 262–67.

Gammel, Irene, and Elizabeth Epperly, eds. *L.M. Montgomery and Canadian Culture*. Toronto: U of Toronto P, 1999.

Gammel, Irene, and Benjamin Lefebvre, eds. *Anne's World: A New Century of Anne of Green Gables*. Toronto: U of Toronto P, 2010.

Garner, Hugh. *Cabbagetown*. Toronto: Collins, 1950. Rev. ed. Toronto: Ryerson, 1968.

Geddes, Gary. "Dennis Lee." *Oxford Companion to Canadian Literature*. Ed. William Toye. Toronto: Oxford UP, 1983. 442–43.

Gerson, Carole. "Anthologies and the Canon of Early Canadian Women Writers." In *Re(Dis)covering Our Foremothers: Nineteenth-Century Canadian Women Writers*. Ed. Lorraine McMullen. Ottawa: Ottawa UP, 1989. 55–76.

———. "The Canon between the Wars: Field-Notes of a Feminist Literary Archaeologist." In *Canadian Canons: Essays on Literary Value*. Ed. Robert Lecker. Toronto: U of Toronto P, 1991. 46–56.

———. "Cultural Darwinism: Publishing and the Canon of Early Canadian Literature in English." *Epilogue* 10.1–2 (1995): 25–33.

———. "Design and Ideology in *A Pocketful of Canada*." *Papers of the Bibliographical Society of Canada* 44.2 (2006): 65–85.

———. "'The Most Canadian of all Canadian Poets': Pauline Johnson and the Construction of a National Literature." *Canadian Literature* 158 (1998): 90–107.

———. *A Purer Taste: The Writing and Reading of Fiction in English in Nineteenth-Century Canada*. Toronto: U of Toronto P, 1989.

———. "The Question of a National Publishing System in English-Speaking Canada: As Canadian as Possible under the Circumstances." In *Les mutations du livre et de l'édition dans le monde, du XVIII^e siècle à l'an 2000.* Ed. Jacques Michon and Jean-Yves Mollier. Québec: Presses de l'Université Laval, 2001. 305–15.

——. "Sarah Binks and Edna Jaques: Gender, Parody, and the Construction of Literary Value," *Canadian Literature* 134 (1992): 62–73.

——. "Seven Milestones: How *Anne of Green Gables* Became a Canadian Icon." In Gammel and Lefebvre 17–34.

——. "Writers without Borders: The Global Framework of Canada's Early Print Culture." *Canadian Literature* 201 (2009): 15–33.

Gerson, Carole, and Jacques Michon, eds. *History of the Book in Canada*, Vol. 3: *1918–80.* Toronto: U of Toronto P, 2007.

Ghandl of the Qayahl Llaanas. *Nine Visits to the Mythworld.* Trans. Robert Bringhurst. Vancouver: Douglas and McIntyre, 2000.

Giroux, Henry A., and Roger Simon. "Popular Culture and Critical Pedagogy: Everyday Life as a Basis for Curriculum Knowledge." In *Critical Pedagogy, the State, and Cultural Struggle.* Ed. Henry Giroux and Peter L. McLaren. Albany: SUNY P, 1989. 236–52.

Gitelman, Lisa. *Always Already New: Media, History, and the Data of Culture.* Cambridge, MA: MIT P, 2006.

Godard, Barbara. "Feminist Periodicals and the Production of Cultural Value: The Canadian Context." *Women's Studies International Forum* 25.2 (2002): 209–23.

Godard, Barbara, and Smaro Kamboureli. "The Critic, Institutional Culture, and Canadian Literature." *Canadian Literature at the Crossroads of Language and Culture: Selected Essays by Barbara Godard, 1987–2005.* Ed. Smaro Kamboureli. Edmonton: NeWest, 2008. 17–52.

Grace, Sherrill. "'The Daily Crucifixion of the Post': Editing and Theorizing the Lowry Letters." In Lennox and Paterson 26–53.

Greenblatt, Stephen. *Shakespearean Negotiations: The Circulation of Social Energy in Renaissance England.* Berkeley: U of California P, 1988.

Greenberg, Susan L. *Editors Talk about Editing.* New York: Peter Lang, 2015.

Greenwald, Marilyn S. *The Secret of the Hardy Boys: Leslie McFarlane and the Stratemeyer Syndicate.* Athens: Ohio UP, 2004.

Greetham, D.C., ed. *The Margins of the Text.* Ann Arbor: U of Michigan P, 1997.

Griffiths, Bill. *A Tract against the Giants.* Toronto: Coach House and Underwhich, 1985.

Groden, Michael. "Contemporary Textual and Literary Theory." In *Representing Modernist Texts: Editing as Interpretation.* Ed. George Bornstein. Ann Arbor: U of Michigan P, 1991. 259–86.

Grondahl, Amanda, with Ramona Brown, Brooke Burns, Tammy Burns, Irene Kavanagh, and Penny McKinlay. "So You Want to Be an Editor: Information about a Career in Editing." *editors.ca.* Editors' Association of Canada, 2011. http://www.editors.ca/join_eac/be_an_editor/so.html

Gross, Robert A. "Books, Nationalism and History." *Papers of the Bibliographical Society of Canada* 36.1 (1998): 107–23.

Gustafson, Ralph. "The Story of the Penguin." *Canadian Poetry* 12 (1983): 71–76.

Halpenny, Francess G., ed. *Editing Canadian Texts.* Toronto: A.M. Hakkert, 1975.

——. "Introduction." In Halpenny, ed. 3–11.

Hammill, Faye. "Martha Ostenso, Literary History, and the Scandinavian Diaspora." *Canadian Literature* 196 (2008): 17–31.

——. "The Sensations of the 1920s: Martha Ostenso's *Wild Geese* and Mazo de la Roche's *Jalna.*" *Studies in Canadian Literature / Études en Littérature Canadienne* 28.2 (2003): 74–97.

Hammill, Faye, and Michelle Smith. *Magazines, Travel, and Middlebrow Culture: Canadian Periodicals in English and French, 1925–1960.* Edmonton: U Alberta P, 2015.

Hancock, Geoff. "The Form of the Thing: An Interview with bpNichol on Ganglia and grOnk." *Rampike* (Autumn 2002): 30–36.

Hardt, Michael, and Antonio Negri. *Empire.* Cambridge, MA: Harvard UP, 2000.

Harnum, Bill. "Re: P.K. Page." Email message to Zailig Pollock. 3 October 2000.

Harrison, Charles Yale. *Meet Me on the Barricades.* New York: Charles Scribner's Sons, 1938.

Hart, Kevin, and Geoffrey H. Hartman. Introduction. *The Power of Contestation: Perspectives on Maurice Blanchot.* Ed. Hart and Hartman. Baltimore: Johns Hopkins UP, 2004. 1–26.

Harvey, Louis-Georges. Rev. of *HBiC*, vol. 1. *Revue d'histoire de l'Amérique française* 59.1–2 (2005): 139–42.

Hegel, G.W.F. *Aesthetics: Lectures on Fine Art.* Trans. T.M. Knox. Vol. 2. Oxford: Clarendon P, 1975.

Hemingway, Ernest. *A Moveable Feast.* New York: Charles Scribner's Sons, 1964.

——. *A Moveable Feast: The Restored Edition.* Ed. Seán Hemingway. New York: Charles Scribner's Sons, 2009.

Henderson, Anna Minerva. *Citadel.* Fredericton: Henderson, 1967.

——. "Parliament Hill, Ottawa." *Canadian Poetry Magazine* 2.1 (1937): 51.

——. "Parliament Hill, Ottawa." *New Harvesting: Contemporary Canadian Poetry, 1918–1938.* Ed. Ethel Hume Bennett. Toronto: Macmillan, 1938. 54.

Henighan, Stephen. "The BookNet Dictatorship." *Geist: North of America*, February 2011. http://www.geist.com/articles/booknet-dictatorship

Henry, Astrid. "Enviously Grateful, Gratefully Envious: The Dynamics of Generational Relationships in U.S. Feminism." *Women's Studies Quarterly* 34: 3–4 (2006): 140–53.

Hinks, John, and Catherine Armstrong, eds. *Worlds of Print: Diversity in the Book Trade.* New Castle and London: Oak Knoll and the British Library, 2004.

"History of the Library." Westmount Public Library. http://www.westlib.org/english/chronology.htm

Hjartarson, Paul, Harvey Quamen, and EMiC UA. "Editing the Wilfred Watson and Sheila Watson Archives: Scholarly Edition ↔ Digital Projects." In Irvine, Lent, and Vautour, eds.

Hockey, Susan. "The History of Humanities Computing." *A Companion to Digital Humanities.* Ed. Susan Schreibman, Ray Siemens, and John Unsworth. Oxford: Blackwell, 2004.

Howsam, Leslie, ed. *The Cambridge Companion to the History of the Book*, Cambridge: Cambridge UP, 2015.

Howsam, Leslie, and James Raven, eds. *Books between Europe and the Americas: Connections and Communities, 1620–1860.* Houndmills: Palgrave Macmillan, 2011.

Hull, Helen. "Love Without Laughter." *McCall's Magazine* 65 (September 1938): 7–9, 48–49, 52–53, 59–60, 62.

Hutchison, Ann M., ed. *Editing Women.* Toronto: U of Toronto P, 1998.

Hutton, June. *Underground.* Toronto: Cormorant Books, 2009.

"Inuktitut syallabary." *Omniglot: The Online Encyclopedia of Writing Systems and Languages.* http://www.omniglot.com/writing/inuktitut.htm

Irvine, Dean. "Editing Canadian Modernism." *English Studies in Canada* 33.1–2 (2007): 53–84.

———. *Editing Modernity: Women and Little-Magazine Cultures in Canada, 1916–1956.* Toronto: U of Toronto P, 2008.

———. "'The Marchbanks Archive': Editing the *Marchbanks* Series." *University of Toronto Quarterly* 78.4 (2009): 949–66.

Irvine, Dean, Vanessa Lent, and Bart Vautour, eds. *Making Canada New: Editing, Modernism, and New Media.* Toronto: U of Toronto P (forthcoming 2016).

Iyer, Pico. "The McLuhan Galaxy." Review of *Marshall McLuhan: You Know Nothing of My Work!*, by Douglas Coupland. *New York Review of Books*, 26 May 2011. http://www.nybooks.com/articles/archives/2011/may/26/mcluhan-galaxy

Jaeger, Peter. "An Interview with Steve McCaffery on the TRG." *Open Letter* 10th ser. 4 (1998): 77–96.

Jameson, Fredric. "Lenin and Revisionism." *Lenin Reloaded: Toward a Politics of Truth.* Ed. Sebastian Budgen, Stathis Kouvelakis, and Slavoj Žižek. Durham: Duke UP, 2007. 59–73.

Johnson, Amelia Etta Hall. *Clarence and Corinne; or, God's Way.* 1890. New York: Oxford UP, 1988.

Johnson, Glen M. "The Teaching Anthology and the Canon of American Literature: Some Notes on Theory in Practice." *The Hospitable Canon: Essays on Literary Play, Scholarly Choice, and Popular Pressures.* Ed. Virgil Nemoianu and Robert Royal. Philadelphia: Benjamins, 1991. 111–35.

Jones, Philip Henry, and Eiluned Rees, eds. *A Nation and Its Books: A History of the Book in Wales.* Aberystwyth: National Library of Wales, 1998.

Joyce-Jones, Susannah. Rev. of *My Dear Mr. M: Letters to G.B. MacMillan from L.M. Montgomery*, ed. Francis W.P. Bolger and Elizabeth R. Epperly. *Atlantis* 7.1 (1981): 144–46.

Justice, Daniel Heath. Letter to Kateri Akiwenzie-Damm. 12 September 2011.

Kadar, Marlene, ed. *Essays in Life Writing.* Toronto: Robarts Centre for Canadian Studies, 1989.

Kamboureli, Smaro. "Canadian Ethnic Anthologies: Representations of Ethnicity." *ARIEL: A Review of International English Literature* 25.4 (1994): 11–52.

———, ed. *Making a Difference: Canadian Multicultural Literature.* 1996. 2nd ed. Toronto: Oxford UP, 2007.

———. Preface. In Kamboureli and Miki, eds. vii–xv.

———. *Scandalous Bodies: Diasporic Literature in English Canada.* Don Mills: Oxford UP, 2000.

Kamboureli, Smaro, and Roy Miki, eds. *Trans.Can.Lit: Resituating the Study of Canadian Literature.* Waterloo: Wilfrid Laurier UP, 2007.

Kanaganayakam, Chelva, ed. *Moveable Margins: The Shifting Spaces of Canadian Literature.* Toronto: TSAR, 2005.

Keats, John. *Complete Poems.* Ed. Jack Stillinger. Cambrige, MA.: Harvard UP, 1978.

Keith, W.J. "How New Was *New Provinces?*" *Canadian Poetry: Studies, Documents, Reviews* 4 (1979): 120–24.

Kertzer, John. *Worrying the Nation: Imagining a National Literature in English.* Toronto: U of Toronto P, 1998.

Klancher, Jon. "Godwin and the Genre Reformers: On Necessity and Contingency in Romantic Narrative Theory." In *Romanticism, History, and the Possibilities of Genre: Re-Forming Literature*. Ed. Tilottama Rajan and Julia M. Wright. Cambridge: Cambridge UP, 1998. 21–38.

Klein, A.M. *The Collected Poems of A.M. Klein*. Ed. Miriam Waddington. Toronto: McGraw-Hill Ryerson, 1974.

———. *The Complete Poems*. Ed. Zailig Pollock. Toronto: U of Toronto P, 1990.

———. *The Letters*. Ed. Elizabeth Popham. Toronto: U of Toronto P, 2012.

———. *Notebooks: Selections from the A.M. Klein Papers*. Ed. Zailig Pollock and Usher Caplan. Toronto: U of Toronto P, 1994.

———. *The Second Scroll*. Ed. Elizabeth Popham and Zailig Pollock. Toronto: U of Toronto P, 2000.

Klein, Ernest. *A Comprehensive Etymological Dictionary of the English Language*. Amsterdam: Elsevier, 1966–67.

Klinck, Carl F. *Giving Canada a Literary History*. Ottawa: Carleton UP, 1991.

Knight, Alan. "Growing Hegemonies: Preparing the Ground for Official Anthologies of Canadian Poetry." In *Prefaces and Literary Manifestoes / Préfaces et manifestes littéraires*. Ed. E.D. Blodgett, A.G. Purdy, and S. Tötösy de Zepetnek. Edmonton: Alberta UP, 1990. 146–57.

Korn, Marianne. "Preface: Ezra Pound and History." In *Ezra Pound and History*. Ed. Korn. Orono: National Poetry Foundation, 1985. 7–11.

Kroller, Eva-Marie. "Cultural Inventories and Nation-Building: Editing the *Cambridge Companion to Canadian Literature*." *Anglistik* 15.2 (2004): 27–42.

Kuipers, Christopher M. "The Anthology as a Literary Creation: On Innovation and Plagiarism in Textual Collections." *Originality, Imitation, and Plagiarism: Teaching Writing in the Digital Age*. Ed. Caroline Eisner and Martha Vicinus. Ann Arbor: U of Michigan P, 2008. 122–32.

———. "The Anthology/Corpus Dynamic: A Field Theory of the Canon." *College Literature* 30.2 (2003): 51–71.

Lai, Larissa. *Slanting I, Imagining We: Asian Canadian Literary Production in the 1980s and 1990s*. Waterloo: Wilfrid Laurier UP, 2014.

Laird, R.G. "Computers in Editing." In Edwards, ed. 58–65.

Lamonde, Yvan. "L'histoire du livre et de l'imprimé au Canada et les percées en histoire culturelle et intellectuelle." *PBSC* 46.1 (2008): 43–54.

Lamonde, Yvan, Patricia Lockhart Fleming, and Fiona A. Black, eds. *History of the Book in Canada*, Vol. 2: *1840–1918*. Toronto: U of Toronto P, 2005.

Lane, Red. *The 1962 Poems of Red Lane*. Intro. George Bowering. *Ganglia* 2. Toronto: Ganglia, 1965.

Latham, Sean. "Unpacking My Digital Library: Programming Modernist Magazines." *Making Canada New: Editing, Modernism, and New Media*. Ed. Dean Irvine, Vanessa Lent, and Bart Vautour. Toronto: U of Toronto P, 2016.

Latham, Sean, and Robert Scholes. "The Rise of Periodical Studies." *PMLA* 121.2 (2006): 517–31.

Lauter, Paul. "Taking Anthologies Seriously." *MELUS: The Journal of the Society for the Study of the Multi-Ethnic Literature of the United States* 29.3–4 (2004): 19–39.

———. "Teaching with Anthologies." *Pedagogy: Critical Approaches to Teaching Literature, Language, Composition, and Culture* 3.3 (2003): 329–39.

Leacock, Stephen. *My Discovery of the West*. Toronto: Allen, 1937.

Lecker, Robert. "The Canonization of Canadian Literature: An Inquiry into Value." *Critical Inquiry* 16.3 (1990): 656–71.

———. "Materialising Canada: National Literature Anthologies and the Making of a Canon." *Australasian Canadian Studies* 26.1 (2008): 23–41.

Ledwell, Jane, and Jean Mitchell, eds. *Anne around the World: L.M. Montgomery and Her Classic*. Montreal and Kingston: McGill-Queen's UP, 2013.

Lefebvre, Benjamin. "Pigsties and Sunsets: L.M. Montgomery, *A Tangled Web*, and a Modernism of Her Own." *English Studies in Canada* 31.4 (2005): 123–46.

———. "'That Abominable War!': *The Blythes Are Quoted* and Thoughts on L.M. Montgomery's Late Style." In *Storm and Dissonance: L.M. Montgomery and Conflict*. Ed. Jean Mitchell. Newcastle: Cambridge Scholars, 2008. 109–30.

Lefebvre, Benjamin, ed. *The L.M. Montgomery Reader*, Vol. 1: *A Life in Print*; Vol. 2: *A Critical Heritage*; Vol. 3: *A Legacy in Review*. Toronto: U of Toronto P, 2013–15.

Leitch, Vincent B., Barbara Johnson, John McGowan, Laurie Finke, and Jeffrey J. Williams. "Editing a Norton Anthology." *College English* 66.2 (2003): 173–77.

Les Figues Press. "I'LL DROWN MY BOOK, Conceptual Writing by Women." *Kickstarter*. http://www.kickstarter.com/projects/1359907001/ill-drown-my-book -conceptual-writing-by-women

Leslie, Kenneth. "The Censored Editor." *New Frontier* 2.3 (1937): 10–11.

———. "Fifth Columnist." In *By Stubborn Stars and Other Poems*. Toronto: Ryerson, 1938. 51–56.

———. "Fifth Columnist." *Protestant Digest* (1939): 24–30.

———. *O'Malley to the Reds, and Other Poems*. Halifax: n.p., 1972.

———. *The Poems of Kenneth Leslie*. Ladysmith: Ladysmith Press, 1971.

Lennox, John, and Michèle Lacombe, eds. *Dear Bill: The Correspondence of William Arthur Deacon*. Toronto: U of Toronto P, 1988.

Lennox, John, and Janet Paterson, eds. *Challenges, Projects, Texts: Canadian Editing*. New York: AMS, 1993.

Lewis, Justin, and Toby Miller, eds. *Critical Cultural Policy Studies: A Reader*. Malden: Blackwell, 2003.

Livesay, Dorothy. "Canadian Poetry and the Spanish Civil War." *CV/II* 2.2 (1976): 12–16.

Loizeaux, Elizabeth Bergmann, and Neil Fraistat, eds. *Reimagining Textuality: Textual Studies in the Late Age of Print*. Madison: U of Wisconsin P, 2002.

Longenbach, James. "The Question of Anthologies." *Raritan: A Quarterly Review* 21.4 (2002): 122–29.

Love, Harold. *Attributing Authorship: An Introduction*. Cambridge: Cambridge UP, 2002.

Lowry, Malcolm. *Under the Volcano*. New York: Reynal and Hitchcock, 1947.

*Lucy Maud Montgomery Research Centre*. U of Guelph. http://www.lmmrc.ca

MacDonald, Bertrum H. "Book-History Studies Come of Age: The Digital Legacy of the *History of the Book in Canada / Histoire du livre et de l'imprimé au Canada* Project." *PBSC* 46.1 (2008): 54–78.

Macdonald, Dwight. "The Responsibility of Peoples." *The Responsibility of Peoples, and Other Essays in Political Criticism*. London: Gollancz, 1957. 9–45.

MacGillivray, S.R. "Bouquets from the Bush Garden: Some Recent Canadian Anthologies." *Lakehead University Review* 7 (1974): 93–101.

Machan, Tibor R. "Boxer's Confusion about Ownership." *Commentaries*. The Future of Freedom Foundation, 4 May 2007. http://fff.org/explore-freedom/article/ boxers-confusion-ownership

Mackey, Eva. *The House of Difference: Cultural Politics and National Identity in Canada.* London: Routledge, 1999.

MacLaren, Eli. "'Against All Invasion': The Archival Story of Kipling, Copyright, and the Macmillan Expansion into Canada, 1900–1920." *Journal of Canadian Studies* 40.2 (2006): 139–62.

MacLean, Heather. "The Canadian Book Industry Supply Chain Initiative: The Inception and Implementation of a New Funding Initiative for the Department of Canadian Heritage." Project Report, Master of Publishing. Vancouver: Simon Fraser U, 2009. https://www.ccsp.sfu.ca/2013/08/the-canadian-book-industry-supply-chain-initiative-the-inception-and-implementation-of-a-new-funding-initiative-for-the-department-of-canadian-heritage

MacLennan, Hugh. "Literature in a New Country." *Scotchman's Return and Other Essays.* Toronto: Macmillan, 1960. 137–41.

———. *The Watch That Ends the Night.* Toronto: Macmillan, 1959.

MacSkimming, Roy. "Charting Canada's Print Culture." *Globe and Mail*, 31 March 2007, D25.

———. *The Perilous Trade: Book Publishing in Canada 1946–2006.* Toronto: McClelland and Stewart, 2003.

Magosci, Paul Robert, ed. *Encyclopedia of Canada's Peoples.* Toronto: U of Toronto P, 1999.

Major, Jean-Louis. "Inventaire et invention d'une littérature: le Corpus d'éditions critiques." In Lennox and Paterson 70–88.

Mandel, Eli. "Masks of Criticism: A.J.M. Smith as Anthologist." *Canadian Poetry: Studies, Documents, Reviews* 4 (1979): 17–28.

Marek, Jayne E. *Women Editing Modernism: "Little" Magazines and Literary History.* Lexington: UP of Kentucky, 1995.

Mason, David. Personal conversation with Irene Gammel. September 2008.

Massumi, Brian. *Parables for the Virtual: Movement, Affect, Sensation.* Durham: Duke UP, 2002.

Maxwell, John. "PEXOD: The Publisher's Extensible Online Database." In *Publishing Studies: Book Publishing 1.* Ed. Rowland Lorimer, John Maxwell, and Jillian G. Shoichet. Vancouver: Canadian Centre for Studies in Publishing, 2009. 326–35.

Mayr, Suzette. *The Widows.* Edmonton: NeWest, 1998.

McCaffery, Steve. "Writing as a General Economy." In *North of Intention: Critical Writings 1973–1986.* Toronto: Nightwood Editions, 1986. 201–21.

McCaffery, Steve, and bpNichol. *Rational Geomancy: The Kids of the Book Machine: The Collected Research Reports of the Toronto Research Group 1973–1982.* Ed. McCaffery. Vancouver: Talonbooks, 1992.

McCall, Sophie. "Double Vision Reading." Rev. of *Moveable Margins: The Shifting Spaces of Canadian Literature*, ed. Chelva Kanaganayakam and *Accounting for Culture: Thinking Through Cultural Citizenship*, ed. Caroline Andrew, Monica Gattinger, M. Sharon Jeannette, and Will Straw. *Canadian Literature* 194 (2007): 95–97.

"McCall's." *Wikipedia, The Free Encyclopedia.* Wikimedia Foundation, Inc. 13 July 2011. http://en.wikipedia.org/wiki/McCall%27s

McCleery, Alistair. "The Book in the Long Twentieth Century." In *The Cambridge Companion to the History of the Book.* Ed. Leslie Howsam. Cambridge: Cambridge UP, 2015. 162–80.

McGann, Jerome. *A Critique of Modern Textual Criticism.* Chicago: U of Chicago P, 1983.

———. "Electronic Archives and Critical Editing." *Literature Compass*. 7.2 (2010): 37–42.

———. "From Text to Work: Digital Tools and the Emergence of the Social Text." *Romanticism on the Net 1996–2006: Celebrating Ten Years of Online Publishing*. Ed. Dino Franco Felluga. Spec. issue of *Romanticism of the Net* 41–42 (2006). http://www.erudit.org/revue/ron/2006/v/n41-42/013153ar.html

———. *Radiant Textuality: Literary Studies after the World Wide Web*. New York: Palgrave Macmillan, 2001.

———. "The Rationale of HyperText." *The Institute for Advanced Technology in the Humanities*, 1995. http://www2.iath.virginia.edu/ public/jjm2f/rationale.html

———. "The Socialization of Texts." In *The Book History Reader*. Ed. David Finkelstein and Alistair McCleery. London: Routledge, 2002. 39–46.

———. *The Textual Condition*. Princeton: Princeton UP, 1991.

McGregor, Hannah, and Michelle Smith. "Martha Osteno, Periodical Culture, and the Middlebrow." *International Journal of Canadian Studies* 48 (2014): 67–83.

McGuigan, Jim. "Cultural Policy Studies." In Lewis and Miller, eds. 23–38.

McKay, Ian. *Reasoning Otherwise: Leftists and the People's Enlightenment in Canada, 1890–1920*. Toronto: Between the Lines, 2008.

———. *Rebels, Reds, Radicals: Rethinking Canada's Left History*. Toronto: Between the Lines, 2005.

McKenzie, Andrea. "Patterns, Power, and Paradox: International Book Covers of *Anne of Green Gables* across a Century." In *Textual Transformations in Children's Literature: Adaptations, Translations, Reconsiderations*. Ed. Benjamin Lefebvre. New York: Routledge, 2013. 127–53.

McKenzie, D.F. *Bibliography and the Sociology of Texts: The Panizzi Lectures*. London: British Library, 1986.

McLeod, Neal. Letter to Kateri Akiwenzie-Damm. 12 October 2011.

McLuhan, Marshall. *The Mechanical Bride: Folklore of Industrial Man*. Boston: Beacon, 1951.

McLuhan, Marshall, with Wilfred Watson. *From Cliché to Archetype*. New York: Viking, 1970.

McMenemy, Siobhan. "Letter of introduction." Email message to Zailig Pollock. 3 December 2001.

Meinecke, Friedrich. *Historicism*. 1959. Trans. J.E. Anderson. New York: Herder and Herder, 1972.

Metcalf, John. *What Is a Canadian Literature?* Guelph: Red Kite, 1988.

Middlebrook, Diane Wood. "Telling Secrets." *The Seductions of Biography*. Ed. Mary Rhiel and David Bruce Suchoff. New York: Routledge, 1996. 123–30.

Miki, Roy. "The Future's Tense: Some Notes on Editing, Canadian Style." *Open Letter* 8.5–6 (1993): 182–96.

Miller, Toby. "From Creative to Cultural Industries." *Cultural Studies* 23.1 (2008): 88–99.

———. *The Well-Tempered Self: Citizenship, Culture, and the Postmodern Subject*. Baltimore: Johns Hopkins UP, 1993.

Miller, Toby, and Alec McHoul. "Helping the Self." *Social Text* 57 (1998): 127–55.

Miller, Toby, and George Yúdice. *Cultural Policy*. London: SAGE, 2002.

Montgomery, L.M. *The Alpine Path: The Story of My Career*. N.p.: Fitzhenry and Whiteside, n.d.

———. *Anne of Green Gables*. Boston: L.C. Page, 1908.

———. *Anne of Green Gables*. 1908. London: Harrap, 1925.

——. *Anne of Green Gables*. 1908. Toronto: Ryerson, 1942.

——. *Anne of Green Gables*. 1908. New Canadian Library. Toronto: McClelland and Stewart, 1992.

——. *Anne of Green Gables*. 1908. Toronto: Seal, 1996.

——. *Anne of Green Gables*. 1908. Ed. Cecily Devereux. Peterborough: Broadview, 2004.

——. *Anne of Green Gables*. 1908. Ed. Mary Henley Rubio and Elizabeth Waterston. New York: Norton, 2007.

——. *Anne of Green Gables*. 1908. New York: Modern Library, 2008.

——. *Anne of Green Gables*. 1908. Toronto: Penguin Canada, 2008.

——. *The Annotated Anne of Green Gables*. Ed. Wendy E. Barry, Margaret Anne Doody, and Mary E. Doody Jones. New York: Oxford UP, 1997.

——. *The Blythes Are Quoted*. Ed. Benjamin Lefebvre. Toronto: Viking Canada, 2009.

——. *The Complete Journals of L.M. Montgomery: The PEI Years, 1889–1900*. Ed. Mary Henley Rubio and Elizabeth Hillman Waterston. Don Mills: Oxford UP, 2012.

——. *The Complete Journals of L.M. Montgomery: The PEI Years, 1901–1911*. Ed. Mary Henley Rubio and Elizabeth Hillman Waterston. Don Mills: Oxford UP, 2013.

——. *The Doctor's Sweetheart and Other Stories*. Ed. Catherine McLay. Toronto: McGraw-Hill Ryerson, 1979.

——. *The Green Gables Letters from L.M. Montgomery to Ephraim Weber, 1905–1909*. Ed. Wilfrid Eggleston. Toronto: Ryerson, 1960.

——. *My Dear Mr. M: Letters to G.B. MacMillan from L.M. Montgomery*. Toronto: McGraw-Hill Ryerson, 1980.

——. *The Poetry of Lucy Maud Montgomery*. Ed. John Ferns and Kevin McCabe. Toronto: Fitzhenry and Whiteside, 1987.

——. *The Road to Yesterday*. Toronto: McGraw-Hill Ryerson, 1974.

——. *The Selected Journals of L.M. Montgomery*, Vol. 1: *1889–1910*; Vol. 2: *1910–1921*; Vol. 3: *1921–1929*; Vol. 4: *1929–1935*; Vol. 5: *1935–1942*. Ed. Mary Rubio and Elizabeth Waterston. Toronto: Oxford UP, 1985–2004.

——. *Una of the Garden*. Ed. Donna J. Campbell and Simon Lloyd. N.p.: n.p., 2010.

——. "The Way to Make a Book." In Lefebvre, ed. 1: 137–43.

Montgomery, L.M., and Nora Lefurgey. "'… where has my yellow garter gone?': The Diary of L.M. Montgomery and Nora Lefurgey." In Gammel, ed., *The Intimate Life* 19–87.

Moodie, Susanna. *Roughing It in the Bush: Or, Life in Canada*. 1852. Toronto: McClelland and Stewart, 1989.

Mookerjea, Sourayan, Imre Szeman, and Gail Farschou, eds. *Canadian Cultural Studies: A Reader*. Durham: Duke UP, 2009.

Moss, Laura, and Cynthia Sugars, eds. *Canadian Literature in English: Texts and Contexts*. 2 vols. Toronto: Pearson/Penguin, 2009.

Mount, Nick. "The Expatriate Origins of Canadian Literature." In *ReCalling Early Canada: Reading the Political in Literary and Cultural Production*. Ed. Jennifer Blair, Daniel Coleman, Kate Higginson, and Lorraine York. Edmonton: U of Alberta P, 2005. 237–55.

Mulhallen, Karen, Susan Bennett, and Russell Brown, eds. *Tasks of Passion: Dennis Lee at Mid-Career*. Toronto: Descant, 1982.

Multineddu, Flavio. "An Interview with bpNichol in Torino, May 6 & 8, 1987." *Open Letter* 8th ser. 7 (1993): 5–35.

Nelson, Cary. "Murder in the Cathedral: Editing a Comprehensive Anthology of Modern American Poetry." *American Literary History* 14.2 (2002): 311–27.

———. *Repression and Recovery: Modern American Poetry and the Politics of Cultural Memory, 1910–1945*. Madison: U of Wisconsin P, 1989.

Nesbitt, Bruce. "Lampmania: Alcyone and the Search for Merope." In Halpenny, ed. 33–48.

New, W.H. "Some Comments on the Editing of Canadian Texts." In Halpenny, ed. 13–32.

"News Notes of Contributors." *Canadian Poetry Magazine* 2.1 (June 1937): 63.

Ngai, Sianne. *Ugly Feelings*. Cambridge, MA: Harvard UP, 2005.

Nichol, bp. *ABC: The Aleph Beth Book*. Ottawa: Oberon, 1971.

———. *The Alphabet Game: A bpNichol Reader*. Ed. Darren Wershler-Henry and Lori Emerson. Toronto: Coach House, 2007.

———. *As Elected*. Ed. Jack David. Vancouver: Talonbooks, 1980.

———. *bp*. Toronto: Coach House, 1967.

———. "bpNichol by John Cannyside" (draft), *Get Set Nemo Te Book, begun March 3, 1982*, MsC 12.d.13, March 11, 1982 and December 2, 1982. bpNichol Fonds, Department of Special Collections, Bennett Library, Simon Fraser U.

———. *bpNichol Comics*. Ed. Carl Peters. Vancouver: Talonbooks, 2002.

———. *The Captain Poetry Poems*. Vancouver: Ganglia and Blew Ointment, 1971.

———. *cold mountain*. Toronto: Ganglia, 1966.

———. *Continental Trance*. Lantzville: Oolichan, 1982.

———. *Critical Frame of Reference*. Toronto: 'Pataphysical Hardware Company, 1985.

———. *A Draft of Book IV of The Martyrology*. Edmonton: bpNichol, 1976.

———. *Familiar*. Toronto: privately printed by Eleanor and bpNichol, 1980.

———. *First Screening*. Toronto: Underwhich Editions, 1984. Floppy Diskette.

———. *Ganglia Press Index*. grOnk 8th ser. 7. Toronto: Ganglia, 1977.

———. *An H in the Heart: A Reader*. Ed. George Bowering and Michael Ondaatje. Toronto: McClelland and Stewart, 1994.

———. *Lament*. Toronto: Ganglia, 1969.

———. *The Langwage The Langwedge*. Toronto: Ganglia, 1966.

———. Letter to Louis Dudek. 8 August 1980. bpNichol Fonds, Department of Special Collections, Bennett Library, Simon Fraser U.

———. *The Martyrology*. Book I. Toronto: Coach House, 1972.

———. *The Martyrology*. Book II. Toronto: Coach House, 1972.

———. *The Martyrology*. Books 3 & 4. Toronto: Coach House, 1976.

———. *The Martyrology*. Book 5. Toronto: Coach House, 1982.

———. *The Martyrology Book 6 Books*. Toronto: Coach House, 1986.

———. *The Martyrology Book(s) 7&: Gifts*. Ed. Irene Niechoda. Toronto: Coach House, 1990.

———. *The Martyrology Book 9: Ad Sanctos*. Musical score by Howard Gerhard. Toronto: Coach House, 1993.

———. *Meanwhile: The Critical Writings of bpNichol*. Ed. Roy Miki. Vancouver: Talonbooks, 2002.

———. Notebook. 27 July 1963 to 8 September 1965. MsC 12a 9.1.1–2. bpNichol Fonds, Department of Special Collections, Bennett Library, Simon Fraser U.

———. *Plaster de Paris*. Toronto: 'Pataphysical Hardware Company, 1985.

———. "The Plunkett Papers." *September 1968 Journal*, MsC12a.10.3, May 1969, July-August 1969; *No Tree Book begun February 18 1983*, MsC12.d.13, July 2, 1983; "The Plunkett Papers" (typescript, n.d.) MsC 12.8.13.2. bpNichol Fonds, Department of Special Collections, Bennett Library, Simon Fraser U.

——. *Still Water.* Vancouver: Talonbooks, 1970.

——. *Truth: A Book of Fictions.* Ed. Irene Niechoda. Toronto: Mercury, 1993.

——, ed. *The Cosmic Chef: An Evening of Concrete.* Ottawa: Oberon, 1970.

Niechoda, Irene. *A Sourcery for Books 1 and 2 of bpNichol's The Martyrology.* Toronto: ECW, 1992.

Norris, Ken. "Interview: Kevin Spenst Talks to Ken Norris." *Prism International,* 13 June 2011. http://prismmagazine.ca/2011/06/13/interview-kevin-spenst-talks-to-ken-norris

"Noted Author Dies Suddenly at Home Here." In Lefebvre, ed. 1: 359–62.

Olson, Charles. *Human Universe and Other Essays.* San Francisco: Auerhahn, 1965.

Ortiz, Simon. "Speaking-Writing Indigenous Literary Sovereignty." Foreword. In *American Indian Literary Nationalism.* By Jace Weaver, Craig S. Womack, and Robert Allen Warrior. Alburquerque: U of New Mexico P, 2006. vii–xiv.

Osborne, Roger. Rev. of *HBiC,* vol. 3. *University of Toronto Quarterly* 78.1 (2009): 368–69.

Ostenso, Martha. "Good Morning, Son." *McCall's Magazine* 65 (September 1938): 12–14, 81–83.

Pacey, Desmond. "At Last – A Canadian Literature." *Cambridge Review* 60 (1938): 146–47.

——. Rev. of *The Green Gables Letters from L.M. Montgomery to Ephraim Weber, 1905–1909,* ed. Wilfrid Eggleston. *Dalhousie Review* 41.3 (1961): 429, 431.

Pacey, Desmond, and Graham Adams, eds. *The Collected Poems of Sir Charles G.D. Roberts.* Wolfville: Wombat, 1985.

Page, P.K. *The Filled Pen: Selected Non-Fiction.* Ed. Zailig Pollock. Toronto: U of Toronto P, 2006.

——. *The Hidden Room.* Ed. Stan Dragland. Erin: Porcupine's Quill, 1997.

——. "Re: Report on meeting." Email message to Zailig Pollock. 10 August 2009.

Parry, John J. "A Plea for Better Anthologies." *College English* 5.6 (1944): 318–24.

Paterson, Dave. Letter to bpNichol. 14 March 1977. bpNichol Fonds, Department of Special Collections, Bennett Library, Simon Fraser U.

Peacock, Alan J. "Pound and Propertius: The Limitations of an Historical Persona." In *Ezra Pound and History.* Ed. Marianne Korn. Orono: National Poetry Foundation, 1985. 83–98.

Pebworth, Ted-Larry. "John Donne, Coterie Poetry, and the Text as Performance." *Studies in English Literature, 1500–1900* 29.1 (1989): 61–75.

Penn, I. Garland. *The Afro-American Press and Its Editors.* 1891. New York: Arno and New York Times, 1969.

Percy, Owen. "Prize Possession: Literary Awards, the GGs, and the CanLit Nation." Diss. U of Calgary, 2010.

Philip, M. NourbeSe. *Frontiers: Selected Essays and Writings on Racism and Culture, 1984–1992.* Stratford: Mercury, 1992.

——. *A Genealogy of Resistance and Other Essays.* Toronto: Mercury, 1997.

*Picturing a Canadian Life: L.M. Montgomery's Personal Scrapbooks and Book Covers.* Confederation Centre Art Gallery, 2002. http://lmm.confederationcentre.com

Piternick, Anne B. "Author Problems in a Collaborative Research Project." *Scholarly Publishing* 24 (1993): 21–37.

Podnieks, Elizabeth. *Daily Modernism: The Literary Diaries of Virginia Woolf, Antonia White, Elizabeth Smart, and Anaïs Nin.* Montreal and Kingston: McGill–Queen's UP, 2000.

Pollock, Zailig. *A.M. Klein: The Story of the Poet.* Toronto: U of Toronto P, 1994.

——. "The Editor as Storyteller." In Lennox and Paterson, eds., 54–69.

——. "Errors in *The Collected Poems of A.M. Klein.*" *Canadian Poetry* 10 (Spring–Summer 1982): 91–99.

——. "Genesis, Exodus, Apocalypse: A Modern Editor's Journey." The Canadian Modernists Meet: A Symposium. University of Ottawa, Ottawa, May 2003.

——. "Sunflower Seeds: A.M. Klein's Hero and Demagogue." *Canadian Literature* 82 (1979): 48–58.

Pomahac, Gertrude C. "Wilfred Watson Fonds Finding Aid." *University of Alberta Archives.* U of Alberta Archives, 21 June 2004. http://archives.library.ualberta.ca/FindingAids/WilfredWatson/WWatson.html

Pratt, E.J. *Complete Poems.* Ed. R.J. Moyles and Sandra Djwa. Toronto: U of Toronto P, 1989.

——. *The Complete Poems and Letters of E.J. Pratt: A Hypertext Edition.* Ed. Zailig Pollock and Elizabeth Popham. Trent U, 1994. http://www.trentu.ca/pratt

——. *Pursuits Amateur and Academic: The Selected Prose of E.J. Pratt.* Ed. Susan Gingell. Toronto: U of Toronto P, 1995.

——. *The Selected Poems of E.J. Pratt.* Ed. Sandra Djwa, W.J. Keith, and Zailig Pollock. Toronto: U of Toronto P, 2000.

"The Press: Man in a Woman's World." *Time Magazine,* 6 January 1947.

Price, Kenneth M. "Edition, Project, Database, Archive, Thematic Research Collection: What's in a Name?" *Digital Humanities Quarterly* 3.3 (2009). http://www.digitalhumanities.org/dhq/vol/3/3/000053/000053.html

Price, Leah. *The Anthology and the Rise of the Novel: From Richardson to George Eliot.* Cambridge: Cambridge UP, 2000.

Rasula, Jed. "The Empire's New Clothes: Anthologizing American Poetry in the 1990s." *American Literary History* 7.2 (1995): 261–83.

Reid, Bill. *Solitary Raven: The Essential Writings of Bill Reid.* Ed. Robert Bringhurst. 2nd ed. Vancouver: Douglas and McIntyre, 2009.

Rider, Peter E. Introduction. *The Magpie.* By Douglas Durkin. Toronto: U of Toronto P, 1974. vi–xxi.

Richler, Mordecai. *Joshua Then and Now.* Toronto: McClelland and Stewart, 1980.

Rifkind, Candida. Rev. of *HBiC,* vol. 3. *Canadian Historical Review* 91.1 (2010): 170–72.

Roberts, Charles G.D. "Those Perish, These Endure." In *Twilight Over Shaugamauk and Three Other Poems.* Toronto: Ryerson, 1937.

——. "Those Perish, These Endure." In *Canada Speaks of Britain.* Toronto: Ryerson, 1941.

Rogers Jr., George C. "The Sacred Text: An Improbable Dream." In *Literary & Historical Editing.* Ed. George L. Vogt and John Bush Jones. Lawrence: U of Kansas Libraries, 1981. 23–33.

"Roots." *The Nathaniel Dett Chorale.* n.pub., 2010. http://www.nathanieldettchorale.org/about/roots

Roy, Fernande. Rev. of *HBiC,* vol 3. *Mens: revue d'histoire intellectuelle de l'Amérique française* 9.2 (2009): 275–82.

Rubio, Mary Henley. "'A Dusting Off': An Anecdotal Account of Editing the L.M. Montgomery Journals." In *Working in Women's Archives: Researching Women's Private Literature and Archival Documents.* Ed. Helen M. Buss and Marlene Kadar. Waterloo: Wilfrid Laurier UP, 2001. 51–78.

——. *Lucy Maud Montgomery: The Gift of Wings*. Toronto: Doubleday Canada, 2008.

——. "Subverting the Trite: L.M. Montgomery's 'Room of Her Own.'" In Lefebvre, ed. 2: 109–48.

Rubio, Mary Henley, and Elizabeth Hillman Waterston. "A Note on the Text." In Montgomery, *The Selected Journals* 4: xxix–xxxi.

Ruecker, Stan. Personal communication with EMiC UA. 16 July 2012.

Ruecker, Stan, and Milena Radzikowska. "The Iterative Design of a Project Charter for Interdisciplinary Research." In *Proceedings of the 7th ACM Conference on Designing Interactive Systems, February 25–27, 2008*. New York: ACM, 2008. 288–94.

Rukavina, Alison. *The Development of the International Book Trade, 1870–1895. Tangled Networks*. Houndmills: Palgrave Macmillan, 2010.

Russ, Joanna. *How to Suppress Women's Writing*. 1st ed. Austin: U of Texas P, 1983.

Said, Edward. *The World, The Text, and the Critic*. Cambridge, MA: Harvard UP, 1983.

Saltman, Judith, and Gail Edwards. *Picturing Canada: A History of Canadian Children's Illustrated Books and Publishing*. Toronto: U of Toronto P, 2010.

Saul, John Ralston. *A Fair Country: Telling Truths about Canada*. Toronto: Viking, 2008.

Scholes, Robert, and Clifford Wulfman. *Modernism in the Magazines: An Introduction*. New Haven: Yale UP, 2010.

Schulze, Robin, G. "How Not to Edit: The Case of Marianne Moore." *Textual Cultures: Texts, Contexts, Interpretation* 2.1 (2007): 119–35.

Schrift, Alan D. "Confessions of an Anthology Editor." *symplokē* 8.1–2 (2000): 164–76.

Sedgwick, Eve Kosofsky. *Touching Feeling: Affect, Pedagogy, Performativity*. Durham: Duke UP, 2003.

Self, Will. "None of This Will Be Yours." *Sore Sites*. London: Ellipsis, 2000. 21–23.

Shadd, Adrienne. *Memory, Race, and Silence: The Poetry of Anna Minerva Henderson (1887–1987)*, N.p.: n. pub, 1996.

Shearer, Karis. "Constructing Canons: Postmodern Cultural Workers and the Canadian Long Poem." Diss. U of Western Ontario, 2008.

Shep, Sydney J. "Imagining Post-National Book History." *PBSA* 104.2 (2010): 253–68.

Sher, Richard. "The Book in the Scottish Enlightenment." In *The Culture of the Book in the Scottish Enlightenment*. Ed. Paul Wood. Toronto: Thomas Fisher Rare Book Library, 2000. 40–60.

Shillingsburg, Peter L. *Scholarly Editing in the Computer Age: Theory and Practice*. Ann Arbor: U of Michigan P, 1996.

Skaay of the Qquuna Qiighawaay. *Being in Being: The Collected Works of a Master Haida Mythteller*. Ed. and trans. Robert Bringhurst. Vancouver: Douglas and McIntyre, 2001.

Slemon, Stephen. Afterword. In Sugars, ed. 517–23.

Smith, Mary Ainslie. "New Tales for the Maud Squad." Rev. of *The Doctor's Sweetheart and Other Stories*, by L.M. Montgomery, selected by Catherine McLay. *Books in Canada* (May 1979): 22.

Smith, Michelle. "Criminal Tales as Cultural Trade: The Production, Reception, and Preservation of Canadian Pulp Magazines." MA thesis. U of Alberta, 2004.

Snyder, Gary. *A Place in Space: Ethics, Aesthetics, and Watersheds*. Berkeley: Counterpoint, 1995.

——. *He Who Hunted Birds in His Father's Village: The Dimensions of a Haida Myth*. Foreword by Robert Bringhurst. 2nd ed. Berkeley: Shoemaker and Hoard, 2007.

Spadoni, Carl. Rev. of *HBiC*, vol. 1. *Fine Books & Collections Magazine*. 20 January 2005. http://www.finebooksmagazine.com/issue/0301/book_review.phtml

Spillers, Hortense. Introduction. In *Clarence and Corinne; or, God's Way*. By Mrs. A.E. Johnson. 1890. New York: Oxford UP, 1988. xxvii–xxxviii.

Spenst, Kevin. "Ken Norris." *Kevin Spenst*. 11 May 2011. http://kevinspenst.com/?p=558

——. "Kevin Spenst Talks to Ken Norris." *Prism International*. 13 June 2011. http://prismmagazine.ca/2011/06/13/interview-kevin-spenst-talks-to-ken-norris

Spivak, Gayatri Chakravorty. *The Post-Colonial Critic: Interviews, Strategies, Dialogues*. Ed. Sarah Harasym. New York: Routledge, 1990.

St. Onge, Anna. "Sheila Watson Finding Guide." *John M. Kelly Library: Special Collections and Archives*. St. Michael's College, U of Toronto, June 2007. http://stmikes.utoronto .ca/kelly/collections/sheila-watson-fonds/sheila-watson-finding-guide.asp

Stillinger, Jack. *Multiple Authorship and the Myth of Solitary Genius*. Oxford: Oxford UP, 1991.

Stone, Marjorie, and Judith Thompson. "Contexts and Heterotexts: A Theoretical and Historical Introduction." Introduction. In *Literary Couplings: Writing Couples, Collaborators, and the Construction of Authorship*. Ed. Stone and Thompson. Madison: U of Wisconsin P, 2006. 3–38.

Stowe, Harriet Beecher. *Uncle Tom's Cabin, or Life Among the Lowly*. 1852. New York: Modern Library, 1948.

Streitfeld, David. "Amazon Pulls Thousands of E-Books in Dispute." *BITS. New York Times*, 28 February 2012. http://bits.blogs.nytimes.com/2012/02/22/amazon-pulls-thousands-of-e-books-in-dispute

Sugars, Cynthia. "Can the Canadian Speak? Lost in Postcolonial Space." *ARIEL: A Review of International English Literature* 32.3 (2001): 115–52.

——, ed. *Home-Work: Postcolonialism, Pedagogy, and Canadian Literature*. Ottawa: U of Ottawa P, 2004.

——. "Postcolonial Pedagogy and the Impossibility of Teaching: Outside in the (Canadian Literature) Classroom." In Sugars, ed. 1–33.

Takaki, Ronald T. *Violence in the Black Imagination: Essays and Documents*. New York: G.P. Putnam's Sons, 1972.

Tartar, Helen. Foreword. In Cullen, ed. ix–xviii.

Teiser, Ruth. *Brother Antoninus: Poet, Printer, and Religious*. 1966. TS BANC 67/92c. Bancroft Library, U of California, Berkeley.

Thagard, Paul. "Collaborative Knowledge." *Noûs* 31.2 (1997): 242–61.

Thomas, Clara, and John Lennox. *William Arthur Deacon: A Canadian Literary Life*. Toronto: U of Toronto P, 1982.

Thompson, John B. *Books in the Digital Age: The Transformation of Academic and Higher Education Publishing in Britain and the United States*. Cambridge: Polity, 2005.

——. *Merchants of Culture: The Publishing Business in the Twenty-First Century*. Cambridge: Polity, 2010.

Tomkins, Silvan. *Shame and Its Sisters: A Silvan Tomkins Reader*. Ed. Eve Kosofsky Sedgwick and Adam Frank. Durham: Duke UP, 1995.

Toronto Research Group. Introduction. *Canadian "Pataphysics*. Spec. issue of *Open Letter* 4th ser. 6–7 (1980–81): 7–8.

Thucydides. *History of the Peloponnesian War*. Trans. Richard Crawley. London: J.M. Dent, 1903.

Tzara, Tristan. *Chanson Dada*. Ed. Lee Harwood. Toronto: Coach House, 1987.

Uricchio, William. "Historicizing Media in Transition." In *Rethinking Media Change: The Aesthetics of Transition*. Ed. David Thorburn and Henry Jenkins. Cambridge: MIT P. 23–38.

Unsworth, John. "Documenting the Reinvention of Text: The Importance of Failure." *Journal of Electronic Publishing* 3.2 (1997). http://dx.doi.org/10.3998/3336451.0003.201

van Gessel, Nina. "'The Art of Life': Editing Domesticity in Margaret Anderson's *My Thirty Years' War*." *American Modernism across the Arts*. Ed. Jay Bochner and Justin D. Edwards. New York: Peter Lang, 1999. 137–54.

van Herk, Aritha. "Blythe Spirits." Rev. of *The Blythes Are Quoted*, by L.M. Montgomery, ed. Benjamin Lefebvre. *Globe and Mail*, 14 November 2009: F12.

———. "Publishing and Perishing with No Parachute." *How Canadians Communicate*. Ed. David Taras, Fritz Pannekoek, and Maria Bakardjieva. Calgary: U of Calgary P, 2003. 121–42.

———. "Robert Kroetsch: A Biocritical Essay." Special Collections. *University of Calgary Library*, 1986. http://www.ucalgary.ca/libold/SpecColl/kroetschbioc.htm

Van Huijstee, Ryan. "PK Page response." Email message to Zailig Pollock. 22 April 2009.

———. "PK Page update." Email message to Zailig Pollock. 7 May 2009.

Vautour, Bart. "From Transnational Politics to National Modernist Poetics: Spanish Civil War Poetry in *New Frontier*." *Canadian Literature* 204 (2010): 44–60.

Verduyn, Christl. *Lifelines: Marian Engel's Writing*. Montreal and Kingston: McGill–Queen's UP, 1995.

———. *Marian Engel's Notebooks: "Ah, mon cahier, écoute …"* Waterloo: Wilfrid Laurier UP, 1999.

———. *Marian and the Major: Engel's Elizabeth and the Golden City*. Montreal and Kingston: McGill–Queen's UP, 2010.

Vulpe, Nicola, ed. *Sealed in Struggle: Canadian Poetry and the Spanish Civil War: An Anthology*. Tenerife: Center for Canadian Studies, U de la Laguna, 1995.

Walcott, Rinaldo. *Black Like Who? Writing Black Canada*. Toronto: Insomniac, 1997.

Warkentin, Germaine. "In Search of 'The Word of the Other': Aboriginal Sign Systems and the History of the Book in Canada." *Book History* 2 (1999): 1–27.

Watson, Sheila. "Antigone." *The Tamarack Review* 11 (1959): 5–13.

———. *The Double Hook*. Toronto: McClelland and Stewart, 1959.

Watson, Wilfred. *Friday's Child*. London: Faber and Faber, 1955.

———. *Plays at the Iron Bridge, or, The Autobiography of Tom Horror*. Ed. Shirley Neuman. Intro. Gordon Peacock. Edmonton: Longspoon, 1989.

Weedon, Alexis, series editor. *The History of the Book in the West*. 5 vols. Farnham and Burlington: Ashgate, 2010.

Wershler-Henry, Darren. "Argument for a Secular *Martyrology*." *Open Letter* 10th ser. 4 (1998): 37–47.

West, James L.W. III. "The Scholarly Editor as Biographer." *Textual Studies and the Common Reader: Essays on Editing Novels and Novelists*. Ed. Alexander Petit. Athens: U of Georgia P, 2000. 81–90.

Whitaker, Muriel. "Literary Pen-Pals." Rev. of *My Dear Mr. M: Letters to G.B. MacMillan from L.M. Montgomery*, ed. Francis W.P. Bolger and Elizabeth R. Epperly. *Canadian Literature* 90 (1981): 141–43.

———. "Women Alone." Rev. of *The Poetry of Lucy Maud Montgomery*, selected by John Ferns and Kevin McCabe; *Proper Definitions: Collected Theograms*, by Betsy Warland;

*People You'd Trust Your Life To,* by Bronwen Wallace. *Canadian Literature* 132 (1992): 228–30.

White, Hayden. *Tropics of Discourse: Essays in Cultural Criticism.* 1978. Baltimore: Johns Hopkins UP, 1985.

"Wild Geese by Martha Ostenso." *Western Home Monthly* July 1925: 27.

"Wilfred and Sheila Watson Collection." *Morris and Helen Belkin Art Gallery.* U of British Columbia, n.d. http://www.belkin.ubc.ca/online/wilfrid-and-sheila -watson-collection

Williams, Raymond. *The Politics of Modernism: Against the New Conformists.* Ed. Tony Pinkney. New York: Verso, 1989.

Willinsky, John. *Learning to Divide the World: Education at Empire's End.* Minneapolis: U of Minnesota P, 1998.

Winship, Michael. Rev. of *HBiC,* vol. 2. *University of Toronto Quarterly* 76.1 (2007): 463–65.

Wirtén, Eva Hemmings. "Surveying the (Battle)field: Book History, SHARP, and the Guerilla Tactics of Research." *SHARP News* 12.1 (2003): 3–4.

Wray, K. Brad. "The Epistemic Significance of Collaborative Research." *Philosophy of Science* 69 (2002): 150–68.

X, Malcolm, and Alex Haley. *The Autobiography of Malcolm X.* New York: Random House, 1965.

York, Lorraine. *Margaret Atwood and the Labour of Literary Celebrity.* Toronto: U of Toronto P, 2013.

Young-Ing, Greg. "Intellectual Property Rights, Legislated Protection, Sui Generis Models, and Ethical Access in the Transformation of Indigenous Traditional Knowledge." Diss. U of British Columbia, 2006.

Zipes, Jack. Introduction. *Anne of Green Gables.* By L.M. Montgomery. 1908. New York: Modern Library, 2008. ix–xxi.

Žižek, Slavoj. *The Sublime Object of Ideology.* London and New York: Verso, 1989.

# About the Contributors

**Kateri Akiwenzie-Damm** is a writer, poet, editor, and publisher from the Chippewas of Nawash First Nation, Saugeen Ojibway Nation, in southwestern Ontario. The publishing house she founded in 1993, Kegedonce Press, is one of four established Indigenous publishers in Canada. Her fiction, poetry, spoken word, libretto, non-fiction, and creative non-fiction have been performed and published around the world. Her collection of short stories, *The Stone Collection,* was published in 2015 by Portage and Main Press.

**Robert Bringhurst** works in many fields. His *Selected Poems* was published in Canada by Gaspereau, in the United States by Copper Canyon, and in London by Jonathan Cape. His Haida trilogy—*A Story as Sharp as a Knife: The Classical Haida Mythtellers and Their World,* with two companion volumes of translation from classical Haida—was named Book of the Year by the *Times* of London and awarded the Edward Sapir Prize from the Society for Linguistic Anthropology. A new edition of *Sharp as a Knife,* with a foreword by Margaret Atwood and illustrations by Haida artist Don Yeomans, was published in London in 2015. Bringhurst's other nonfiction works include *The Tree of Meaning* and *Everywhere Being Is Dancing* and *The Elements of Typographic Style.* Among many honours is the lifetime achievement award of the American Printing History Association. In 2013 he was named an Officer of the Order of Canada.

The Poet Laureate of Toronto (2012–15), **George Elliott Clarke** is an Africadian (African Nova Scotian). A prized poet, his fourteenth work is *Extra Illicit Sonnets* (Exile, 2015), a set of amatory lyrics. His forthcoming title is the epic "Canticles," whose subject is slavery and imperialism, to be published, over five years, in three parts, beginning in Fall 2016. Currently the inaugural E.J. Pratt Professor of Canadian Literature at the University of Toronto, Clarke has also taught at Duke University (1994–99), McGill University (1998–99), the University of British Columbia (2002), and Harvard University (2013–14). He has won several awards for his poetry and a novel, and received eight honorary doctorates, plus appointments to the Order of Nova Scotia and the Order of Canada at the rank of Officer. In 2016, Clarke was appointed Canada's 7th Parliamentary Poet Laureate.

**Frank Davey**, FRSC, is Professor Emeritus at Western University and author of twenty collections of poetry and ten books on Canadian literature, including the biography of bpNichol, *aka bpNichol*, in 2010. He edited the poetry newsletter *Tish* from 1961 to 1963 and the journal *Open Letter* from 1965 to 2013. His "Frank Davey's Blog" began in April 2013.

**Kate Eichhorn** is Associate Professor of Culture and Media Studies at the New School University. Her recent books include *Adjusted Margin: Xerography, Art and Activism in the Late 20th Century* (MIT, 2016) and *The Archival Turn in Feminism* (Temple UP, 2013).

**Irene Gammel** holds a Canada Research Chair in Modern Literature and Culture at Ryerson University in Toronto, where she is Professor of English and also directs the Modern Literature and Culture Research Centre. She is the author of many articles and books, including *Looking for Anne of Green Gables* (St. Martin's Press) and *Baroness Elsa: Gender, Dada, and Everyday Modernity* (MIT Press) and most recently co-editor of *Body Sweats: The Uncensored Writings of Elsa von Freytag-Loringhoven* (MIT Press) and *Anne's World: A New Century of Anne of Green Gables* (University of Toronto Press). Her current research focuses on the literature and visual culture of the First World War with a focus on Canada.

**Carole Gerson** is a Professor in the Department of English at Simon Fraser University. With Jacques Michon, she co-edited volume 3 (1918–1980) of *History of the Book in Canada / Histoire du livre et de l'imprimé au Canada*. Her extensive publications on Canada's literary and cultural history focus on women writers, and her recent book, *Canadian Women in Print, 1750–1918* (2010), won the Gabrielle Roy Prize for Canadian criticism. In 2013 she received the Marie Tremaine Medal from the Bibliographical Society of Canada.

**Paul Hjartarson** is Professor Emeritus in English and Film Studies at the University of Alberta, where he leads the Editing Modernism in Canada research group (EMiC UA). His most recent book, co-authored with S.C. Neuman and EMiC UA, is *The Thinking Heart: The Literary Archive of Wilfred Watson* (2014). With

Gregory Betts and Kristine Smitka, he has co-edited *Counterblasting Canada: Marshall McLuhan, Wyndham Lewis, Sheila Watson, and Wilfred Watson* (2016).

**Dean Irvine** is an Associate Professor at Dalhousie University. He is director of Editing Modernism in Canada and the open-source software and design company Agile Humanities Agency. His publications include *Editing Modernity: Women and Little Magazine Cultures in Canada, 1916–1956* (2008) as well as the edited collections *The Canadian Modernists Meet* (2005), *Making Canada New: Editing, Modernism, and New Media* (2016), co-edited with Vanessa Lent and Bart Vautour, and *Translocated Modernisms: Paris and Other Lost Generations* (2016), co-edited with Emily Ballantyne and Marta Dvořák. He is the series editor for the Canadian Literature Collection from the University of Ottawa Press.

**Smaro Kamboureli** is Avie Bennett Chair in Canadian Literature at the University of Toronto. The director of TransCanada Institute, which she founded via her Canada Research Chair Tier 1 in Critical Studies in Canadian Literature at the University of Guelph (2005–2013), she is the author of *On the Edge of Genre: The Contemporary Canadian Long Poem* (1991) and *Scandalous Bodies: Diasporic Literature in English Canada* (2000, 2009). The editor of the Writer as Critic series (NeWest Press, 1987–) and TransCanada Series (Wilfrid Laurier University Press, 2007-), she has published two editions of *Making a Difference: Canadian Multiculture Literatures in English* (1996, 2007) and is the author of numerous chapters and articles. Her most recent publication is Lee Maracle's *Memory Servies: Oratories* (2015), which she edited and to which she contributed an Afterword.

**Robert Lecker** is Greenshields Professor English at McGill University, where he specializes in Canadian literature. He is the former editor of *Essays on Canadian Writing* and the editor and author of numerous books and articles, including *Anthologizing Canadian Literature: Theoretical and Cultural Perspectives*; *Open Country: Canadian Literature in English*; *Canadian Writers and Their Works: Essays on Form, Context, and Development*; *The Annotated Bibliography of Canada's Major Authors*; *On the Line: Readings in the Short Fiction of Clark Blaise, John Metcalf, and Hugh Hood*; *Robert Kroetsch*; *Another I: The Fictions of Clark Blaise*; *Making It Real: The Canonization of English-Canadian Literature*; *Dr. Delicious: Memoirs of a Life in CanLit*; *The Cadence of Civil Elegies*; and *Keepers of the Code: English-Canadian Literary Anthologies and the Representation of Nation*. He is currently completing a history of Canadian authors and their literary agents.

**Benjamin Lefebvre** teaches in the graduate certificate program in publishing at Ryerson University, the Department of English and Film Studies at Wilfrid Laurier University, and the Youth and Children's Studies program at Laurier Brantford. His books include an edition of L.M. Montgomery's rediscovered final book, *The Blythes Are Quoted* (2009), and the critical anthology *The L.M. Montgomery Reader*, Volume 1: *A Life in Print* (2013), Volume 2: *A Critical Heritage* (2014), and Volume 3: *A Legacy in Review* (2015). He is also Series Editor of the Early Canadian Literature series of rediscovered primary texts published by Wilfrid Laurier University Press and director of the Web resource L.M. Montgomery Online (lmmonline.org). His current project is a book-length study of child characters in English-language Canadian fiction for adults.

**Hannah McGregor** is an instructor in English and Film Studies at the University of Alberta, where she completed a SSHRC-funded postdoctoral fellowship focusing on periodical studies, the middlebrow, and digital humanities. Her current research project, *Modern Magazines Project Canada* (modmag.ca), explores new methods for reading digitized periodical archives, with a focus on the Winnipeg-based magazine *The Western Home Monthly* (1899–1932). Her work has been published in *Archives & Manuscripts*, *University of Toronto Quarterly*, *Canadian Literature*, and *International Journal of Canadian Studies*.

**Heather Milne** is an Associate Professor in the Department of English at the University of Winnipeg. She is currently completing a book manuscript on neoliberalism and dissent in contemporary Canadian and American feminist poetics. She is the co-editor of *Prismatic Publics: Innovative Canadian Women's Poetry and Poetics*.

**Laura Moss** is an Associate Professor at UBC, where she teaches Canadian and African literatures. Having served as associate editor of the journal *Canadian Literature* since 2004, Moss became the editor of the journal in 2015. She is the co-editor, with Cynthia Sugars, of the two-volume anthology *Canadian Literature in English: Texts and Contexts*. She also edited a collection of essays titled *Is Canada Postcolonial?*, a selected edition of the poetry of F.R. Scott, and a scholarly edition of *The History of Emily Montague*. In addition to her edited books, Moss has published articles on work by M.G. Vassanji, Salman Rushdie, Zadie Smith, Margaret Atwood, Chinua Achebe, Rohinton Mistry, and Antje Krog, among others, and has written on literary pedagogy, public arts policy in Canada, Canadian broadcasting, and public memorials in Vancouver's Downtown Eastside. Her current book project concerns the intersections of public policy and the history of arts culture in Canada.

**Zailig Pollock** is Professor Emeritus at Trent University. He received his BA at the University of Manitoba and his PhD from the University of London. He was principal investigator of *The Collected Works of A.M. Klein*, and he has been directly involved in editing Klein's poetry and notebooks, as well as his novel, *The Second Scroll*. He has also written a study of Klein's work, *A.M. Klein: The Story of the Poet*. He was principal investigator of *The Collected Works of E.J. Pratt*; and has co-edited *Selected Poems of E.J. Pratt*. He is principal investigator of the digital edition of the collected works of P.K. Page, *The Digital Page* (digitalpage.ca), and has edited *Kaleidoscope: Selected Poems of P.K. Page*.

**Harvey Quamen** is an Associate Professor of English and Humanities Computing at the University of Alberta. He specializes in digital humanities and is a member of many research teams, including Editing Modernism in Canada, Implementing New Knowledge Environments, and the Canadian Writing Research Collaboratory. In the past, he has served as the Electronics and Design Editor for *English Studies in Canada* and is a editorial board member for the Map of Early Modern London research project.

**Cynthia Sugars** is a Professor of English at the University of Ottawa. She is the author of *Canadian Gothic: Literature, History, and the Spectre of Self-Invention* (2014) and the editor of *The Oxford Handbook of Canadian Literature* (2015). She is the editor of numerous other collections, including *Canadian Literature and Cultural Memory* (with Eleanor Ty; 2014); the historical anthology *Canadian Literature in English: Texts and Contexts* (with Laura Moss; 2009); *Unsettled Remains: Canadian Literature and the Postcolonial Gothic* (with Gerry Turcotte; 2009); *Unhomely States: Theorizing English-Canadian Postcolonialism* (2004); and *Home-Work: Postcolonialism, Pedagogy, and Canadian Literature* (2004). She is the co-editor, with Herb Wyile, of the journal *Studies in Canadian Literature*.

**Bart Vautour** is an Assistant Professor at Dalhousie University. His research considers Canadian cultural production, literary history, textual studies, and modernism. He is editor of Ted Allan's Spanish Civil War novel *This Time a Better Earth* (2015) and co-editor, with Emily Robins Sharpe, of Charles Yale Harrison's *Meet Me on the Barricades* (2016). With Erin Wunker, Travis V. Mason, and Christl Verduyn, he is co-editor of *Public Poetics: Critical Issues in Canadian Poetry and Poetics* (2015). With Dean Irvine and Vanessa Lent, he is the co-editor of *Making Canada New: Editing, Modernism, and New Media* (2016). He co-directs, with Emily Robins Sharpe, Canada and the Spanish Civil War (spanishcivilwar.ca).

**Christl Verduyn** is a Professor of English and Canadian Studies at Mount Allison University, where she holds the Davidson Chair in Canadian Studies and is director of the Centre for Canadian Studies. Her teaching and research interests include Canadian and Québécois literatures, women's writing and criticism, multiculturalism and minority writing, life writing, and Canadian studies. She is the author, editor, or co-editor of over a dozen volumes in these areas, most recently *Canadian Studies, Past, Present, Praxis* (with Jane Koustas, 2012) and *Critical Collaborations: Indigeneity, Diaspora, and Ecology in Canadian Literary Studies* (with Smaro Kamboureli, 2014).

**Darren Wershler** is an Associate Professor at Concordia University, the University Research Chair in Media and Contemporary Literature, the Provost's Fellow for Interdisciplinarity and, with Charles Acland, the co-founder and co-coordinator of the Concordia Media History Research Centre. He is the editor of over thirty-five books and the author or co-author of twelve books, including *The Iron Whim: A Fragmented History of Typewriting* and *Guy Maddin's My Winnipeg*.

# Index

McClelland, Jack, 64

McClelland and Stewart, 5, 6, 57, 80, 83, 217; archives, 90

McClung, Nellie, 182–84

McCrae, John, 72

McGann, Jerome: and archives, 24; on collaborative editing, 79, 80, 89; and digital technology, 128, 135; influence of, 8, 19–20, 76, 96; and social text, 22, 108–9, 141, 176–77; and textual history, 82, 91, 146

McGee, Thomas D'Arcy, 171

McGregor, Hannah, 4, 8, 13, 103

McGuigan, Jim, 15, 226

McGuire, Shannon, 103

McKenzie, D.F., 8, 102, 108

McLay, Catherine, 83

McLeod, Neal, 32, 34, 38–39, 240n1

McLuhan, Marshall, 118, 121–22, 128–29, 136

mentoring, 2, 34, 35, 137, 192; of authors, 6, 7, 36, 39, 111, 240n1; of scholars, 12, 125. See also curating

metadata, 14, 115, 120, 132–35. See also database

metamorphosis, 5, 158

Metcalf, John, 163, 187

methodology. See editorial methods

Métis, 31, 32, 178, 180–81. See also Gabriel Dumont Institute; Pemmican Publications

Michaels, Anne, 184, 245n5 (Keeping)

Michon, Jacques, 60, 61, 67

middlebrow: literature, 106, 111, 116, 119; studies, 88, 108, 119–20, 243n2. See also cultural production; culture; Ostenso, Martha; periodical studies

migration. See immigration

Miki, Roy, 126–27

Mi'kmaq (language), 72, 177

Miller, Toby, 7, 225, 228–31, 237

Milne, Heather, 4, 7, 191, 193

mimesis: in anthologies, 152–53, 155–56, 161, 163, 166, 182; as nationalism, 150–51; and occasional literature, 140

Mistry, Rohinton, 245n3

modernism, 17, 43; in Canada, 57, 146, 160, 163, 186, 204; and editing, 13, 75, 86, 98, 132; literary, 22, 44, 84, 143, 200, 208; masculine, 58; scholarship on, 12, 114, 115, 119, 127. See also Dadaism; digital

modernist studies; Editing Modernism in Canada; Freudian analysis; *Little Review*; modernity; Textual Editing and Modernism in Canada

*Modernist Journals Project*, 114, 119

modernity, 45, 118, 145, 245n4 (The Politics)

Modern Language Association, 9, 13, 102

*Monodromos* (Engel), 8, 17, 19

Montgomery, L.M., 6; editing of, 79–86, 88–91; as editor, 75–79; Research Centre, 86; studies, 87–88. See also *Anne of Green Gables*; *Blythes Are Quoted, The*; life writing; Page, L.C.

Montreal, 26, 63, 68, 162

Moodie, Susanna, 46

Moore, Henry, 131

Mootoo, Shani, 184

Morrissey, Stephen, 206

Moses, Daniel David, 15

Moss, Laura, 4, 8, 11

Mouré, Erin, 162, 184

*Moveable Feast, A* (Hemingway), 89

Moyles, Gordon, 96

Murphy, Emily, 183

Naipaul, V.S., 217

nation: and citizenship, 139, 225, 237; disarticulations of, 11, 44, 106; and identity, 71, 149, 155–56, 161, 163–64, 170, 186; as plural, 152; writing about, 54, 176. See also book history; Canada; liberalism; nationalism

nationalism: cultural, 9, 127, 208; and editing Canadian literature, 11; and emotion, 197–98; literary, 29, 149–52, 186, 218; Quebec, 66. See also Black nationalism; Canadian literature; mimesis; postcolonialism; realism; transnationalism

national literature, 106, 127, 142, 175, 226; anthologies of, 42, 55, 58, 149–67, 170–74, 186–87, 198. See also Canadian literature; canon; mimesis; nationalism; occasional literature; realism

Native. See Indigenous

Negri, Antonio, 193

neoliberalism, 7, 139, 233, 245n4 (The Politics); and cultural policy, 237–38

Neruda, Pablo, 141

networks, 71, 86–88; academic, 156; Actor-, 236; author, 116, 120, 140, 143; of

**Books in the TransCanada Series**
Published by Wilfrid Laurier University Press

Smaro Kamboureli and Roy Miki, editors
*Trans.Can.Lit: Resituating the Study of Canadian Literature* / 2007 / xviii + 234 pp. /
ISBN 978-0-88920-513-0

Smaro Kamboureli
*Scandalous Bodies: Diasporic Literature in English Canada* / 2009 / xviii + 270 pp. /
ISBN 978-1-55458-064-4

Kit Dobson
*Transnational Canadas: Anglo-Canadian Literature and Globalization* / 2009 / xviii +
240 pp. / ISBN 978-1-55458-063-7

Christine Kim, Sophie McCall, and Melina Baum Singer, editors
*Cultural Grammars of Nation, Diaspora, and Indigeneity in Canada* / 2012 / viii +
276 pp. / ISBN 978-1-55458-336-2

Smaro Kamboureli and Robert Zacharias, editors
*Shifting the Ground of Canadian Literary Studies* / 2012 / xviii + 350 pp. / ISBN
978-1-55458-365-2

Kit Dobson and Smaro Kamboureli
*Producing Canadian Literature: Authors Speak on the Literary Marketplace* / 2013 /
xii + 208 pp. / ISBN 978-1-55458-355-3

Eva C. Karpinski, Jennifer Henderson, Ian Sowton, and Ray Ellenwood, editors
*Trans/acting Culture, Writing, and Memory* / 2013 / xxix + 364 pp. / ISBN
978-1-55458-839-8

Smaro Kamboureli and Christl Verduyn, editors
*Critical Collaborations: Indigenity, Diaspora, and Ecology in Canadian Literary Studies* /
May 2014/ viii + 288 pp. / ISBN 978-1-55458-911-1

Larissa Lai
*Slanting I, Imagining We: Asian Canadian Literary Production in the 1980s and 1990s* /
2014 / xii + 262 pp. / ISBN 978-1-77112-041-8

Bart Vautour, Erin Wunker, Travis V. Mason, and Christl Verduyn, editors
*Public Poetics: Critical Issues in Canadian Poetry and Poetics* / 2015 / x + 366 pp. /
ISBN 978-1-77112-047-0

Dean Irvine and Smaro Kamboureli, editors
*Editing as Cultural Practice in Canada* / 2016 / x + 296 pp. / ISBN 978-1-77112-111-8